Optimise

Teacher's Book Premium Pack

A2

Key
for Schools

macmillan education

Welcome

ABOUT *OPTIMISE*

- *Optimise* is a fantastic new secondary-level exam-preparation course. The course is designed to prepare teenagers for international exams (A2 Key for Schools, etc.) or local state exams.
- *Optimise*'s highly respected authors Malcolm Mann and Steve Taylore-Knowles brought their exam expertise and many years of experience of official exams as Course Consultants on this level of the course, ensuring your students achieve exam success.
- *Optimise* offers attractive images, stimulating, age-appropriate topics and carefully guided skills development, which prepare students for everyday life as well as exams.
- *Optimise*'s print and digital package gives you the flexibility to choose the approach that works best for your teaching situation: from print to blended to a fully interactive digital approach.

For students

Student's Book or Digital Student's Book

See pages 4–13 for details of the Student's Book content.

See page 14 for more on the Digital Student's Book.

Workbook with/without answer key or Online Workbook

See pages 17–20 for details of the Workbook content.

See page 21 for more on the Online Workbook.

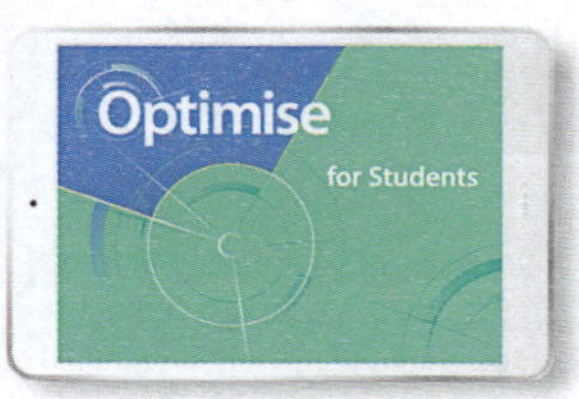

Student's Resource Centre

See page 22 for a full list of resources available on the Student's Resource Centre.

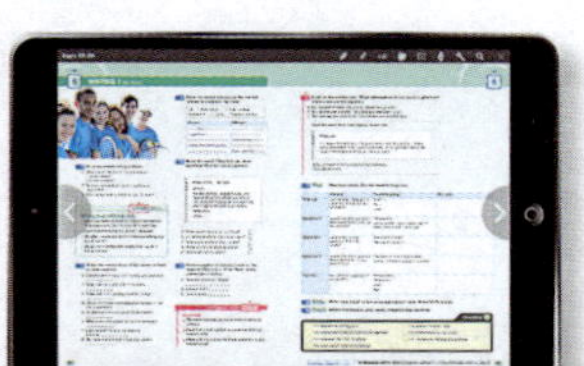

Student's eBook

An eBook version of the Student's Book is included.

For teachers

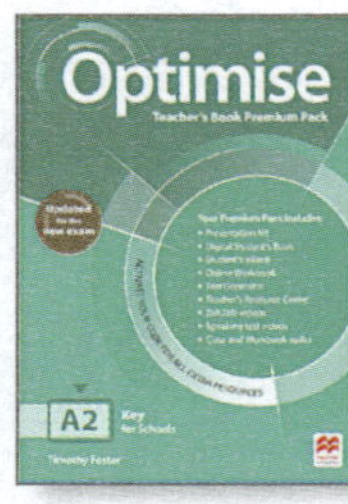

Teacher's Book

Your Teacher's Book Premium Pack includes:

- Presentation Kit
- Digital Student's Book
- Student's eBook
- Online Workbook
- Test Generator
- Teacher's Resource Centre
- *Talk2Me* videos
- Speaking test videos
- Class and Workbook audio

See pages 22–23 for details of the worksheets and tests available.

Presentation Kit

See page 15 for more information about the Presentation Kit.

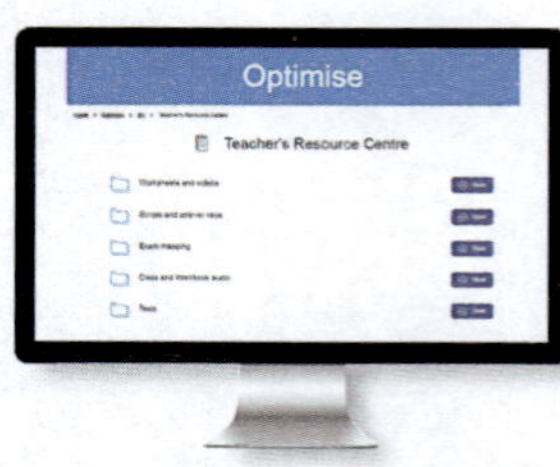

Teacher's Resource Centre
Digital Student's Book
Online Workbook
Test Generator
Student's eBook

See page 22 for a full list of resources available on the Teacher's Resource Centre.

Class Audio CDs

Class audio on CDs. Also available on the Resource Centres.

ABOUT THE *OPTIMISE* COURSE DEVELOPERS

Malcolm Mann and Steve Taylore-Knowles have written a number of exam courses for teenagers, including the highly successful *Laser* series. They are also the series editors of Macmillan's *Improve your Skills for First (FCE)* and *Improve your Skills for Advanced (CAE)* series.

Malcolm

Malcolm lives and works in Athens, Greece. He's responsible for the production of the LAAS exam suite, and is a former Chairperson of TESOL Greece.

Steve

Steve lives and works in the UK. He is a former Cambridge speaking examiner and also provides government-endorsed teacher training in many countries throughout Europe, Asia and South America.

A MESSAGE FROM THE *OPTIMISE* COURSE DEVELOPERS

Thank you for choosing to use *Optimise*.

Optimise is an exam course with a difference.

In *Optimise*, we effectively combine exam training and language development to prepare students not only for language exams, but also for life beyond the classroom.

Below we have listed our principles and the key features which we believe make *Optimise* an outstanding exam-preparation course.

We very much hope you and your students enjoy using *Optimise A2* and benefit from its motivating content, syllabus and structure.

All the very best for the school year!

Malcolm and Steve

Principles

The following principles are at the heart of the *Optimise* series:

- **Motivation:** The more teens are motivated by engaging and interesting content (texts, topics, tasks, etc.), the more likely they are to improve their skills, and develop their linguistic competence.
- **Practice:** Exam practice is essential. In order for students to feel confident and perform at their optimum, they need to be familiar with exam tasks. Language and exam skills tested in the exam have to be practised and developed.
- **Guidance:** The most effective way to help students develop their language and exam skills is to deal with them in a systematic and guided way, through a carefully-planned course syllabus.
- **Coverage:** Vocabulary does not only consist of individual words; it also includes collocations, phrasal verbs, word formation and word patterns, as well as topic vocabulary, which all need to be covered comprehensively.
- **Support:** Students require expert guidance and support in order to produce exam-level pieces of writing. The process of writing involves different drafts, proofreading and feedback, and is essential in helping students develop their skills.
- **Consolidation:** Regular consolidation makes a vital contribution towards ensuring students understand and retain the information they need to prepare for exams.
- **Personalisation:** Personalisation is key in enabling students to relate the material in their Student's Book to their own lives, opinions and culture.

Key features

- An extensive range of print and digital materials, providing you with a variety of flexible options for your students.
- Strong focus on exam-skills development, with each lesson focusing on a specific skill and offering detailed advice on how to complete the task effectively.
- Resource Centres for both students and teachers, with a wide variety of worksheets including CLIL and Culture, Grammar and Vocabulary.
- Unit tests, Progress tests, End-of-year test, all set at two levels – Standard and Higher – are available as PDFs and also adaptable to suit your own requirements on the Test Generator.
- A Placement test to check your students' level and a Diagnostic test to highlight students' strengths and weaknesses.
- A2 Key for Schools Practice tests: one at the back of the Workbook and another complete Practice test available on the Teacher's Resource Centre as a printable PDF.
- Systematic language and exam-preparation development throughout every lesson.
- Personalisation tasks to develop skills, such as critical analysis, collaboration and learning strategies, presented through the Think, Research, Culture, Learn and Me features.
- *Talk2Me* videos in every Speaking lesson feature teenagers using everyday functional language in a variety of situations that students will relate to. The Flipped classroom approach is suggested as an alternative approach for this video to encourage learner autonomy and create more time to focus on activating the target language.
- A Speaking test video with an examiner shows a pair of students completing a speaking test. This video is exploited in the *Optimise your Speaking* section of the Student's Book *Optimise your exams* pages, along with an additional worksheet on the Resource Centre, which encourages students to analyse the video further.
- Systematic Writing lessons which include a writing model, a paragraph planner and a writing exam task, along with a post-writing Checklist for students to refer to.
- A Progress check, after every two units, reviews the grammar and vocabulary of the preceding two units and includes a self-assessment tool for students to chart their learning.

Course components

STUDENT'S BOOK | Reading lesson

Every unit starts with a 2-page Reading lesson.

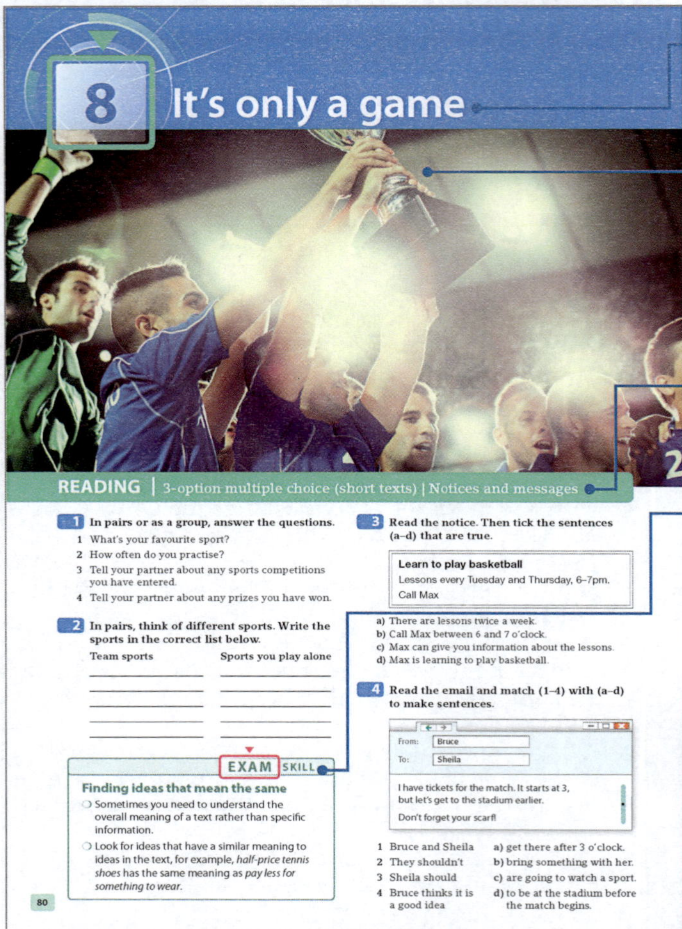

8 It's only a game

READING | 3-option multiple choice (short texts) | Notices and messages

1 In pairs or as a group, answer the questions.

1 What's your favourite sport?
2 How often do you practise?
3 Tell your partner about any sports competitions you have entered.
4 Tell your partner about any prizes you have won.

2 In pairs, think of different sports. Write the sports in the correct list below.

Team sports	Sports you play alone
______	______
______	______
______	______
______	______

EXAM SKILL

Finding ideas that mean the same

- Sometimes you need to understand the overall meaning of a text rather than specific information.
- Look for ideas that have a similar meaning to ideas in the text, for example, *half-price tennis shoes* has the same meaning as *pay less for something to wear.*

3 Read the notice. Then tick the sentences (a–d) that are true.

Learn to play basketball
Lessons every Tuesday and Thursday, 6–7pm.
Call Max

a) There are lessons twice a week.
b) Call Max between 6 and 7 o'clock.
c) Max can give you information about the lessons.
d) Max is learning to play basketball.

4 Read the email and match (1–4) with (a–d) to make sentences.

From: Bruce
To: Sheila

I have tickets for the match. It starts at 3, but let's get to the stadium earlier.
Don't forget your scarf!

1 Bruce and Sheila	a) get there after 3 o'clock.
2 They shouldn't	b) bring something with her.
3 Sheila should	c) are going to watch a sport.
4 Bruce thinks it is a good idea	d) to be at the stadium before the match begins.

80

Unit topics and themes chosen to be interesting and engaging for teenage students.

The opening spread of each unit has colourful and impactful images connected to the unit topic, which can be used at the start of the lesson to stimulate on-topic discussion.

Clear labelling of the exam task and text type in the lesson will help you and your learners.

All Reading lessons feature an *Exam skill* box, with targeted advice on how to approach different exam tasks and the specific sub-skills required.

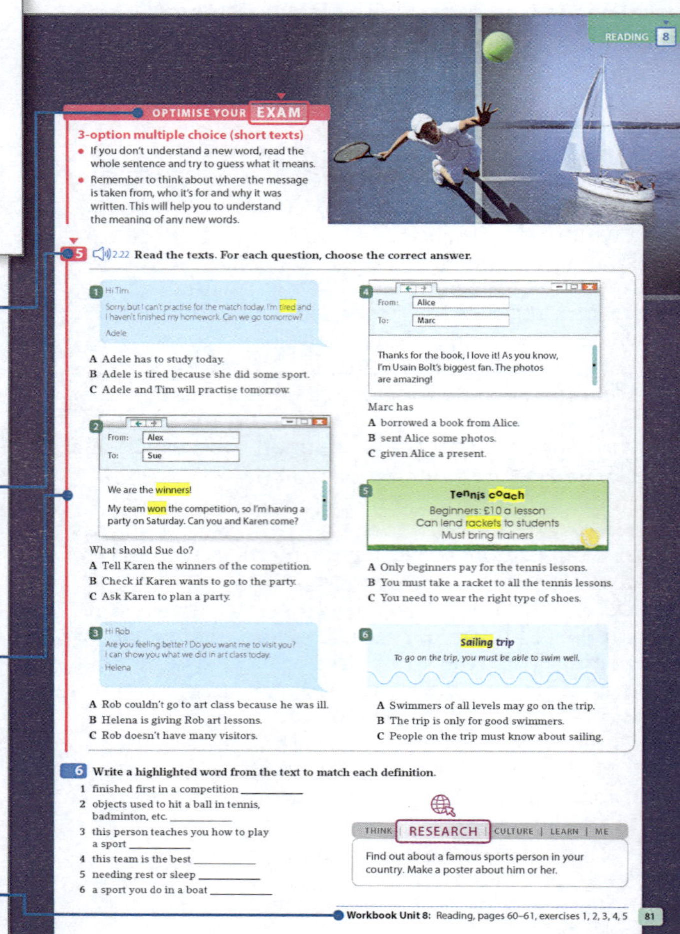

READING 8

OPTIMISE YOUR EXAM

3-option multiple choice (short texts)

- If you don't understand a new word, read the whole sentence and try to guess what it means.
- Remember to think about where the message is taken from, who it's for and why it was written. This will help you to understand the meaning of any new words.

5 2.22 Read the texts. For each question, choose the correct answer.

1 Hi Tim
Sorry, but I can't practise for the match today. I'm tired and I haven't finished my homework. Can we go tomorrow?
Adele

A Adele has to study today.
B Adele is tired because she did some sport.
C Adele and Tim will practise tomorrow.

2 From: Alex
To: Sue
We are the winners!
My team won the competition, so I'm having a party on Saturday. Can you and Karen come?

What should Sue do?
A Tell Karen the winners of the competition.
B Check if Karen wants to go to the party.
C Ask Karen to plan a party.

3 Hi Rob
Are you feeling better? Do you want me to visit you? I can show you what we did in art class today.
Helena

A Rob couldn't go to art class because he was ill.
B Helena is giving Rob art lessons.
C Rob doesn't have many visitors.

4 From: Alice
To: Marc
Thanks for the book, I love it! As you know, I'm Usain Bolt's biggest fan. The photos are amazing!

Marc has
A borrowed a book from Alice.
B sent Alice some photos.
C given Alice a present.

5 Tennis coach
Beginners: £10 a lesson
Can lend rackets to students
Must bring trainers

A Only beginners pay for the tennis lessons.
B You must take a racket to all the tennis lessons.
C You need to wear the right type of shoes.

6 Sailing trip
To go on the trip, you must be able to swim well.

A Swimmers of all levels may go on the trip.
B The trip is only for good swimmers.
C People on the trip must know about sailing.

6 Write a highlighted word from the text to match each definition.

1 finished first in a competition ______
2 objects used to hit a ball in tennis, badminton, etc. ______
3 this person teaches you how to play a sport ______
4 this team is the best ______
5 needing rest or sleep ______
6 a sport you do in a boat ______

THINK | RESEARCH | CULTURE | LEARN | ME

Find out about a famous sports person in your country. Make a poster about him or her.

Workbook Unit 8: Reading, pages 60–61, exercises 1, 2, 3, 4, 5 81

All Reading lessons include an *Optimise your exam* feature, which gives students tips and strategies to help them prepare for the lesson exam task.

Every Reading lesson has an exam task. These tasks are level-appropriate and reflect the tasks students are likely to encounter in most official exams.

All reading texts are relevant to teenage students. Some focus on stimulating, out-of-the-ordinary topics, which will be of interest to teenagers. Some, like these, present authentic short texts that students come across in their daily lives.

All lessons include references to the Workbook, and other relevant reference material.

STUDENT'S BOOK | Grammar lessons

Every unit has two separate Grammar lessons.

8 GRAMMAR 1 | Modals (1): ability, necessity, obligation, possibility

Every Grammar lesson presents a different grammar point.

Grammar in context

The *Grammar in context* box introduces the grammar lesson by asking students to identify the target structures in a context they have already seen.

Find these sentences in Exercise 5 on page 81 and then choose the correct words to complete sentences a–e.

1 *People on the trip* ***must*** *know about sailing.*
2 *You* ***need to*** *wear the right type of shoes.*
3 *Swimmers of all levels* ***may*** *go on the trip.*
4 ***Can*** *you and Karen come?*
5 *Adele* ***has to*** *study today.*
6 *Rob* ***couldn't*** *go to art class because he was ill.*

a) We use *can* to talk about **ability / necessity**.
b) We use *have to* to talk about **possibility / obligation**.
c) We use *may* to talk about **possibility / ability**.
d) We use *must* to talk about **possibility / obligation**.
e) We use *need(n't)* to talk about **necessity / ability**.

REMEMBER

- Modal verbs do not change their form and are followed by the bare infinitive (without *to*) of another verb.
- We use *can/can't (cannot)* to talk about ability in the present and *could/couldn't* to talk about ability in the past.
- We can use *must / have to* for rules made by other people or when the person doing the action believes it is necessary. There is no past form of *must*, we use *had to*. The negative form is *don't have to*.

▶ See Grammar reference, Unit 8, page 151

1 Choose the correct words.

1 When my dad was at school, he **can't / couldn't** understand maths.
2 All football players **may / must** follow the rules of the game.
3 The weather forecast says it's going to snow tomorrow so we **might / needn't** go snowboarding.
4 Sports people **could / have to** train every day.
5 We **couldn't / needn't** go for a run today if we don't want to.
6 You **can't / must** tell the sports teacher if you don't feel well.

2 Complete the conversation with the words in the box.

can	can't	don't have
have	might	needn't

Robert: (1) __________ you see who's got the ball?
Anna: No, I (2)__________. I think it's number 10.
Robert: Oh, that's Harry Kane. He's an amazing player. But dad says he (3) __________ move to a different team next year. I hope not.
Anna: Oh, you (4) __________ worry. He loves this team so I don't think he'll want to leave.
Robert: Look! He's scored a goal! That's 1-1.
Anna: That's great! There's only a few more minutes left, so shall we go now?
Robert: No way! We (5) __________ to stay until the end. There's still time for another goal.
Anna: OK, then. We (6) __________ to hurry, anyway. We've got lots of time until the next bus.
Robert: That's good. Now let's enjoy the end of the game!

3 Complete the text with the correct form of the modals *can('t), could(n't), had (to), have (to), may/might, need(n't)*.

Exercises are staged so as to be progressively more challenging as students work through the lesson.

Keep on running...!

At 15, Emil Zátopek was a young Czech who worked in a shoe factory. When he was younger he **(1)** __________ do any sports particularly well, so he **(2)** __________ never have become a runner. However, one day, the factory sports coach told him he **(3)** __________ to run in a race. Everyone was surprised when he came second. Zátopek then started to think that he **(4)** __________ work in the factory forever. He thought maybe he could be a runner instead!

Everyone knows that to be the best at any sport you **(5)** __________ to train hard, and he did. Zátopek ran in the 1952 Olympic Games, and he won the 5,000- and 10,000-metre races. He also ran in the marathon, the longest race in the Games. It was his first marathon, but he ran the 42-kilometre race and won! Today most people still **(6)** __________ believe he did this ... but he did! Zátopek showed that if you really want something, you **(7)** __________ worry about what other people **(8)** __________ think. Just believe in yourself.

82 ▶ **Workbook Unit 8:** Grammar 1, page 62, exercises 1, 2, 3

GRAMMAR 2 | Modals (2): advice, permission, polite requests, prohibition 8

Grammar in context

Look at these sentences from the audio in the listening lesson then match them to the descriptions (a–e).

1 *You* ***should*** *start playing again, Dad – it's good exercise ...*
2 *Camp rules say we* ***mustn't*** *swim if there's a strong wind ...*
3 *...* ***could*** *you take some photos of the boats, please?*
4 *You* ***shouldn't*** *be out all day in the sun if it's very hot.*
5 *The camp leader says we* ***can*** *go to the pool today instead.*

a) something is not allowed ____
b) we have permission ____
c) someone is making a request ____
d) something is a good idea ____
e) something isn't a good idea ____

REMEMBER

- We use modals to:
  - ask for / give advice: *should/shouldn't*
  - ask for / give permission: *can/could*
  - refuse permission: *can't/couldn't*
  - make a polite request: *could*
  - say something is prohibited: *mustn't*
- To make the negative form, you add 'not' after the modal verb and this is usually contracted, e.g. *need not = needn't*.
- Sometimes the negative form changes the modal's meaning: *In the UK, you* ***must*** *drive on the left.* (obligation) *In the UK, you* ***mustn't*** *drive on the right.* (prohibition)
- To make a question, the subject and modal swap position: ***Could you*** *pass me my racket, please?*

▶ See Grammar reference, Unit 8, page 158

Remember boxes on the grammar pages present additional information in a clear way for students to remember, and end with a signpost to the *Grammar reference* at the back of the Student's Book, where further explanations and examples are provided.

1 Choose the correct words.

1 We're very happy because the teacher says we **shouldn't / can** all watch a video for the last half hour this afternoon.
2 'Amber, come back and get your helmet! You **could / mustn't** ever go out on your bike without it.'
3 Ed, **should / could** you help me with my school project, please?
4 Please turn the computer off. You **shouldn't / can** play video games all evening. It's not a good thing to do!
5 You look very tired. You **mustn't / should** go to bed earlier.

Whenever possible, short texts are included on the grammar pages, to give your students the opportunity to see and practise grammar in realistic contexts.

2 Choose the correct words (a, b or c) to complete each sentence.

1 I'm not sure how to do this. ____ you help me, please?
a) Could b) Should c) Shouldn't
2 You ____ eat for 30 minutes before you go swimming.
a) could b) can c) shouldn't
3 I think you ____ try learning a new sport. It's fun!
a) mustn't b) couldn't c) should
4 The teacher says we ____ use her tennis rackets. That's kind of her.
a) can b) shouldn't c) couldn't
5 The boys ____ go to the match last night because their dad said no.
a) shouldn't b) couldn't c) mustn't
6 The rule here is that you ____ do any water sports if you ____ swim 500 metres.
a) should, can b) mustn't, can't c) could, mustn't

3 Complete the text about a summer camp with the phrases from the word box.

can use	can't do	could you ask
could you bring	mustn't leave	
should bring (×2)	should have	
shouldn't arrive		

A WELCOME from our Camp Manager

We're really excited about meeting everyone at Super Sports Summer Camp next month. Before you come, I want to give you some important information.

- **What to bring** First of all, everyone **(1)** __________ these things to camp: a pair of trainers, shorts or leggings and a T-shirt. You **(2)** __________ sports without them. Secondly, don't bring your best clothes, because we don't want them to get dirty. So **(3)** __________ some old clothes for art activities, please? People often ask us if they **(4)** __________ their own rackets, bats or balls. The answer is no. We have all the equipment here and you **(5)** __________ it whenever you want.
- **When to arrive** The camp starts at 11:30 am on Saturday 7th July. You **(6)** __________ too early, as the leaders won't all be here until 10, so please try and arrive at about 10:30 if possible.
- **And finally ...** When you arrive, **(7)** __________ your parents to park in the Rees Lane car park. There's plenty of room there for everyone. And, one last thing ... always remember the camp rule while you're here – you **(8)** __________ the camp at any time without permission. See you on Saturday!

▶ **Workbook Unit 8:** Grammar 2, page 63, exercises 1, 2, 3 85

The Vocabulary lesson in each unit has three separate word sets, one of which is always topic vocabulary.

Each lesson has three clearly-labelled vocabulary areas.

VOCABULARY | Topic vocabulary | Word formation | Collocations **8**

Topic vocabulary sections increase students' lexical knowledge in topics that commonly appear in exams.

Words connected with *sport*

1 2.24 **Write a word from the box to match each definition. There are two extra words you do not need. Listen and check.**

badminton | cricket | kit | pool | skiing | stadium | table tennis | winner

1 You need a small plastic ball to play this game. __________
2 You can go swimming here. __________
3 You can do this sport on snow in the mountains. __________
4 You can watch a football game here. __________
5 This is the person who is first in a competition or race. __________
6 You need a racket to play this game. __________

2 2.25 **Choose the best word to complete each sentence. Listen and check.**

1 The __________ told us what exercises to do and helped us play better.
A team B coach C member
2 Can you __________ a horse?
A play B skate C ride
3 You need a __________ to go to the basketball game tonight.
A ticket B bat C club
4 I can't go swimming because I haven't got my __________.
A swimsuit B beach C pool
5 Ed was the winner of the 800-metre __________.
A race B bat C club
6 They played in a rugby __________ yesterday, and won 35-3!
A club B goal C match

Verbs/nouns

3 2.26 **Complete the table. Listen and check.**

verb	noun
win	winner
(1) __________	surfer
swim	(2) __________
(3) __________	runner
play	(4) __________

Word formation tasks appear regularly to extend students' word knowledge as well as serving to prepare them for common exam tasks.

4 **Complete the sentences with the correct form of some of the words from Exercise 3.**

1 There are over 50 __________ in the pool today!
2 Novak Djokovic __________ the tennis match.
3 The eight best __________ waited in the stadium to start the 500-metre race.
4 Who do you think is the best football __________ in the world this year?
5 If you want to learn to __________, it's important that you can swim.

Collocations with verbs

5 2.27 **Complete the sentences with the correct form of the verbs in the box. Listen and check.**

climb | enter | go | play | throw | win

1 Greg __________ the ball into the road.
2 My class __________ swimming at the city pool every Wednesday.
3 Everyone can __________ the competition but only one person can win.
4 In the summer, lots of people in England __________ cricket.
5 Do I need to practise a lot before I __________ a mountain?
6 Emil Zátopek was very happy when he __________ the 5,000-metre race at the Olympic Games.

Collocations help students increase their vocabulary competence and prepare for a number of different exam tasks.

► Vocabulary reference, page 166 ► Workbook Unit 8: Vocabulary, pages 62–63, exercises 1, 2, 3

Lessons include details of the *Vocabulary reference* at the back of the Student's Book. This provides reference materials to support students during vocabulary tasks and also acts as a revision tool.

TOPIC VOCABULARY | Words connected with *sport*

Word	Example sentence
badminton (n)	Badminton is the best sport I have ever played!
cricket (n)	My grandpa is very good at cricket and plays every weekend in the summer.
kit (n)	Mum, where's my kit? I'm going to play football.
pool (n)	The pool near my school is busy on Saturdays because lots of children go swimming at the weekend.
skiing (n)	She loves skiing, but it doesn't snow very often where she lives.
stadium (n)	We enjoyed going to the stadium to watch the rugby match.
table tennis (n)	Will you teach me to play table tennis?
winner (n)	And Will is the winner of the competition!

The Listening lesson in each unit focuses on a specific exam skill and always includes an exam task.

All class audio material is available on CDs as well as being provided on the Resource Centres.

Listening lessons always feature a specific exam skill and provide support and guidance to help students develop the skill further.

The initial task helps students to start thinking about the topic of the lesson in more depth.

The *Exam skill* boxes in Listening lessons focus on specific sub-skills needed to achieve success in listening.

8 LISTENING | Matching

1 Work in pairs. Look at the poster for a summer camp and answer the questions.

1 What sports are the young people doing?
2 Would you like to do the sports in the poster? Why / Why not?
3 What other sports would you like to do at a summer camp?

EXAM SKILL

Listening for important information

- You don't need to understand every word to answer the questions.
- The first time you listen, think about the important words.
- When you listen again, think carefully about what the speakers mean.

2 2.27 Listen to five people talking about sports. Match each speaker to a sport.

Speaker 1 ___ a) running
Speaker 2 ___ b) windsurfing
Speaker 3 ___ c) badminton
Speaker 4 ___ d) cycling
Speaker 5 ___ e) table tennis

3 2.27 Listen again and write the names of the other sports the people talk about in each conversation.

Conversation 1 *football*
Conversation 2 ___
Conversation 3 ___
Conversation 4 ___
Conversation 5 ___

OPTIMISE YOUR EXAM

Matching

- Read the question and all the possible answers carefully.
- Remember that there are three possible answers that you don't need.
- When you listen again, check the three possible answers you didn't choose, to make sure they aren't correct.

4 2.28 You will hear Bea talking to her dad about her summer camp. What sport did she do on each day?

Example:
Monday morning *H*

1 Monday afternoon ___
2 Tuesday ___
3 Wednesday ___
4 Thursday ___
5 Friday ___

A swimming
B badminton
C volleyball
D tennis
E sailing
F football
G cricket
~~H running~~

5 2.28 Listen again and check your answers.

THINK | RESEARCH | CULTURE | LEARN | ME

Work in pairs and answer the questions.

- How popular are summer camps in your country?
- What sports and other activities can you do there?

84 ► Workbook Unit 8: Listening, page 64, exercises 1, 2, 3

The *Optimise your exam* box in the Listening lessons always gives students advice on how to approach this kind of task.

Every Listening lesson includes an exam task which allows students an opportunity to apply the advice given in the preceding *Optimise your exam* box.

Personalisation tasks at the end of the Listening lessons relate to the unit topic, giving students a chance to develop the topic further.

There is a reference to the relevant Workbook pages at the end of each Listening lesson.

STUDENT'S BOOK | Speaking lesson

Talk2Me video in every Speaking lesson

Speaking lessons include a video which features target functional language.

Speaking lessons focus on one of two task types which students will need to develop in preparation for a speaking test.

All Speaking lessons suggest using an optional Flipped classroom approach, in which students watch the video and complete some exercises at home in order to prepare for the lesson.

The *Exam skill* box in the Speaking lesson highlights one of the sub-skills that are required for success in speaking tests.

Every unit contains a *Say it right* feature, which develops a specific aspect of pronunciation that appears in one of the lessons. The worksheet for this is available on the Resource Centre.

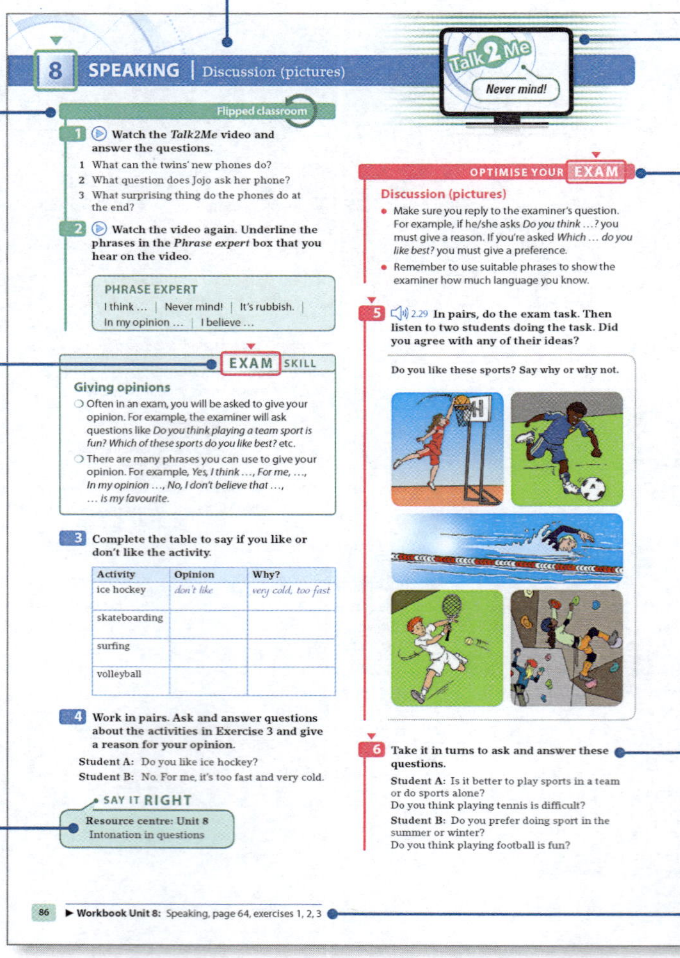

8 **SPEAKING** | Discussion (pictures)

Talk 2 Me
Never mind!

Flipped classroom

1 **Watch the *Talk2Me* video and answer the questions.**

1 What can the twins' new phones do?
2 What question does Jojo ask her phone?
3 What surprising thing do the phones do at the end?

2 **Watch the video again. Underline the phrases in the *Phrase expert* box that you hear on the video.**

PHRASE EXPERT
I think … | Never mind! | It's rubbish. | In my opinion … | I believe …

EXAM SKILL

Giving opinions

- Often in an exam, you will be asked to give your opinion. For example, the examiner will ask questions like *Do you think playing a team sport is fun? Which of these sports do you like best?* etc.
- There are many phrases you can use to give your opinion. For example, *Yes, I think …, For me, …, In my opinion …, No, I don't believe that …, … is my favourite.*

3 **Complete the table to say if you like or don't like the activity.**

Activity	Opinion	Why?
ice hockey	*don't like*	*very cold, too fast*
skateboarding		
surfing		
volleyball		

4 **Work in pairs. Ask and answer questions about the activities in Exercise 3 and give a reason for your opinion.**

Student A: Do you like ice hockey?
Student B: No. For me, it's too fast and very cold.

SAY IT RIGHT
Resource centre: Unit 8
Intonation in questions

OPTIMISE YOUR EXAM

Discussion (pictures)

- Make sure you reply to the examiner's question. For example, if he/she asks *Do you think …?* you must give a reason. If you're asked *Which … do you like best?* you must give a preference.
- Remember to use suitable phrases to show the examiner how much language you know.

5 2.29 **In pairs, do the exam task. Then listen to two students doing the task. Did you agree with any of their ideas?**

Do you like these sports? Say why or why not.

6 **Take it in turns to ask and answer these questions.**

Student A: Is it better to play sports in a team or do sports alone?
Do you think playing tennis is difficult?
Student B: Do you prefer doing sport in the summer or winter?
Do you think playing football is fun?

86 ▶ **Workbook Unit 8:** Speaking, page 64, exercises 1, 2, 3

All Speaking lessons include a *Talk2Me* video, featuring native speakers. They discuss topics related to the unit, modelling target functional language, which students then practise and use in their final task.

The *Optimise your exam* box develops the lesson skill in order to prepare students for the exam task that follows.

The lesson ends in a speaking-test task consolidating the skill developed on this page.

There is a reference to the relevant pages in the Workbook at the end of every Speaking lesson.

STUDENT'S BOOK | Language in Use

All Language in Use lessons provide comprehensive coverage of all aspects of grammar and vocabulary that students need in order to prepare for exams.

Every Language in Use lesson is based on a specific task type that students will be tested on in their English exams.

Language in Use exam skills are language-focused for exam preparation, but also for students' general language development.

The *Optimise your exam* box develops the lesson skill in order to prepare students for the exam task that follows.

Exercises build up throughout the lesson, preparing students for the final A2 Key for Schools Reading and Writing exam task.

All the common A2 Key for Schools Reading exam tasks are covered: open cloze, 3-option multiple-choice cloze, 3-option multiple matching, and 3-option multiple choice.

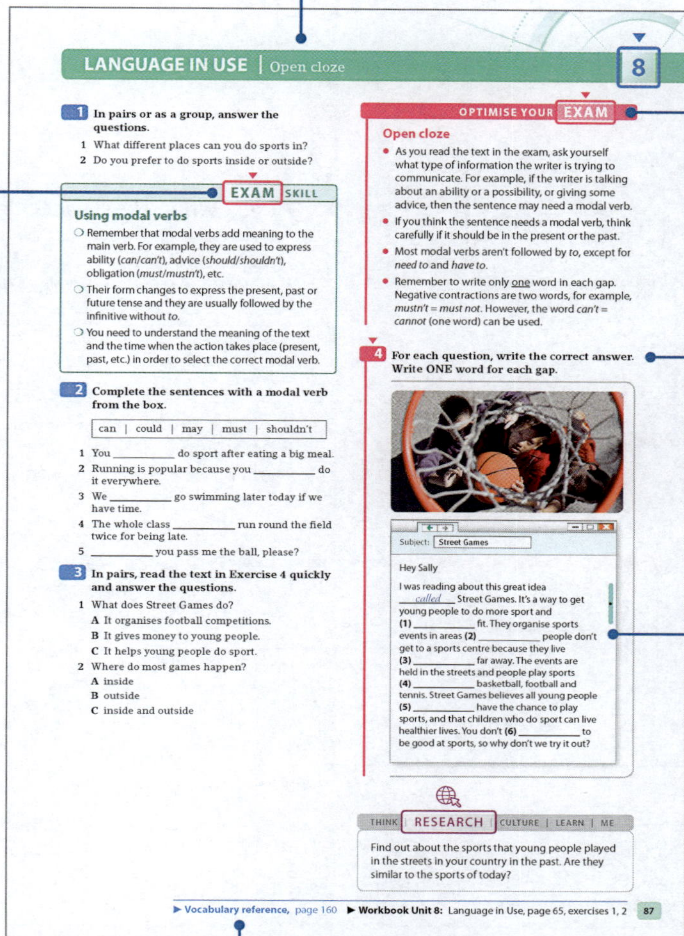

8

LANGUAGE IN USE | Open cloze

1 In pairs or as a group, answer the questions.

1 What different places can you do sports in?
2 Do you prefer to do sports inside or outside?

EXAM SKILL

Using modal verbs

- Remember that modal verbs add meaning to the main verb. For example, they are used to express ability (*can/can't*), advice (*should/shouldn't*), obligation (*must/mustn't*), etc.
- Their form changes to express the present, past or future tense and they are usually followed by the infinitive without *to*.
- You need to understand the meaning of the text and the time when the action takes place (present, past, etc.) in order to select the correct modal verb.

2 Complete the sentences with a modal verb from the box.

can | could | may | must | shouldn't

1 You ________ do sport after eating a big meal.
2 Running is popular because you ________ do it everywhere.
3 We ________ go swimming later today if we have time.
4 The whole class ________ run round the field twice for being late.
5 ________ you pass me the ball, please?

3 In pairs, read the text in Exercise 4 quickly and answer the questions.

1 What does Street Games do?
A It organises football competitions.
B It gives money to young people.
C It helps young people do sport.
2 Where do most games happen?
A inside
B outside
C inside and outside

OPTIMISE YOUR EXAM

Open cloze

- As you read the text in the exam, ask yourself what type of information the writer is trying to communicate. For example, if the writer is talking about an ability or a possibility, or giving some advice, then the sentence may need a modal verb.
- If you think the sentence needs a modal verb, think carefully if it should be in the present or the past.
- Most modal verbs aren't followed by *to*, except for *need to* and *have to*.
- Remember to write only one word in each gap. Negative contractions are two words, for example, *mustn't* = *must not*. However, the word *can't* = *cannot* (one word) can be used.

4 For each question, write the correct answer. Write ONE word for each gap.

Subject: Street Games

Hey Sally

I was reading about this great idea *called* Street Games. It's a way to get young people to do more sport and (1) ________ fit. They organise sports events in areas (2) ________ people don't get to a sports centre because they live (3) ________ far away. The events are held in the streets and people play sports (4) ________ basketball, football and tennis. Street Games believes all young people (5) ________ have the chance to play sports, and that children who do sport can live healthier lives. You don't (6) ________ to be good at sports, so why don't we try it out?

THINK | RESEARCH | CULTURE | LEARN | ME

Find out about the sports that young people played in the streets in your country in the past. Are they similar to the sports of today?

▶ Vocabulary reference, page 160 ▶ Workbook Unit 8: Language in Use, page 65, exercises 1, 2

87

Any extra material in the *Vocabulary reference* which is relevant to the Language in Use lesson is signposted at the bottom of the page.

Every unit ends with a two-page Writing lesson.

8 **WRITING** | Guided writing (an email)

1 In pairs, answer the questions.

1 What sports do you do at your school:
- in the winter?
- in the summer?

2 Do boys and girls do sports together or separately?
3 How many hours a week do you do sport?

EXAM SKILL

Writing in an informal style

- When you write an email to a friend or family member, use informal language, for example, *Hello!, Hi, See you soon, Write soon, Bye.*
- In informal writing we can use contractions, for example, *I'm, he can't, we've got, they didn't.*
- We often also use more exclamation marks than we do in formal writing, for example, *I've got a great idea!*

2 Write the contractions of the words in bold in each sentence.

1 I **would** like to learn how to play golf next year. *I'd*
2 Sally **has** got a new pair of trainers. ______
3 They **will** start playing baseball in May. ______
4 Those two teams **were not** good enough to win the competition. ______
5 He **did not** score any goals in the match. ______
6 **Who is** the new player in the cricket team? ______
7 I **am** excited because my team is winning! ______
8 We **have** trained really hard this winter. ______

3 Write F (formal) or I (informal) next to the words and phrases, as in the example.

Example: Dear *F* Hi *I*

1 I suggest we … ___
2 How about … ___
3 Can't wait to … ___
4 I would like to thank you for … ___
5 See you soon ___
6 Love ___
7 I am looking forward to … ___
8 Yours sincerely, ___
9 Thanks a lot for … ___
10 Best wishes ___

4 Read the email from Chris to his English friend Sam. Then answer the questions.

From: Chris
To: Sam

Hi Sam,

Thanks for your email. My school is really cool!

We play football, cricket, hockey and basketball and do athletics at school. Yes, everyone's got to do at least one sport each term! We often go to the park to do sports when the weather is good, but when it rains we use the gym.

Write soon,
Chris

1 What sports does Chris have at his school?
2 How many sports do you have to play each term?
3 When do they go to the park?
4 What do they do when it rains?

5 Find examples of informal style in the email in Exercise 4. Write them in the correct place below.

1 informal words or phrases ______, ______
2 a contraction ______

OPTIMISE YOUR EXAM

Guided writing (an email)

- In the exam, you can invent details in your emails – what you write doesn't have to be true.
- Use your imagination and use a variety of adjectives to make your email interesting to read.
- Remember that your email should be short. You only need to write one paragraph of 25 words or more.

88

Writing lessons focus on the different types of writing that students may be expected to produce in an exam situation.

Every Writing lesson includes a model, which students can use to inform and guide their own writing when they complete the exam task later in the lesson.

The *Exam skill* box develops key language functions that students will need to apply in writing tasks.

In Writing lessons, the *Optimise your exam* box provides guidance and advice to help students prepare for the lesson exam task.

8

6 Look at this exam task. What information do you need to include in your email? Choose the correct answers.

You want to join your English friend Lee's tennis club this summer. Write an email to Lee.

In your email:
- tell Lee you have all the kit
- say your dad will give you the money
- ask Lee how often they practise.

Write 25 **words** or more.

1 the clothes he has / the clothes he needs to buy
2 the person who will give you the money / how much the club costs
3 the amount of time / the places where they practise

7 **Plan** Plan your email. Use the table to help you.

	Details	My notes
First line	use informal language to greet the person you are writing to	
Point 1	Tell	
Point 2	Say	
Point 3	Ask	
Last line	use informal language to say goodbye	

8 **Write** Write your email to Lee in an appropriate style. Write 25 words or more.

9 **Check** Before you hand in your email, complete this checklist.

Checklist

- I've followed my writing plan.
- I've started and ended my email in the right way.
- I've used all three points.
- I've used a good range of vocabulary.
- I've used an informal style.
- I've written 25 words or more.
- I've checked my spelling, grammar and punctuation.

► Writing reference, page 163 ► Workbook Unit 8: Writing, page 66, exercises 1, 2, 3, 4 and Progress check 8, page 67 89

Students analyse the task and make notes to prepare for the writing in each unit.

After writing, students are encouraged to check their work carefully.

There is a Checklist at the end of every Writing lesson so that students take responsibility for reviewing and assessing their work.

In the *Writing reference*, there are longer writing tasks covering a range of different text types, to offer more extensive practice to students.

STUDENT'S BOOK | Progress check

There is a two-page Progress check after every two units.

PROGRESS CHECK UNITS 7–8

GRAMMAR AND VOCABULARY

The *Progress checks* cover grammar and vocabulary from the preceding two units.

1 Complete the conversation using the correct form of *will* or *going to*.

Simona: What (1) ______ you ______ do in the summer holidays?
Martin: I (2) ______ stay with my cousins in France for two weeks. After that, I (3) ______ visit my grandparents. (4) ______ you ______ go on holiday?
Simona: No, I'm not. I (5) ______ study English at a summer school in London. But I need to pass an exam first.
Martin: You're one of the best students in the class. I'm sure you (6) ______ pass.
Simona: I hope so. I have to go now. I (7) ______ do my history homework in the library.
Martin: I'm really bad at history. (8) ______ you help me?
Simona: OK. I (9) ______ help you find the information you need, but I (10) ______ tell you the answers.
Martin: That's great. Thanks a lot.

__/10

2 Choose the correct answers (A, B or C).

1 What do I need to play tennis?
A It's a good idea.
B A racket and some trainers.
C Don't forget your bat and ball.

2 I want to take an English course in September.
A You should speak to my teacher. He's great.
B I don't think so.
C Can you help me?

3 Have you seen my dictionary?
A I have to go.
B It's on the bookshelf.
C It's after lunch.

4 Who won the race?
A Not at the moment.
B It doesn't take long.
C I don't know. They're still running.

5 I'm going to enter this competition.
A I hope you win.
B You don't have to run.
C Wait until it finishes.

__/5

The *Progress checks* include a variety of task types, all designed to provide extra exam preparation as well as reviewing the Student's Book material.

3 Choose the correct modal verb to complete each sentence.

1 My sister **could / may / should** play tennis when she was five.
2 My cousin **can't / couldn't / shouldn't** read or write until he was eight.
3 I **can / have to / may** need your help with my homework, but I'm not sure yet.
4 You **can't / needn't / couldn't** use your mobile phone during the exam. Leave it in your bag.
5 You **don't have to / should / may** wear a coat to school because it might be cold later on.
6 In football, only the goalkeeper **doesn't have to / has to / can** touch the ball with his hands.
7 You **have to / shouldn't / couldn't** eat too much before you do sport.
8 The runners **don't have to / can / shouldn't** stop for water, but it is a good idea.
9 You **can / needn't / have to** use a dictionary during French lessons if you want to find a word.
10 Everyone **could / may / has to** wear a swimsuit in the pool.
11 You **can / may / don't have to** go to school in the holidays.
12 I **may / couldn't / can't** come to the match on Saturday, but at the moment I don't know. I'll tell you tomorrow.

__/12

90

The *Progress checks* include exam-type tasks.

4 Complete the blog post with one word in each gap.

I'm Paz Nevado, I'm 14 years old, I'm from Spain (**1**) ______ I love sport. I (**2**) ______ tennis three times a week and I'm also in the school team. Every year, we enter a big competition (**3**) ______ May. This year, it's (**4**) ______ to be in Madrid. We have (**5**) ______ practise a lot (**6**) ______ we go to the competition. We've never won it, (**7**) ______ last year we came second. It's great fun and I always (**8**) ______ lots of new friends there. I also love swimming. I can't swim very often (**9**) ______ there isn't a pool in my town. Every summer, we (**10**) ______ to the beach and I swim in the sea. I love it!

__/10

5 Complete the sentences with the verbs in the box.

climb | do | go | make | ride | take | throw | win

1 When you're at school, you need to ______ homework every night.
2 It's really useful to ______ notes when the teacher is talking.
3 Cora wants to ______ a really high mountain when she is older.
4 Who do you think will ______ the 10,000-metre race at the Olympics?
5 Lots of young people ______ to university when they're 18.
6 Don't ______ the ball into the road. It's dangerous.
7 It's OK to ______ mistakes when you're learning something new.
8 I'd really like to learn how to ______ a horse next year.

__/8

6 Read the descriptions about sports. What is the word for each one? The first letter is already there.

1 Two or four people play this game with a ball and rackets. t_ _ _ _ _
2 You hit a ball with a bat in this English summer game. c_ _ _ _ _ _ _
3 Moving through water. s_ _ _ _ _ _ _ _
4 You hit a ball with your hands in this team game. v_ _ _ _ _ _ _ _ _ _
5 Riding a board on the sea. s_ _ _ _ _ _ _

__/5

Total score __/50

There is a total of 50 marks for every *Progress check*.

Every *Progress check* ends with an *Exam skills can-do* checklist. This gives students the opportunity to assess what they can now do, having completed two more units of their Student's Book, and also provides references of where to look if there are any areas students feel they need to review.

EXAM SKILLS

Tick the statements that are true for you. Review the skills in the unit if you need more help.

I can …	Unit/page
☐ develop strategies to answer the question in multiple-choice activities	Unit 7 p70
☐ think about the missing information I need to listen for	Unit 7 p74
☐ talk about the future and make predictions	Unit 7 p76
☐ identify commonly confused words	Unit 7 p77
☐ use adjectives in a story	Unit 7 p78
☐ find ideas that mean the same in the text	Unit 8 p80
☐ listen for important information	Unit 8 p84
☐ give opinions in a discussion	Unit 8 p86
☐ use modal verbs	Unit 8 p87
☐ write an email using an informal style	Unit 8 p88

91

STUDENT'S BOOK | Optimise your exams

The 8-page *Optimise your exams* section at the back of the Student's Book brings together exam strategies for each of the key skills, plus advice on how to perform well under exam conditions.

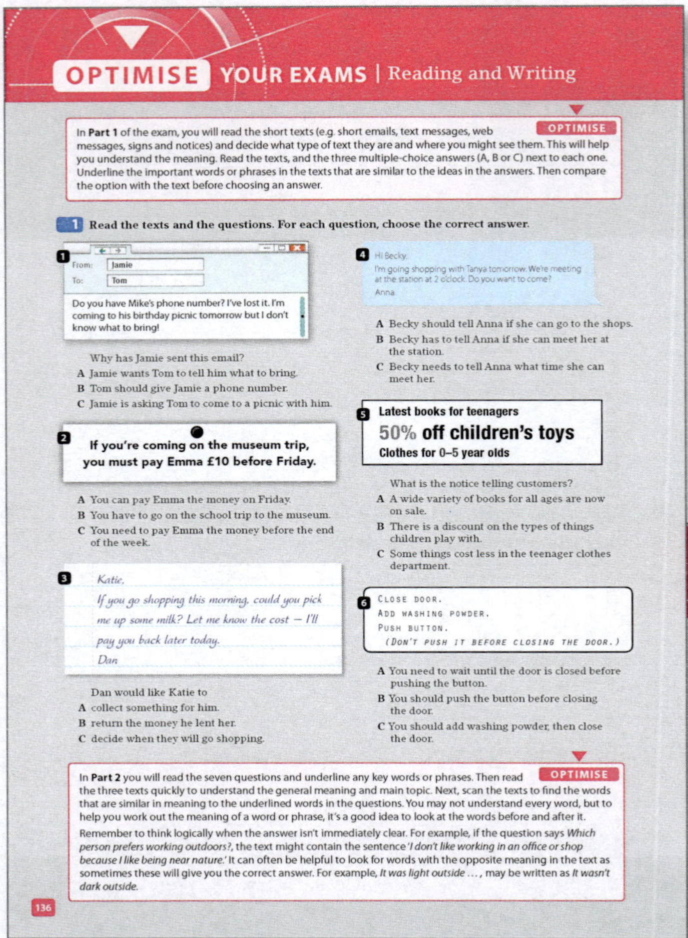

OPTIMISE YOUR EXAMS | Reading and Writing

OPTIMISE In **Part 1** of the exam, you will read the short texts (e.g. short emails, text messages, web messages, signs and notices) and decide what type of text they are and where you might see them. This will help you understand the meaning. Read the texts, and the three multiple-choice answers (A, B or C) next to each one. Underline the important words or phrases in the texts that are similar to the ideas in the answers. Then compare the option with the text before choosing an answer.

1 Read the texts and the questions. For each question, choose the correct answer.

1 From: Jamie To: Tom
Do you have Mike's phone number? I've lost it. I'm coming to his birthday picnic tomorrow but I don't know what to bring!

Why has Jamie sent this email?
A Jamie wants Tom to tell him what to bring.
B Tom should give Jamie a phone number.
C Jamie is asking Tom to come to a picnic with him.

2 If you're coming on the museum trip, you must pay Emma £10 before Friday.

A You can pay Emma the money on Friday.
B You have to go on the school trip to the museum.
C You need to pay Emma the money before the end of the week.

3 Katie,
If you go shopping this morning, could you pick me up some milk? Let me know the cost – I'll pay you back later today.
Dan

Dan would like Katie to
A collect something for him.
B return the money he lent her.
C decide when they will go shopping.

4 Hi Becky,
I'm going shopping with Tanya tomorrow. We're meeting at the station at 2 o'clock. Do you want to come?
Anna

A Becky should tell Anna if she can go to the shops.
B Becky has to tell Anna if she can meet her at the station.
C Becky needs to tell Anna what time she can meet her.

5 Latest books for teenagers
50% off children's toys
Clothes for 0–5 year olds

What is the notice telling customers?
A A wide variety of books for all ages are now on sale.
B There is a discount on the types of things children play with.
C Some things cost less in the teenager clothes department.

6 CLOSE DOOR.
ADD WASHING POWDER.
PUSH BUTTON.
(DON'T PUSH IT BEFORE CLOSING THE DOOR.)

A You need to wait until the door is closed before pushing the button.
B You should push the button before closing the door.
C You should add washing powder, then close the door.

OPTIMISE In **Part 2** you will read the seven questions and underline any key words or phrases. Then read the three texts quickly to understand the general meaning and main topic. Next, scan the texts to find the words that are similar to the underlined words in the questions. You may not understand every word, but to help you work out the meaning of a word or phrase, it's a good idea to look at the words before and after it. Remember to think logically when the question isn't immediately clear. For example, if the question says *Which person prefers working outdoors?*, the text might contain the sentence *'I don't like working in an office or shop because I like being near nature.'* It can often be helpful to look for words with the opposite meaning in the text as sometimes these will give you the correct answer. For example, *It was light outside …*, may be written as *It wasn't dark outside.*

136

OPTIMISE YOUR EXAMS | Listening

OPTIMISE In **Part 1** of the exam, you should look carefully at what the pictures are showing and think about what words you might hear. Think about what is different in the pictures and what words or phrases you might hear about each one. For example, you might hear words to describe different places, things or activities. Then read the questions and underline the important words. Use the first listening to listen for the specific information, and then the second time to check your answers.

1 3.33 For each question, choose the correct picture.

1 Where is Kara's bag? A B C

2 What time does the film start? A 7:15 B 7:45 C 8:15

3 Where are Kevin and his sister going at the weekend? A B C

4 What is Dad going to buy Mum for her birthday? A B C

5 What's the weather going to be like tomorrow? A B C

OPTIMISE In **Part 2** of the exam, you will need to complete a note with specific information from a monologue, such as prices, times, dates or telephone numbers. First, read the note to see what type of information you need to listen for. Then, listen for specific information and finally listen again to check your answer or to complete the gaps you have missed. Spell words correctly when they are spelt out by the speaker. It's important to write only one word in each gap.

2 3.34 Listen to a teacher telling his students about a trip to the theatre. For each question, write the correct answer in the gaps. Write one word or a number or a date or a time.

You will hear a boy telling his friend about a trip to the theatre.

SCHOOL TRIP TO THEATRE

City:	London
Day of trip:	(1) ______
Play starts:	(2) ______ pm
Name of the play:	(3) ______
Name of the theatre:	(4) ______ Theatre
Cost of ticket:	(5) £ ______

OPTIMISE In **Part 3** of the exam, you will listen to an informal conversation between two speakers and then choose the correct answer from three options (A, B or C). Read the questions and options and think about the context of the conversation. This part of the test includes questions about specific details, opinions and feelings of the speakers. First, listen to try and understand the gist of the conversation and think about the best option for each question. Then, listen again for specific information and then check all your answers carefully.

140

Optimise your exams features:

- Sections dedicated to each of the exam papers.
- Exercises to improve students' understanding of common exam tasks.
- Clear, targeted advice on how to approach specific exam tasks.
- Exercises to encourage analysis of sample answers.
- A Speaking test video in which real candidates complete an authentic Speaking test, to watch and analyse.
- Advice on how much time to spend on different parts of the exams.

STUDENT'S BOOK | Reference material

There is a bank of reference material at the back of the Student's Book, designed to support students as they work through the lessons, and also intended to act as a revision tool when required.

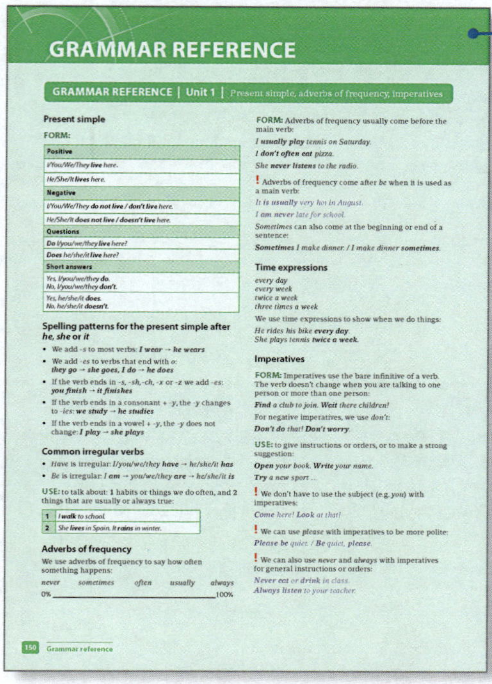

GRAMMAR REFERENCE

The *Grammar reference* pages provide more detailed explanations of the grammar points covered in every unit, along with example sentences showing how the structures can be used.

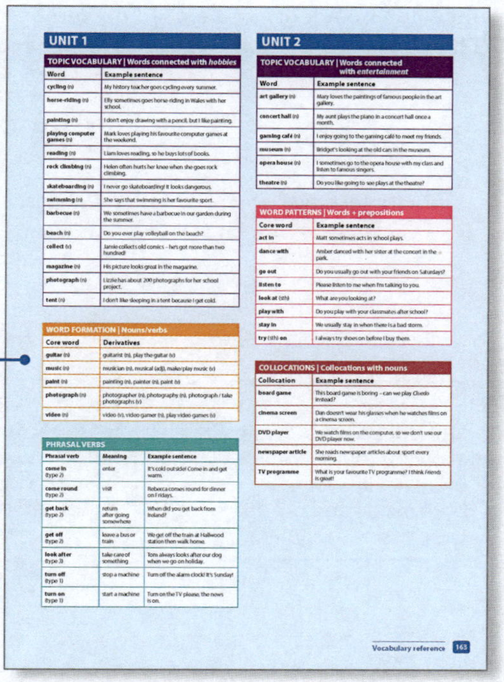

UNIT 1 UNIT 2

All three vocabulary sections from each unit are expanded upon in the *Vocabulary reference*. The sections on Topic vocabulary, Phrasal verbs, Collocations and Word patterns all include example sentences. The Word formation sections include a list of derivatives.

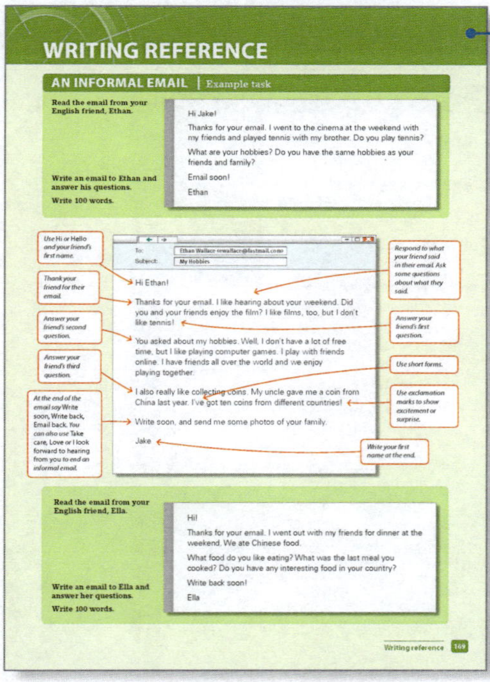

WRITING REFERENCE

There is a model text for each common writing genre, with annotations to highlight key points that students need to remember.

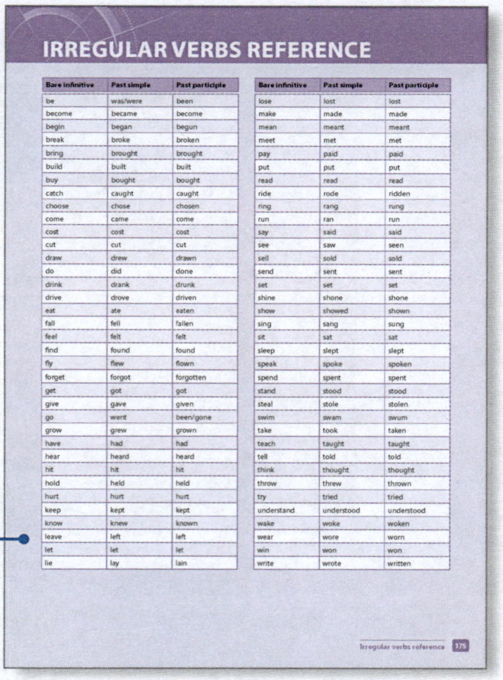

IRREGULAR VERBS REFERENCE

A list of irregular verbs used throughout the A2 Student's Book is provided at the end of the reference material.

DIGITAL STUDENT'S BOOK SB

Includes an access code for the Student's Resource Centre

The *Optimise* Digital Student's Book offers students the possibility of an interactive learning experience, which engages the class as a whole and enables lessons to be dynamic and motivating. The material is easily downloadable and, once downloaded, can be used offline.

The *Optimise* Digital Student's Book includes:

Interactive Student's Book Activities
Interactive versions of the Student's Book activities, allowing the option of more flexible learning both inside and outside the classroom situation.

Complete class audio and **Integrated video**
Easy-to-navigate digital reproduction of the Student's Book pages, which includes embedded audio and video material.

Note-taking function
A notes facility, which enables students to make their own notes about all aspects of the Digital Student's Book material.

Score report (Scores)
A score report facility, which means exercises will be automatically marked and scores will be sent through to you when the student next goes online.

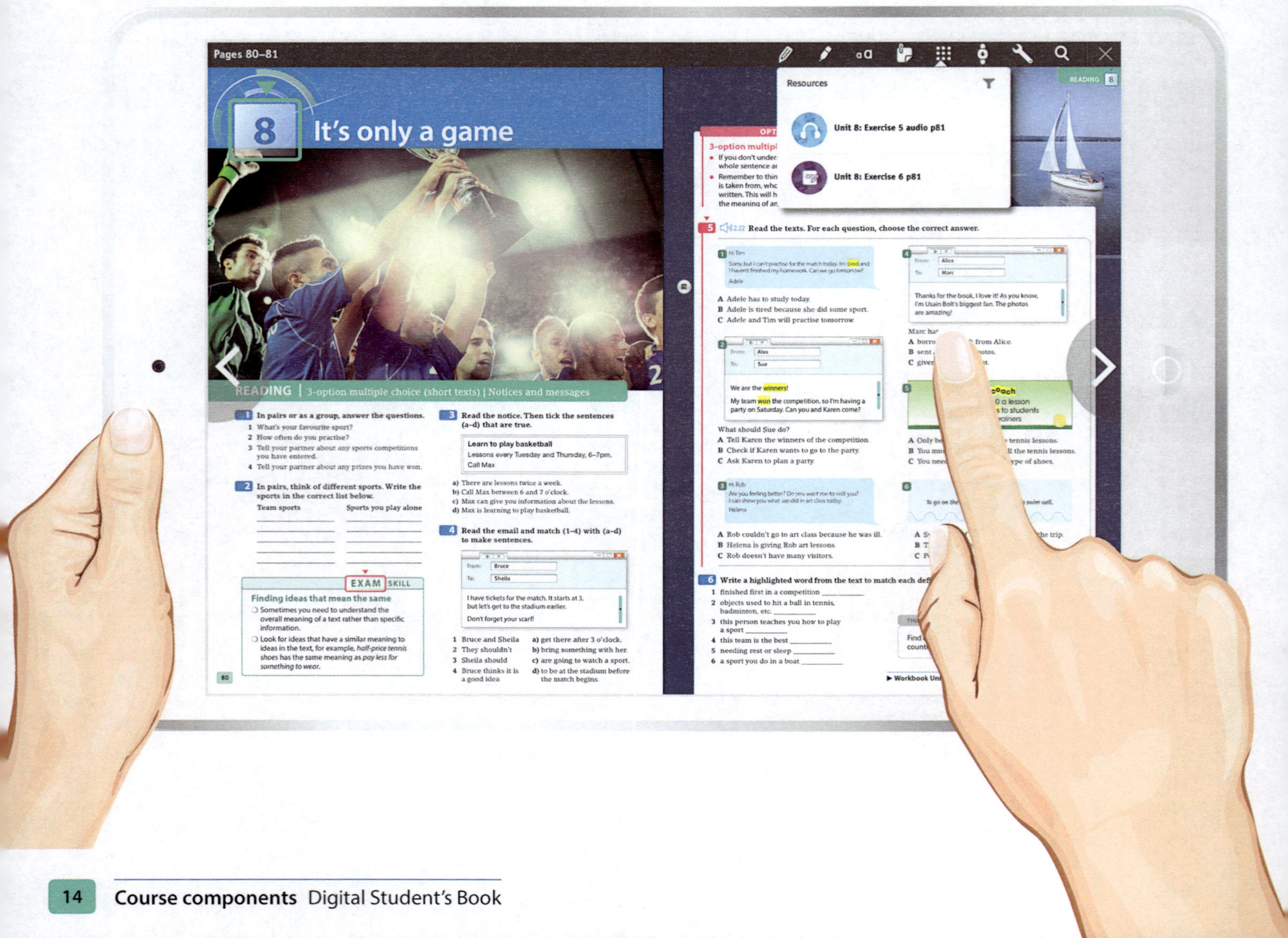

PRESENTATION KIT

Includes digital versions of the Student's Book and Workbook

You can use the *Optimise* Presentation Kit in the classroom to promote interactive, heads-up lessons, allowing for the option of collaborative learning. The Presentation Kit provides you with a versatile, digital presentation and teaching tool. Built-in functionality enables you to annotate and customise your presentation in advance, making the lesson more suited to the needs of your class. The Presentation Kit can be easily downloaded and, once downloaded, can be used offline.

The *Optimise* Presentation Kit includes:

Interactive Student's Book activities

Interactive versions of the Student's Book activities, giving you the opportunity to complete activities and check answers as a whole class.

Complete Class and Workbook audio / **Integrated video**

All class audio and video material, which can be played instantly by clicking on the hotspots throughout the Presentation Kit material.

Student's Book and Workbook Answer key feature

Answer keys for the Student's Book and Workbook are embedded within each activity, meaning you can show the next answer at the touch of a button. Additional answer key pop-ups are also provided, with suggested answers for open activities.

Note pad feature

A notes facility, enabling you to add your own comments on the material. This helps you deliver more effective and engaging lessons.

VIDEOS

Use in class or for self-study

Optimise videos provide comprehensive support for students to develop their speaking skills. The course features two different video strands, both of which are flexible and versatile resources that can be used in a number of different ways to support and extend listening and speaking skills.

Talk2Me

1 *Talk2Me* videos

Every Speaking lesson includes a *Talk2Me* video. These exciting videos feature three teenagers (twins Jojo and Max and their best friend, Evie) in a variety of everyday situations, where things sometimes don't go quite as planned!

The videos present key functional language in a natural and original context.

Flipped classroom

Flipped classroom option

You can choose to use the Flipped classroom approach for these videos and set them for homework. Students watch the videos and complete the exercises in the Student's Book at home to prepare for the Speaking lesson. This allows more class time to activate the functional language and develop fluency for the exam task.

Classroom option

Of course, the videos can be watched together as a class with students completing the exercises individually or sharing their ideas with other students.

The videos are available on the Resource Centre and are accompanied by additional worksheets, transcripts and answer keys.

2 Speaking test videos

Optimise includes Speaking test videos as part of the *Optimise your exams* section. The videos provide students with a chance to observe the performance of candidates doing complete Speaking tests under exam conditions.

Watching and discussing the video also enables students to have a greater understanding of the format and processes involved in speaking tests, giving them more confidence and helping them to feel better prepared for the exam.

WORKBOOK | Reading lesson

Each Workbook unit has eight pages, with a section for each separate lesson in the Student's Book, and one page for an end-of-unit Progress check.

Complete *Optimise Practice test* at the back of the Workbook

All exam skills match the corresponding Student's Book lesson.

Every unit includes a reference to the corresponding Student's Book lesson.

Exercises check students' comprehension of the reading text and are designed to develop students' reading skills.

New vocabulary from the Workbook reading text is highlighted.

The Reading lessons feature exam-type reading texts.

8 It's only a game

READING | 3-option multiple choice (short texts) | Notices and messages

→Student's Book, pages 80–81

1 **Read the email and complete the sentences with the words in the box.**

doesn't know | don't usually
some information | tells | usually

From: Coach
To: Team

Basketball practice tomorrow is outside, not in the sports centre, as usual. Don't forget your kit. I'll tell you where our next practice is then.

1 The players ________________ practise in the sports centre.
2 The coach ________________ them to bring something.
3 The players ________________ practise outside.
4 The coach ________________ where next week's basketball practice will be.
5 The coach will give them ________________ later.

2 **Read the message and circle the correct words.**

Jack,
I have some news! The school sports club is now open every day after school, except for holidays! Why don't we go on Friday?
Becky

1 They **can / can't** go to the sports club during the holidays.
2 Becky is **asking for / giving** Jack some news.
3 The sports club is **open all day / opens after the last lessons.**
4 Becky **would like to go on Friday / doesn't want to go on Friday.**
5 Jack should **go to the club on Friday / write back to Becky.**

3 **Choose the best answer, a or b, to show what the sentences mean.**

1 Basketball: for under 14s only
a) Children who are not older than 14 can do this activity.
b) Children who are not younger than 14 can do this activity.
2 Free entry for members and one friend
a) Only members don't have to pay.
b) A friend of a member doesn't have to pay.
3 To join the club, fill in the form.
a) Complete the form and become a member of the club.
b) Become a member of the club and then complete the form.
4 Are you still interested in going rock-climbing?
a) Do you think rock-climbing is interesting?
b) Do you want to do the activity?

60

It's only a game 8

4 **Read the texts. For each question, choose the correct answer.**

Hi Liz
The basketball team is having a meeting on Friday about the last match of the year. We all have to be there!
May

1 A Liz and May are not meeting the basketball team.
B The team will play the last match on Friday.
C Every player must go to the meeting.

From: Jo
To: Leo

I want to look after my health and get fit. How did you do it? Can you give me some advice? Thanks!

4 What should Leo do?
A try to exercise more often
B suggest things Jo should do/try
C ask Jo if she is feeling any better

Tim,
I need your swimming cap. I can't find mine and the coach doesn't let us swim without it. Is it in your room?
Ellie

2 What should Tim do?
A Look for Ellie's swimming cap.
B Tell Ellie where to find something.
C Let the teacher know about the cap.

VOLLEYBALL TEAMS NEED BEGINNERS
Ages 12–15
We always play every Saturday

5 A You should have experience playing volleyball.
B You need to be a good player.
C You must be free once a week.

CRICKET CLUB
No matches tomorrow afternoon. Will play on Sunday if grass isn't wet.

3 A The team will not be able to play cricket tomorrow.
B The team isn't sure if they will play cricket on Sunday.
C The team have decided not to play cricket tomorrow.

From: John
To: Andy

Do you want to go to the football competition? I've got tickets. If not, I'll ask Lucy. Call me by 6pm.

6 John is asking Andy
A to decide if he wants to go to the competition.
B to give his ticket to Lucy for the competition.
C to tell John why he cannot go to the competition.

5 **Match the highlighted words in the texts to the definitions 1–6.**

1 take care of someone or something ________________
2 a teacher for a sport team ________________
3 people who are starting to learn something ________________
4 an event where people talk ________________
5 an event where people try to be the best or the fastest ________________
6 covered in water ________________

61

WORKBOOK | Grammar lessons | Vocabulary lesson

Grammar lessons throughout the Workbook reflect the material covered in the Student's Book and provide students with more opportunities to consolidate and practise the structures.

The page number of the Student's Book *Grammar reference* is included in the Workbook so that students can refer back if they need to.

8 GRAMMAR 1 | Modals (1): ability, necessity, obligation, possibility

→ Student's Book, page 82 → Grammar reference, Unit 8, Student's Book, page 157

1 Complete the sentences with *can, can't, could* or *couldn't*.

1 All my friends __________ ride horses, but I can't.
2 My brother __________ go skiing last weekend because his leg hurt.
3 __________ you ride a bike when you were five?
4 When Laura was young, she __________ swim really well and she won prizes.
5 Can you speak more slowly, please? I __________ understand you.
6 I __________ play volleyball yesterday because I was ill in bed.
7 We __________ go swimming with you. We're studying for a test.
8 __________ you run faster than your friends or are they faster than you?

2 Complete the swimming club rules with the correct form of *have to* or *don't have to*.

Langton Swimming Club

1 If you are under 16, you __________ come with an adult or you can't use the club.
2 The club is free for members. They __________ pay.
3 Swimmers __________ wear a swimming cap in the pool. You can't swim without one.
4 Everyone __________ have a shower before going into the pool, or they can't go in.
5 You __________ bring your own towel or shampoo. We have everything you need here.
6 You __________ put your wet towels in the bins. Please do not leave them on the floor.

Every grammar section contains two or three exercises, and where possible texts are included, giving students another chance to see the unit grammar in a realistic context.

3 Complete the sentences with the correct form of *may, must* or *need to* and the verbs in brackets.

1 I __________ **(stay)** at home today and watch the athletics on TV. I'm not sure.
2 We're playing at 11am, but you __________ **(drive)** us to the match. We're going by bus.
3 You __________ **(run)** near the swimming pool.
4 You can't leave now! You __________ **(stay)** and see the end of the match.
5 __________ I __________ **(bring)** my own tennis balls or can I borrow some?
6 My brother's won all his matches easily. I'm not sure, but I think he __________ **(win)** the final.

8 VOCABULARY | Topic vocabulary | Word formation | Collocations

→ Student's Book, page 83 → Vocabulary reference, Student's Book, page 166

The corresponding page of the *Vocabulary reference* is included throughout the Workbook wherever relevant.

1 Read the descriptions of some words about sport. What is the word for each one? The first letter is there to help you. There is one space for each other letter in the word.

1 You hit a tennis ball with this. r _ _ _ _ _
2 Women wear this to swim. s _ _ _ _ _ _ _ _
3 You need to buy this to get into a match. t _ _ _ _ _
4 You sit on a horse and do this. r _ _ _
5 This person tells the team what to do in a match. c _ _ _ _
6 The clothes or things you need to play a sport. k _ _

2 Complete the sentences with the correct form of the words in the box.

play | run | surf | swim | win

1 Every morning, my mum __________ in the pool before she goes to work.
2 Our team were better, so we __________ the basketball match 45-32.
3 My brother loves to run. He is a fast __________. He won the 400-m race in the stadium yesterday.
4 I like tennis, but I'm a terrible __________.
5 I want to go to Hawaii with my surfboard and __________ in the sea there.

62

Each of the three vocabulary sections is covered separately in the Workbook, giving your students another chance to reinforce their lexical knowledge.

It's only a game 8

3 Match to make sentences.

1 In basketball, you need to throw ___
2 You can't climb ___
3 My sister may enter ___
4 I've never played ___
5 In the summer, we often go ___
6 I hope I win ___

a) badminton, but I want to.
b) the race, but I can't run very fast.
c) swimming in the lake.
d) the skiing competition. She's very good.
e) the ball to someone in your team.
f) that mountain without good boots.

A second grammar section in the Workbook corresponds to the second grammar lesson in the Student's Book.

8 GRAMMAR 2 | Modals (2): advice, permission, polite requests, prohibition

→ Student's Book, page 85 → Grammar reference, Unit 8, Student's Book, page 158

1 Look at the table and complete the conversation with the correct form of *can*.

Ride a bike	Play tennis	Go swimming
?	✓	✗

Kim: (1) __________ I come with you to the sports centre this afternoon?
Sue: Yes, sure. Today we (2) __________ play tennis, but we (3) __________ go swimming unfortunately.
Kim: That's a shame. Last week, we (4) __________ do both activities.
Sue: Yes, but the pool is closed today. (5) __________ you ride a bike? I'm going to cycle there.
Kim: I can, but I'm not sure if I'm allowed. I'll check with my parents. But (6) __________ you possibly lend me a bike? Mine is broken.

2 Complete the sentences with *should* or *shouldn't* and a verb from the box.

eat | get | play | talk | wear | worry

1 You __________ a big meal before you go swimming. It may make you feel ill.
2 Runners __________ comfortable shoes when they go running.
3 If we need to buy tickets, we __________ to the stadium early.
4 Shh! You __________ loudly at a tennis match.
5 Your sister __________ about the match. I'm sure she'll win!
6 If you think football is boring, you __________ basketball. I think it's more exciting.

3 Complete the second sentence so that it has a similar meaning to the first. Use the correct form of *can, have to, must* or *should* and any other words you need.

Example: It is prohibited to wear outdoor shoes in the sports hall.
You *mustn't wear* outdoor shoes in the sports hall.

1 We weren't allowed to go into the gym because the teacher wasn't there.
We __________ into the gym because the teacher wasn't there.
2 Is it possible for you to open the window, please? It's hot in here.
__________ you __________ the window, please? It's hot in here.
3 It's a good idea to buy tickets for the match early.
We __________ tickets for the match early.
4 It is prohibited for students under 16 to use the gym.
You __________ the gym if you are under 16.

63

Exercises in the Workbook are staged so as to be progressively more challenging.

WORKBOOK | Listening lesson | Speaking lesson | Language in Use lesson

8 LISTENING | Matching

→ Student's Book, page 84

The listening exam skill in the Student's Book is practised again in the Workbook.

1 Match the phrases a–e to the words 1–5 with a similar meaning.

1 running ___ a) walking to the top of a mountain
2 tennis ___ b) going out in a boat
3 climbing ___ c) riding a bike
4 sailing ___ d) moving very quickly on foot
5 cycling ___ e) playing a racket sport

2 10 Listen to five people talking about sport. As you listen, choose each person's favourite sport, a or b.

Speaker 1 ___ a) sailing b) swimming
Speaker 2 ___ a) tennis b) table tennis
Speaker 3 ___ a) running b) cycling
Speaker 4 ___ a) football b) rugby
Speaker 5 ___ a) skiing b) climbing

3 11 Listen to two people talking about their friends. For each friend, choose his or her favourite sport. There are three extra letters you do not need.

The Workbook listening exercises have their own dedicated audio material, available on the Resource Centres and on the Online Workbook.

Friends	Sports
1 Ben ___	A table tennis
2 Harry ___	B swimming
3 Paula ___	C cricket
4 Lisa ___	D rugby
5 Steve ___	E surfing
	F sailing
	G basketball
	H skiing

Workbook exercises give students more practice in exam-type tasks.

8 SPEAKING | Discussion (pictures)

→ Student's Book, page 86

1 Complete the conversation with the words in the box.

As the Workbook is designed for independent use, the speaking lessons consist of written exercises specifically designed to provide essential preparation that will further improve students' speaking skills.

about | agree | boring | do | prefer | really | think | you

Carla: Let's discuss these different ways of getting fit. What do you (1) __________ about jogging?
Mark: I've never tried it, but I think it would be (2) __________ . What about (3) __________ ?
Carla: Yes, I (4) __________ . I don't (5) __________ like exercising alone.
Mark: Well, what (6) __________ going to a sports centre?
Carla: That might be OK. You can do different things there. What (7) __________ you think?
Mark: Well, it could be expensive. As an activity, I think it's good but I (8) __________ using my exercise bike at home.

2 Look at the pictures. Do you like these different ways of getting fit? Why / Why not?

3 Write your answers to the questions below.

1 Do you think going to the gym is fun? Why?
2 Which of these activities do you like best? Why?
3 Do you prefer to exercise alone or with friends? Why?

64

It's only a game 8

8 LANGUAGE IN USE | Open cloze

→ Student's Book, page 87

Workbook exercises give students the chance to examine and practise language in more detail.

1 Complete the sentences with the correct modal verb in the positive or negative form.

can | could | may | must | should

Example: You *should* only go swimming in the sea when there are other people with you.

1 At school we ____________________ walk in the corridors, not run.
2 ____________________ you help me, please?
3 When I was three, I ____________________ ride a bike. I learnt when I was five.
4 You ____________________ go swimming straight after eating.
5 Ask Lauren, she ____________________ be able to help you.

The Language in Use lessons in the Workbook include an exam-type task, so students get a further opportunity to apply the language skills they developed in the Student's Book lesson.

2 Read the text and write the correct answer in each gap. Write ONE word for each gap.

To: greg@home.com
Subject: The World Alternative Games

Hi Greg,

I've *just* read an article about the World Alternative Games. You really (1) __________ read about this event too. I think the Games are a lot of fun! They started in Llanwrtyd Wells, a small town in Wales. The people decided to have their (2) __________ sporting event, like the Olympic Games. One of the events is the Man versus Horse race. It's for runners and people riding horses, and they race for 35 km. The horses (3) __________ 15 minutes after the runners. I (4) __________ not go to Wales last year, but I (5) __________ go this year, I'm not sure yet. If I do, I'll watch that race! You should (6) __________ about the games online.

alternative different, not the usual

Engaging images attract students' attention and interest in the text.

65

8 WRITING | Guided writing (an email)

→ Student's Book, pages 88–89

1 Read the exam task. What information do you need to give Becca? Tick the correct answers (1–6).

Write an email to Becca and answer her questions.

From: Becca
To:

You haven't told me about your PE lessons at school. How often do you do PE at school? Who's your teacher? What clothes do you have to wear?

Write **25 words** or more.

1 how often ☐
2 the place ☐
3 the person who teaches ☐
4 the sports kit ☐
5 the other students ☐
6 the name of the school ☐

> Writing lessons begin by re-focusing students on the exam advice given in their Student's Book.

2 Read the model emails below (A, B and C). Then complete the checklist. Which is the best email?

A
Dear Becca,
Thank you for your email. Im going to tell you about my PE lessons at school. My teacher is called Mr Hampton and he is very nice. Sometimes we can choose the sport and other times he tells us what we are going to do. I would like to try badminton next.
Best wishes,
Jack

B
PE's three times on week. The teacher's name are Mrs Roberts. We don't have wear special clothes.

C
Hi Becca,
We've got PE twice a week. Our teachers called Mr Thomas. We have to wear a white T-shirt and blue shorts. We don't have to bring racket or balls!
Write soon,
Danny

Checklist ✓

		A	B	C	ME
1	The email uses informal style, including contractions.	○	○	○	○
2	It starts and ends in the right way.	○	○	○	○
3	It answers all of Becca's questions.	○	○	○	○
4	It's 25 words or more.	○	○	○	○
5	The spelling and grammar is correct.	○	○	○	○

The best email is ___ .

> The Workbook includes a model answer in addition to the one found in the Student's Book.

3 Read these sentences from the emails in Exercise 2. Rewrite the underlined words correctly.

1 Im going to tell you about my PE lessons. ______
2 Our teachers called Mr Thomas. ______
3 PE's three times on week. ______
4 The teacher's name are Mrs Roberts. ______
5 We don't have wear special clothes. ______

> Exercises in the Workbook will help students to consolidate and develop their writing skills in general.

4 Write your own email to Becca. Then check your email using the checklist in Exercise 2.

______

> Students usually do a complete writing task in the Workbook.

66

> Every Workbook lesson ends with a one-page *Progress check*.

It's only a game 8

PROGRESS CHECK

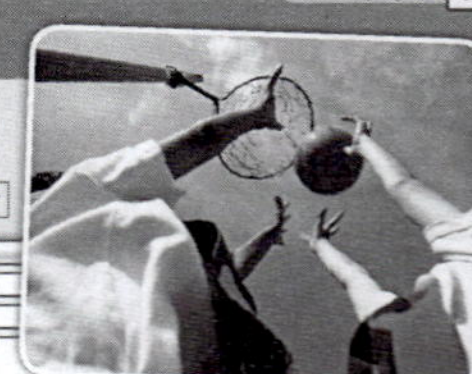

1 Complete the email with the words in the box. There are two extra words you do not need.

club | coach | go | kit | members | play | teams | throw | ticket | winner

From: Natalie
To: Emily

Hi Emily,

Thanks for your email. You asked me about my favourite sport. I've got two actually – tennis and netball. I know you (1) ______ tennis, so let me tell you about netball. There are two (2) ______ of seven players. It's like basketball, you get points by putting the ball, into a ring – the team with the most points is the (3) ______ . In basketball, you can move with the ball, but in netball you can't, you have to (4) ______ the ball to another player. The sports (5) ______ is similar to tennis – girls wear a T-shirt, a skirt and trainers, but the ball is much bigger and heavier than a tennis ball. I started playing on the school netball team about three years ago. Then our town's netball (6) ______ asked me to play in their under-16 team. Our (7) ______ is amazing; she never gets angry even when we lose. The next Netball World Cup is going to be near my home. I hope I can buy a (8) ______ to watch a match.

I hope this answers your question.

Write soon,

Natalie

2 Choose the correct answers.

1 A: Are you going to play tennis after school?
B: **I don't have to / can't / couldn't** play. I've hurt my hand.
2 A: I want to watch the match on TV.
B: You **should / don't have to / can't** tidy your room first. There are clothes everywhere!
3 A: When did you learn to climb trees?
B: I **can / could / should** climb them when I was six.
4 A: My brother would like to try a new exciting sport.
B: Well, he **shouldn't / couldn't / doesn't have to** play rugby. It's really dangerous.
5 A: **Can / Could / Should** your brother run as fast as you?
B: No, he isn't a fast runner. I'm much faster.
6 A: I need some new trainers.
B: You **should / can / don't have to** look online. They're much cheaper.
7 A: **Can I / Should I / I have to** go swimming with my friends?
B: Yes, but remember we're going to have dinner with Grandma later.
8 A: I'll never finish this homework and I've got a match this afternoon.
B: Don't worry, we **shouldn't / couldn't / don't have to** give it to the teacher until Monday.

> The *Progress Check* always has one exercise based on the vocabulary from the unit, and one exercise based on the unit grammar.

Cumulative progress 1 2 3 4 5 6 7 8 9 10 11 12

3 Choose the best answer (A, B or C) to complete the conversations.

1 You should get a new racket from Sports World.
A Yes, of course it is. B That's a good idea. C I have to buy a new racket.
2 Have you ever been to a basketball match?
A We're going to be there soon. B I went to one last summer. C You've been to a match.
3 Are you going to enter the competition?
A I'm not sure. B I won't play. C I didn't.
4 Shall we go surfing later?
A I'm sorry. I can't swim. B You don't have to. C We couldn't go.
5 We couldn't play tennis because it was raining.
A Were you playing tennis? B Did you play tennis? C What did you do?

67

> The final part of the *Progress check* is a *Cumulative progress* exercise, which includes vocabulary and grammar items from any of the preceding units.

ONLINE WORKBOOK OWB

For students PLUS Gradebook for teachers

The *Optimise* Online Workbook includes all the print Workbook content in a fully-interactive digital format, which students can use for independent self-study.
The *Optimise* Online Workbook includes:

- Interactive Workbook activities
- Complete Workbook audio
- Automated marking for instant feedback
- Gradebook

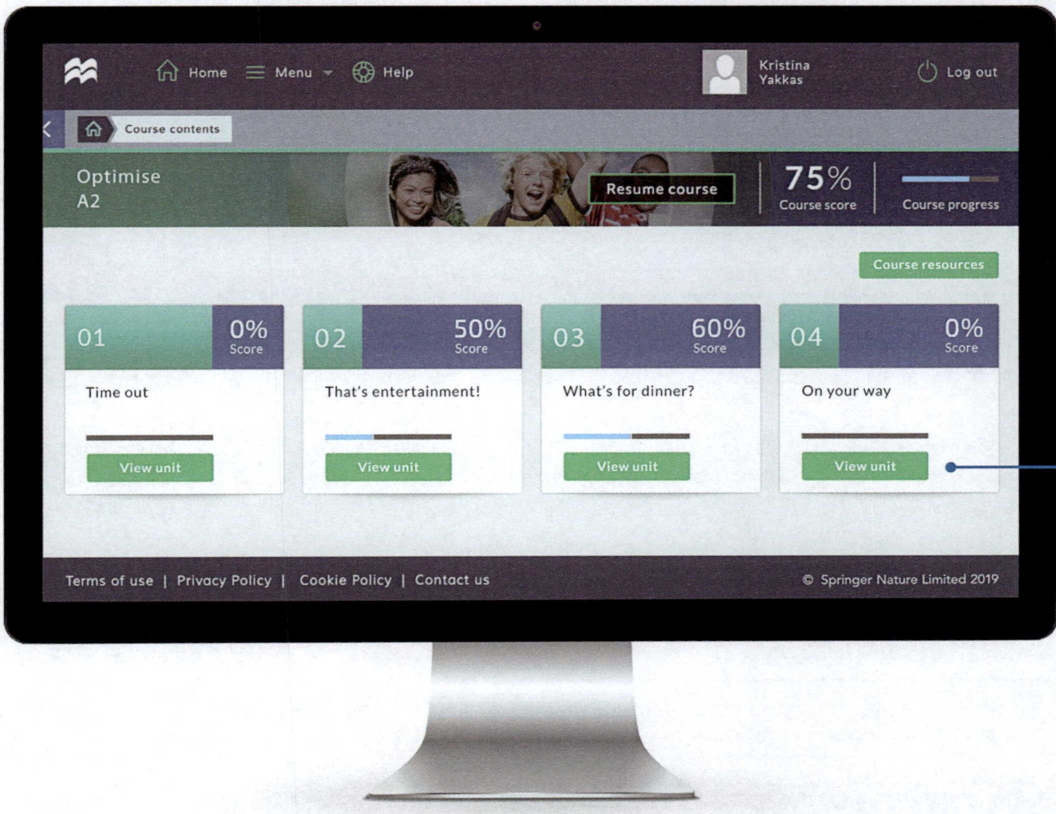

The Online Workbook enables you to manage multiple classes in a single location, and the content-locking facility gives you control over how you manage the tasks for your class.

The automatic Gradebook facility will save you valuable marking time.

Students have the chance to make multiple attempts at answering questions, enabling them to effectively consolidate their learning.

Scores are automatically collated and clearly displayed in the Gradebook, so it is easy to compare students and classes. Students' progress can be monitored at a glance, highlighting areas where they may require additional support.

The messaging and notification features allow you to correspond with your students, send homework reminders, and notify your classes when scores are available.

Detailed feedback on scores and progress creates a highly personalised self-study environment.

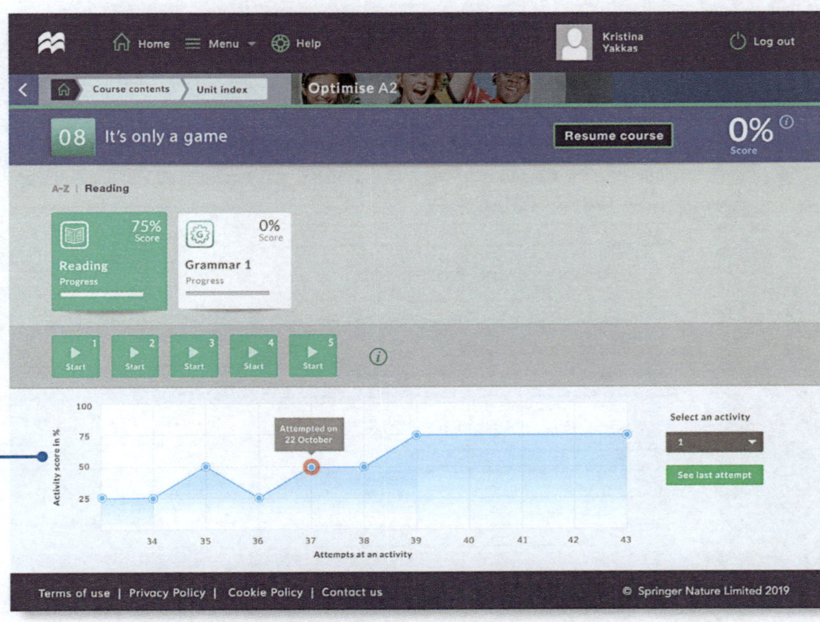

TEACHER'S AND STUDENT'S RESOURCE CENTRES

For teachers and students

The *Optimise* Resource Centres offer a huge bank of additional downloadable material and tests that have been designed to comprehensively support and enhance the core Student's Book and Workbook material.

For students, the Student's Resource Centre provides complementary materials to consolidate learning and encourage independent study.

STUDENT'S RESOURCE CENTRE

- *Optimise your grammar* worksheets (Standard and Higher)
- *Optimise your vocabulary* worksheets (Standard and Higher)
- *Talk2Me* videos and worksheets
- *Say it right* pronunciation worksheets
- Culture and CLIL worksheets
- Speaking test videos
- Class and Workbook audio

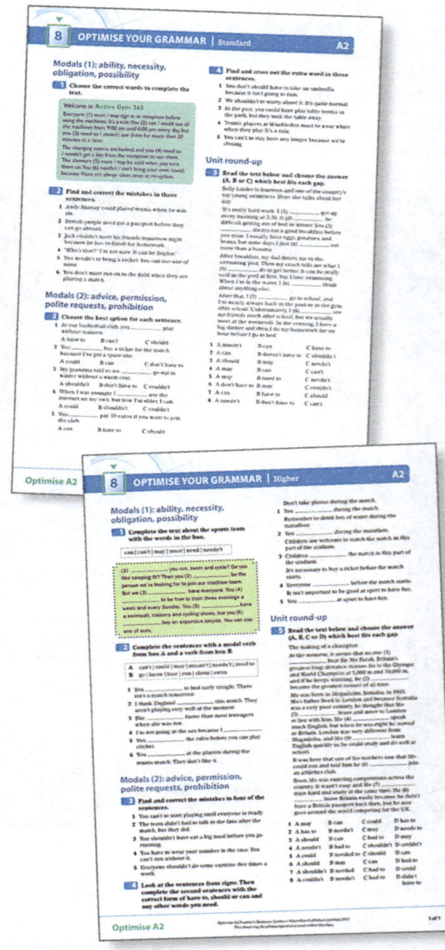
8 OPTIMISE YOUR GRAMMAR | Standard A2

Modals (1): ability, necessity, obligation, possibility

Unit round-up

Modals (2): advice, permission, polite requests, prohibition

Optimise A2

8 OPTIMISE YOUR GRAMMAR | Higher A2

Modals (1): ability, necessity, obligation, possibility

Unit round-up

Modals (2): advice, permission, polite requests, prohibition

Optimise A2

The Teacher's Resource Centre is your go-to place for resources to deliver dynamic lessons, assign tasks for homework, and for support in the classroom.

TEACHER'S RESOURCE CENTRE

- *Optimise your grammar* worksheets (Standard and Higher)
- *Optimise your vocabulary* worksheets (Standard and Higher)
- *Talk2Me* videos and worksheets
- Speaking test videos
- *Say it right* pronunciation worksheets
- *Everyday English* worksheets
- Grammar communication worksheets
- Culture and CLIL worksheets
- Class and Workbook audio
- Answer keys
- Audioscripts
- Placement and Diagnostic tests, Unit and Progress tests
- A2 Key for Schools Practice test
- Wordlists

TESTING MATERIALS

Complete testing package

Optimise provides an extensive range of testing materials, which can be used throughout the school year to assess your students' progress and to prepare them for exams.

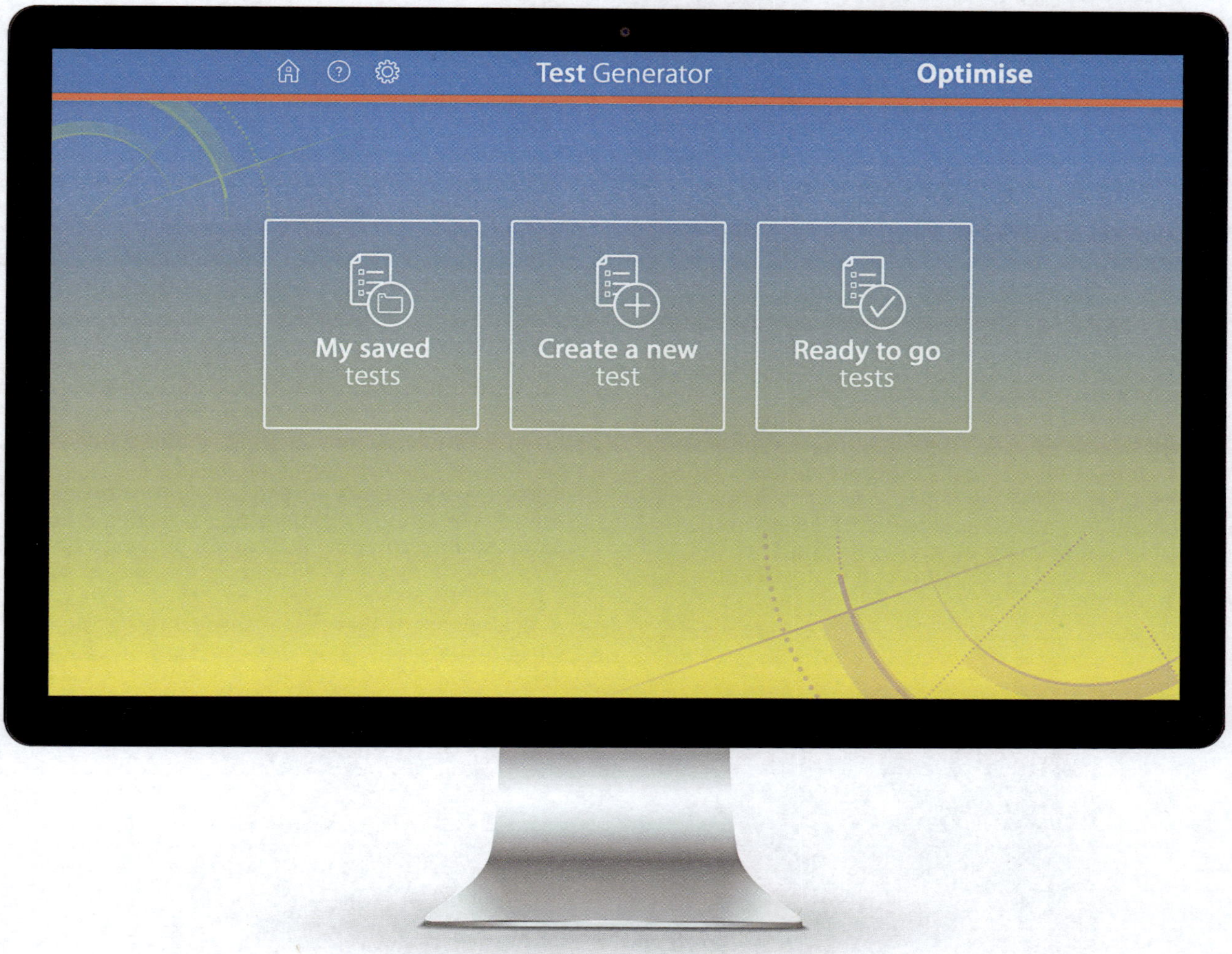

Printable tests

Optimise offers a comprehensive range of printable tests, available on the Teacher's Resource Centre in PDF format.

All the *Optimise* tests correspond to the course level.

Tests are aligned closely to the CEFR and to competency levels for international and state exams.

Tests include:

- *Diagnostic* and *Placement tests*
- *Unit tests*, *Progress tests* and *End-of-year tests* (Standard and Higher)
- A2 *Key for Schools* practice tests:
  - an *Optimise Practice test* at the back of the Workbook
  - A2 *Key for Schools Practice test* on the Teacher's Resource Centre, which can be taken under test conditions.

Complete answer keys, audio and audioscripts are provided for all tests.

Test Generator

The *Optimise* Test Generator allows you to create customised tests from the pre-prepared Unit and Progress tests.

- Tests are aligned to CEFR levels.
- The content reflects Reading and Writing, Listening and Speaking tasks from international and state exams.
- The Test Generator comes with the option to save tests in progress and to preview them before printing.
- With Standard and Higher levels available, it also allows for maximum flexibility in choosing the test content.

Teacher support

PREPARING STUDENTS FOR EXAMS

Knowing your exam

- It's important that students become as familiar as possible with the different parts of the exam they are preparing for and understand what is required of them in each exam task.
- Carry out timed practice tests regularly with your students. As well as being excellent training, it's also an important way of highlighting specific areas for improvement.
- *Optimise* includes two Practice tests: one at the back of the Workbook and another on the Teacher's Resource Centre.
- After each test, draw up a class checklist of basic reminders or issues related to the exam.
- The *Optimise your exams* section at the back of the Student's Book provides detailed information about each of the different parts of the exam, so students know what to expect.
- Many students associate exams with stress and panic, but if they are well prepared, students will generally feel more confident and that will show in their performance.

Reading preparation

- It's important that students develop key strategies for dealing with a variety of question types. These include skimming, scanning, reading for detail and understanding the main idea of the text, as well as being able to identify lexical and structural words.
- Encourage students to refer to dictionaries or the *Grammar* and *Vocabulary references* at the back of the Student's Book. However, students also need to learn strategies for working independently, as reference material cannot be used in exams.
- Students should create an efficient system for recording all new vocabulary they learn. Encourage them to think about how they can record words and phrases in as much detail as possible.
- Remind students that spelling is important, especially in tasks such as *Word completion*.
- Encourage students to read a variety of texts outside the classroom, e.g. online articles, graded readers, short stories and novels. This should help to increase their knowledge of vocabulary, grammatical structures and writing styles.
- Ask students to share ideas for recording and learning vocabulary, and to give short presentations about what they have read or learnt outside the classroom.

PREPARING STUDENTS FOR EXAMS

Writing preparation

- Make sure students have regular opportunities throughout the year for writing. They can write things like short messages, invitations, plans for meeting, etc.
- Writing in another language can be challenging for most young students, so make sure they have plenty of practice, both in class and as homework, at writing the different types of Key Test tasks.
- Make sure students always read the question carefully and underline the key points. If they don't answer the question, respond to specific prompts or include all relevant information, they may lose marks.
- Remind students to think carefully about who they are writing for, and if the style required will be formal or informal.
- Encourage students to plan their work before writing. As well as planning their work, students should leave time at the end to check spelling and punctuation.
- Timing is important in a real exam and practice under timed conditions in class is the best way to prepare students for writing tasks.
- Students should try to write within the correct word limit. They won't lose marks for writing more words than the suggested amount (25–35), but will lose marks if they write fewer. Advise your students to try and write the required number of words.
- Encourage students to read each other's pieces of writing to give them ideas and develop their own writing further.

Listening preparation

- It's important that students develop key strategies for dealing with a variety of listening question types. These include answering multiple-choice questions on pictures, dialogues and on longer conversations, matching items and completing gap fills based on conversations and monologue.
- Classroom discussions can help prior to doing a listening task. For example, ask students what they think the speakers will talk about, and if they will hear any specific information, such as times, names, dates and places.
- It can also be useful to vary the focus of a task in class before students attempt a set of exam questions. For example, students could listen once to give an overall summary of what was said on the audio, then listen again for specific information.
- When listening to short conversations, students need to look carefully at multiple-choice options in questions and underline key words. When the options are pictures, encourage students to think about what each of the three picture options have in common and what key words they might hear in the conversation.
- When listening to longer conversations or monologues, encourage students to listen for the overall idea(s) first before they focus on the actual words and phrases. Make sure students listen to stressed or key words that have an important message, rather than focusing on every individual word.
- Encourage students to listen to audio material outside class, for example on English-language digital radio or TV stations. They also need to hear a variety of accents, styles and age groups.
- When students listen to authentic material, encourage them to develop strategies such as picking out key information, or deducing meaning from context by focusing on key words and ignoring unimportant or unknown words.

Speaking preparation

- Some students may feel especially nervous about taking a speaking exam, so one way to reassure them is to make them familiar with the structure of the exam they are going to take.
- In some speaking exams, students are tested in pairs and there are two examiners: one interlocutor, who speaks to the candidates and directs the test as well as giving marks, and one assessor, who marks the students on specific criteria.
- It is important for students to understand the different types of interaction that will take place. For example, students need to know when they will speak with their partner or with the interlocutor.
- All classroom activities that encourage students to ask and answer questions, discuss issues in pairs or groups, or talk about themselves and their own experiences will give them practice in skills they will need in an exam, and will also help to build their confidence when speaking.
- When practising any activities for speaking, encourage students to speak clearly and to ask for clarification if they don't understand or aren't sure about something.
- Ask students to work in pairs or groups to do some simple role plays. They should use everyday language to ask and answer questions about things like their family, daily routines, hobbies and interests. It's helpful for them to also practise exchanging information about things like prices, dates, opening times, etc. of a local library or sports centre, for example.
- Encourage students to expand on their ideas and give examples or reasons when speaking.
- Give students as much practice as possible in talking with partners in class. Encouraging them to discuss different exercises as they work on them or their ideas for writing tasks all provide good speaking opportunities and, again, build confidence.

TEACHING MIXED-ABILITY CLASSES

Introduction

All classes have students of different abilities and with a range of different learning needs. The teacher's challenge is to engage the more advanced students at the same time as helping those who are finding lessons more difficult. Here are some practical tips to create a more inclusive classroom.

Group dynamics

Begin the whole class together with a lead-in activity to provide a sense of community and a foundation for the levelled tasks that will follow. Lead-in activities preview, present and practise language in a way that lends itself perfectly to whole-class, multi-level instruction. At the end of a lesson, always bring the class back together and assign a whole-class activity.

Group, pair and individual work

Vary the way students work in the class to address different levels and needs. Organise students to work in pairs, small groups and teams. It is less stressful for weaker students to work with other classmates because they have more time to think about tasks, and students can help and learn from each other.

In some schools, it may be possible to divide classes into two groups according to ability. The two groups can be given the same work to complete, or they can work on differentiated material.

Games and activities, such as brainstorming vocabulary, help to increase collaboration in the mixed-ability classroom. For example, ask students to work together to produce spidergrams as a way to help them remember topic vocabulary.

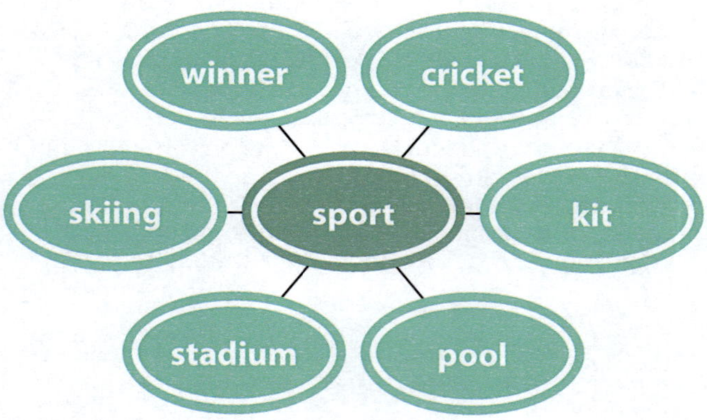

No matter what the level of the student, they all get better results through collaboration than they would have got by working on their own.

Pair work is usually successful in the mixed-ability classroom because it is easy to control and there is greater student participation. Depending on the task, decide how you organise your students into pairs: students with a similar level can work together at their own pace, or a stronger student can pair with a weaker student and help to support them. There are plenty of opportunities for pair work throughout *Optimise*.

Individual work allows for variations in speed and level. By giving a time limit rather than a quantity-of-work limit (e.g. '*Do as much as you can in three minutes.*' instead of, '*Do exercise 3.*'), students are able to work at their own pace.

Specific strategies for dealing with above-level students

- **Reading**

Set advanced students more challenging work to keep them motivated. For example, they could write their own comprehension questions to ask the class, select six new words from the reading text to write definitions for and learn, or create their own sentences using new vocabulary from the reading text.

- **Grammar and Vocabulary**

Ask stronger students to try to work out the meaning of new words from the context and to elicit grammar rules by looking at the language in context.

Encourage a higher level of fluency and accuracy from the stronger students.

Encourage students to support weaker classmates by explaining the grammar point to them or by clarifying the meaning of a new vocabulary item.

- **Listening**

Ask students to summarise what they heard after listening to it the first time (as a whole class or in pairs).

Encourage students to write their own comprehension questions to ask the class.

- **Speaking**

Demand a higher level of fluency and accuracy and ask stronger students to justify and defend their opinions.

Practise paraphrasing and brainstorm other phrases to use in the functional language (*Phrase expert*) boxes.

Encourage students to write their own conversations to act out in pairs.

- **Writing**

Indicate where something could be said in a more interesting or more complex way, and set creative tasks that students can do at their level.

Encourage peer correction by asking them to look at each other's work and suggest improvements. However, where more advanced students are reviewing work from below-level students, always make sure they are sensitive and constructive in their advice.

TEACHING MIXED-ABILITY CLASSES

Specific strategies for dealing with below-level students

- **General classroom organisation**

Make sure weaker students don't sit at the back, where it's more difficult for you to make eye contact with them.

Give clear instructions and check students have understood the task before they begin. For more complex tasks, ask stronger students to do an example of the task to check understanding.

- **Reading**

Ask weaker students easier questions, alternating with harder questions for stronger students.

Simplify multiple-choice tasks by reducing the number of options. Then gradually increase to exam level.

- **Grammar and Vocabulary**

Simplify gap-fill tasks by introducing optional answers, so students can identify the correct answer rather than having to produce it.

Be selective in your error correction and praise students for what they have managed to do, regardless of what others have produced.

Use homework to address weaknesses and consolidate classwork by using the mixed-ability Grammar and Vocabulary worksheets on the Teacher's Resource Centre.

- **Listening**

Pause the audio regularly to check understanding and explain if anything remains unclear. For more difficult texts, provide audioscripts after the first two listenings.

- **Speaking**

Provide useful phrases and model answers for less-able students to use as a basis for their answers.

- **Writing**

Additional model answers can assist students with their writing tasks. For students who need more support, provide a gapped or jumbled model answer for them to complete or put in order instead of asking them to write a text from scratch.

Mixed-ability features in *Optimise*

The **Mixed-ability** features in the *Optimise* Teacher's Book help to engage different groups of students using the same class material as the starting point, but with multi-level instruction. This way, you avoid increased preparation time, and the student group can still work together for most of the class.

As well as the **Mixed-ability** features in the *Optimise* Teacher's Book, the **Optional extension** and **Fast finishers** boxes also offer teachers a range of suggestions for ways to differentiate activities for stronger students.

Mixed ability

Ask stronger students to cover Exercise 5 and look at the highlighted words in the text and to try to work out what they mean purely from the context. Have less confident students complete the task as it appears in the Student's Book. Then pair stronger students with weaker students and have them share their ideas. Give students this model to follow: *I think* online *means* on the internet. *Do you agree?*

Optional extension

Have students play ***Preposition tennis*** in groups of three. Tell two students to work together with their books closed (Students A and B) and tell the third student (Student C) to act as the judge. Explain that Student A says a verb, e.g. *go*, and Student B has to say the corresponding preposition *out* and then a new verb, e.g. *stay*. Student A has to respond with the preposition *in* and so on. Student C monitors and checks they are using the correct prepositions and maintaining a regular rhythm. Monitor the groups in case Student C is unsure about the correct answer. If one student pauses for too long or repeats a verb, the other student wins a point. Have students change roles so they all take turns as judge.

Fast finishers

Ask students to explain what the incorrect alternatives mean and how they could be used, e.g. *a team* refers to a group of people who play a sport together, whereas *a member* is someone who belongs to a club or group: *Some members of the hockey team are friends of mine.*

The *Optimise* Teacher's Resource Centre provides additional Grammar and Vocabulary worksheets in addition to the Unit and Progress tests, all available at two levels (Standard and Higher).

The *Optimise* Test Generator also allows teachers to custom-build their own tests according to their students' needs.

Encourage students to use the Online Workbook. Students get immediate feedback on their work and they can do the tasks as many times as necessary in order to get them correct. It's perfect for students of all abilities.

TEACHING TIPS

Here are some useful teaching tips for you to refer to throughout the school year.

Encouraging language development

Optimise A2 provides your students with an excellent opportunity to consolidate and build on the language they have learnt up to this point. The material is rich with new vocabulary and presents comprehensive coverage of a full range of grammar structures. Lessons include a wide range of strategies that you can use to help your students develop their language. Exploiting all this material in as many ways as possible will help to consolidate the language and make students comfortable and confident about using it in other contexts.

Useful expressions

One important aspect of language development which you can help your students focus on at this level is learning expressions. Expressions are high-frequency, multi-word phrases that function as a unit. Very often, expressions are pronounced as if they were one word. Fixed expressions, such as expressions of opinion, perform specific functions and they can't always be defined by looking them up in a dictionary as individual words. Such expressions are important in helping students improve their fluency. If they can learn these fixed expressions, students can develop language competency by transferring them to a variety of different contexts.

It is often the case that students learn these expressions, use them in the class and then go back to using just one expression they were already familiar with. Point out to students they can gain more points in Speaking exams if they use a variety of expressions.

Developing accuracy and fluency in speaking

Accuracy is the ability to produce correct sentences with correct grammar and vocabulary. Fluency is the ability to read, speak or write easily, smoothly and with the correct intonation. The accuracy/fluency question depends on the purpose of the activity students are doing in the class. Controlled and semi-controlled speaking practice such as drills and information exchanges are working on accuracy. More open discussion should focus on fluency.

In general, try not to correct speaking too often in class as it interrupts the student's train of thought and can undermine their confidence. It's important to encourage students to talk and to keep talking. It's useful to note down errors while students are speaking then to take a few minutes at the end of class for a quick feedback session.

Memory and learning

Students are far more likely to remember words that they have analysed or focused on in some way than words they have learnt in isolation. If they have learnt the word in context and have fully understood it, rather than just learning it based upon a definition, it is much easier for students to remember the word in the long-term. Ask your students how they learn words best – do they need to hear them, see them written down or write them down themselves? Some students memorise vocabulary by associating new words with ideas or anecdotes. Help students to create mnemonic devices such as short phrases, tunes or poems to support their learning. In order to internalise vocabulary, students should also review vocabulary regularly. For strong lexical ability, students need to study vocabulary in context and that is best done by reading in English. Try to encourage your students to do this as much as possible. You could invite them to bring English books and magazines to class for group discussion or presentations. When your students come across a new word, encourage them to look at its place in the sentence, and to look at the words that appear either side of it. Remind them to think about the context and who the text is written for, and to look out for word patterns. They should always try to deduce meaning, but where they can't, point out that it's fine to use a dictionary as a tool for vocabulary building.

Teacher-talking time

As a teacher, you're always aware of how much time you spend speaking during the lesson. This is especially important in speaking lessons, where the key purpose is to encourage students to speak. That's not to say your speech isn't invaluable in providing models for pronunciation, functional language and appropriate discourse. But sometimes a large amount of teacher-talking time can slow the pace of a lesson and students can lose concentration and become bored or disinterested.

Some useful strategies to avoid this are:

- Wait for an answer when you ask a question. Students need 'thinking' time.
- Ask open-ended questions (e.g. *Wh-* questions) to encourage students to give longer answers, e.g. *What did you do last weekend?* instead of *Did you have a good weekend?*
- Vary the way students get feedback: they can check activities in pairs, for example.
- Encourage students to give explanations instead of giving them yourself.
- Present students with clear examples and guided questions so that they do not need to be 'told'. Guided discovery is a better and more rewarding way for students to learn.
- A useful guideline is to limit your talking to 30% of class time and no more than ten minutes at a time.

Pairwork

Pairwork is another opportunity for students to practise their speaking skills. Pairwork activities enable all students to have much more speaking time than if each student had an individual turn at speaking. When students are working in pairs, it also provides teachers with a chance to walk round and listen, and to give advice to students in a more discreet and personal way, rather than in front of the whole class.

If you ask students to work in pairs, they are likely to pair up with their friends or the person they sit nearest. It's a good idea to put students into 'new' pairs from time to time, so they can work with classmates of different abilities and with different approaches.

Certain speaking skills are necessary when working with another person, so it's useful to teach phrases that help students interrupt politely (*Yes, I agree, but … / May I … So you think …*, etc.).

Another idea to put students at their ease when they're speaking is to play some quiet music in the background. This helps students feel less self-conscious.

Personalisation

Students are more likely to want to speak when they are speaking about something they know about, are interested in or have experienced. Personalisation is important in learning a second language as it makes language more meaningful and therefore memorable to learners. There are plenty of personalisation opportunities throughout *Optimise*. Where possible, extend and adapt other activities to give students even more speaking opportunities.

Developing writing skills

Students are required to produce a short piece of writing (email, note, story or article). Whatever they write, the basic steps for all writing tasks are the same. This is reinforced by the approach used throughout *Optimise* – ***Plan, Write, Check***.

There are some extra points to keep in mind when helping students with writing tasks:

Before beginning to write, students need to consider the purpose of the text and who the text is for, as both things will affect the tone (formal or informal).

During the ***Plan*** phase, students should read the questions and any prompts carefully to make sure they know exactly what they have to include in their writing and/or what questions they have to answer. It is important to encourage students to spend time on this stage as it makes the writing task easier.

Next is the ***Write*** phrase. Students write a first draft as quickly as they can, including all the main points from the brainstorming phase. They should make sure they include all required information and that they fully answer the question.

The final stage is the ***Check*** phase, where students need to look closely at spelling, grammar, punctuation and word choice. They can use the *Optimise* **Checklist** for this.

Classroom management

It can be particularly challenging with larger class groups to keep all students engaged in the lesson.

Here are some ideas to consider:

- Move around and teach the class from different points in the classroom to give the students the feeling of being in the middle of the 'action' rather than an observer. Moving around the class makes the room feel smaller and encourages student involvement. It also means students who are furthest away from the front of the classroom can feel more involved.
- Check understanding regularly, and give students feedback to clarify points they haven't understood.
- Set up some class routines (weekly homework assignments of 20 minutes, class discussions every Friday, etc.). Where possible, involve students in deciding what these routines should be.
- Find ways to link what students have learnt to the exam, so they can clearly see their progress and the fact that they are achieving a common goal.
- Give regular short tests and dictations.
- Change the pace of the lesson from time to time and change delivery methods (speaking, using digital materials, playing video, etc.)
- Start lessons by writing a lesson outline on the board so students know what to expect.
- Give fast finishers something to do (see the unit teaching notes for suggestions) or direct them to the Workbook.

Games

As a useful change of pace, and sometimes to refocus students, games can be an excellent teaching tool. Students generally enjoy games and tend to remember more as a result. Vocabulary games are helpful for practising and reviewing language. Always make the 'rules' clear, and check understanding before playing the game. For example, after explaining what to do, ask the students to explain the game back to you. Or demonstrate the game by playing it yourself with a few students while the others watch.

When planning games you need to consider what your aims and objectives are. Games are particularly useful for reviewing work from the previous lesson, checking what students know before teaching a new language item, practising a new language item you have just presented, warming up at the beginning of the lesson or filling in at the end of a lesson. There are a variety of games suggested throughout the *Optimise* teaching notes.

LISTENING	SPEAKING	LANGUAGE IN USE	WRITING
Identifying differences 3-option multiple choice (pictures)	Talking about yourself Questions Talk2Me	Using prepositions Open cloze	Understanding the task Guided writing (an email)
Listening for words that mean the same Matching	Talking about free time activities Questions Talk2Me	Predicting the answer 3-option multiple-choice cloze	Using your own words Guided writing (a note)
Predicting what the speaker will say 3-option multiple choice (dialogue)	Explaining likes and dislikes Questions Talk2Me	Using conjunctions Open cloze	Making and replying to suggestions Guided writing (a note)
Listening for important information Gap fill	Asking someone to explain Discussion (pictures) Talk2Me	Choosing the right word 3-option multiple-choice cloze	Punctuation and spelling Guided writing (an email)
Understanding when things happen 3-option multiple choice (pictures)	Talking about preferences Discussion Talk2Me	Using determiners Open cloze	Using linking words Picture story
Listening for the main idea 3-option multiple choice (monologues and dialogues)	Describing and expressing opinions Discussion (pictures) Talk2Me	Identifying words that go together 3-option multiple-choice cloze	Using a variety of tenses Guided writing (a note)
Thinking about the missing information Gap fill	Talking about the future Questions Talk2Me	Commonly confused words 3-option multiple-choice cloze	Using adjectives Picture story
Listening for important information Matching	Giving opinions Discussion (pictures) Talk2Me	Using modal verbs Open cloze	Writing in an informal style Guided writing (an email)
Understanding the speakers' questions Multiple choice (pictures)	Talking about a topic Questions Talk2Me	Identifying conditional sentences 3-option multiple-choice cloze	Expressing preferences An email
Identifying incorrect answers 3-option multiple choice (monologues and dialogues)	Giving yourself time to think Discussion Talk2Me	Using the present perfect Open cloze	Writing a good ending Picture story
Taking notes Gap fill	Talking about jobs Questions Talk2Me	Using indefinite and relative pronouns Open cloze	Planning an article An article
Checking your answers 3-option multiple choice (dialogue)	Agreeing and disagreeing Discussion (pictures) Talk2Me	Identifying words that show the order of events 3-option multiple-choice cloze	Writing a story A story

▶ LISTENING p 140–141 ▶ SPEAKING / SPEAKING TEST VIDEO p 142–143

Student's Resource Centre

- *Talk2Me* videos (flipped classroom)
- Speaking test video
- *Optimise your grammar* worksheets
- *Optimise your vocabulary* worksheets
- *Say it right* pronunciation worksheets
- Culture and CLIL worksheets
- Class and Workbook audio

1 Time out

UNIT AIMS

Exam preparation in Unit 1:

- scan an article
- identify differences between three pictures
- talk about yourself
- use prepositions
- understand the task

TEACHER'S PRESENTATION KIT

- *Talk2Me* videos
- Speaking test videos
- Class and Workbook audio
- Workbook pages and answer key

UNIT OVERVIEW

Student's Book / Digital Student's Book SB		Workbook / Online Workbook OWB
LESSON / EXAM TASK	EXAM SKILLS / LANGUAGE FOCUS	CONSOLIDATION
Reading **3-option multiple matching**	Scanning Online article	Workbook, pp 4–5, Exercises 1, 2, 3, 4, 5 Unit 1, Reading, Exercises 1, 2, 3, 4, 5
Grammar 1	Present simple, adverbs of frequency, imperatives	Workbook, p 6, Exercises 1, 2, 3 Unit 1, Grammar 1, Exercises 1, 2, 3
Vocabulary	Words connected with *hobbies* Nouns/verbs Phrasal verbs	Workbook, p 7, Exercises 1, 2, 3 Unit 1, Vocabulary, Exercises 1, 2, 3
Listening **3-option multiple choice (pictures)**	Identifying differences	Workbook, p 8, Exercises 1, 2 Unit 1, Listening, Exercises 1, 2
Grammar 2	Possessive *'s*, prepositions of time and place	Workbook, p 7, Exercises 1, 2 Unit 1, Grammar 2, Exercises 1, 2
Speaking **Questions**	Talking about yourself	Workbook, pp 8–9, Exercises 1, 2, 3 Unit 1, Speaking, Exercises 1, 2, 3
Language in Use **Open cloze**	Using prepositions	Workbook, p 9, Exercises 1, 2 Unit 1, Language in Use, Exercises 1, 2
Writing **Understanding the task**	Guided writing (an email)	Workbook, p 10, Exercises 1, 2, 3, 4 Unit 1, Writing, Exercises 1, 2, 3, 4
		Workbook, p 11, Progress check and Cumulative progress Progress check and Cumulative progress

Additional material

PRESENTATION KIT	TEACHER'S / STUDENT'S RESOURCE CENTRE RC	TEST GENERATOR
Talk2Me video *My surname is …*	**Unit 1 worksheets:** *Optimise your grammar* (Standard and Higher), *Optimise your vocabulary* (Standard and Higher), *Talk2Me* video, *Say it right* **Units 1–2 worksheets:** CLIL, Culture, Everyday English (TRC only), Grammar communication (TRC only)	Unit Test 1 (Standard and Higher)

READING
3-option multiple matching | Online article

→ Student's Book, pages 4–5 SB

Lesson aims

- Focus on words which mean the same
- Practise a 3-option multiple matching task
- Discuss which activity you would like to do

Lead-in

Ask students to look at the unit title ***Time out*** and the photos below it, and elicit what the phrase means (*a break from working or studying to do something else or rest*). Elicit what activities the teenagers in the photos are doing (*abseiling / rock climbing, dancing/gymnastics, mountain biking, tennis and painting*) and then ask students what they think the unit will be about (*hobbies and free-time activities*).

1 Divide the class into pairs or groups to complete the task. Have students share their ideas with the class, giving reasons why they like or would like to do their chosen hobbies.

2 Explain to students that they need to scan the text quickly to see which teenagers give advice about how to choose a hobby. Have them work in pairs to check answers before checking answers as a class.

Answers
Jake and Amaya

3 1.01 **Note: The reading text is also available on the audio CD. You may want to have students listen as they read the text.** Have students complete the task individually. Ask them to rewrite any false sentences so that they are true. Then have volunteers share their answers with the class.

Answers
1 F (Kareem says he doesn't spend all of his free time playing online.) **2** T **3** F (Jake thinks that people don't usually find the perfect hobby immediately.) **4** T **5** T **6** F (Amaya's photography club meets every Thursday evening.)

4 Go through the first definition as a class and elicit the correct answer. Then ask students to complete the exercise individually.

Answers
1 camera **2** simple **3** blog **4** perfect **5** different **6** hobby **7** member **8** discuss

EXAM SKILL

Scanning

Ask students to read the tips.

- Point out that learning to identify synonyms can help students in all aspects of exams, not just in Reading tasks.
- Explain to students that it is very important to read the task carefully, look at all the material given and then reread the task to make sure that they understand it clearly.
- Point out that underlining important words and phrases is particularly useful when they have to match or find specific information (e.g. Exercise 6 question 3 take part in a group = became a member of a photography club).

5 Explain to students that they need to scan the text and make a note of the hobbies. Have them work in pairs to check answers before checking answers as a class.

Answers
playing video games, blogging, skateboarding, taking photos / photography

OPTIMISE YOUR EXAM

3-option multiple matching

Ask students to read the tips.

- Students need to read seven questions and then three short texts that are about the same topic (e.g. hobbies). They have to match each question to one of the texts.
- Students should read each question carefully to find out what information they need to look for in the three texts.

▼ Exam task

6 Ask students to complete the exercise and then ask them to justify their answers before showing the answer key to the class. Discuss if there are any discrepancies between their answers and the key.

Answers
1 B **2** A **3** C **4** A **5** A **6** B **7** C

Optional extension

Ask students to think about their hobby and why they like it. Then ask them to draft a short article about their hobby saying how often they do it, who they do it with and why they like doing this hobby. Then ask students to swap their articles and peer correct, checking for any spelling or grammar errors before completing the final draft.

THINK | RESEARCH | CULTURE | LEARN | **ME**

In pairs or groups, students discuss the different activities. Invite them to share their ideas with the class.

Homework

OWB

Assign students Reading exercises 1, 2, 3, 4 and 5 on pages 4–5 of their Workbook.

GRAMMAR 1

Present simple, adverbs of frequency, imperatives

→ Student's Book, page 6 SB

Lesson aims

- Focus on the present simple, adverbs of frequency and imperatives
- Describe habits/regular actions and things that are usually/always true
- Express how often something happens
- Give instructions and orders

Lead-in

Write these notices on the board:
Only speak in English.
No mobile phones in class.
Put your hand up if you want to ask a question.

Ask students where they can see notices like these (*in a classroom*). Have students work in pairs to think of more notices they expect to see in a classroom. Then ask students to share the items they chose with the class.

Grammar in context

Ask students where the sentences come from (*the article on page 5*). Elicit what tense the two sentences are in by asking *Are the sentences about the present or the past?* (*present*). Have students complete the exercise and refer them to the *Remember* box if they aren't sure.

Remind students that they can find more information in the Grammar reference, Unit 1, page 144.

Answers
a) 1 **b)** 2; often

Language note

The present simple is used to talk about habits and routines (*He has his lunch at school.*) and things that are usually or always true (*Her name is Julie.*). Explain the general rule that adverbs of frequency go in the middle position within a sentence (*The park is always open.*) and time expressions go at the end of a sentence (*I ride my bike to school every day.*).

1 Go through the first sentence with the class and then have students complete the exercise individually. Check answers with the class.

Answers
2 goes **3** have **4** plays **5** play **6** go

2 Ask students to complete the exercise. Check answers with the class.

Answers
a do **b** do **c** does **d** have **e** gets **f** play

3 Ask students to match the questions and answers and then ask and answer the questions in pairs. Check answers with the class.

Answers
1 c **2** e **3** d **4** f **5** b **6** a

Optional extension

Write these questions on the board: ***1*** *Who is your best friend?* ***2*** *What do you like to do in the evenings?* ***3*** *What time does school start and finish?* ***4*** *How often do you walk to school?* ***5*** *What do you do at weekends?* In pairs, students ask and answer the questions. Walk round, monitoring students for good use of the present simple.

4 Elicit the rules for the position of adverbs of frequency within a sentence, encouraging students to refer to the *Remember* box if they are unsure. Then ask students to complete the exercise. Check answers in open class.

Answers
1 It's often very cold in the winter.
2 I usually watch TV with my sister.
3 He always goes to bed at 9 o'clock.
4 I never drink cola for breakfast.

Grammar in context

Explain to students that imperative forms are the bare infinitive of the verb and don't change in the third person. Tell students to refer to the information in the *Remember* box and then encourage them to give you more examples of giving instructions and orders.

Remind students that they can find more information in the Grammar reference, Unit 1, page 144.

Language note

- Use the infinitive without *to* for imperatives (*Take off your shoes.*). There is usually no subject.
- Make negatives by placing *don't* in front (*Don't talk in the library.*).

5 Ask students to complete the exercise. Check their answers in open class.

Answers
1 Remember **2** Don't **3** Please open

Mixed ability

Ask less confident students to think of three everyday situations and write an imperative sentence for each situation, e.g. *on a bus – Please give your seat to an older person.* Ask more confident students to write sentences to describe three situations in which people might need to use an imperative sentence, e.g. *Your mum works in a museum and someone is taking photos with flash.* Then, pair less confident students with more confident students. The less confident students read their imperative sentences and their partner has to guess the context. The more confident students read their sentences and their partner has to decide what to say.

6 Have students look at the title of the text and elicit what it refers to (*they go cycling and make films at the same time*). Then ask students to complete the exercise. Have students compare their answers in pairs before you check with the class.

Answers

1 lives **2** ride **3** put **4** Be **5** has **6** hits **7** watch **8** love

Cultural note

Videoing your surroundings and/or yourself while doing adventure sports is extremely popular these days. People use selfie sticks to see their reactions doing things or to get images of themselves and their friends in beautiful places. However, at times people prefer to film themselves hands-free, and in those cases they use small cameras which can be fitted to a helmet to capture the action when the person is doing an activity like climbing, surfing, cycling or running.

Homework

OWB

Assign students Grammar 1 exercises 1, 2 and 3 on page 6 of their Workbook.

VOCABULARY

Topic vocabulary | Nouns/verbs | Phrasal verbs

→ Student's Book, page 7 SB

Lesson aims

Understand the correct usage of:

- words connected with hobbies
- nouns and verbs from the same word family
- phrasal verbs

Lead-in

Draw a picture on the board to illustrate a hobby, e.g. a picture of a stick person with a camera and elicit the phrase (*taking photos*). Ask students to think of hobbies they know in English, then take turns to come up to the board and draw these for the other students to guess. For students who are not good at drawing, give them the option of miming doing the hobby instead.

Words connected with *hobbies*

1 1.02 Ask students what activities they recognise. Then play the audio for students to check their answers.

Answers/Audioscript

1 rock climbing **2** cycling **3** skateboarding **4** horse-riding **5** swimming **6** reading **7** playing computer games **8** painting

2 1.03 Ask students to complete the exercise. Play the audio for students to listen and check their answers.

Answers/Audioscript

1 You can take one of these with a camera. *photograph*
2 People who like swimming in the sea often go here. *beach*
3 A thin paper book with photographs, articles, stories, etc. *magazine*
4 When you buy and keep books or magazines, for example, you do this. *collect*
5 A meal when you cook and eat food outdoors. *barbecue*
6 You stay in this when you go camping. *tent*

Refer students to the Vocabulary reference, page 157, for more information on topic vocabulary.

Nouns/verbs

3 1.04 Complete the first two items as an example. Then ask students to complete the exercise. Play the audio for students to listen and check their answers. Check the spelling of all the missing words by writing them on the board.

Answers/Audioscript

object: painting, **person:** *painter*, **verb:** to paint
object: photograph, **person:** *photographer*, **verb:** to photograph / take photographs
object: music, **person:** *musician*, **verb:** to make / play music
object: guitar, **person:** guitarist, **verb:** to *play* the guitar
object: *video game*, **person:** video *gamer*, **verb:** to play video games

4 Ask students to complete the exercise individually. Check their answers in open class.

Answers

1 painting / to paint **2** music **3** plays (the guitar) **4** photographer **5** musician **6** (video) gamer

Extra support

Before students start Exercise 4, ask them to look at sentences 1–6 in pairs and decide if the words they need are objects, people or verbs. Check answers in open class before continuing.

Answers

1 object/verb **2** object **3** verb **4** people **5** people **6** people

SAY IT RIGHT

Word stress

TRC

For the *Say it right* pronunciation activity and instructions, go to the Teacher's Resource Centre.

Refer students to the Vocabulary reference, page 157, for more information on word formation.

Phrasal verbs

5 1.05 Present the idea of the phrasal verb *come in* by leaving the classroom and coming in again. Elicit the meaning from the class (*to enter*). Then have students complete the exercise individually and check their answers in pairs. Play the audio for students to listen and check their answers.

Answers/Audioscript

1 (e) come in: to enter
2 (g) come round: to visit
3 (a) get back: to return after going somewhere
4 (d) get off: to leave a bus or train
5 (f) look after: to take care of someone or something
6 (c) turn off: to stop a machine
7 (b) turn on: to start a machine

Language note

These phrasal verbs belong to three different categories.

Come in, *come round* and *get back* are intransitive phrasal verbs (with no object). *Get off* (*the bus*) and *look after* (*this book*) are both non-separable phrasal verbs, and the object, whether it is a noun or pronoun, will always come after the particle.

Turn off/on could be problematic as the object can go between the verb and the particle (*turn the radio off*) or after the particle (*turn off the radio*) when it is a noun but has to go between the verb and the particle when it is a pronoun (*turn it off*).

6 Ask students to complete the exercise individually. Have students compare their answers in pairs before you check them in open class.

Answers

1 off **2** in **3** on **4** off **5** round **6** after **7** back

Refer students to the Vocabulary reference, page 157, for more information on phrasal verbs.

Homework OWB

Assign students Vocabulary exercises 1, 2 and 3 on page 7 of their Workbook.

LISTENING
3-option multiple choice (pictures)

→ Student's Book, page 8 SB

Lesson aims

- Listen to identify factual information
- Practise answering a picture multiple-choice exam task

Lead-in

Write these numbers, dates and times on the board:
£25 4:30 pm $15 Monday 7th 75 31st August €99 1:15 am

Divide the class into pairs or small groups to discuss how to say them. Have a feedback session with the whole class and point out any options students didn't think of. For example, *half past four* or *four thirty*.

1 Have students continue working with their partner or group to complete the exercise. Elicit answers from different students around the class. Ask them to give reasons for their answers and encourage the rest of the class to comment.

Answers

1 **1** all games **2** all are something to read **3** all are times **4** all are food **5** all are days of the week
2 **1** the games are different **2** the magazines and book are not the same **3** different times **4** different meals **5** different days of the week

EXAM SKILL

Identifying differences

Ask students to read the tips.

- Explain to students that it is important to answer questions (who, where, when, etc.) when making notes in order to create a good description of what they see.
- Tell students that picture multiple-choice exercises with short conversations can test a lot of different areas in a single exercise. In this particular exam task, students are being tested on prepositions of place, types of reading material, times, foods and days of the week. Remind them that, as each question is independent, they shouldn't panic if they don't understand some parts of the audio very well – they might have problems with the prepositions of place but understand the information about days of the week in the first audio, for example.
- Encourage students to brainstorm all the prepositions they can think of so that they are aware of all the possibilities before they listen.

2 Have students look at the pictures and elicit the differences. Then have them complete the exercise. Check answers with the class.

Answers

1 C **2** B **3** A

3 1.06 Before students listen, have them predict possible words and phrases to complete the conversation. Then play the audio for students to check their predictions. Elicit which students' predictions were correct and incorrect. Ask the students to share their predictions with the class.

Answers

1 near **2** in the middle **3** under

OPTIMISE YOUR EXAM

3-option multiple choice (pictures)

Ask students to read the tips.

- Remind students that, as well as underlining important words in the question, they should also look carefully at the pictures and try to predict words/phrases they expect to hear in the audio.
- Explain to students that it is common to hear words that sound the same but have a different meaning. Therefore, it is important to listen specifically for words/phrases which mean the same as the words they predicted or underlined.

Extra support

Before students complete the exam task, split the class into five groups. Assign each group one of the questions in Exercise 4 and ask them to prepare a set of notes to match the pictures, using the notes in Exercise 2 as a model. Regroup students into new groups and have them share their notes and check if the others in their new groups can match them to the correct pictures.

Exam task

4 1.07 Have students put their notes away before listening. Then play the track for students to complete the exercise.

5 1.07 Tell students to read through the questions one more time before you play the track again. Tell them to listen to any questions they were not sure about. After the second listening, elicit answers from students around the class.

Answers

1 A **2** C **3** B **4** C **5** A

Optional extension 1.07

Play the track again and ask students to call out *Stop!* when they hear the phrases that confirm the answers in Exercise 4. Repeat the specific phrases as a dictation for students to write them down and see exactly how the phrases in the recording relate to the questions.

Answers

1 The adventure game, please. **2** … my book! It's great. **3** It always begins at 9.30. **4** What about fish and chips? … OK. **5** I have art on Wednesday, yes.

Homework OWB

Assign students Listening exercises 1 and 2 on page 8 of their Workbook.

GRAMMAR 2

Possessive *'s*, prepositions of time and place

→ Student's Book, page 9 SB

Lesson aims

- Distinguish possessive *'s* from the verb *to be*
- Identify the use of prepositions of time and place
- Practise using possessive *'s* and prepositions of time and place

Lead-in

Ask each student in the class to give you an item from their desk, bag or pocket, e.g. a pen or a notebook. Take each item, show it clearly to the class and say whose it is, e.g. *This is John's pen.* Place the items on your desk. Then test students' knowledge by holding up an item and asking *Whose is this?* Elicit a sentence, e.g. *That is John's pen.* before returning each item to its owner. Write the sentence on the board, without a contraction for *to be*, and circle the *'s* in the sentence. Tell students that the apostrophe plus *s* shows possession.

Grammar in context

Confusion with the use of *s* and *'s* at the end of words is common, even amongst native speakers (e.g. *it's* and *its*), so it is natural English language students will have problems too. Clarify that the possessive *'s* takes the place of the structure *the … of …* which is used in other languages. Write *the tent of your cousin* on the board and elicit from students how this phrase changes to include the possessive *'s* (*your cousin's tent*).

Also clarify that *'s* is also used as as a contraction to indicate missing letters for the third person singular forms of the verbs *to be* and *to have* (*got*), e.g. *He's my brother.* = *He is my brother. She has got a car.* = *She's got a car.*

Remind students that they can find more information in the Grammar reference, Unit 1, page 145.

Answer

statement b

1 Go through the first sentence with the class before asking students to complete the exercise. Have students compare their answers in pairs before you check answers with the whole class.

Answers

1 Anna's book **2** boys' bags **3** my parents' **4** children's desks

2 Ask students if the apostrophe in the first sentence represents a contraction or possession (*possession*). Have students complete the exercise in pairs. Then elicit answers with the class.

Answers

1 P **2** B **3** P **4** B

Optional extension

Revise family vocabulary by drawing a simple family tree on the board using stick figures and writing names under each person. Use the family tree to elicit different sentences about the family, e.g. *Francisco is Alicia's brother.* Check that students use the possessive *'s* correctly in the sentences.

Grammar in context

Ask students what the words in bold are (*prepositions*) and then have them complete the task. Refer them to the information in the *Remember* box if they aren't sure. Then check their answers.

Remind students that they can find more information in the Grammar reference, Unit 1, page 145.

Answers

a in, near, under **b** at, on

3 Ask students to complete the exercise. Have students check their answers with a partner before you check with the whole class.

Answers

1 last week **2** to, on **3** in **4** In **5** in, today **6** on

4 Ask students to complete the exercise. Have students compare answers in pairs before you check their answers in open class.

Answers

1 on **2** in **3** near **4** next **5** At **6** in front

Fast finishers

Have fast finishers extend the table in the *Remember* box with additional items to make the lists more complete, e.g. *at lunchtime, in winter,* etc. After you check the answers to Exercise 4, ask students to share the words/phrases they thought of.

Homework OWB

Assign students Grammar 2 exercises 1 and 2 on page 7 of their Workbook.

Assign students the Flipped classroom tasks on page 10 of their Student's Book if you'd like them to prepare for the next lesson. To complete this task, students need to watch the *Talk2Me* video which can be found on the Resource Centre.

SPEAKING
Questions

→ Student's Book, page 10 SB

Lesson aims

- Focus on talking about yourself
- Practise answering personal questions in an interview

The *Talk2Me* video in this unit focuses on free time, hobbies and activities. The people in the video talk about a dance competition. They discuss their timetables and when they can arrange to practise for the competition.

Students answer some comprehension questions and then listen for key phrases in the video.

The video can be used in one of two ways:

Flipped classroom

Flipped classroom option

Using this approach, students watch the video and complete the exercises for homework. This prepares students for the speaking lesson by introducing them to the topic and the key phrases to use in the exam task. Teachers who use this method will find they have more class time to spend on activating the target language and developing fluency for the final task.

***Talk2Me* worksheet**

Ask students to also complete the *Talk2Me* worksheet from the Resource Centre for more detailed comprehension exercises and more practice of the key phrases.

Classroom option

1 Ask students to spend a minute or two reading the questions. Play the *Talk2Me* video for students to complete the exercise. Play the video again, if necessary, before checking their answers.

2 Play the *Talk2Me* video again, so students underline the words and phrases in the *Phrase expert* box. Pause the video from time to time if necessary. Check answers in open class.

***Talk2Me* worksheet**

Ask students to complete the *Talk2Me* worksheet on the Resource Centre for more detailed comprehension exercises and more practice of the key phrases.

Answers

The transcript and answer key for the *Talk2Me* video exercises and Worksheet can be found on the Teacher's Resource Centre.

Lead-in

Show students a photo of you and your family. Describe when and where it was taken, who the people are and a little about them. Use the text in Exercise 4, on Student's Book page 10 as a model and use possessive *'s* and prepositions where appropriate.

3 1.08 Play the track for students to listen and repeat. Then write some letters at random on the board and elicit their names. In pairs, students ask and answer the three questions.

EXAM SKILL

Talking about yourself

Ask students to read the tips.

- Encourage students to practise talking about where they live, daily routines, personal interests, likes, dislikes, etc. Point out that in the first part of the exam, the examiner will ask each person two short-answer questions about these types of topics followed by one longer 'Tell me something about …' question.
- Remind students that it is really important to be proactive rather than reactive as language learners. Students should find out the vocabulary they need to talk about things in 'their world' if this is not covered in class.
- Elicit ways students can practise in their free time and encourage them to be autonomous.

4 1.09 Before you play the track, ask students what they are going to listen to. Remind them to identify factual information while they are listening. After students complete the exercise, ask them to compare their answers in pairs before you check with the whole class.

Answers

Student A
Name: Victor
Hobbies: swimming, skateboarding
Evenings: gets home 6pm, homework, meal, bed 9pm
Last weekend: visited grandparents, saw animals, helped in garden
Student B
Name: Eleanor
Weekends: beach, swim, play volleyball
People: brothers, friends

Extra support

Give students the first word of each question to guide them in Exercise 5 (**1** *What*, **2** *How*, **3** *Do*, **4** *What*, **5** *What*, **6** *Who*, **7** *Tell*).

5 1.09 Ask students what questions the examiner asks before playing the track again. Have students write down the questions they remember. Then have them listen and check or complete their answers.

Answers

1 What's your name? **2** How old are you? **3** Do you have any hobbies? **4** What do you usually do in the evenings? **5** What do you like doing at the weekends? **6** Who do you usually spend time with at weekends? **7** Tell me about what you did last weekend.

6 Ask students if they can remember the words or phrase the student used. If necessary, play the phrase again for students to check their ideas.

Answer

Sorry, can you say that again, please?

OPTIMISE YOUR EXAM

Questions

Ask students to read the tips.

- Remind students that it is extremely important that they ask the examiner to repeat the question if they haven't understood. Explain that no marks will be deducted as long as a candidate uses an appropriate phrase to do this. Also explain that if candidates answer a different question to the one they are asked, the examiners will assume they don't understand the language being used and they will lose marks.
- Remind students that Speaking exams are principally designed to test their ability to communicate, and adding some extra information, even if they make a few mistakes, gives a very positive impression.

▼ Exam task

7 Divide the class into pairs to complete the exercise. Walk round the class, monitoring students for good use of language and errors to go over at the end of the activity.

Write any errors on the board and go through them with students, eliciting corrections from them where possible. After the class feedback, students could then repeat this activity with another partner, to try to improve their performance.

Optional extension

Have students work in pairs or groups to brainstorm other personal questions they could be asked in Speaking exams, e.g. *How old are you? Where do you live? Do you like studying English? Why? / Why not?* Have pairs practise asking and answering these questions.

Homework OWB

Assign students Speaking exercises 1, 2 and 3 on pages 8–9 of their Workbook.

LANGUAGE IN USE
Open cloze

→ Student's Book, page 11 SB

Lesson aims

- Focus on a part of speech (prepositions) that can be tested in an open-cloze exam task
- Practise an open-cloze exam task
- Discuss places for young people to do activities

Lead-in

Write this notice on the board:

The s_ _ _ _ _ _ _ _ _ _ _ _ club

1 *Come to the p_ _ _. Open all day, every day!*

2 *Be c_ _ _ _ _ _! Always wear a h_ _ _ _ _.*

3 *Don't forget your b_ _ _ _!*

Then have students work in pairs and decide what words complete the gaps. Invite volunteers to come to the board and complete the notice.

Answers
skateboarding **1** park **2** careful, helmet **3** board

1 Focus students' attention on the text and ask them where they would see a similar text. Then have them answer the questions in pairs.

Answers
1 Make new friends, try new activities, climb trees, ride your bike, build dens, join an art class, learn nature photography, cook wild food, go to barbecues and mini music festivals, go camping
2 No, only children aged 11 and over. **3** It's free but special classes cost £10. **4** Students' own answers

EXAM SKILL

Using prepositions

Ask students to read the tips.

- Remind students that before doing open-cloze exam tasks, it is important to skim the text to find out the topic and general meaning.
- Students should only write one word for each gap and should check their spelling is correct.

2 Ask students to complete the exercise. Have students check answers in pairs before checking as a class.

Answers
Time: on
Place: at, between
Before noun/pronoun: for
Phrasal verb: fill in

3 Ask students to complete the exercise. Students compare in pairs before you check in open class.

Answers
1 with **2** at **3** of **4** up **5** out **6** on

OPTIMISE YOUR EXAM

Open cloze

Ask students to read the tips.

- Tell students that in an actual exam task, there would only be a few gaps which might test prepositions or phrasal verbs as this task tests a range of grammatical forms (e.g. verb forms, determiners, pronouns, prepositions, etc.).
- Highlight to students that the same word would never be tested in more than one gap, so all six answers must be different words for their answers.

Exam task

4 Ask students to complete the exercise. Check their answers.

Answers
1 on **2** with **3** go **4** but **5** to **6** Do

Fast finishers

Have students identify which part of speech they use in their answers to Exercise 4.

Answers
1 preposition **2** preposition **3** verb/fixed phrase **4** conjunction
5 preposition/fixed phrase **6** auxiliary verb

THINK | RESEARCH | **CULTURE** | LEARN | ME

Divide the class into groups to discuss the question. Open out the discussion to a class debate if there is time.

Homework OWB

Assign students Language in Use exercises 1 and 2 on page 9 of their Workbook.

WRITING
Guided writing (an email)

→ Student's Book, pages 12–13 SB

Lesson aims

- Focus on identifying and noting down key information
- Plan which information to include in an email
- Write an email exam task

Lead-in

Have students practise giving each other personal information to register for an after-school club. Give them these prompts and elicit the questions they will need:

Activity booking form: *name? surname? spell? age? from? activity?*

Answers
What's your name? What's your surname? How do you spell that? How old are you? Where do you come from? What activity/activities do you like?

Have students ask and answer the questions in pairs. Explain that they can use their imagination.

1 Have students work in different pairs or groups to ask and answer the questions. Elicit answers from different students around the class.

Answers
Students' own answers

Mixed ability

Pair stronger students with less confident students for exercises 2–5. This will allow stronger students to help less confident students as necessary and ensures stronger students do not race ahead.

2 Ask students to read the email to identify how many pieces of information are given in the email. Check their answers.

Answers
Three: meet at the sports club, meet on Saturday, play basketball

3 Ask students to complete the exercise and then get them to compare their answers in pairs before going over the answer key with the whole class.

Answers
Students should tick:
1, 2, 3, 4

EXAM SKILL

Understanding the task

Ask students to read the tips.

- Tell students that for exams it is important to be able to identify key information quickly and to respond to all three prompts in the email.
- Remind students that they should look for words that mean the same wherever possible. They practised this technique in the Reading lesson on pages 4–5.

4 Ask students to complete the exercise and then check their answers.

Answers
1 no (he doesn't say what date he wants to meet) **2** three **3** yes

5 Ask students to complete the exercise and then have pairs check their answers before going over the answers as a whole group.

Answers
1 near the school. **2** at 3 o'clock. **3** because it's so much fun!

Fast finishers

Ask students to write down alternative ways to complete the sentences in questions 1–3. Get them to compare their answers in pairs to see if they have the same, similar or completely different endings to the sentences.

OPTIMISE YOUR EXAM

Guided writing (an email)

Ask students to read the tips.

- Tell students that they need to follow typical email conventions, such as how they start and end their email depending on who they are writing to (e.g. *Hi/ Dear …*, *Bye for now*/*Best wishes*, etc.).
- Students need to consider what kind of information is needed for the three prompts.
- Encourage students to write a rough draft before writing the final answer on their answer sheet and to check their spelling.

Exam task

6 Ask students to complete the exercise in pairs or groups. Check their answers.

Answers
1 35 words **2** Jo uses 'Hi Pat' to start her email and 'See you soon' to end it. **3** Yes; Jo gives information on all three bullet points, in the correct order, and writes at least 25 words. Jo also gives a reason for why he/she wants to try the art class (it sounds interesting).

7 Plan Have students work in pairs or small groups to complete the exercise. Encourage students to share what they ticked on the list and give reasons for their answers.

8 Write Have students complete their email individually. Remind them that spelling and correct use of capital letters are both important in writing exams.

9 Check Have students complete the checklist. Explain that they should plan to leave a few minutes at the end of the exam for this. Tell them that they will be provided with a specific checklist in each writing lesson in the book in order to improve different writing skills.

Optional extension

For a slightly longer writing task, refer students to the task in the Writing reference (SB page 163). It includes an annotated sample text and related writing task to challenge your students a little more.

Homework

OWB

Assign students Writing exercises 1, 2, 3 and 4 on page 10 of their Workbook and Progress check 1 on page 11.

2 That's entertainment!

UNIT AIMS

Exam preparation in Unit 2:

- skim a longer text
- listen for words that mean the same
- talk about free-time activities
- predict the answer
- use your own words in an email

TEACHER'S PRESENTATION KIT

- *Talk2Me* videos
- Speaking test videos
- Class and Workbook audio
- Workbook pages and answer key

UNIT OVERVIEW

Student's Book / Digital Student's Book SB		Workbook / Online Workbook OWB
LESSON / EXAM TASK	EXAM SKILLS / LANGUAGE FOCUS	CONSOLIDATION
Reading **3-option multiple choice (long text)**	Skimming A magazine article	Workbook, pp 12–13, Exercises 1, 2, 3, 4, 5 Unit 2, Reading, Exercises 1, 2, 3, 4, 5
Grammar 1	Present simple and present continuous	Workbook, p 14, Exercises 1, 2 Unit 2, Grammar 1, Exercises 1, 2
Vocabulary	Words connected with *entertainment* Words + prepositions Collocations with nouns	Workbook, p 14, Exercises 1, 2, 3 Unit 2, Vocabulary, Exercises 1, 2, 3
Listening **Matching**	Listening for words that mean the same	Workbook, p 16, Exercises 1, 2, 3 Unit 2, Listening, Exercises 1, 2, 3
Grammar 2	Present continuous for future use	Workbook, p 15, Exercises 1, 2 Unit 2, Grammar 2, Exercises 1, 2
Speaking **Questions**	Talking about free-time activities	Workbook, pp 16–17, Exercises 1, 2 Unit 2, Speaking, Exercises 1, 2
Language in Use **3-option multiple-choice cloze**	Predicting the answer	Workbook, p 17, Exercises 1, 2, 3 Unit 2, Language in Use, Exercises 1, 2, 3
Writing **Guided writing (a note)**	Using your own words	Workbook, p 18, Exercises 1, 2, 3, 4 Unit 2, Writing, Exercises 1, 2, 3, 4
Progress check	Check language progress for Units 1 and 2	Workbook, p 19, Progress check and Cumulative progress Progress check and Cumulative progress

Additional material

PRESENTATION KIT	TEACHER'S / STUDENT'S RESOURCE CENTRE RC	TEST GENERATOR
Talk2Me video *It starts at …*	**Unit 2 worksheets:** *Optimise your grammar* (Standard and Higher), *Optimise your vocabulary* (Standard and Higher), *Talk2Me* video, *Say it right* **Units 1–2 worksheets:** CLIL, Culture, Everyday English (TRC only), Grammar communication (TRC only)	Unit Test 2 (Standard and Higher)

READING

3-option multiple choice (long text) | A magazine article

→ Student's Book, pages 14–15 SB

Lesson aims

- Focus on understanding important words
- Practise a 3-option multiple-choice exam task (long text)
- Discuss the most popular forms of entertainment

Lead-in

Ask students to look at the unit title ***That's entertainment!*** and elicit what they think the theme of the unit will be (*different types of entertainment*). Ask students for a couple of examples of forms of entertainment, e.g. the cinema, the theatre, etc.

Draw students' attention to the photos in the article / on page 15 and elicit what form of entertainment they think the magazine article is about (*the world of video gaming*).

1 Divide the class into pairs or groups to discuss the questions. Then have students share their ideas with the class. Encourage them to give reasons for their answers.

EXAM SKILL

Skimming

Ask students to read the tips.

- Tell students they are going to practise the technique of skimming to read a text quickly to find out where the text is from (e.g. a newspaper, a blog, a magazine, etc.), the topic, and understand the general gist of the article.
- Reinforce that they don't need to read and understand every word when they skim a text and not to get distracted when they read new words.

2 Ask students to complete the exercise individually. Check the answer as a class.

Answer

A

OPTIMISE YOUR EXAM

3-option multiple choice (long text)

Ask students to read the tips.

- Explain to students that they should: (1) read the text quickly for gist; (2) read the questions carefully and underline important information; (3) go back to the beginning of the text and read the relevant sections more carefully to check if they have chosen the correct answer.
- Emphasise that when students choose an answer, they should check the other two options and decide why they are wrong.

▼ Exam task

3 1.10 **Note: The reading text is also available on the audio CD. You may want to have students listen and read the text before doing the exam task.**

Before students complete the exercise, go through the instructions as a class. Remind them to underline key words in the text as they read. After the students have finished the exercise, have them compare their answers in pairs before checking with the class. Encourage students to justify their answers with evidence from the text.

Answers

1 B (*Video gaming is … not quite as popular as listening to music and watching TV*)

2 C (*Gfinity Arena …, where hundreds of people go to play online games with other fans around the world*)

3 A (*He started playing [computer games] when he was 10.*)

4 C (*He designed and built fantastic digital worlds using Minecraft.*)

5 B (*Brandon still designs attractive [digital] worlds, but now people buy them and use them in adverts.*)

6 A (*Florian and … friends … are making ads for YouTube, gaming channels and films.*)

Mixed ability

Ask stronger students to cover Exercise 4 and look at the highlighted words in the text and to try to work out what they mean purely from the context. Have less confident students complete the task as it appears in the Student's Book. Then pair stronger students with weaker students and have them share their ideas. Give students this model to follow: *I think* online *means* on the internet. *Do you agree?*

4 Remind students to use the skills they have learnt to guess the meaning of vocabulary through context before completing the exercise. Have students check their answers with a partner.

Answers

1 alone **2** fan **3** attractive **4** ads **5** competitions **6** online

Cultural note

Brandon Relph lives with his family in Eastbourne, UK. Around the age of ten, he bought a copy of *Minecraft* and was inspired by the virtual worlds he was able to create. In 2014, he founded *goCreative*, which helps companies advertise their products through virtual worlds of *Minecraft*. He is now the CEO of his own rapidly-growing business. He has also been successful academically and hopes one day to study at either Oxford or Cambridge.

Minecraft is a hugely successful computer game in which players create worlds out of 3-D cubes. It has won numerous awards for innovation and was purchased by Microsoft in 2014 for £1.5 billion.

Homework
OWB
Assign students Reading exercises 1, 2, 3, 4 and 5 on pages 12–13 of their Workbook.

GRAMMAR 1
Present simple and present continuous

→ Student's Book, page 16 SB

Lesson aims

- Understand the correct usage of the present simple and present continuous
- Practise talking about habits, routines, facts, permanent situations and actions in progress
- Discuss favourite types of entertainment

Lead-in

Describe a picture from the Student's Book using the present simple and present continuous, e.g. page 53: *This is a picture of three children working together, probably in school or in a class somewhere else. They are working on some kind of electronic equipment and they are all wearing goggles to protect their eyes. They look very interested in their activity.* Tell students to listen without taking notes. When you have finished the description, say *Go!* and encourage the students to look through the book and find the picture you were describing.

Grammar in context

Ask students to look back at the text to find the sentences and discuss the questions in pairs. Remind students to refer to the information in the *Remember* box if they aren't sure. Check their answers in open class.

Remind students that they can find more information in the Grammar reference, Unit 2, page 145.

Answers

a 2 **b** 3 **c** 1

Language note

Make a list of words and phrases we commonly use with the two tenses for students, e.g. present simple – *always, sometimes, every day/month, once a day/week*; present continuous – *at the moment, now, right now, this week, today.*

1 Ask students to complete the exercise. Check their answers.

Answers

1 'm learning **2** goes **3** plays **4** 're doing **5** usually spend
6 's wearing **7** never read **8** doesn't like

2 Before students complete the exercise, revise some short forms if necessary (*I'm, you're, he's, she's, we're, they're, isn't, aren't*). Remind students to use them where possible. Then have students complete the exercise in pairs and check answers with the class.

Answers

1 Dad reads an online newspaper every week.
2 I'm playing a video game at the moment. / At the moment, I'm playing a video game.
3 Mum isn't working this week.
4 Chris comes from Slovenia and speaks three languages.
5 I usually like his books, but I'm not enjoying this one.
6 I like fruit, but I don't eat it every day.

Fast finishers

Have fast finishers look at the article on page 15 again and find more examples of the present simple and the present continuous. Have them classify each sentence according to its function: *habit, routine, fact, actions in progress*, etc.

SAY IT RIGHT

Pronunciation of *-ing*
TRC
For the *Say it right* pronunciation activity and instructions, go to the Teacher's Resource Centre.

3 Ask students to look at the photo and say what the people are doing (*They are watching a musical show.*) and where they are (*They are in a theatre.*) Ask students to complete the exercise. Then have students compare in pairs before checking their answers with the class.

Answers

1 loves **2** spends **3** plays **4** goes **5** 's dancing **6** prefers
7 's enjoying **8** is doing **9** 's smiling **10** isn't watching **11** 's sleeping

THINK | RESEARCH | CULTURE | LEARN | **ME**

Ask students to talk about their favourite types of entertainment in pairs. Elicit interesting or unusual answers from students around the class.

Homework
OWB
Assign students Grammar 1 exercises 1 and 2 on page 14 of their Workbook.

VOCABULARY
Topic vocabulary | Word patterns | Collocations

→ Student's Book, page 17 SB

Lesson aims

Understand the correct usage of:

- words connected with entertainment
- verb + preposition word patterns
- noun + noun collocations

Lead-in

Play the game ***Stop*** with the class. Explain that you will start saying the alphabet and students have to say the word 'Stop'. Repeat the last letter and have students say a form of entertainment beginning with that letter. For example, *m – musicals*, *c – concerts*. Have the student who answers first say the alphabet next. Continue the same process so that other students can participate.

Words connected with *entertainment*

1 1.11 Have students describe what they see in the pictures. Then have them complete the exercise individually. Play the audio for students to listen and check their answers. Then elicit which of the activities students like to do.

Answers/Audioscript

1 (C) *see an exhibition of famous paintings – at an art gallery*
2 (D) *see a play – at a theatre* **3** (A) *learn about a period in history – at a museum* **4** (F) *listen to a famous classical singer – at an opera house*
5 (E) *download a game – at a gaming café* **6** (B) *see a well-known band – at a concert hall*

2 Have students complete the exercise individually. Then they compare their answers in pairs before you check them in open class.

Answers

1 art gallery **2** concert hall **3** opera house **4** gaming café
5 museum **6** theatre

Fast finishers

Ask fast finishers to write alternative sentences for the words in Exercise 1. Then encourage volunteers to read their sentences out loud after you check the answers to Exercise 2.

Refer students to the Vocabulary reference, page 157, for more information on topic vocabulary.

Words + prepositions

3 1.12 Ask students to complete the exercise. Play the audio for students to listen and check their answers.

Answers/Audioscript

1 On Friday nights I stay *in* and listen *to* music. Every Saturday evening I go *out* with my friends.

2 We like looking *at* the new fashions. Sometimes we try *on* different clothes.

3 I really like the theatre. I go to an after-school drama club. I want to act *in* a play.

4 I love street dancing. Most kids I know prefer to play video games, but they thought it was cool when I danced *with* my club in a competition. And we won!

Optional extension

Have students play ***Preposition tennis*** in groups of three. Tell two students to work together with their books closed (Students A and B) and tell the third student (Student C) to act as the judge. Explain that Student A says a verb, e.g. *go,* and Student B has to say the corresponding preposition *out* and then a new verb, e.g. *stay*. Student A has to respond with the preposition *in* and so on. Student C monitors and checks they are using the correct prepositions and maintaining a regular rhythm. Monitor the groups in case Student C is unsure about the correct answer. If one student pauses for too long or repeats a verb, the other student wins a point. Have students change roles so they all take turns as judge.

Refer students to the Vocabulary reference, page 157, for more information on word patterns.

Collocations with nouns

4 1.13 Ask students to complete the exercise. Play the audio for students to listen and check their answers.

Answers/Audioscript

1 Chess is a well-known board *game*. I love playing it.

2 Did you see the newspaper *article*? There are some good photographs in it.

3 I'm watching a great TV *programme* about the history of rock music.

4 I'm getting a new MP3 *player* soon – I want one I can record films on, too.

5 I'm going to watch a film on the big new 3-D cinema *screen* in town.

Refer students to the Vocabulary reference, page 157, for more information on collocations.

Homework OWB

Assign students Vocabulary exercises 1, 2 and 3 on page 14 of their Workbook.

LISTENING
Matching

→ Student's Book, page 18 SB

Lesson aims

- Listen for words with the same meaning
- Practise a matching exam task
- Discuss how the internet is changing entertainment

Lead-in

Ask students to brainstorm different types of TV programmes in pairs. Encourage them to give an example of a programme for each type, e.g. *reality show – Big Brother, cartoon – The Simpsons*. Then have students look at the photo on page 18 and see which types of TV programmes they can identify. Compare the programmes in the book with the ones students thought of.

1 Divide the class into pairs or groups to answer the questions. Elicit answers from different students around the class, encouraging them to give reasons for their answers.

EXAM SKILL

Listening for words that mean the same

Ask students to read the tips.

- Remind students of the work they did on finding words that mean the same in Unit 1 and tell them that they are going to continue to develop that technique here.
- Tell students that in Listening exams, they will always have time to read the questions before they hear the audio. Stress the importance of using this preparation time to read the questions carefully and think of vocabulary they would expect to hear in the recording.

2 After students complete the exercise, have volunteers come to the front of the class and write their ideas on the board. Go through students' answers and explain that more than one answer is possible.

3 Have students complete the exercise individually and then compare their answers with a partner.

Answers

1 c **2** a **3** b

4 Have students continue working in pairs to complete the exercise. Check answers with the class.

Answers

1 not very interesting = a bit boring, hard = difficult **2** nice = pleasant, a bit slow = not very fast **3** not excellent = terrible, unusual = strange

5 Ask students to complete the exercise by taking notes. Encourage them to compare their ideas with a partner before checking ideas with the class.

Suggested answers

A clever – intelligent **B** excellent – great **C** exciting – fantastic **D** funny – crazy **E** terrible – awful **F** noisy – loud **G** unhappy – sad **H** interesting – original

OPTIMISE YOUR EXAM

Matching

Ask students to read the tips.

- Remind students that it is unlikely they will hear the exact words (A–H) given in the exam task and that if they do, they should be suspicious as the word may have been included to distract them. Stress the importance of understanding the speaker's general opinion or feeling about each item and that they should use words that mean the same to help them do this.
- After listening the first time, students should have an idea of which opinions/feelings match which TV watching habits. The second time they listen they should focus very carefully on the specific words or phrases that confirm their ideas.

Mixed ability

Ask stronger students to turn their backs to the board and complete the exercise. Write *awful, crazy, fantastic, great, intelligent, loud, sad, original* on the board for weaker students to match to the opinions/feelings. When both groups have finished, wipe the board and pair stronger students with weaker students. Ask the stronger students to guess the words their partner has. Have pairs report their answers back to the class.

Exam task

6 1.14 Before playing the audio, tell students that they are going to listen to a conversation between a boy and his cousin. Play the audio for students to complete the exercise. Don't check answers at this stage as students will check their answers in Exercise 7.

Extra support

If students are struggling, guide them to the words/phrases that mean the same. Write these extracts on the board and tell students to listen for them very carefully.

They're exciting.

a good … channel

They're really bad.

… that make me laugh

They make me feel sad.

7 1.14 Play the track again for students to check if their answers are correct or change them for new ones. Elicit answers from students around the class.

Answers

1 D **2** C **3** G **4** B **5** E

THINK | RESEARCH | CULTURE | LEARN | ME

Ask students how often they use the internet for entertainment purposes. Then divide the class into pairs or groups to discuss the questions. Extend to a class discussion and ask students to justify their ideas where possible.

Homework OWB

Assign students Listening exercises 1, 2 and 3 on page 16 of their Workbook.

GRAMMAR 2
Present continuous for future use

→ Student's Book, page 19 SB

Lesson aims

- Understand how to use the present continuous to talk about the future
- Practise talking about future plans and arrangements

Lead-in

Tell students about your present and future actions using the present continuous, e.g. *I'm studying Spanish in my free time. Next weekend, a Spanish friend is coming to stay.* Some actions should be actions happening now or temporary/changing situations and some should use the present continuous for future plans/arrangements. Then elicit which actions refer to the present and which refer to the future.

Grammar in context

Ask students to read the sentences and complete the task individually. Remind students to refer to the information in the *Remember* box if they aren't sure. Check answers with the class. Elicit more examples of future time expressions, e.g. *next week, tomorrow night,* etc.

Remind students that they can find more information in the Grammar reference, Unit 2, page 146.

Answers

a 1 **b** 2

Language note

Explain that the present continuous is used for the future when we have made firm plans or arrangements, often involving other people, so we are very confident that they are going to happen.

Check the present continuous *yes/no* question form and short answer. Write *Is he visiting his grandparents on Saturday?* and ask students to identify the verbs. Then elicit the short answer: *Yes, he is. / No, he isn't.*

1 Go through the first set of questions with the class. Ask students to complete the exercise. Check their answers in open class.

Answers

2 Are, meeting, are you meeting **3** are you playing, are you playing **4** Are, cooking, are you cooking **5** Are, doing, are you doing **6** Are, studying, are you studying

2 Have students practise asking and answering the questions in pairs or groups. Walk round, monitoring students for good use of language and errors to go over at the end of the activity. Invite volunteers to practise the dialogues in front of the class.

3 Have students complete the exercise individually. Then have them compare their answers in pairs before checking answers with the class.

Answers

A 1 follow **2** 'm/am learning **3** 'm/am starting **4** have **5** 're/are going **6** leaves

B 1 'm/am listening **2** 'm/am making **3** are starting **4** 're/are going **5** 'm/am spending **6** 'm/am getting

C 1 are playing **2** live **3** build **4** play **5** 're/are meeting **6** are designing

Cultural note

Carcassonne is a medieval French town near Toulouse, famous for its city walls and fortifications. It was listed as a World Heritage Site in 1997. It is also famous for inspiring the successful board game.

Homework

OWB

Assign students Grammar 2 exercises 1 and 2 on page 15 of their Workbook.

Assign students the Flipped classroom tasks on page 20 of their Student's Book if you'd like them to prepare for the next lesson. To complete this task, students need to watch the *Talk2Me* video which can be found on the Resource Centre.

SPEAKING
Questions

→ Student's Book, page 20 SB

Lesson aims

- Focus on talking about times
- Practise using useful phrases to give factual or personal information in an exam task

The *Talk2Me* video in this unit focuses on entertainment. The people in the video talk about entertainment. They discuss going to the cinema, the times of the films and which films they would like to see and why.

Students answer some comprehension questions and then listen for key phrases in the video.

The video can be used in one of two ways:

Flipped classroom

Flipped classroom option

Using this approach, students watch the video and complete the exercises for homework. This prepares students for the speaking lesson by introducing them to the topic and the key phrases to use in the exam task. Teachers who use this method will find they have more class time to spend on activating the target language and developing fluency for the final task.

***Talk2Me* worksheet**

Ask students to complete the *Talk2Me* worksheet on the Resource Centre for more detailed comprehension exercises and more practice of the key phrases.

Classroom option

1 Ask students to spend a minute or two reading the questions. Play the *Talk2Me* video for students to complete the exercise. Play the video again, if necessary, before checking their answers.

2 Play the *Talk2Me* video again, so students underline the phrases in the *Phrase expert* box. Pause the video from time to time if necessary. Check answers in open class.

Talk2Me worksheet

Ask students to complete the *Talk2Me* worksheet on the Resource Centre for more detailed comprehension exercises and more practice of the key phrases.

Answers

The transcript and answer key for the *Talk2Me* video exercises and Worksheet can be found on the Teacher's Resource Centre.

Lead-in

Draw a horizontal line on the board and draw a stick figure of a girl at one end and a boy at the other. Give students a form of entertainment, e.g. *video gaming*, and ask students where on the line they would put it. Aim to challenge the stereotypes, so if students want to put it on the scale near the boy, ask them questions like *Do you know any girls who play video games?* or if you have a mixed class, ask the girls, *What do you think about that?* Aim to provoke discussion wherever possible. Continue with different activities, e.g. *dancing, going to the cinema, playing board games,* etc.

3 Focus students' attention on the poster and elicit what they can see. Then have students work in pairs or groups to discuss the questions. Elicit answers from different students around the class.

Answers

1 on Wednesday **2** It starts at 5 pm/5 o'clock
3 It lasts (for) 1.5 hours

EXAM SKILL

Talking about free-time activities

Ask students to read the tips.

- Remind students that they will have to speak about free-time and routine activities in the first part of the exam. Encourage students to think about the places they go to and the activities they enjoy doing and to practise speaking about them.
- Using appropriate phrases to talk about time and the correct prepositions to use with time phrases can improve a candidate's mark in an exam.
- Remind students that it is extremely important that they use appropriate phrases to answer the questions the examiner asks them or to ask the examiner to repeat something if they have not understood it correctly.

4 1.15 Tell students that this exercise will help them to practise formulating questions to ask about an event. After they've finished the exercise, play the track for students to listen and check.

Answers/Audioscript

1 What time does the concert start? It starts at 8pm **2** What are the opening hours of the museum? The opening hours are 10am until 5pm. **3** How long does the film last? It lasts 90 minutes. **4** When is football training? It's on Saturdays from 9am until 11am. **5** What time does the concert finish? It finishes at 10pm.

OPTIMISE YOUR EXAM

Questions

Ask students to read the tip.

- Candidates are not usually given time to prepare what they are going to say in speaking exams, so learning useful phrases related to routine and free-time activities will help them to feel prepared for the first part of the exam and to get off to a good start.
- Give students some additional phrases in case they need to stall for time, e.g. *Just give me a moment, Well, …, That's a good question*, and elicit more ideas from the class.

Exam task

Extra support

In pairs, ask students to write down a list of free-time activities they enjoy doing. Then ask pairs to swap their lists and think of questions to find out more information about their partner's hobbies. Elicit from the class some questions they might ask each other (e.g. *How often do you play football? Where …? Who …?*, etc.) Then get pairs to ask each other their questions.

5 Assign each student a letter, A or B, and put them into A/B pairs. Give them a moment to look at the questions they are going to ask each other. Remind students to use phrases to allow themselves more time to answer, if necessary, and to ask their partner to repeat any of the questions they don't understand. Walk around, monitoring students for good use of language and errors to go over at the end of the activity.

Write any errors on the board and go through them with students, eliciting corrections from them where possible. After the class feedback, students could then repeat this activity with another partner, to try to improve their performance.

Answers

Students' own answers

Homework

Assign students Speaking exercises 1 and 2 on pages 16–17 of their Workbook. OWB

LANGUAGE IN USE

3-option multiple-choice cloze

→ Student's Book, page 21 SB

Lesson aims

- Practise predicting answers for multiple-choice cloze texts
- Practise a 3-option multiple-choice cloze exam task
- Discuss things people talk about when they meet

Lead-in

Write *The news* on the board. Ask students to brainstorm all the different sections of the news they can think of, e.g. *local, national, international, culture, business* and all the places people can access the news from, e.g. *TV, podcasts, newspapers, Facebook, Twitter, internet, news apps*.

1 Before students read the text, have them predict what they think the text will be about (*how people access the news*). After students complete the exercise, encourage them to share their ideas with the class.

Answers
Students' own answers

EXAM SKILL

Predicting the answer

Ask students to read the tips.

- Explain to students that they can read a text with missing words and still understand the general idea of the text.
- While students read through the text the first time, encourage them to read through the text and to think of their own ideas of what word might fit into each gap without looking at the options.
- When students read through the text and options the second time, see if they thought of any of the words that appear in the options. This prediction strategy may help them to identify the correct words for the gaps.

2 Ask students to complete the questions individually and then compare their answers with a partner before going over the answers in open class.

Answers
1 a **2** b **3** b **4** b **5** a **6** b

Fast finishers

Have stronger students work individually or pair up to identify which parts of speech appear in Exercise 3 questions 1–6.

Answers
1 nouns **2** nouns **3** verbs **4** verbs **5** verbs **6** adjectives

OPTIMISE YOUR EXAM

3-option multiple-choice cloze

Ask students to read the tips.

- Ask students to predict which words might fit into the six gaps before looking at any of the options.
- After reading the text and options, ask students to choose their answers and decide why the other two options are wrong for each of the six questions.
- Once all the gaps are completed, they should read the whole text again to ensure it makes sense.

Exam task

3 Ask students to complete the exercise individually. Then have students compare their answers in pairs before eliciting answers from the class.

Answers
1 B **2** A **3** C **4** C **5** A **6** A

Extra support

Ask students to identify what is in common for each of the options. Then get them to identify what parts of speech are being tested in questions 1–6 and tell them that these are some of the parts of speech that are tested in this part of the exam.

Answers
The three options in each question are always the same part of speech.
1 nouns **2** nouns **3** verbs **4** verbs **5** verbs **6** adjectives

THINK | RESEARCH | **CULTURE** | LEARN | ME

In groups, students discuss the question.

Homework

Assign students Language in Use exercises 1, 2 and 3 on page 17 of their Workbook.

OWB

WRITING
Guided writing (a note)

→ Student's Book, pages 22–23 SB

Lesson aims

- Focus on using your own words
- Plan and write a note

Lead-in

Play ***Hangman*** with some of the words from the unit. Invite students to come to the front of the class to lead the game, if appropriate. Students may still struggle with the alphabet at this level, so correct them and clarify how we say problem letters if necessary.

1 Encourage students to share note-writing habits in pairs or groups. Elicit answers from the class.

EXAM SKILL

Using your own words

Ask students to read the tips.

- Remind students that they have done a lot of work on words that have the same meaning in Units 1 and 2. Tell them that it is also important to think about this area when writing too, as it will mean they can avoid repeating exact words from the exam text. Repeating, or 'lifting', words/phrases from exam texts lowers candidates' marks.
- Tell students to use part of their planning time to brainstorm alternative words and phrases, which they can use in their answers to demonstrate how much English they know.

2 After students complete the exercise, elicit why this type of exercise may be important (*to find out what the sender wants*).

Answers

What are you doing this afternoon? Can you come to the art gallery? Are you free then?

3 In pairs, students compare the two notes. Check their answers in open class.

Answers

Note B is better because it answers all three questions and gives extra information.

Note A is too short (22 words) and the information is not very clear.

Optional extension

Point out that in English it is rude to reply to an invitation simply by saying 'No'. People usually expect a reason. Have students write an invitation individually, e.g. *I'm meeting a friend at the cinema on Friday night. Do you want to come with me?* Elicit some ways to refuse invitations, e.g. *I'm sorry, I can't … because … / I'd love to, but I'm …* Then have students stand up and invite each other to do something or go somewhere. Everybody should refuse at least four invitations, giving a reason why, e.g. *Friday night? Oh, what a pity! I'm going to a party with my friend Claire.*

4 Elicit another way to say *really like* from students. Then have them complete the exercise with a partner. Check students' answers in open class.

Suggested answers

really like = love
later today = later on
See you later = Meet you later
I'm busy = I'm not free
go to = visit
Have fun! = Enjoy yourself!

OPTIMISE YOUR EXAM

Guided writing (a note)

Ask students to read the tips.

- Tell students that planning is an essential part of successful task completion. Advise them to take the time to think carefully about the context, check exactly what information they need to include and brainstorm useful language to show how much English they know before they start writing.
- Inform students that they will be given enough time to plan and write their text when in an exam.

Exam task

5 Ask students to complete the exercise and remind them of the importance of answering the questions. Check answers in open class.

Answers

1 What are you doing tonight? Do you want to see a new comedy at the cinema at 6:30? Do you want to come?

2 see a new comedy / go to the cinema

3 go for a pizza

6 Ask students to decide which plan they will follow when writing the note to Kris.

7 Plan Ask students to complete the writing plan. You may want to look at students' plans to check them and give advice and suggestions for improvement before they take the next step.

8 Write After students write their note, remind them to proofread their work. If there is not enough time, set this and the subsequent checklist exercise for homework.

9 Check Students complete the checklist before handing in their note.

Homework OWB

Assign students Writing exercises 1, 2, 3 and 4 on page 18 of their Workbook and Progress check 2 on page 19.

Answers PROGRESS CHECK Units 1–2

Exercise 1
1 tent **2** painting **3** article **4** swimming **5** out **6** musician **7** game **8** art gallery **9** gamer **10** café

Exercise 2
1 plays **2** 'm/am looking **3** starts **4** 're/are practising **5** 's/is watching **6** 're/are doing **7** live **8** tries

Exercise 3
1 A **2** B **3** C **4** C **5** A **6** C **7** B **8** A

Exercise 4
1 get **2** come **3** go **4** look **5** turn **6** stay

Exercise 5
1 in **2** have **3** them **4** We **5** to **6** go **7** the **8** don't **9** 'm/am **10** It

Exercise 6
1 camping **2** competition **3** camera **4** guitarist **5** attractive **6** member **7** advert **8** popular

3 What's for dinner?

UNIT AIMS

Exam preparation in Unit 3:

- understand *'who'* and *'what'* in a gapped text
- predict what the speaker will say
- explain likes and dislikes
- use conjunctions
- make and reply to suggestions

TEACHER'S PRESENTATION KIT

- *Talk2Me* videos
- Speaking test videos
- Class and Workbook audio
- Workbook pages and answer key

UNIT OVERVIEW

Student's Book / Digital Student's Book SB		Workbook / Online Workbook OWB
LESSON / EXAM TASK	EXAM SKILLS / LANGUAGE FOCUS	CONSOLIDATION
Reading **Gapped text**	Understanding *'who'* and *'what'* A gapped text	Workbook, pp 20–21, Exercises 1, 2, 3, 4 Unit 3, Reading, Exercises 1, 2, 3, 4
Grammar 1	Past simple: regular verbs, *Wh-* words	Workbook, p 22, Exercises 1, 2, 3 Unit 3, Grammar 1, Exercises 1, 2, 3
Vocabulary	Words connected with *food* Verbs/adjectives Collocations with verbs	Workbook, pp 22–23, Exercises 1, 2, 3 Unit 3, Vocabulary, Exercises 1, 2, 3
Listening **3-option multiple choice (dialogue)**	Predicting what the speaker will say	Workbook, p 24, Exercises 1, 2, 3, 4 Unit 3, Listening, Exercises 1, 2, 3, 4
Grammar 2	Past simple: irregular verbs	Workbook, p 23, Exercises 1, 2, 3 Unit 3, Grammar 2, Exercises 1, 2, 3
Speaking **Questions**	Explaining likes and dislikes	Workbook, p 24, Exercises 1, 2, 3, 4 Unit 3, Speaking, Exercises 1, 2, 3, 4
Language in Use **Open cloze**	Using conjunctions	Workbook, p 25, Exercises 1, 2 Unit 3, Language in Use, Exercises 1, 2
Writing **Guided writing (a note)**	Making and replying to suggestions	Workbook, p 26, Exercises 1, 2, 3, 4 Unit 3, Writing, Exercises 1, 2, 3, 4
		Workbook, p 27, Progress check and Cumulative progress Progress check and Cumulative progress

Additional material

PRESENTATION KIT	TEACHER'S / STUDENT'S RESOURCE CENTRE RC	TEST GENERATOR
Talk2Me video *It's my favourite because …*	**Unit 3 worksheets:** *Optimise your grammar* (Standard and Higher), *Optimise your vocabulary* (Standard and Higher), *Talk2Me* video, *Say it right* **Units 3–4 worksheets:** CLIL, Culture, Everyday English (TRC only), Grammar communication (TRC only)	Unit Test 3 (Standard and Higher)

READING
Gapped text | A magazine article

→ Student's Book, pages 26–27 SB

Lesson aims

- Identify pronouns and who or what they are referring to
- Practise a gapped text exam task
- Write a recipe and compare work with peers

Lead-in

Ask students to look at the unit title ***What's for dinner?*** and say what they think the unit is going to be about (*food, cooking, places to eat*). In pairs, ask students to brainstorm 'international' foods, e.g. *pizza, paella, tacos, curry, sushi*. Encourage students to share their ideas with the rest of the class.

1 Divide the class into pairs or groups to discuss the questions. Elicit some answers in open class to develop a class discussion.

EXAM SKILL

Understanding *who* or *what*

Ask students to read the tips.

- Elicit some more examples of pronouns that belong in the categories of *who* (*his, hers, yours*, etc.) and *what* (*it, this, that*, etc.).
- Remind students that pronouns are often important to help work out who is doing an action. Pronouns like *he, she* and *they* may refer to someone already mentioned, or we may need to use common sense and world knowledge to work out who the pronouns refer to.

2 Ask students to complete the exercise and then check answers in open class.

Answers

1 everybody **2** busy people **3** people who don't eat fish **4** the person reading the article

3 Ask students to complete the exercise in pairs. Check answers in open class, eliciting justification for answers.

Suggested answers

1 eating in restaurants **2** (working as / being) a waiter **3** being the head chef of a famous hotel

4 Ask students to read the sentences in Exercise 3 to complete the exercise. Then check answers in open class.

Answers

1 present **2** past **3** future

5 Have students skim the magazine article on page 27 quickly to answer the question and then compare their answers in pairs. Have a feedback session in open class and find out how many students know how to cook and how old they were when they started learning.

Answer

B

OPTIMISE YOUR EXAM

Gapped text

Ask students to read the tips.

- Encourage students to skim the text first to find out the topic and general meaning and then read the text again, but more carefully.
- Tell students that it's important to deal with the gaps one by one so they can compare each option (A–H) with the text before choosing one.
- Remind students to focus on the sentences before and after each gap and to pay special attention to tenses and pronouns that are being used in them. This will help students to decide which option fits the text best both grammatically and cohesively.

▼ Exam task

6 Before students complete the exam task, remind them to use all the tips they remember from this and previous units. Tell them to read the instructions carefully and follow the example. Check each answer in open class or have students listen to the audio to check their own answers.

7 1.16 **Note: The reading text is also available on the audio CD. You may want to have students listen and read the text after doing the exam task to check their answers.**

Answers

1 D ('The programme' is referring to the TV show *Junior MasterChef* in the first sentence.)

2 C (Sentence C continues the description of what happens in the show. 'The one' means one of the 'young people' in the show will be the winner.)

3 G (The idea of 'sharing recipes online' in the line before the key is reinforced by an example of someone learning 'to cook by watching YouTube videos'.)

4 A (The name 'Ben' is male so the pronoun is correct and we know that Ben is interested in music and isn't a chef so 'He's a successful rapper …' fits this gap.)

5 E (Sentence E gives another suggestion for learning how to cook and follows on naturally from 'look up the recipe' or 'watch a video about how to cook it'.)

Fast finishers

Have students write down why the answers are correct, e.g. *1 is 'The programme' is referring to the TV show Junior MasterChef in the first sentence.* As you check the answers to Exercise 6, ask fast finishers to explain the reasons behind the correct answers.

8 Ask students to complete the exercise. Students compare in pairs before you check in open class.

Answers

1 chef **2** prepare **3** famous **4** idea **5** study **6** meals **7** recipes **8** show

THINK | RESEARCH | **CULTURE** | LEARN | ME

If you have access to the internet, students can research their recipes themselves. If not, be prepared to provide vocabulary and language students need to explain their recipes clearly.

Cultural note

MasterChef was first broadcast in 1990 by the BBC. A new version of the programme was created in Australia in 2009 and this is the version which many countries around the world have adopted. The spin-off *Junior MasterChef* was first seen in 1994 and *Celebrity MasterChef* in 2006.

The 'ADHD Cooking School' (ADHD – Attention Deficit Hyperactivity Disorder) was set up in August 2015 by Goma with rapper Loyle Carner (Ben Coyle-Larner). Goma works on a range of social projects and wanted to create a cookery school for teenagers with ADHD. Loyle Carner has suffered from the disorder since childhood and finds he can channel it through his music and cooking, hence his involvement in the project.

Homework OWB

Assign students Reading exercises 1, 2, 3 and 4 on pages 20–21 of their Workbook.

GRAMMAR 1
Past simple: regular verbs, *Wh-* words

→ Student's Book, page 28 SB

Lesson aims

- Understand the correct usage of past simple, regular verbs and *Wh-* question words
- Practise talking about the past and asking questions

Lead-in

Write these unusual food items on the board:

bat soup, alligator chilli, kangaroo steak, chicken feet, mosquito eggs

Have students work in pairs and discuss which of the foods they would eat and which they wouldn't. Have a feedback session in open class.

Grammar in context

Ask students to complete the task. Check their answers and ask them to read more about past simple, regular verbs in the *Remember* box.

Remind students that they can find more information in the Grammar reference, Unit 3, page 146.

Answers

1 started **2** helped **3** opened

1 Focus students' attention on the text and ask them where they might find it (*in a magazine*). Then have them complete the exercise. Check their answers and spelling in open class.

Answers

1 started **2** watched **3** practised **4** preferred **5** used **6** baked **7** asked **8** wanted

Mixed ability

Give weaker students the verbs in the order they appear in the text (*start, watch, practise, prefer, use, bake, ask, want*) so that they can focus purely on the correct spelling. Have fast finishers circle all the words in the text related to food and cooking, e.g. *baking (n), cook (v), bake (v).*

SAY IT RIGHT

Pronunciation of *-ed* TRC

For the *Say it right* pronunciation activity and instructions, go to the Teacher's Resource Centre.

Cultural note

Amy's Baking Year was first published in 2014 when Amy-Beth Ellice was just 14 years old. The book contains numerous recipes organised according to the seasons and special occasions through the year.

Grammar in context

Students at A2 level are expected to be able to use the basic *Wh-* question words correctly to refer to the present, past and future. Ask students to complete the task. Remind them to refer to the information in the *Remember* box if they aren't sure. Then check their answers.

Remind students that they can find more information in the Grammar reference, Unit 3, page 146.

Answers

a past **b** a time

2 Go through the example. Then have students complete the exercise. Check their answers.

Answers

2 c **3** d **4** a **5** e **6** b

3 Read the title of the text and elicit what it means (*A start-up is a small business that has just started up.*). Ask students to complete the exercise. Elicit answers from different students around the class.

Answers

1 talking **2** When **3** travelled **4** decided **5** Who **6** talked **7** Where **8** What **9** Which **10** What

Homework

OWB

Assign students Grammar 1 exercises 1, 2 and 3 on page 22 of their Workbook.

VOCABULARY

Topic vocabulary | Word formation | Collocations

→ Student's Book, page 29 SB

Lesson aims

Understand the correct usage of:

- words connected with food
- verbs and adjectives from the same word family
- verb + noun collocations

Lead-in

Write these jumbled questions on the board and ask students to put them in the correct order and complete the *Wh-* question word.

1 house / in / wh_ / your / the cooking / does / usually
2 to Friday / wh_ / have / do / you / lunch / from Monday
3 was / the last time / a meal / for / wh_ / you / went out

Answers

1 Who usually does the cooking in your house?
2 Where do you have lunch from Monday to Friday?
3 When was the last time you went out for a meal?

Words connected with *food*

1 1.17 Before students complete the exercise, elicit which food they like/dislike or which food is healthy/unhealthy. Play the audio for students to listen and check their answers. (Potatoes as carbohydrates and tomatoes as fruit are also acceptable answers.)

Answers/Audioscript

Vegetables: beans, *carrots, lettuce, onions, potatoes* (could also go in the 'carbohydrates' list), *tomatoes*
Fruit: apple, *banana, oranges, strawberries*
Carbohydrates: bread, *cereal, pasta, rice*
Meat: beef, *chicken, steak*
Dairy: cheese, *milk, yoghurt*
Other: honey, *oil, salt, vinegar*

2 Ask students what snacks they like. Then have them complete the exercise individually. Have students compare answers in pairs before checking answers in open class.

Answers

1 cereal **2** yoghurt **3** bread **4** honey **5** beef/steak **6** oil/salt **7** cheese **8** onions **9** lettuce **10** strawberries

Refer students to the Vocabulary reference, page 158, for more information on topic vocabulary.

Verbs/adjectives

3 1.18 Ask students to complete the exercise. Play the audio for students to listen and check their answers. Then have students close their books. Call out the verbs and have volunteers say the correct adjectives to check their pronunciation.

Answers/Audioscript

verb: bake, **adjective:** *baked*
verb: boil, **adjective:** *boiled*
verb: *fry*, **adjective:** fried
verb: grill, **adjective:** *grilled*
verb: roast, **adjective:** *roasted*

Language note

Both *bake/baked* and *roast/roasted* refer to preparing food in an oven. The difference is that foods that are baked are cooked 'dry', e.g. cakes and bread, while those that are roasted are baked in oil or fat, e.g. potatoes, beef.

4 1.19 Ask students to complete the exercise individually. Then play the audio for students to listen and check their answers.

Answers/Audioscript

1 I ate some delicious *fried* fish at the new Thai restaurant.
2 He *boiled* the pasta for a long time. It tasted terrible.
3 We need to *grill* this chicken for 20 minutes.
4 I like *baked* potatoes with cheese and beans.

5 Ask students to complete the exercise. Check their answers.

Answers

I ate some delicious fried fish at the new Thai restaurant. Then I had some cold coconut ice cream with fresh green grapes.

6 Have students complete the exercise. Remind students to refer to the information in the *Remember* box if they aren't sure. Check answers in open class.

Answers

1 A **2** A **3** B

Extra support

Read the following items and ask students to decide if the adjectives are in the correct order. Ask students to correct the ones that sound strange.

1 *some baked horrible pasta*
2 *a young Japanese chef*
3 *a green small apple*
4 *some fantastic new recipes*
5 *an Indian old cookbook*

Answers

1 horrible baked **3** small green **5** old Indian

Refer students to the Vocabulary reference, page 158, for more information on word formation.

Collocations with verbs

7 1.20 Remind students that collocations are word combinations that go together. Have students complete the exercise. Then play the audio for them to listen and check their answers.

Answers/Audioscript

1 *have* lunch / *have* a drink / *have* a good time
2 *take* an exam / *take* a train / *take* a photo
3 *do* homework / *do* the washing-up / *do* sports
4 *make* breakfast / *make* a picnic / *make* a mistake
5 *bake* bread / *bake* a cake / *bake* a potato

8 Ask students to complete the exercise. Check answers in open class.

Answers

2 bake, make/have **3** ✓ **4** ✓ **5** do, make

Refer students to the Vocabulary reference, page 158, for more information on collocations.

Homework OWB

Assign students Vocabulary exercises 1, 2 and 3 on pages 22–23 of their Workbook.

LISTENING
3-option multiple choice (dialogue)

→ Student's Book, page 30 SB

Lesson aims

- Listen for detail after predicting content
- Practise a multiple-choice exam task
- Research places to eat

Lead-in

Divide the class into teams. Call out one of the verbs for preparing food from the previous lesson, e.g. *bake*. Set teams a time limit of 30 seconds to think of phrases with the verb, e.g. *biscuits, cakes, bread*. Repeat the process with *boil, fry, grill* and *roast*. Check answers, giving one point for each correct answer. The team with the most points wins.

1 Have students ask and answer the questions in pairs or groups. Elicit answers from around the class to see which restaurant is the most popular.

EXAM SKILL

Predicting what the speaker will say

Ask students to read the tips.

- Remind students of the work they have already done on predicting. In Unit 1 they practised predicting content for a picture multiple-choice listening exam task. Here they will be practising the same techniques, but with words rather than pictures.
- Remind students that they should prepare to listen for words that have the same meaning. Taking notes can be a valuable part of the predicting process and help organise a candidate's ideas, and students will be looking at this in detail in exercises 3 and 4.

2 Ask students to look at the exam question and tell you what it will be about (*a new café*). Then have them complete the exercise. Check their answers in open class.

Suggested answers

reason, likes, café, cheap cake, good coffee, friendly staff

3 Have students complete the exercise in pairs. Then discuss the two sets of notes as a class and make sure students understand why B is much better.

Answers

B are the better notes. They use the information from the questions to predict what the speaker might say.

4 1.21 Remind students how important it is to listen very carefully and not just choose the first word they hear. Play the track for students to listen and answer the question. Check in open class.

Answer

1 B

5 Before the exercise, remind students that this is a pre-listening task. After students complete the exercise, elicit answers from different students around the class and accept all sensible suggestions.

OPTIMISE YOUR EXAM

3-option multiple choice (dialogue)

Ask students to read the tips.

- Tell students that in this part of the exam they will hear a conversation between two speakers. Tell them to look at the questions and underline key words to help them predict what the speakers might discuss. This will help them to follow the conversation.
- Remind students to listen carefully to both speakers because the answers to the questions can come from either of the speakers.

▾ Exam task

6 1.22 Ask students who they will listen to (*two friends talking: Clare and Simon*). Play the track for students to listen and complete the exercise. Don't check answers at this stage, as students will do this in Exercise 7.

7 1.22 Play the track again for students to check their answers. Remind them to always choose an answer, even if they are not totally sure. Check their answers in open class.

Answers

1 B **2** C **3** A **4** B **5** A

Optional extension 1.22

Play the track again, pausing where necessary, for students to listen and note down words from the answer options that were mentioned in the recording but were not the correct answers.

Answers

1 Simon asked if they went to the café on Friday evening (A), but Clare says they went on Saturday afternoon (B).

2 Clare says there were only five tables (C), but she also says there were *two* people in her group (A).

3 Clare says the food *wasn't great* (C), but Simon says the food he ate *was good* (A).

4 Simon had *an omelette* (A) when he went to the cafe and Kristy had *a curry* (C), but Clare had fish (B).

5 Clare had a drink (A), but she also mentions *fruit* (B) and *dessert* (C).

THINK | **RESEARCH** | CULTURE | LEARN | ME

In pairs or groups, students research to answer the questions.

Homework OWB

Assign students Listening exercises 1, 2, 3 and 4 on page 24 of their Workbook.

GRAMMAR 2
Past simple: irregular verbs

→ Student's Book, page 31 SB

Lesson aims

- Focus on past simple irregular verbs
- Understand the use of the auxiliary *did* for negative statements and questions in the past
- Practise using irregular verbs to talk about the past
- Discuss interesting restaurants

Lead-in

Play the memory game: *Yesterday, I went to the shops and bought …* with the class. Start by saying a food with an adjective, e.g. *Yesterday, I went to the shops and bought some fresh fish.* Nominate a strong student to repeat the sentence and add an item, e.g. *… some fresh fish and some small tomatoes.* Continue with more students. Have students who cannot repeat all the food sit down. The last student standing wins. With a large class, divide students into groups.

Grammar in context

Ask students what they remember about Clare and Simon's conversation in the previous lesson. Then have them complete the task. Check their answers and ask students to read the information in the *Remember* box. Remind them that they need to learn irregular verbs off by heart. Encourage them to study the Irregular verbs reference on page 167.

Remind students that they can find more information in the Grammar reference, Unit 3, page 147.

Answers

1 go **2** thought **3** had **4** pay **5** said

Language note

Some irregular verbs can be organised into groups that behave in a similar way, e.g.

- verbs where /ɪ/ changes to /æ/, e.g. *begin* > *began*, *drink* > *drank*, *swim* > *swam*
- verbs where the past form ends in /ɔːt/, e.g. *buy* > *bought*, *teach* > *taught*, *think* > *thought*
- verbs where /iː/ changes to /e/, e.g. *keep* > *kept*, *meet* > *met*, *sleep* > *slept*

Highlighting similarities between irregular verbs can help students remember them.

Mixed ability

Pair stronger students with less confident students. Ask the less confident students to test their partners' knowledge of irregular verbs. Less confident students refer to the Irregular verbs reference on page 167 and ask questions, e.g. *What's the past of 'bring'? How do you spell it?* This activity will help both groups reinforce their knowledge of the verbs. In Exercise 1, allow less confident students to refer to the Irregular verbs reference.

1 Go through the example sentence as a class and then ask students to complete the exercise. Check answers in open class, eliciting both the spelling and pronunciation of the irregular verbs.

Answers

2 Helen didn't go to the restaurant last week.

3 Paul got up early this morning.

4 He saw his friends after school last night.

5 Rob couldn't come for dinner last Monday.

6 She bought a sandwich at the local shop this morning.

7 We met in the park in 2018.

8 I had a lot of comics as a child.

2 Have students complete the exercise individually. Walk round the class, helping if necessary. Have students compare their sentences in pairs. Invite volunteers to share their answers in open class.

Answers

Students' own answers with:

2 … taught me English last year.

3 The best programme I saw on TV yesterday was … / … was the best programme I saw on TV yesterday.

4 I went to … with my friends at the weekend.

5 I … before bed last night.

6 The best meal I had last week was … / … was the best meal I had last week.

3 Ask a strong student: *What did you eat for breakfast this morning?* Then divide the class into pairs to practise speaking. After the exercise, ask students to share any interesting answers they heard.

Mixed ability

Pair stronger students with weaker students and have the stronger students ask the questions first. This way the weaker students have a chance to hear the questions before having to formulate them. Alternatively, elicit the questions from the class before students start to ask and answer.

4 Ask students to complete the exercise. Have students compare in pairs before you check their answers in open class.

Answers

1 went **2** saw **3** got **4** didn't have **5** heard **6** thought **7** said **8** understood **9** ate **10** didn't leave

THINK | RESEARCH | CULTURE | LEARN | **ME**

In pairs, students tell each other about their experience.

Cultural note

The Little Yellow Door café is in Notting Hill Gate in London. In summer 2016, they launched a special Emoji Menu where customers can order using text messages from their phones.

Homework OWB

Assign students Grammar 2 exercises 1, 2 and 3 on page 23 of their Workbook.

Assign students the Flipped classroom tasks on page 32 of their Student's Book if you'd like them to prepare for the next lesson. To complete this task, students need to watch the *Talk2Me* video which can be found on the Resource Centre.

SPEAKING
Questions

→ Student's Book, page 32 SB

Lesson aims

- Talk about your likes, dislikes and daily life
- Practise answering personal questions

The *Talk2Me* video in this unit focuses on food and drink. The people in the video talk about preparing food for Mother's Day, their favourite cakes and cleaning the house. Students answer some comprehension questions and then listen for key phrases in the video. The video can be used in one of two ways:

Flipped classroom

Flipped classroom option

Using this approach, students watch the video and complete the exercises for homework. This prepares students for the speaking lesson by introducing them to the topic and the key phrases to use in the exam task. Teachers who use this method will find they have more class time to spend on activating the target language and developing fluency for the final task.

***Talk2Me* worksheet**

Ask students to also complete the *Talk2Me* worksheet on the Resource Centre for more detailed comprehension exercises and more practice of the key phrases.

Classroom option

1 Ask students to spend a minute or two reading the questions. Play the *Talk2Me* video for students to complete the exercise. Play the video again, if necessary, before checking their answers.

2 Play the *Talk2Me* video again, so students underline the phrases in the *Phrase expert* box. Pause the video from time to time if necessary. Check answers in open class.

***Talk2Me* worksheet**

Ask students to also complete the *Talk2Me* worksheet on the Resource Centre for more detailed comprehension exercises and more practice of the key phrases.

Answers

The transcript and answer key for the *Talk2Me* video exercises and Worksheet can be found on the Teacher's Resource Centre.

Lead-in

Make sure students have their books closed. Answer the two questions in Exercise 3 with examples. Ask students to listen carefully to your answers and work out what they think the questions are. Have students make notes and compare their ideas in pairs. Then have students check their questions with the ones on Student's Book page 32.

EXAM SKILL

Explaining likes and dislikes

Ask students to read the tips.

- Remind students that it is extremely important to ask the examiner to repeat questions they don't understand. Explain that reformulating (repeating what you think the examiner is asking for) is a good technique, as it shows that the candidate was paying attention and wants to confirm before answering, e.g. *So, you want me to talk about the meal I like most?* (in response to *What is your favourite meal of the day?*).
- Remind students that adding some extra information in the form of examples or opinions, even if it has a few mistakes in it, makes a very positive impression on examiners.

3 Divide the class into pairs or groups to ask and answer the questions. Elicit answers from different pairs or groups around the class.

4 1.23 Tell students that they will hear an extract from a speaking exam, and have them read the questions. Play the track for students to listen and answer. Have them compare their answers in pairs before checking answers with the class.

Answer

1 pasta **2** pears **3** hot bread, meat

5 1.23 Play the track again, pausing where necessary, for students to listen and note down the reasons the student gives.

Answers

1 It's tasty and easy to make.
2 He has to eat so many of them.
3 It's cold and dark so they make hot things.

6 Elicit or point out that the categories in the mind map relate to the questions from the speaking exam in Exercise 4. Give students time to complete the mind map with their own answers and a reason for each one. Monitor students and help where necessary.

OPTIMISE YOUR EXAM

Questions

Ask students to read the tips.

- Remind students to find the vocabulary they need to talk about their personal likes and dislikes. They can use dictionaries or ask the teacher and should try to use this vocabulary whenever they get an opportunity.
- Explain that students need to be prepared for all sorts of questions. Remind them that they should also think about asking and answering relevant questions in their head.

Exam task

7 Divide the class into pairs to ask and answer the questions in Exercise 4. Ask students to use their notes from Exercise 6 and the words and phrases in the *Phrase expert* box to help them give extra information in their answers. Walk round and monitor students, noting down errors and good use of language to go over at the end of the activity.

Write any errors you hear on the board and go through them with students, eliciting corrections from them where possible. If there is time, have students repeat the task with another partner to help improve their performance.

Fast finishers

Ask students to brainstorm other topics connected to food, which they think might come up in the exam, e.g. *Special food in your country, Special food for special times of the year, The worst meal ever.* When everyone has finished, have students share their ideas in open class.

Homework

OWB

Assign students Speaking exercises 1, 2, 3 and 4 on page 24 of their Workbook.

LANGUAGE IN USE
Open cloze

→ Student's Book, page 33 SB

Lesson aims

- Focus on thinking about grammar
- Practise an open-cloze exam task
- Describe food

Lead-in

Tell students about a place where you like to eat. Use the sentences in Exercise 1 to guide you and try to cover all the areas mentioned there. Explain that they can take notes if they wish. Afterwards, put students in pairs to look at the sentences in Exercise 1 and, based on what you told them, they should try to agree on what the most important thing is for you. Then give them feedback on their ideas.

1 Have students complete the exercise individually. If necessary, encourage them to think about the example you gave when they are deciding the order.

2 Divide the class into pairs or groups of students who don't usually work together to promote a little diversity in the class. Ask them to discuss and explain their opinions.

3 In the same pairs or groups, have students come to a consensus on a final order. Then have them present their ideas to the class with reasons for their decision.

Optional extension

Give students the name of a local restaurant they all know. Have a brainstorming session for students to describe it, e.g. *Nino's – delicious (pasta), cheap (menu), top quality (ingredients), tasty (pizzas).* Repeat the process with two or three different local restaurants to elicit as much vocabulary as possible.

EXAM SKILL

Using conjunctions

Ask students to read the tips.

- Explain that different tasks in exams focus on different areas, and open-cloze tasks like the one on this page focus particularly on grammar.
- Tell students that the open-cloze task tests a range of grammatical structures. One of the structures that are tested is conjunctions; they are also known as linking words because they link two ideas.
- Tell students that knowing how sentences are linked together can help them figure out what the missing conjunctions are in an open-cloze task.

4 Ask students to complete the exercise. Check their answers and elicit the reasons for each one.

Answers

1 or (choice) **2** and (addition) **3** and (addition) **4** but (opposite ideas) **5** because (reason) **6** but (opposite ideas)

OPTIMISE YOUR EXAM

Open cloze

Ask students to read the tips.

- Point out that open-cloze exam tasks look similar to multiple-choice cloze tasks. Explain that the only obvious difference is that students are not given options beneath the text in open-cloze tasks. However, multiple-choice cloze places more emphasis on vocabulary, and open cloze focuses mainly on grammar.
- Tell students to think only about the type of words they could use in each space the first time they read and not to get distracted by exact words. It's important that they get a general understanding of the whole text before completing the task.

Exam task

5 Go through the example and then have students complete the exam task. Elicit answers and ask them to identify the types of words for each gap.

Answers

1 on (preposition) **2** an (article) **3** but (conjunction)
4 to (preposition) **5** because (conjunction)
6 some (determiner)

THINK | RESEARCH | CULTURE | LEARN | ME

Monitor the task and help students with vocabulary. Have groups share their sentences and try to guess each other's food.

Homework

OWB

Assign students Language in Use exercises 1 and 2 on page 25 of their Workbook.

WRITING
Guided writing (a note)

→ Student's Book, pages 34–35 SB

Lesson aims

- Focus on using your own vocabulary
- Plan and write a note

Lead-in

Play a spelling game with the class. Ask all students to stand up. Choose a strong student and ask *What's the past of* teach? *How do you spell it?* If the student does not answer both questions correctly, he or she sits down. Repeat the process, nominating students at random. Have students who hesitate also sit down. Include both regular and irregular verbs and continue until only one student is left standing.

1 As students answer the questions, make a list of their ideas on the board.

2 Ask students who the note is from (*Toni*). Then have them complete the exercise.

Answers

Toni asks three questions.

Students should underline: What/like eating, Where/go, What/time/meet

EXAM SKILL

Making and replying to suggestions

Ask students to read the tips.

- Tell students that they need to answer the three questions in 25 words or more. They need to make sure they address each of the questions in their reply; otherwise they will receive lower marks.
- Remind students to use their preparation time effectively. Also remind them that planning is an essential part of successful task completion.

3 After students have read both texts, have them highlight the main differences between the two. Check the answers in open class and ask students to justify their answers.

Answers

1 Note A (20 words)

2 Note B; Note A doesn't answer the first and second questions

3 Both. Note A *Let's eat some …*; Note B *How about …?*, *Would you like to …?*

4 Note B *… on Bond Street, fantastic … cheap*

4 Ask students to complete the exercise. Then check their answers in open class.

Suggested answers

1 I'm also free today. **2** I love pizza. / Pizza is my favourite food. **3** Let's try it. / How about going there? / Why don't we go there? **4** How about meeting there at one o'clock? / Why don't we meet there at one o'clock?

OPTIMISE YOUR EXAM

Guided writing (a note)

Ask students to read the tips.

- Remind students they have worked with words that have the same meaning and have used their own words rather than repeating or lifting words/phrases from the exam texts.
- Tell students that writing is an opportunity for candidates to show examiners how much English they know, so taking time to think of interesting vocabulary can make a real difference. Explain that the more they can show their knowledge of vocabulary, the more marks they will get.

Exam task

5 Invite different volunteers to read the instructions and the note. Monitor students and help where necessary. Then have students share their answers in pairs.

Answers

1 Ella

2 25 words or more

3 three

4 What the cookery classes were like. What you learnt to cook.

5 past simple for the first and second questions and present tenses to answer the third question

6 phrases for food and cooking

6 Plan Tell students to use all the tips they have seen so far to complete the plan. You may want to look at students' plans to check them and give advice and suggestions for improvement before they take the next step.

Extra support

Look at the plan with students. Elicit suggestions for how to complete the *Detail* column from the class and prompt them to write the questions that they need to answer. Give them a couple of minutes to write down some ideas in the *My notes* column. Then have students brainstorm ideas in pairs or small groups for the *Useful language* column. Collate these on the board so all students have plenty of ideas to choose from before they start writing.

7 Write Make sure students understand what is meant by the appropriate style (*informal language that is used for writing notes*). Offer help where needed. If there is not enough time, set this and the subsequent checklist exercise for homework.

8 Check Students complete the checklist before they hand in their note. Tell students that this is an important part of every task they do.

Homework OWB

Assign students Writing exercises 1, 2, 3 and 4 on page 26 of their Workbook and Progress check 3 on page 27.

4 On your way

UNIT AIMS

Exam preparation in Unit 4:

- understand words from context
- listen for important information
- ask someone to explain
- choose the right word
- punctuation and spelling in an email

TEACHER'S PRESENTATION KIT

- *Talk2Me* videos
- Speaking test videos
- Class and Workbook audio
- Workbook pages and answer key

UNIT OVERVIEW

Student's Book / Digital Student's Book SB		Workbook / Online Workbook OWB
LESSON / EXAM TASK	EXAM SKILLS / LANGUAGE FOCUS	CONSOLIDATION
Reading **3-option multiple matching**	Understanding words from context Blog posts	Workbook, pp 28–29, Exercises 1, 2, 3, 4 Unit 4, Reading, Exercises 1, 2, 3, 4
Grammar 1	Past continuous, linking words	Workbook, p 30, Exercises 1, 2 Unit 4, Grammar 1, Exercises 1, 2
Vocabulary	Words connected with *travel* Compound nouns Phrasal verbs	Workbook, pp 30–31, Exercises 1, 2, 3 Unit 4, Vocabulary, Exercises 1, 2, 3
Listening **Gap fill**	Listening for important information	Workbook, p 32, Exercises 1, 2, 3 Unit 4, Listening, Exercises 1, 2, 3
Grammar 2	Past simple and past continuous	Workbook, p 31, Exercise 1 Unit 4, Grammar 2, Exercise 1
Speaking **Discussion (pictures)**	Asking someone to explain	Workbook, pp 32–33, Exercises 1, 2, 3 Unit 4, Speaking, Exercises 1, 2, 3
Language in Use **3-option multiple-choice cloze**	Choosing the right word	Workbook, p 33, Exercises 1, 2 Unit 4, Language in Use, Exercises 1, 2
Writing **Guided writing (an email)**	Punctuation and spelling	Workbook, p 34, Exercises 1, 2, 3, 4 Unit 4, Writing, Exercises 1, 2, 3, 4
Progress check	Check language progress for Units 3 and 4	Workbook, p 35, Progress check and Cumulative progress Progress check and Cumulative progress

Additional material

PRESENTATION KIT	TEACHER'S / STUDENT'S RESOURCE CENTRE RC	TEST GENERATOR
Talk2Me video *Did you say …?*	**Unit 4 worksheets:** *Optimise your grammar* (Standard and Higher), *Optimise your vocabulary* (Standard and Higher), *Talk2Me* video, *Say it right* **Units 3–4 worksheets:** CLIL, Culture, Everyday English (TRC only), Grammar communication (TRC only)	Unit Test 4 (Standard and Higher) Progress Test (Standard and Higher)

READING

3-option multiple matching | Blog posts

→ Student's Book, pages 36–37 SB

Lesson aims

- Focus on reading for general meaning and strategies for understanding new words or phrases
- Practise a matching exam task

Lead-in

Ask students to look at the unit title ***On your way*** and the photo and say what they think the unit will be about (*transport, travel*). Ask them if they like to travel and, if so, where and how they like to travel. Also ask them about their favourite places, when they last visited and why they liked them. Encourage students to give reasons and examples with their answers if possible.

1 Before students complete the task, make sure they understand all the vocabulary. Then elicit answers from different students around the class.

2 1.24 **Note: The reading text is also available on the audio CD. You may want to have students listen and read the text after doing the scanning task.**

Ask students to look at the photos on page 37 and describe what they see. Then have them complete the exercise. Check answers in open class.

Answers

1 C **2** A **3** B

3 Invite a volunteer to read out the first definition. Elicit the correct word from the text. Then have students complete the exercise individually. Check answers in open class.

Answers

1 sightseeing **2** pack **3** trip **4** journeys **5** storm **6** wet **7** flight **8** festival

EXAM SKILL

Understanding words from context

Ask students to read the tips.

- Tell students that to help understand a text fully, it is important to think about the context it is written in. Explain that figuring out where texts are from and who is likely to read them can make exam tasks much easier.
- Remind students that when they don't know a word in a text, they should look at the words before and after the word to help understand what it might mean. They can also read the sentence after the word as this may make the meaning of the word clearer.

4 Ask students to complete the exercise and then go over the answers in open class.

Answers

1 a **2** b **3** a

OPTIMISE YOUR EXAM

3-option multiple matching

Ask students to read the tips.

- Remind students that thinking about the topic vocabulary before completing an exercise will help them complete the exam task more successfully.
- Remind them that there are always some additional items they do not need to use in multiple-matching tasks. Tell them to be careful as some of the items may look like the correct answer even though they are not.

▼ Exam task

5 Ask students to complete the exercise individually. Check answers in open class and elicit the key words and phrases in the blog posts which helped them to answer each question.

Answers

1 B (I went to a language school) **2** C (Edinburgh Castle … it was really busy because it's so popular) **3** A (our flight was delayed because there was a terrible storm) **4** C (I decided to stay in the hotel to rest … a tour guide took them on an exciting night tour of the city) **5** B (music festival … raining all day/wet and muddy) **6** A (our flight was delayed … I was reading an exciting story so the time went quickly) **7** A (I hate long journeys)

Optional extension

Split the class into six groups. Assign each group one of the following places: *airport, bus station, campsite, park, petrol station, train station* and ask them to brainstorm topic vocabulary for that place. Regroup students so that everyone is in a different group and have students share their vocabulary with each other. Encourage them to explain the meaning of any unfamiliar words to their new groups if necessary.

Cultural note

Note that American English has different names for some of these places: *petrol station = gas station; train station = railroad station; bus station = bus terminal; campsite = campground.*

Homework

OWB

Assign students Reading exercises 1, 2, 3 and 4 on pages 28–29 of their Workbook.

THINK | RESEARCH | CULTURE | LEARN | **ME**

Students answer the questions.

GRAMMAR 1
Past continuous, linking words

→ Student's Book, page 38 SB

Lesson aims

- Understand the correct usage of the past continuous and linking words
- Practise talking about actions that were happening over a specific period of time in the past
- Practise using linking words to connect ideas

Lead-in

Tell the class that you want each student to stand up and simultaneously mime an action to you, e.g. play the piano, kick a football. Ask one student to time 30 seconds and then call out 'Stop'. Students immediately stop miming their actions. Try to remember what each student was doing and formulate it as a past continuous sentence, e.g. *Ahmed was playing the piano.* The student then sits down. You win if you are able to remember what everyone was doing, but the class wins if any students are left standing. Write the last sentence you said on the board, circle the past continuous verb form and elicit the name for the tense before continuing. Students can play this game again in small groups after Exercise 2.

Grammar in context

Have students complete the task and check their answers. Ask them if they got their answers correct and, if not, encourage them to read more about the past continuous in the *Remember* box.

Remind students that they can find more information in the Grammar reference, Unit 4, page 147.

Answers
1 was reading **2** wasn't studying **3** were my friends doing

1 Ask students who's speaking in the conversation and what they are talking about (*Joe and Ben, a trip to France*). Check their answers and have students practise the conversation in pairs.

Answers
1 was walking **2** were you going **3** was driving **4** was taking
5 was doing **6** were both cycling **7** were being **8** wasn't looking

2 Go through the example as a class and then have students complete the exercise individually. Have students compare in pairs before you check answers in open class.

Answers
2 She was playing music last night.
3 James was studying in London last year.
4 No, I was sightseeing.

Grammar in context

Ask students to complete the task. Refer them to information in the *Remember* box if they aren't sure. Check their answers.

Remind students that they can find more information in the Grammar reference, Unit 4, page 147.

Answers
1 because **2** when **3** but

3 Before students complete the exercise, ask them why they think the web page is called *Around the world in 80 ways* (the posts are always about unusual ways to travel and the title also makes reference to the famous novel *Around the World in Eighty Days*, by Jules Verne). Check answers in open class.

Answers
1 was feeling **2** but **3** were travelling **4** when **5** was speaking
6 was working **7** because **8** were leaving

Fast finishers

Have fast finishers read the text again and underline all the words for people (*travellers, parents, Dad, Mum, driver, mechanic, son, football fan*).

SAY IT RIGHT

TRC

/ə/

For the *Say it right* pronunciation activity and instructions, go to the Teacher's Resource Centre.

Homework OWB

Assign students Grammar 1 exercises 1 and 2 on page 30 of their Workbook.

VOCABULARY
Topic vocabulary | Word patterns | Phrasal verbs

→ Student's Book, page 39 SB

Lesson aims

Understand the correct usage of:

- words connected with travel
- noun + noun word patterns (compound nouns)
- phrasal verbs

Lead-in

Write *Places in town* on the board and put students into small groups to brainstorm ideas, e.g. *chemist, bus station, supermarket, car park*, etc. Then encourage the class to write them on the board. Ask students questions about some of the items, e.g. *Where can you get a stamp and post a letter?* (*the post office*), *Where do you go if you want a magazine?* (*the newsagent*).

Words connected with *travel*

1 1.25 Ask students who they think Amelie is (*a new pupil*). Then have students complete the exercise individually. Play the audio for students to listen and check their answers.

Answers/Audioscript

Hi Amelie,

Here is the information about getting to school tomorrow. We can catch the bus at the *bus stop* outside my house at 7:40 am. We arrive at school at about 8:15, unless the bus is *delayed* or we *miss* it. ☹ We don't need tickets because we have student ID cards. We cross the *bridge* over the river, then Kelly gets on the bus in town. We go through three *traffic lights,* then arrive at Jamie's stop. Then we go past the *railway station*, where we pick up passengers from the train – so, Yasmin and Leo get on the bus there. Next, the bus goes round a *roundabout* and then after a few more stops we arrive at school. Sometimes there's a lot of *traffic* and the journey's slow – but then we get more time to chat! ☺

2 Ask students to complete the exercise. Have them compare their answers in pairs before checking them in open class.

Answers

1 roundabout **2** traffic **3** bridge **4** bus stop **5** traffic lights

Refer students to the Vocabulary reference, page 158, for more information on topic vocabulary.

Compound nouns

3 1.26 Elicit what compound nouns are (*two words that go together to form one noun*). Give a few examples, e.g. *railway station, bus stop.* Then ask students to complete the exercise. Play the audio for students to listen and check their answers.

Answers/Audioscript

1 (d) car park **2** (e) driving licence **3** (a) helicopter ride
4 (c) petrol station **5** (b) sailing boat **6** (g) ticket machine
7 (f) tour guide **8** (h) traffic news

4 Ask students to complete the exercise. Check their answers.

Answers

1 traffic news **2** tour guide **3** helicopter ride **4** driving licence
5 ticket machine **6** car park **7** petrol station **8** sailing boat

Refer students to the Vocabulary reference, page 158, for more information on word patterns.

Phrasal verbs

5 1.27 Have a volunteer go outside the classroom and knock on the door. Say *come in,* and elicit the meaning of *come in*. Then have students complete the exercise. Play the audio for students to listen and check their answers.

Answers/Audioscript

1 to enter a place: *go in*
2 to leave the ground and go into the sky: *take off*
3 to start a journey: *set off*
4 what somebody says to invite you into a place: *come in*
5 to collect something or somebody, often in a car: *pick up*
6 to leave a main road: *turn off*

Language note

These phrasal verbs belong to three different categories.

Come in, *go in* and *set off* are intransitive phrasal verbs (with no object). Note that when these verbs are followed by a place, this is introduced with *to*. *Turn off (the road)* is a non-separable phrasal verb, and the object, whether it is a noun or pronoun, will always come after the particle.

Pick up is taught with two meanings and in both cases the object can go between the verb and the particle (*pick the children up*) or after the particle (*pick up the children*) when it is a noun, but a pronoun has to go between the verb and the particle (*pick them up*).

Take off could be problematic when it means 'how a plane leaves' as it works in the same way as *come in*, *go in* and *set off*. However, when it means 'to remove something', it works in the same way as *pick up*.

6 Ask students what the message is about (*a school trip update*). Then have them complete the exercise. Check their answers.

Answers

1 take off **2** pick up **3** set off **4** come in **5** turn off

Refer students to the Vocabulary reference, page 158, for more information on phrasal verbs.

Homework

OWB

Assign students Vocabulary exercises 1, 2 and 3 on pages 30–31 of their Workbook.

LISTENING
Gap fill

→ Student's Book, page 40 SB

Lesson aims

- Listen for important information
- Practise a gap-fill exam task
- Discuss ways to check spelling

Lead-in

Books closed. Explain to students that you are going to describe a photo and that they have to listen to your description and try to draw what you describe. Use the photo at the top of Student's Book page 40, e.g. *In the top half of the photo there's an open suitcase with clothes in it. In front of …* Have students compare their drawings in pairs or small groups before looking at the Student's Book.

1 Ask students what tourists usually do when they visit a new place. Brainstorm ideas on the board. Then have students complete the exercise in pairs or as a group.

Answers
Students' own answers

EXAM SKILL

Listening for important information

Ask students to read the tips.

- Remind students that it is important to predict the possible format(s) of the numbers they are going to hear. For example, the way we say numbers in a time (1:15 could be *one fifteen* or *quarter past one*) is very different to the way we say numbers in a date (15/01 could be *the fifteenth of January* or *January the fifteenth*) and students should try to prepare for this.
- Tell students that if they are unsure about a number they heard, they should listen very carefully in the second listening to check their understanding.

Extra support

Play ***Bingo*** with the class. Write the following pool of numbers on the board and ask students to draw a grid (three columns by two rows) and choose six items to complete it.

32 £2.50 16th 4:30 pm 30 October 3.8 230.5 44 £9.99 17 15 60th 14 70

Read out numbers at random, making a note of the order to check the winner's answers at the end. Before you call out the numbers, explain that the number *44* can also be said as 'double four' and the number zero as 'oh'. The first student to call 'bingo' wins.

2 1.28 Tell students they are going to listen to five short conversations. Then play the audio for them to complete the exercise. Play the track again for students to check their answers.

Answers
1 32a **2** 4 **3** 786 934 **4** 16th **5** 12:14

3 1.28 Tell students they are going to listen to the same five short conversations again. Then play the audio for them to complete the exercise. Play the audio again for students to check their answers.

Answers
1 F **2** T **3** T **4** T **5** F

4 1.29 Explain that students will hear eight short conversations and have to write down the words that are spelt out. Play the audio and then have them compare their answers in pairs before checking them in open class.

Answers
2 Solomon **3** Cambourne **4** Alisha Pieters **5** Leicester **6** Clapham Junction **7** Borough **8** Tom Maltravers

OPTIMISE YOUR EXAM

Gap fill

Ask students to read the tips.

- Point out that if the speaker spells a word out in listening exam tasks, that means students are expected to spell the word correctly. However, if they hear a word that is not spelt out, they should write it how they think it is spelt.
- When speaking, point out that a useful technique is to say a word that begins with the letter causing problems, e.g. *No, not 'z' for 'zoo', it's 'c' for 'Canada'.*

Exam task

5 1.30 Have students read the information before they listen. Play the audio. Don't check answers at this stage, as students will listen again to check in Exercise 6.

6 1.30 Have students review their answers. Play the track again. Elicit answers from students around the class.

Answers
1 8:30 **2** Nunthorpe **3** island **4** pairs **5** water

THINK | RESEARCH | CULTURE | **LEARN** | ME

Point out that many web search engines and some online dictionaries / dictionary apps now have 'fuzzy searches', so even if you don't spell the word correctly, it will still offer suggestions of what it thinks the word you are looking for might be.

Homework

OWB

Assign students Listening exercises 1, 2 and 3 on page 32 of their Workbook.

GRAMMAR 2
Past simple and past continuous

→ Student's Book, page 41 SB

Lesson aims

- Understand the differences between the past simple and past continuous
- Practise using the past simple and past continuous
- Discuss things different people were doing in the past

Lead-in

Write this sentence starter on the board:

I was doing my homework last night when …

Tell students you want to hear the most ridiculous excuse possible for why they haven't done their homework, e.g. *I was doing my homework last night when a spaceship landed and aliens took my school bag.* Have students think of ways to complete the sentence in pairs. Elicit the best ideas from different pairs around the class.

Grammar in context

Ask students to complete the task. Refer them to the information in the *Remember* box if they aren't sure. Check their answers.

Remind students that they can find more information in the Grammar reference, Unit 4, page 148.

Answers

a were sailing, fell **b** were sailing **c** fell (into the water)

1 Go through the first sentence as a class. Elicit the continuous activity that was interrupted (*everyone was having a good time*). Have students complete the exercise individually. Then check answers as a class.

Answers

1 arrived, was having **2** was listening, called **3** did you break, Were you running **4** was riding, fell **5** stopped, was driving **6** was shopping, lost

2 Ask students to complete the exercise. Check answers in open class.

Answers

1 said, were looking **2** were walking, saw, was shopping **3** didn't want, was raining **4** were driving, stopped **5** changed, were chatting

Mixed ability

Give weaker students the tenses they need for each item (e.g. ***1** past simple, past continuous; **2** past continuous, past simple*) and ask them to focus on choosing the correct form of the verb *to be* in the past continuous, and on spelling the *-ing* and past simple forms correctly. Ask stronger students to write additional sentences using different combinations of the verbs in item 2, e.g. *drive + begin – We were driving home yesterday when it began to snow.*

3 Tell students to look at the travel blog and describe what they see in the picture (*a person looking at the sky*). After students complete the exercise, have them compare their answers in pairs. Then check answers in open class.

Answers

1 didn't post **2** were staying **3** didn't stream **4** weren't camping **5** took **6** was beginning **7** was looking **8** flew **9** were taking **10** started **11** kept **12** was standing

Cultural note

The Uyuni Salt Flats (*Salar de Uyuni* in Spanish) are in the south-west of Bolivia, high in the Andes. They cover over 10,000 km² and are at an altitude of just over 3,500 m. They were formed from a giant prehistoric lake tens of thousands of years ago and contain large quantities of lithium, which is extracted for use in batteries. Tourism is becoming more popular in the area and hotels are often built from blocks of salt.

THINK | RESEARCH | CULTURE | LEARN | ME

In pairs, students discuss what they were doing.

Homework

OWB

Assign students Grammar 2 exercise 1 on page 31 of their Workbook.

Assign students the Flipped classroom tasks on page 42 of their Student's Book if you'd like them to prepare for the next lesson. To complete this task, students need to watch the *Talk2Me* video which can be found on the Resource Centre.

SPEAKING
Discussion (pictures)

→ Student's Book, page 42 SB

Lesson aims

- Focus on asking someone to explain
- Practise asking for repetition
- Practise discussing pictures in a collaborative exam task

The *Talk2Me* video in this unit focuses on exercise. The people in the video talk about the best type of exercise and the benefits of cycling, then arrange to buy some bikes.

Students answer some comprehension questions and then listen for key phrases in the video.

The video can be used in one of two ways:

Flipped classroom

Flipped classroom option

Using this approach, students watch the video and complete the exercises for homework. This prepares students for the speaking lesson by introducing them to the topic and the key phrases to use in the exam task. Teachers who use this method will find they have more class time to spend on activating the target language and developing fluency for the final task.

***Talk2Me* worksheet**

Ask students to also complete the *Talk2Me* worksheet on the Resource Centre for more detailed comprehension exercises and more practice of the key phrases.

Classroom option

1 Ask students to spend a minute or two reading the questions. Play the *Talk2Me* video for students to complete the exercise. Play the video again, if necessary, before checking their answers.

2 Play the *Talk2Me* video again, so students underline the phrases in the *Phrase expert* box. Pause the video from time to time if necessary. Check answers in open class.

EXAM SKILL

Asking someone to explain

Ask students to read the tips.

- Point out that, in the same way as it is very important to understand what the examiner says, students also need to understand what their partner says in order to successfully complete the collaborative task.
- Remind them that they can ask for general clarification with questions like *Could you say that again, please?* or they can ask about a specific piece of information again, e.g. *How much did you say?*

***Talk2Me* worksheet**

Ask students to also complete the *Talk2Me* worksheet on the Resource Centre for more detailed comprehension exercises and more practice of the key phrases.

Answers

The transcript and answer key for the *Talk2Me* video exercises and Worksheet can be found on the Teacher's Resource Centre.

Lead-in

Ask students to work in teams to brainstorm as many words as possible related to travel and transport in one minute.

3 Divide the class into pairs. Student A should talk about different ways they travel and why they use this type of transport. Student B will use phrases from the *Phrase expert* box to get their partner to repeat or explain what they are talking about.

4 1.31 Tell students they are going to listen to a discussion about holidays and then answer the questions. Ask students to compare their answers with a partner before playing the audio a second time and checking answers in open class.

Answers

1 cycling holiday **2** cruise/ship **3** coach trip **4** walking holiday **5** horse-riding holiday

OPTIMISE YOUR EXAM

Discussion (pictures)

Ask students to read the tips.

- Remind students that in many speaking exams there is a part where students work together on a collaborative task.
- One of the marking criteria in many speaking exams is interactive communication. This refers to the students' ability to participate actively in a two-way conversation at an appropriate level without intervention from the examiner.
- Tell students that in this exam task type, both candidates are being assessed all the time. Examiners will be listening both for the candidates' ability to form questions correctly, and their ability to answer questions in full sentences with the correct information.

Exam task

5 Have students read the information before they do the collaborative exam task. If possible, use a timer and let students know that they must speak about the different types of holidays for two minutes. Then change partners and try the timed task again.

6 Put students in pairs and allocate which student is Student A and which is Student B and ask them to do the task in about two minutes. Use a timer if possible. Then ask students to swap roles and time the task again.

Optional extension

Ask students to think about the best holiday they have ever been on. Elicit what kinds of questions they should ask their partner to find out information about their holiday. Write down some questions (e.g. *Where did you go? Who did you go with? How did you travel there? Why did you enjoy this holiday?*). Get pairs to ask each other questions about their favourite holiday. Finally, ask students to feed back to the class something they learnt about their partner's holiday.

Homework

OWB

Assign students Speaking exercises 1, 2 and 3 on pages 32–33 of their Workbook.

LANGUAGE IN USE
3-option multiple-choice cloze

→ Student's Book, page 43 SB

Lesson aims

- Focus on vocabulary related to travel
- Practise a 3-option multiple-choice exam task

Lead-in

Write *Down Under* on the board and ask students if they know what it means. If they don't, draw a globe on the board with the United Kingdom at the top and Australia at the bottom. Draw an arrow to the UK and another to the bottom of the globe and ask students what country it is. Explain that 'down under' refers to Australia. Ask students to tell you everything they can think of about Australia, e.g. *koala bears, kangaroos, Sydney Opera House, barbecues, surfing, Uluru (Ayers Rock).*

1 Ask students what the difference between a tour and a journey is and elicit the correct option for the first sentence. Have students complete the exercise and compare their answers in pairs. Then check the answers in open class and make sure that students are clear about the meaning of all the words.

Answers
1 A **2** B **3** A **4** C **5** C **6** A **7** C **8** A

Language note

Some commonly confused words

A *tour* is the act of travelling round a place to see interesting things; a *journey* is the act of travelling from one place to another.

A *chair* is a piece of furniture you sit on. You sit on a *seat* on a form of transport.

Luggage means all the bags you take on holiday. A *suitcase* is one piece of luggage; it has flat sides and a handle.

EXAM SKILL

Choosing the right word

Ask students to read the tips.

- Tell students that in each set of answer options A, B and C are the same part of speech, for example, nouns, verbs, adjectives, etc. In this part of the exam, the focus is on testing vocabulary rather than grammatical knowledge.
- Each set of answer options will have a similar meaning, but students need to decide which of the three options is correct.
- Encourage students to look at the words that are before and after the gap to help them decide which is the correct answer. Sometimes the correct option must collocate with the word after the gap.

2 Have students complete the exercise and then compare their answers in pairs before you check them in open class.

Answers
1 big (meal) **2** (railway) station **3** (beach) holidays **4** really (late) **5** going (away)

OPTIMISE YOUR EXAM

3-option multiple-choice cloze

Ask students to read the tips.

- Make sure students understand they need to read all the sentences or text before they start answering, as the context may help them to choose the correct answers.
- Remind students that multiple-choice tasks often test their knowledge of vocabulary (e.g. nouns, verbs, adjectives). Point out that they need to look at the whole sentence and remember that the clues could be before or after each gap.

▾ Exam task

3 Ask students what they know about Australia before completing the exercise. Tell students to complete the exam task using the tips from the Exam skill box to help them. Check answers in open class.

Answers
1 C **2** A **3** A **4** A **5** B **6** C

Fast finishers

Have fast finishers write the reasons why their answers are correct, e.g. *'1 is 'went' as 'went away' is another way to say that Réka went on holiday'*. As you check the answers to Exercise 3, ask the students who wrote reasons to share them with the class.

Homework

OWB

Assign students Language in Use exercises 1 and 2 on page 33 of their Workbook.

WRITING
Guided writing (an email)

→ Student's Book, pages 44–45 SB

Lesson aims

- Focus on punctuation and spelling
- Plan and write an email

Lead-in

Write these sentences on the board and ask students to tell you what this information is about (where someone lives):

1 People love visiting my town because it's next to the sea.

2 Many tourists love going to the cafés and shops in the harbour.

3 The easiest way to get here is by boat.

Ask students where they might read sentences like these. Elicit that they are all sentences that might appear in an email describing where someone lives.

Answers

1 France **2** Brazil **3** India

1 Have students discuss the questions, and then elicit answers from different students around the class.

2 Draw students' attention to the photo and elicit information about the place, e.g. *it's a town near the sea*. Then have them read the task and answer the questions. Check the answers in open class.

Answers

1 Why do people visit your town? How do people get there (to your town)? What's the best way to get around (it/your town)?

2 a photo of your town

3 Heres → Here's, how → How, round → around

EXAM SKILL

Punctuation and spelling

Ask students to read the tips.

- Explain that an error in punctuation or spelling could have an effect on the message they want to send. Students should make sure they read their work after they have finished.
- Remind students to look back at the spelling rules for regular verbs and tell them to revise the Irregular verbs reference so that they don't confuse regular and irregular verbs.

3 Tell students to think about the possible mistakes they can find. Check answers in open class.

Answers

1 most → Most **2** Their → There **3** ariving → arriving
4 walks → walk **5** Its → It's

4 Have two volunteers read the emails out loud before students complete the exercise. Elicit ideas from students around the class.

Suggested answer

B is the better answer. Jordi answers all three questions clearly, although he also gives information about the airport, which isn't relevant. It is easy to understand what he means, and he uses a better range of vocabulary.

Julia uses more informal language and it is easy to understand what she means, but she doesn't answer the second question.

OPTIMISE YOUR EXAM

Guided writing (an email)

Ask students to read the tips.

- Remind students of the importance of replying to specific questions. Tell them that they need to reply to the three questions in 25 words or more.
- Tell students that while it is good to experiment with new language in class (trying out new words and finding new ways to say things), an exam is not the place to do this. Explain that it should be written using informal language.

Exam task

5 Invite volunteers to read the exam task and the questions before students answer the questions. Monitor and help where necessary before checking answers in open class.

Answers

1 George
2 25 words or more
3 about George's last holiday
4 where you are on holiday, what the place is like
5 present and past tenses
6 words related to holidays and travel

6 Plan Ask students to complete the plan individually. You may want to look at students' plans to check them and give advice and suggestions for improvement before they take the next step.

Extra support

Look at the plan with students. Elicit suggestions for how to complete the *Detail* column from the class and prompt them to write the questions that they need to answer. Give them a couple of minutes to write down some ideas in the *My notes* column. Then have students brainstorm ideas in pairs or small groups for the *Useful language* column. Collate these on the board so all students have plenty of ideas to choose from before they start writing.

7 Write Tell students that they can use their plan as a starting point, but it is OK to change this while they are writing. If there is not enough time, set this and the subsequent checklist exercise for homework.

8 Check Students complete the checklist before they hand in their email.

Fast finishers

For students who finish their email, ask them to pair up. Ask them to swap their emails to peer correct. Get them to underline any grammar, punctuation or spelling mistakes in their partner's email. They then return their emails and correct any errors that were identified.

Optional extension

For a slightly longer writing task, refer students to the task in the Writing reference (SB page 163). It includes an annotated sample text and related writing task to challenge your students a little more.

Homework

OWB

Assign students Writing exercises 1, 2, 3 and 4 on page 34 of their Workbook and Progress check 4 on page 35.

Answers PROGRESS CHECK Units 3–4

Exercise 1
1 stop **2** near **3** in **4** on **5** outside **6** ride **7** off **8** there

Exercise 2
1 up **2** in **3** off **4** in **5** off **6** bake **7** take **8** have

Exercise 3
1 C **2** B **3** A **4** B **5** A **6** C **7** B **8** B

Exercise 4
1 asked, was shouting **2** was travelling, ate **3** decided, was shining **4** bought, were cooking

Exercise 5
1 What **2** Did **3** who **4** whose **5** was **6** why **7** Where **8** weren't **9** which **10** when

Exercise 6
1 recipes **2** fried **3** prepare **4** journey **5** traffic light **6** petrol station **7** railway station **8** tour guide

5 Technology talks

UNIT AIMS

Exam preparation in Unit 5:

- understand text type
- understand when things happen
- talk about preferences
- use determiners
- use linking words

TEACHER'S PRESENTATION KIT

- *Talk2Me* videos
- Speaking test videos
- Class and Workbook audio
- Workbook pages and answer key

UNIT OVERVIEW

Student's Book / Digital Student's Book SB		Workbook / Online Workbook OWB
LESSON / EXAM TASK	EXAM SKILLS / LANGUAGE FOCUS	CONSOLIDATION
Reading **3-option multiple choice (short texts)**	Understanding text types Notices and short messages	Workbook, pp 36–37, Exercises 1, 2, 3, 4, 5 Unit 5, Reading, Exercises 1, 2, 3, 4, 5
Grammar 1	Quantifiers with countable and uncountable nouns	Workbook, p 38, Exercises 1, 2 Unit 5, Grammar 1, Exercises 1, 2
Vocabulary	Words connected with *communication and technology* Compound nouns Collocations with verbs	Workbook, pp 38–39, Exercises 1, 2, 3 Unit 5, Vocabulary, Exercises 1, 2, 3
Listening **3-option multiple choice (pictures)**	Understanding when things happen	Workbook, p 40, Exercises 1, 2 Unit 5, Listening, Exercises 1, 2
Grammar 2	Comparatives and superlatives	Workbook, p 39, Exercises 1, 2 Unit 5, Grammar 2, Exercises 1, 2
Speaking **Discussion**	Talking about preferences	Workbook, pp 40–41, Exercises 1, 2, 3 Unit 5, Speaking, Exercises 1, 2, 3
Language in Use **Open cloze**	Using determiners	Workbook, p 41, Exercises 1, 2, 3 Unit 5, Language in Use, Exercises 1, 2, 3
Writing **Picture story**	Using linking words	Workbook, p 42, Exercises 1, 2, 3, 4, 5, 6, 7 Unit 5, Writing, Exercises 1, 2, 3, 4, 5, 6, 7
		Workbook, p 43, Progress check and Cumulative progress Progress check and Cumulative progress

Additional material

PRESENTATION KIT	TEACHER'S / STUDENT'S RESOURCE CENTRE RC	TEST GENERATOR
Talk2Me video *It's better to …*	**Unit 5 worksheets:** *Optimise your grammar* (Standard and Higher), *Optimise your vocabulary* (Standard and Higher), *Talk2Me* video, *Say it right* **Units 5–6 worksheets:** CLIL, Culture, Everyday English (TRC only), Grammar communication (TRC only)	Unit Test 5 (Standard and Higher)

READING

3-option multiple choice (short texts) | Notices and short messages

→ Student's Book, pages 48–49 SB

Lesson aims

- Identify different types of text
- Practise a 3-option multiple-choice exam task
- Discuss owning a mobile phone

Lead-in

Ask students to look at the unit title ***Technology talks*** and the photo and ask them what they think the unit will be about (*communications and technology*). Elicit what functions and icons they recognise in the photo , e.g. *mail, cloud*. Then ask students approximately how much time they spend communicating using technology every day.

1 Hold up your phone and elicit ways people can communicate information with each other. Write students' ideas on the board. Have students discuss the questions in pairs or groups and then elicit answers in open class.

EXAM SKILL

Understanding text type

Ask students to read the tips.

- Tell students that they should try to identify what type of text they are reading (a public notice, text message, sign, etc.) and to decide which context it would appear in (at school, on a phone, at a shop, etc.).
- Tell students that they can use the visual information (layout, location, image, etc.) to help identify the context.
- Students need to know that different types of texts have different kinds of information. For example, a public sign usually gives instructions, while a text message from a friend might be asking questions or giving information about something.

2 Have students complete the exercise. Check answers in open class.

Answers

a) 2 **b)** 1 **c)** 3

3 Read out the first text in Exercise 2 and the two possible answers to the class. Elicit the correct answer. Then have students complete the exercise. Check answers in open class.

Answers

1 b **2** a **3** b

4 Put students in pairs to complete the exercise. Monitor to check pronunciation.

Answers

1 Lucy should reply to Jane / tell Jane if she has her book.

2 To take part in the photo show, you should be aged 12 to 15. You should also print your photos and write your name and age on the back of the photos.

3 Becky should tell Anna if she can go shopping with her.

Optional extension

Put students into teams and tell them that they need to write a list of as many different kinds of communicative messages (texts, notices, etc.) as they can think of. Then ask students to compare their lists and add any items they didn't include. Finally, get teams to write down the kinds of information commonly found on their list of communicative messages (an email from a teacher – important information about homework, an advert – what is being sold, price, contact information, etc.).

SAY IT RIGHT

Missing vowel sounds in questions

For the *Say it right* pronunciation activity and instructions, go to the Teacher's Resource Centre. TRC

OPTIMISE YOUR EXAM

3-option multiple choice (short texts)

Ask students to read the tips.

- Tell students that in this part of the exam they will have to read six short emails, notices, signs, texts or messages. For each question, students have to match the meaning of one of the three sentences to the short text.
- Remind students that they should underline the key words or phrases in the text and in the options. This can help them decide if the paraphrase in an option correctly matches the meaning of the text.
- Encourage students to compare each option with the text before choosing their answer carefully.

▼ Exam task

5 2.01 **Note: The reading text is also available on the audio CD. You may want to have students listen and read the text before doing the exam task.**

Ask students to complete the exercise. Have students compare in pairs before you check in open class.

Answers

1 B **2** C **3** A **4** C **5** C **6** A

Optional extension

Ask students to discuss how often they send emails and text or instant messages (WhatsApp, Messenger, etc.) and who they generally send their messages to. Invite students to discuss which is better, sending messages or speaking to someone in person.

6 Have students scan the six texts for the words and phrases that match the definitions. Check students' answers in open class.

Answers

1 collect **2** chat **3** let me know **4** store **5** spending **6** home number

Fast finishers

Ask students to write a short message to a friend using the vocabulary in Exercise 6 (*collect, chat, let me know, story, spending, home number*).

THINK | RESEARCH | CULTURE | LEARN | ME

Tell students to brainstorm all of their ideas. Then have pairs or groups present their ideas to the class, giving reasons for their answers.

Homework OWB

Assign students Reading exercises 1, 2, 3, 4 and 5 on pages 36–37 of their Workbook.

GRAMMAR 1

Quantifiers with countable and uncountable nouns

→ Student's Book, page 50 SB

Lesson aims

- Focus on quantifiers with countable and uncountable nouns
- Practise talking about the quantities of things

Lead-in

Divide the board in half down the centre and write *a/an* at the top of the left side and *some* at the top of the right side. Have students copy this in their notebooks. Read out the following items for students to decide which group they belong to:

singer steak bridge computer game honey beach traffic musician exhibition cereal oil bus stop

Have students compare their answers in pairs before you check answers in open class and collate the items on the board. Ask students what the difference is between the words on the left and the words on the right, and explain that the words on the left can also be used with *some* if these are made plural.

Answers

a/an (+ countable noun): singer, steak, bridge, computer game, beach, musician, exhibition, bus stop

some (+ uncountable noun): honey, traffic, cereal, oil

Grammar in context

Ask students to complete the task and look at the text to check their answers. Tell students to read the information in the *Remember* box if their answers are incorrect.

Remind students that they can find more information in the Grammar reference, Unit 5, page 148.

Answers

1 Lots **2** a few **3** some **4** any

Language note

Countable nouns are items we can count using numbers. We cannot count uncountable nouns, but we can measure them, for example, in weight: *100 grams of sugar*; or with containers *a bag of potatoes, a box of cereal*, etc. Uncountable nouns don't take *-s* or other plural forms; they take the singular form of verbs.

1 Ask students to complete the exercise individually. Remind them to refer to the information in the *Remember* box if they aren't sure. Ask students to compare their answers with a partner before checking in open class.

Answers

1 a little **2** a lot of **3** A few **4** any **5** a lot of **6** much **7** Some **8** A few **9** many **10** any

2 Focus students' attention on the photo and have them describe what they see before they complete the exercise. Then check answers in open class.

Answers

1 B **2** A **3** B **4** B **5** C **6** C **7** B **8** C **9** A

Fast finishers

Ask students to look again at the gaps and see if any other quantifiers could be used in each space. Elicit ideas while going through the answers.

Suggested answers

1 a lot **2** many / lots of / a lot of **3** Lots **4** any **5** lots of / some **6** some **7** a few **8** some **9** lots of

3 Ask students what they can write about modern technology. Elicit ideas and then have students complete the exercise individually. Walk round the class, helping students and monitoring for good use of the quantifiers. Elicit some answers from different students around the class.

Homework OWB

Assign students Grammar 1 exercises 1 and 2 on page 38 of their Workbook.

VOCABULARY

Topic vocabulary | Word patterns | Collocations

→ Student's Book, page 51 SB

Lesson aims

Understand the correct usage of:

- words connected with communication and technology
- noun + noun word formation (compound nouns)
- verb + noun collocations

Lead-in

Play the memory game *In my room at home I have …* with the class. Start by providing a model sentence, e.g. *In my room at home I have a lot of papers.* Nominate a strong student to repeat the sentence and add an item, e.g. … *a lot of papers and some books*, and then another student, e.g. … *a lot of papers, some books and a computer.* Highlight that every item should use a suitable quantifier. When students have understood the activity, put them in small groups to play. Walk round the class, monitoring students' use of language. Make a note of any errors you hear.

Words connected with *communication and technology*

1 2.02 Ask students what parts of a computer they can name. Then have them complete the exercise individually. Play the audio for students to check their answers.

Answers/Audioscript

1 screen **2** keyboard **3** laptop **4** printer **5** camera **6** mouse

2 2.03 Ask students what the text type is (*a blog*) and have them complete the exercise individually. Play the audio for students to check their answers. Ask students if they regularly read blogs and, if so, what they are about.

Answers/Audioscript

Hi everyone! Sorry I've been quiet! I've just moved house. It's good to get *online* again – I missed *blogging*! I have a lovely big desk for my *laptop* in the new house. So, I can use that when I'm at home. It's got a really big *screen*, which is perfect for watching videos. I decided to get a *printer* as well, so I can print the photos I like. The laptop is good for gaming too. The *graphics* in the games look much better. The *keyboard* is a bit different from my last one, so sorry if I make any spelling mistakes! The wireless *mouse* is great and isn't noisy when you click it. I still need to *download* my files from the old computer. And I need some new *software* so that I can *stream* music faster.

Tomorrow, I'll use the *camera* and upload some new photos of me at my new desk!

Refer students to the Vocabulary reference, page 159, for more information on topic vocabulary.

Compound nouns

3 2.04 Ask students to complete the exercise. Play the audio for students to listen and check their answers.

Point out that *website* is written as one word, but that all the other words are written as two. Highlight that for most of these items the main stress is on the first word, except for *mobile phone, laptop computer* and *personal computer* where the main stress is on the second word.

Answers/Audioscript

1 *player*: CD player, DVD player, MP3 player

2 *phone*: camera phone, cell phone, mobile phone

3 *web*: web address, web page, website

4 *computer*: laptop computer, personal computer, computer file, computer software

Language note

A 'mobile phone' and a 'cell phone' are the same thing – the term *mobile phone* is British English whereas *cell phone* is used mainly in American English.

4 Write the sentences *His mobile / camera phone is really old. You can't even take pictures with it.* on the board and elicit the correct option to complete it (*mobile*). Then ask students to complete the exercise. Elicit answers from different students around the class.

Answers

1 MP3 **2** website **3** page **4** software

Refer students to the Vocabulary reference, page 159, for more information on word patterns.

Collocations with verbs

5 2.05 Ask students to cover items 1–6 and to suggest words which might come after each of the verbs in the box. Have students complete the exercise individually. Play the audio for students to check their answers.

Answers/Audioscript

1 *make* a phone call / *take* a phone call **2** download a piece of software **3** *download* a file / *open* a file **4** *download* a photograph / *take* a photograph **5** *send* a text message **6** *start* a conversation

6 Remind students to use the skills they learnt in previous lessons when completing multiple-choice activities. Have them compare ideas in pairs before checking answers in open class.

Answers

1 started a conversation **2** making a phone call **3** open/download a file **4** download a piece of software **5** take a photograph **6** send a text message

Mixed ability

To check the answers to Exercise 6, pair strong students with weak students and have stronger students close their books. Ask weaker students to read the first part of the sentence, up to the verb in the correct form, e.g. *1 I met her on the train and she…* Tell their partner to say the rest of the sentence from memory. Have weaker students help their partners by giving them some of the key words from the second part of the sentence if they get stuck, e.g. *1 social networking sites, 2 brother, Canada, talk*, etc.

Refer students to the Vocabulary reference, page 159, for more information on collocations.

Homework OWB

Assign students Vocabulary exercises 1, 2 and 3 on pages 38–39 of their Workbook.

LISTENING
3-option multiple choice (pictures)

→ Student's Book, page 52 SB

Lesson aims

- Listen and understand when things happen
- Practise a 3-option multiple-choice (pictures) exam task

Lead-in

Write the number *3* on the board. Put students into pairs and tell them to write down:

three words you can use before 'player'
three things you can do with a file
three words you can use after 'web'
three things you can download
three words you can use before 'phone'

Check their answers.

Suggested answers

CD/DVD/MP3 player; open/save/close a file; web page / website / web address; download music/films/apps; cell/ mobile/camera phone

1 Ask students if they are creative and, if so, what they like to create. Then have them look at the photo and discuss the questions. Elicit answers from different students around the class.

EXAM SKILL

Understanding when things happen

Ask students to read the tips.

- Remind students that they have used language to talk about the past (with the past simple and past continuous), the present (with the present simple and present continuous) and the future (with the present simple and present continuous). Elicit an example of each and remind students that they are now prepared to identify these tenses when listening.
- Explain that, as well as the tenses, there are usually other clues to help students understand when things happen and the exact order of events. Tell students not to panic if they don't hear the tense clearly, and to simply focus on the rest of the sentence for specific words in these cases.

2 Invite two volunteers to read out the conversation. Then ask students to complete the exercise individually. Check their answers in open class.

Answers

1 I looked **2** I'm writing **3** It says

3 Tell students to refer back to the conversation in Exercise 2. In pairs, students put the events in order. Check answers in open class.

Answers

a 3 **b** 4 **c** 2 **d** 1

OPTIMISE YOUR EXAM

3-option multiple choice (pictures)

Ask students to read the tips.

- Opinions are an expression of a person's feelings and are based on facts or emotions but can't be proven to be true or false. Opinions can be preceded with terms such as *I think* (which students will see on the *Speaking* page in this unit), or with adjectives, comparatives and superlatives (which students will see on the next *Grammar* page).
- Point out that the word *like* is a commonly used word in English, but it does not always mean 'something we enjoy'. Highlight that in questions such as *What's X like?* we use it to ask for descriptions. Also explain that students might hear the word *like* within a negative sentence, in which case the meaning is the opposite, or could even be as extreme as *hate*, depending on the exact words chosen.

Exam task

4 2.06 Before students listen, tell them that they will hear five situations and need to identify the correct image for each one. Then play the audio for students to complete the exercise. Ask them to compare their choices in pairs. Don't check the answers at this stage as students will check them in Exercise 5.

5 2.06 Play the audio again for students to check their answers and then discuss as a class.

Answers
1 C **2** A **3** B **4** C **5** A

Homework
Assign students Listening exercises 1 and 2 on page 40 of their Workbook.

OWB

GRAMMAR 2
Comparatives and superlatives

→ Student's Book, page 53

SB

Lesson aims

- Understand the correct usage of comparatives and superlatives
- Practise comparing two or more things
- Discuss useful pieces of technology

Lead-in

In pairs, students race to make a list of adjectives for every letter of the alphabet in a three-minute time limit. Do a feedback session in open class and ask students to share the items they chose for each letter. Check that they have spelt them correctly. Write the adjectives on the board, if possible using one colour for adjectives which form the comparative/ superlative with *-er/-est* and a different colour for adjectives which take *more / the most*. At the end, ask students to tell you why you have used the two colours.

Possible answers
High-level items in brackets
angry, **b**ad, **c**omfortable, **d**irty, **e**arly, **f**ast, **g**ood, **h**igh, **i**mportant, (**j**ealous), **k**ind, **l**oud, **m**odern, **n**ew, **o**ld, **p**retty, **q**uiet, (**r**ude), **s**mall, **t**hin, **u**nusual, (**v**ictorious), **w**orried, (**x**enophobic), **y**oung, (**z**ealous)

Grammar in context

Tell students that the sentences are extracts from the listening they heard in the previous lesson. Ask students to complete the task and refer them to the information in the *Remember* box if they aren't sure. Then check their answers.

Remind students that they can find more information in the Grammar reference, Unit 5, page 149.

Answers
1 better **2** nicer **3** more

Language note

Students are tested on comparative and superlative forms in all parts of official exams at this level. Remind students that this language point is also useful in speaking exams, e.g. when giving full answers to personal questions and for discussing things with a partner in collaborative tasks.

1 If students aren't confident doing this type of 'sentence transformation', as this is their first appearance in the book, consider doing the second item together as a class. Ask students to complete the exercise individually. Have students compare answers in pairs before checking in open class.

Answers
2 The PC is more expensive than the laptop.
3 Rap is more popular than rock music.
4 Her blog is more interesting than yours / your blog.
5 The video of the surfer is stranger than the video of the skateboarder.
6 My computing class is bigger than the photography class.
7 His email was longer than hers / her email.
8 The design of the laptop is more modern than the PC.

2 Ask students to complete the exercise. Check answers in open class.

Answers
1 newer than **2** bigger than **3** more expensive **4** the best **5** more **6** heavier than **7** the most popular

3 Before students complete the exercise, remind them to think carefully about whether the adjectives form the comparative/superlative with *-er/-est* or with *more / the most* and to be very careful with spelling. Have students compare their answers in pairs before you check answers with the class.

Answers
1 more exciting **2** the most interesting **3** better **4** more careful **5** more difficult **6** the best **7** busier **8** the most unusual

THINK | RESEARCH | CULTURE | LEARN | **ME**

Tell students to think about what inventions have had the biggest impact on the world and what they think it would be difficult to live without. Have students discuss their ideas with a partner. Then elicit answers from different students in the class and try to develop a class discussion.

Homework

Assign students Grammar 2 exercises 1 and 2 on page 39 of their Workbook.

Assign students the Flipped classroom tasks on page 54 of their Student's Book if you'd like them to prepare for the next lesson. To complete this task, students need to watch the *Talk2Me* video which can be found on the Resource Centre.

SPEAKING

Discussion

→ Student's Book, page 54

Lesson aims

- Focus on talking about preferences
- Practise answering personal questions in an interview task

The *Talk2Me* video in this unit focuses on communications and technology. People in the video talk about the advantages of online shopping and they order some food items online.

Students answer some comprehension questions and then listen for key phrases in the video.

The video can be used in one of two ways:

Flipped classroom

Flipped classroom option

Using this approach, students watch the video and complete the exercises for homework. This prepares students for the speaking lesson by introducing them to the topic and the key phrases to use in the exam task. Teachers who use this method will find they have more class time to spend on activating the target language and developing fluency for the final task.

***Talk2Me* worksheet**

Ask students to also complete the *Talk2Me* worksheet on the Resource Centre for more detailed comprehension exercises and more practice of the key phrases.

Classroom option

1 Ask students to spend a minute or two reading the questions. Play the *Talk2Me* video for students to complete the exercise. Play the video again, if necessary, before checking their answers.

2 Play the *Talk2Me* video again, so students underline the phrases in the *Phrase expert* box. Pause the video from time to time if necessary. Check answers in open class.

***Talk2Me* worksheet**

Ask students to also complete the *Talk2Me* worksheet on the Resource Centre for more detailed comprehension exercises and more practice of the key phrases.

Answers

The transcript and answer key for the *Talk2Me* video exercises and Worksheet can be found on the Teacher's Resource Centre.

Lead-in

Write some commonly used text-messaging abbreviations on the board and put students into pairs to discuss what they think they mean (answers in brackets).

2moro (tomorrow)* *2nte* (tonight)* *BFF* (Best friends forever!) *BTW* (by the way) *CTN* (Can't talk now.) *CU* (See you!)* *GR8* (Great!)* *IDK* (I don't know.) *TMI* (Too much information!) *L8R* (later)* *LOL* (laughing out loud) *P911* (Parent alert!)* *THX* (thanks) *TTYL* (Talk to you later.) W8 (wait)*

Explain that not all text-messaging abbreviations are simply the first letters of the words. In some cases (marked with *), they are a play on the sounds (e.g. 'two'morrow), or rely on common knowledge (e.g. *P911*, 911 is the emergency number in a variety of countries). Have students share the abbreviations they know with the class and elicit their favourite one.

3 Have students look at the photos and say where the people are (*The people in photo A are possibly at school and the people in photo B are at home*). Then have them complete the exercise in pairs or groups. Elicit answers from the class.

EXAM SKILL

Talking about preferences

Ask students to read the tips.

- Tell students they should be able to talk about their personal preferences. They should avoid giving one-word answers and try to extend their answers by giving reasons and examples for their preferences.
- Encourage students to practise using appropriate phrases to express preferences like the ones in the *Phrase expert* box.

4 2.07 Have students read through the questions before you play the audio. Check answers in open class.

Answers

1 be with your friends **2** watch a film **3** shopping with friends **4** playing games online

5 2.07 Tell students they are going to listen to the audio again so they can number the phrases in order. Elicit answers from different students around the class, encouraging them to repeat the information they heard.

Answers

A 4 **B** 3 **C** 2 **D** 1

OPTIMISE YOUR EXAM

Discussion

Ask students to read the tips.

- Remind students that when they are revising, they should look back through the topics in the book, check they feel confident talking about each of the areas and make sure they have personal examples for each topic to talk about.
- Encourage them to think about the type of questions that they may be asked – they can do this by looking through the Speaking lessons in their Student's Book and making a few notes about each topic. They should include past experiences, present situations and future plans.
- Remind them that they need to listen carefully to the question they are being asked. Point out that the examiner will be impressed if they can give reasons for their preferences. For example, if they are asked *What do you like doing in your free time?*, they could answer *I love playing football because I like doing sport. Playing football is more exciting than playing video games.*

▼ Exam task

6 Divide the class into pairs and have them complete the exercise. Remind students to use phrases for talking about preferences from the *Phrase expert* box. Walk round the class, monitoring students for good use of language and errors to go over at the end of the exercise.

Write any errors you hear on the board and go through them with students, eliciting corrections from them. After the class feedback, you could have students repeat this activity with another partner, to try to improve their performance.

Extra support

Answer one of the questions in Exercise 4 yourself as a model for students. Ask students to listen to you carefully and identify the question you are answering and make a note of what your preference is. Make sure your answers are not overcomplicated, so that students can see how they might be able to answer the questions themselves and not feel your model is intimidating.

Mixed ability

With a weaker class, give students the verb tense they need to form *Do you …?* questions and give them time to work in pairs formulating each question together. Check the questions and drill them for correct pronunciation and intonation before continuing. Ask stronger classes to think of two additional items to 'surprise' their partner with; one *Do you …?* question and one item with *Tell me …*

Homework

OWB

Assign students Speaking exercises 1, 2 and 3 on pages 40–41 of their Workbook.

LANGUAGE IN USE

Open cloze

→ Student's Book, page 55 SB

Lesson aims

- Focus on determiners
- Practise an open-cloze exam task
- Discuss communication

Lead-in

Ask students *How many different forms of communication did you use yesterday?* Have students make a list of all the different ways they remember communicating individually and then compare lists with their partner. Find out which student used the most forms of communication and ask him or her to share them with the class. Have the other students listen and add to their lists.

1 2.08 Before students listen, tell them what the teenagers will be talking about (*communication*). Play the track. Check answers in open class.

Answers

1 C **2** A **3** B

2 Divide the class into pairs or groups to answer the questions. Elicit some ideas and have a discussion in open class.

EXAM SKILL

Using determiners

Ask students to read the tips.

- Remind students that determiners are particularly important in multiple-choice open-cloze tasks, but that they are also important in other parts of the exam as they give information about the nouns they precede.
- Encourage students to memorise the most common determiners (articles, pronouns, possessives and quantifiers) as they are high-frequency words and are often tested in open-cloze tasks.

3 Ask students to complete the exercise and then compare their answers in pairs. Elicit answers from the class.

Answers

1 mine **2** This **3** a lot **4** the

OPTIMISE YOUR EXAM

Open cloze

Ask students to read the tips.

- Remind students that this type of exam task focuses on candidates' understanding of grammar rather than their lexical knowledge of content words, such as nouns, verbs, adjectives, etc.
- Point out that determiners are a grammatical structure that can be tested in this part of the exam along with other grammatical structures, such as conjunctions, infinitive markers, prepositions, interrogative adverbs, etc.

Exam task

4 Ask students to complete the exercise. Have them compare their answers in pairs before checking them in open class.

Answers

1 an **2** to **3** lots **4** them **5** because/as/and **6** Why

Fast finishers

Ask students to identify the five different parts of speech for the answers (1–6) in Exercise 4.

Answers

1 indefinite article **2** infinitive marker **3** quantifier **4** pronoun **5** conjunction **6** interrogative adverb

THINK | RESEARCH | CULTURE | LEARN | ME

Students work in small groups to discuss the questions. Remind students that questions like these, asking for opinions, are often part of a speaking exam. Remind them of the importance of giving examples to support their ideas.

Homework

OWB

Assign students Language in Use exercises 1, 2 and 3 on page 41 of their Workbook.

WRITING
Picture story

→ Student's Book, pages 56–57 SB

Lesson aims

- Focus on using linking words
- Plan and write a short story

Lead-in

Ask students to discuss the types of technology they use at school and at home. Then ask them to talk about how much time they use technology each day. Finally, get them to negotiate how much time they think young people should be able to use technology each day. Monitor group discussions and then invite a spokesperson from each group to feed back what their group has decided.

1 Give students an example of a form of technology you use at home and how you use it differently at school. Then have students discuss the questions in pairs or groups. Elicit answers from students around the class.

2 Focus students' attention on the three pictures. In pairs or groups, ask them to discuss what they think the story is about and then elicit answers in open class.

Answers

Students' own answers

3 Ask students to complete the table about the three pictures. Monitor and offer suggestions if needed.

Suggested answers

Picture 1

Who?: brother and sister (provide names)

Where?: at home, in the living room

What?: he's watching TV (bored), while she's listening to music and singing

Picture 2

Who?: same boy and girl

Where?: at home, in the living room

What?: boy is talking on the phone, looking happy, girl is listening to what boy is saying

Picture 3

Who?: same boy and girl + friend of boy (provide name)

Where?: at home, in the living room

What?: the boys and the girl are playing a video game, all three are laughing

EXAM SKILL

Using linking words

Ask students to read the tips.

- Remind students that the sequence of events in a story needs to be clear to the reader. Encourage them to use linking words as they will help make their stories easier to follow from start to finish.
- There is almost always more than one way of giving the same information, so students should think about this when reading texts or listening to recordings. They should also bear this in mind when writing and speaking, as it will allow them to use a greater variety of language, rather than repeating themselves unnecessarily.

4 Ask students to complete the exercise. Then have them peer check their answers before going over the answers in open class.

Answers
after (that), afterwards, before, finally, first, later, next, then

5 Ask students to complete the exercise and then check answers in open class.

Answers
1 First **2** Next **3** After

6 Individually or in pairs, ask students to answer the questions. Then go over the answers in open class.

Answers
1 watching TV and listening to music **2** talking on the phone and listening to a conversation **3** past continuous **4** while

7 Tell students to refer to the notes they have made in Exercise 3 before drafting a story. Encourage them to use linking words and to refer to all three images in 35 words or more. Then get peers to correct each other's work before drafting a final copy. If there is time, show students the sample answer to see if their stories are similar or different.

Sample answer
It was Saturday afternoon and Max was at home. He was watching TV, but he was bored. His sister Jo was listening to music and singing. Then Max decided to call his friend Tom. A little later, Tom arrived and they played video games. They all had fun!

OPTIMISE YOUR **EXAM**

Picture story

Ask students to read the tips.

- Tell students that they need to look at the pictures carefully and identify the three main events of the story, who is in the story (friends, family members, classmates, etc.) and the tenses they will use in their narrative.
- Encourage students to use linking words so the sequence of events in their stories is clear to the reader.
- They should write a draft of the story on rough paper before writing the final copy and should check their spelling, grammar and punctuation.

Exam task

8 Have students complete the exercise and then check answers in open class.

Answers
1 three **2** 35 or more **3** past simple and past continuous **4** with an introductory sentence **5** Students' own answers

9 **Plan** Tell students to use the questions in Exercise 8 to help them complete the table. You may want to look at the students' plans to check them and give advice and suggestions for improvement before students take the next step.

10 **Write** Ask students to use the information they put in the table to help them write a story in 35 words or more.

11 **Check** Students complete the checklist before they hand in their stories.

Optional extension

Have students draw three pictures or find three pictures from magazines or newspapers. Then ask them to draft and write a story about the sequence of events in their three images.

Homework

OWB

Assign students Writing exercises 1–7 on page 42 of their Workbook and Progress check 5 on page 43.

6 Teen fashion

UNIT AIMS

Exam preparation in Unit 6:

- understand linking words and phrases
- listen for the main idea
- describe and express opinions
- identify words that go together
- use a variety of tenses

TEACHER'S PRESENTATION KIT

- *Talk2Me* videos
- Speaking test videos
- Class and Workbook audio
- Workbook pages and answer key

UNIT OVERVIEW

Student's Book / Digital Student's Book SB		Workbook / Online Workbook OWB
LESSON / EXAM TASK	EXAM SKILLS / LANGUAGE FOCUS	CONSOLIDATION
Reading **Gapped text**	Understanding linking words and phrases An online article	Workbook, pp 44–45, Exercises 1, 2, 3 Unit 6, Reading, Exercises 1, 2, 3
Grammar 1	Present perfect simple with *ever* and *never*	Workbook, p 46, Exercises 1, 2, 3 Unit 6, Grammar 1, Exercises 1, 2, 3
Vocabulary	Words connected with *fashion, clothes and shopping* Verbs + prepositions Collocations with verbs	Workbook, p 47, Exercises 1, 2, 3 Unit 6, Vocabulary, Exercises 1, 2, 3
Listening **3-option multiple choice (monologues and dialogues)**	Listening for the main idea	Workbook, p 48, Exercises 1, 2, 3 Unit 6, Listening, Exercises 1, 2, 3
Grammar 2	Present perfect simple and past simple	Workbook, p 47, Exercises 1, 2 Unit 6, Grammar 2, Exercises 1, 2
Speaking **Discussion (pictures)**	Describing and expressing opinions	Workbook, p 48, Exercises 1, 2 Unit 6, Speaking, Exercises 1, 2
Language in Use **3-option multiple-choice cloze**	Identifying words that go together	Workbook, p 49, Exercises 1, 2, 3 Unit 6, Language in Use, Exercises 1, 2, 3
Writing **Guided writing (a note)**	Using a variety of tenses	Workbook, p 50, Exercises 1, 2, 3, 4 Unit 6, Writing, Exercises 1, 2, 3, 4
Progress check	Check language progress for Units 5 and 6	Workbook, p 51, Progress check and Cumulative progress Progress check and Cumulative progress

Additional material

PRESENTATION KIT	TEACHER'S / STUDENT'S RESOURCE CENTRE RC	TEST GENERATOR
Talk2Me video *The address is ...*	**Unit 6 worksheets:** *Optimise your grammar* (Standard and Higher), *Optimise your vocabulary* (Standard and Higher), *Talk2Me* video, *Say it right* **Units 5–6 worksheets:** CLIL, Culture, Everyday English (TRC only), Grammar communication (TRC only)	Unit Test 6 (Standard and Higher)

READING
Gapped text | An online article

→ Student's Book, pages 58–59 SB

Lesson aims

- Focus on linking words
- Practise a gapped exam task
- Discuss change in fashion

Lead-in

Write the unit title ***Teen fashion*** on the board and elicit what the title refers to (*clothes, accessories, shopping, trends, fashion magazines, fashion vloggers/bloggers*).

1 Focus students' attention on the photos and elicit which of the styles of clothes they like. Encourage them to give reasons for their answers. Then have students discuss the questions. Elicit some answers from the class and try to develop a class discussion.

EXAM SKILL

Understanding linking words and phrases

Ask students to read the tips.

- Tell students to pay attention to any linking words they see in the gaps in the text and in the options (A–H) to help them choose the correct answer.
- Stress that students should know the function of linking words and phrases. If there is a linking word or phrase in an option, then students must figure out if it makes sense when they put the option in the gap.

2 Ask students what they have to do to complete the exercise (*choose the correct linking words*). Then have them complete the exercise and check their answer in pairs.

Answers

1 Then **2** So **3** also

3 Ask students to complete the exercise. Check their answers.

Answers

1 Because **2** Finally **3** For example

4 Ask students to complete the exercise and then check their answers in open class.

Answers

1 so **2** also **3** finally **4** then **5** because **6** for example

OPTIMISE YOUR EXAM

Gapped text

Ask students to read the tips.

- Remind students that for all text-based exam tasks, they should read the text first quickly and ask themselves questions like: *What is the text about? Where is the text from (blog, email, magazine article, etc.)? Who is the author's intended audience?* etc.
- Many students overlook titles and pictures, but these can often give context. Look at the title together and elicit what they can see in the photos and how this relates to the title. Elicit or explain the meaning of trend (*a fashion that apppears quite quickly and usually disappears just as quickly*).

▾ Exam task

5 Have students read the article and the possible answers before completing the exercise. Remind them to use all the tips they remember from this and previous units. Tell them to read the instructions carefully. Don't check answers at this stage, as students check their answers in Exercise 6.

6 2.09 **Note: The reading text is also available on the audio CD but contains the missing sentences. You may want to have students listen and read the text after doing the exam task to check their answers.**

Check each answer in open class or have students listen to the audio to check their own answers.

Answers

1 C ('some of them' in the sentence after the gap refers to the 'people starting new trends')

2 F ('so' is followed by an action which results from the sentence before the gap)

3 A ('A' supports the question asked before the gap and then a further explanation is given in the sentence after the gap 'this is because …')

4 H ('And now' links the main idea in this part of the text with the two sentences surrounding the gap)

5 D ('For example' supports the preceding sentence and 'it' in the sentence after the gap refers to 'Johnny Cupcakes' clothes shop)

7 Tell students to read through the definitions and try to guess the correct words before looking for them in the text. After the exercise, check answers in open class.

Answers

1 hungry **2** normal **3** prices **4** follow **5** busy **6** shop assistant **7** unusual **8** customers

Mixed ability

Ask stronger students to cover the text and look at the definitions in Exercise 7 and try to work out what the words are. Have less confident students complete the task as it appears in the Student's Book. Pair stronger students with less confident students and ask less confident students to check their ideas by saying, for example, *I think the word that means 'feeling that you want food' is 'hungry'. Do you agree?*

THINK | RESEARCH | **CULTURE** | LEARN | ME

Check students know the meaning of *vlogger* (= *video blogger, i.e. someone who, rather than writing a blog, posts a series of video posts talking to the camera*). Tell students to start by brainstorming ideas. Then tell them to come to a consensus with their partner / in their groups. Have students present their ideas and opinions to the class, giving reasons for their answers.

Cultural note

Vlogging has become more and more popular over the last decade. Numerous sites, including YouTube, actively encourage vloggers to upload their content and offer them support to help them make money from their work. The most popular vloggers can accumulate millions of followers and be paid large sums of money to promote products and services to their subscribers.

Homework

OWB

Assign students Reading exercises 1, 2 and 3 on pages 44–45 of their Workbook.

GRAMMAR 1

Present perfect simple with *ever* and *never*

→ Student's Book, page 60 SB

Lesson aims

- Understand the correct usage of the present perfect simple with *ever* and *never*
- Practise describing life experiences

Lead-in

Have a class discussion about fashion trends amongst young people. Ask students to tell you which fashion brands are popular at the moment, classify them and then ask them to organise them in order of preference.

Grammar in context

Tell students that the sentences are extracts from the article they read in the previous lesson. If students need extra support, remind them to refer to the information in the *Remember* box. Check answers in open class.

Remind students that they can find more information in the Grammar reference, Unit 6, page 149.

Answers

1 has **2** changed **3** Have **4** never

1 Go through the example sentence as a class before students complete the exercise. Check answers by having volunteers read out their answers.

Answers

2 Have you ever travelled by train alone? **3** Have you ever seen the Eiffel Tower? **4** Have you ever worn socks in bed? **5** Have you and your friends ever eaten together in a restaurant? **6** Have you and your family ever moved house?

2 Read the example question from Exercise 1 out loud and encourage students to give you the correct answer (***d*** *Yes, I have. I've made pizza and salad for my mum a few times.*). Students complete the exercise. Check answers in open class.

Answers

1 d **2** e **3** f **4** c **5** b **6** a

3 Draw students' attention to the example question and answer. Ask students to complete the exercise in pairs. Walk round the class, monitoring students' use of the present perfect and *ever/never*. Invite volunteers to ask and answer one of the questions in front of the class.

4 Focus students' attention on the dialogue and ask them what word they think they'll need to use to complete most of the gaps (*different forms of the auxiliary* have *and* ever *and* never). After completing the exercise, have students practise reading it in pairs.

Answers

1 been **2** haven't **3** has **4** ever **5** hasn't **6** Have **7** never **8** have

5 Check that students know what the UAE stands for (*the United Arab Emirates*) and ask them what they know about the country. After students complete the exercise, have volunteers read the text to check answers.

Answers

1 've/have had **2** Have you ever heard **3** 've/have never seen **4** 've/have eaten **5** 've/have ridden **6** 've/have never tried **7** haven't / have not written **8** haven't / have not forgotten

SAY IT RIGHT

TRC

Pronunciation of *have*

For the *Say it right* pronunciation activity and instructions, go to the Teacher's Resource Centre.

Homework

OWB

Assign students Grammar 1 exercises 1, 2 and 3 on page 46 of their Workbook.

VOCABULARY

Topic vocabulary | Word patterns | Collocations

→ Student's Book, page 61 SB

Lesson aims

Understand the correct usage of:

- words connected with fashion, clothes and shopping
- verb + preposition word patterns
- verb + noun collocations

Lead-in

Draw two human figures on the board, one male and one female. Divide the class in half and assign one half to the male figure and one half to the female figure. Have students work in pairs or small groups to brainstorm all the clothes worn by that gender and what clothes can be worn by both. Elicit vocabulary from the class. Write the words students suggest on the board with arrows pointing to the part of the body where the clothes are worn.

Words connected with *fashion, clothes and shopping*

1 2.10 Ask students to look at the words in the box and check that they know the meaning of each one before completing the exercise. Play the audio for students to listen and check their answers.

Answers/Audioscript

people: customer, *shop assistant, shopper*
places: *department store, market, shopping centre, supermarket*
money (verbs): *buy, change, cost, spend*
money (nouns): *bill, cash, change, cheque, credit card, receipt*

2 Ask students to complete the exercise. Then have them compare their answers in pairs before checking them in open class.

Answers

1 cash, credit card(s) **2** buy, spend **3** department stores, shopping centres **4** shoppers, customers **5** bill, change **6** receipt, cost

Optional extension

Ask students to work in pairs and write a short vox pop (a short idea or opinion about a topic collected by people who make radio and television programmes) about fashion, clothes and shopping using the words from Exercise 1 that weren't used in Exercise 2 (*shop assistant, market, supermarket, cheque* and *change* as a verb). Ask pairs to read their vox pops to the class.

Refer students to the Vocabulary reference, page 159, for more information on topic vocabulary.

Verbs + prepositions

3 2.11 Remind students that word patterns are groups of words that frequently appear together. Ask students to complete the exercise. Play the audio for students to check their answers. Then have students say which answer they got correct and incorrect in order to check the similarities/differences in students' understanding.

Answers/Audioscript

1 When I go shopping, I always pay *in* cash.
2 Write *down* what you want and I'll go to the supermarket for you.
3 Please take *off* your wet boots before you go into the house.
4 It's raining so put *on* your raincoat before you go out.
5 Did you pay *for* the online shopping by credit card?
6 Most shops give you 30 days to take *back* anything you don't want.

Language note

Note that all the word patterns in this section include phrasal verbs, and that these belong to three different categories. *Pay for (something)* and *pay in* (e.g. *cash*) are non-separable phrasal verbs so the object will always come after the particle. However, with *take back, put on, take off* and *write down*, the object can go between the verb and the particle (*put your coat on*) or after the particle (*put on your coat*) when it is a noun, but has to go between the verb and the particle when it is a pronoun (*put it on*).

4 Ask students to complete the exercise. Then have them compare their answers in pairs before checking them in open class. Ask students what they found easy or difficult about the exercise.

Answers

1 pay for **2** take off **3** pay in **4** write down

Refer students to the Vocabulary reference, page 159, for more information on word patterns.

Collocations with verbs

5 2.12 Ask students to complete the exercise. Play the audio for students to listen and check their answers.

Answers/Audioscript

1 Do you prefer to *go* shopping with your friends or with your mum?
2 You can *save* money for a new computer game if you stop buying chocolate and cakes!
3 We usually *catch* the bus when we want to go to the shopping centre.
4 The bill was nine pounds and twenty pence, so Dad gave the waiter £10 and told him to *keep* the change.
5 'Mum, there's no milk left.' 'It's OK–I'm going to *do* the shopping later.'
6 There are some lovely clothes *for* sale in that shop.

Refer students to the Vocabulary reference, page 159, for more information on collocations.

Homework

OWB

Assign students Vocabulary exercises 1, 2 and 3 on page 47 of their Workbook.

LISTENING

3-option multiple choice (monologues and dialogues)

→ Student's Book, page 62 SB

Lesson aims

- Listen to identify the right answers from various options
- Practise a 3-option multiple-choice exam task
- Discuss changes in buying habits

Lead-in

Play a game to recycle the word patterns from the previous lesson (*pay for …, take off …, pay in …, take back …, write down, put on …*). Split the class into two teams. Call out a word pattern and ask teams to think of a grammatically correct sentence using the word pattern. The first team to write a sentence and hold it up gets a point. After you have used all the word patterns, the team with the most points is the winner.

1 Ask students to look at the photo and say which of the things they enjoy buying and which they are not interested in at all. After students discuss the questions, elicit some answers from different students around the class.

EXAM SKILL

Listening for the main idea

Ask students to read the tips.

- Explain to students that they shouldn't worry if they don't understand every word and detail to understand what someone is saying. In this part of the exam, they need to understand the main idea or gist of a conversation or monologue.
- Encourage students to note down any key words or phrases that they hear. This will help them to form an overall picture of what is being said. They need to listen to the whole conversation carefully.

2 2.13 Tell students to read the instructions before they hear the audio. Play the audio so students can listen and answer the questions. Then check their answers in open class.

Answers

a) speaker 3 **b)** speaker 2 **c)** speaker 4 **d)** speaker 1

OPTIMISE YOUR EXAM

3-option multiple choice (monologues and dialogues)

Ask students to read the tips.

- Encourage students to pay attention to the sentence before each question. This will help them to understand the context of who is speaking, what they are going to talk about and possibly the relationship of the speakers.
- Tell students they should underline key words in the question and three options. They should listen for similar information or paraphrases that match one of the options.
- Point out that they should pay attention each time they listen. Then they can check for any information they may have missed or misunderstood during the first listening.

▼ Exam task

3 2.14 Tell students they will hear five audios. Play the audio. Don't check answers at this stage, as students check their answers in Exercise 4.

4 2.14 Tell students to read through their answers before you play the track again for them to check.

Answers

1 B (*I'm afraid my son needs blue ones*) **2** A (*But I've saved that time for practising the piano*) **3** C (*I need you to put the luggage in the car!*) **4** C (*I'm really pleased that I can bring my dog – I miss him when he can't come with me*) **5** B (*… all I need now is the team's shirt …*)

THINK | RESEARCH | CULTURE | LEARN | ME

Encourage students to think of things like credit cards and how they have made an impact on people's spending. Invite some students to share their ideas with the class.

Homework

OWB

Assign students Listening exercises 1, 2 and 3 on page 48 of their Workbook.

GRAMMAR 2

Present perfect simple and past simple

→ Student's Book, page 63 SB

Lesson aims

- Understand the correct usage of the present perfect simple and past simple
- Practise talking about things that happened at specific and unspecified times in the past
- Share some recent news with a partner

Lead-in

Write *Have you ever …?* in large letters on the board. Ask a question, e.g. *Have you ever given me your homework late?* Ask several students to reply to elicit the responses, e.g. *Yes, I have. / No, I haven't.* Now ask students to come up with three of their own questions beginning with *Have you ever …?* Monitor students' work, making any necessary corrections. Students then ask other students in the class their questions and make a note of their answers. Once completed, ask for some feedback about what information students have gathered about their classmates.

Grammar in context

Ask students to complete the task individually before checking their answers with a partner. Then ask pairs to give reasons for their answers. Tell them to use the information in the *Remember* box to help them explain.

Remind students that they can find more information in the Grammar reference, Unit 6, page 150.

Answers

a) 2 **b)** 1

Language note

The present perfect is often used as a 'conversation starter' as it allows us to ask about life experiences, or introduce a new topic, as students saw in Grammar 1. We usually switch to the past simple to ask for more details and discuss the topic further.

In this section, students will see how the present perfect can be used to give a sense of immediacy to actions. This is usually because we want to emphasise the results of something and we consider these more important than exactly when the action happened, e.g. *I've opened the window. I've moved house.* In cases like this, we use the present perfect without *ever/never.*

1 Ask students to complete the exercise individually. Check students' answers.

Answers

1 've done **2** bought **3** 've lost **4** started **5** Did you sell **6** 've had

2 Go through the example with the class and remind students that the normal structure is to introduce a situation with the present perfect and then give details or explanations in the past simple. After students complete the exercise, have them compare their answers in pairs.

Answers

2 The boys have walked into town. They left at 2 o'clock.

3 I've/have got Mum a present for her birthday. I paid €10 for it.

4 He didn't like his old flat. He's lived in three different flats this year.

5 She's/has lost an earring. She dropped it in the street.

6 I haven't / have not worn these boots before. My old ones were very comfortable.

3 Ask students to complete the exercise individually. Have them compare their answers in pairs before you check them with the class. Check the spelling of all the past simple verbs and past participles.

Answers

1 Have you ever made **2** started **3** looked **4** decided **5** told **6** wanted **7** thought **8** 've/have helped **9** began **10** 've/have learnt **11** met **12** 've/have shared

THINK | RESEARCH | CULTURE | LEARN | **ME**

Ask students to tell their partner about real things that have happened to them recently. If necessary, remind students not to bring up or ask about sensitive areas.

Homework

OWB

Assign students Grammar 2 exercises 1 and 2 on page 47 of their Workbook.

Assign students the Flipped classroom tasks on page 64 of their Student's Book if you'd like them to prepare for the next lesson. To complete this task, students need to watch the *Talk2Me* video which can be found on the Resource Centre.

SPEAKING
Discussion (pictures)

→ Student's Book, page 64 SB

Lesson aims

- Focus on describing and expressing opinions
- Practise a discussion (pictures) exam task
- Research interesting places to shop

The *Talk2Me* video in this unit focuses on clothes and a clothes sale. The people in the video talk about what style of clothes they like and what they would like to buy and sell at a clothes sale.

Students answer some comprehension questions and then listen for key phrases in the video.

The video can be used in one of two ways:

Flipped classroom

Flipped classroom option

Using this approach, students watch the video and complete the exercises for homework. This prepares students for the speaking lesson by introducing them to the topic and the key phrases to use in the exam task. Teachers who use this method will find they have more class time to spend on activating the target language and developing fluency for the final task.

***Talk2Me* worksheet**

Ask students to also complete the *Talk2Me* worksheet on the Resource Centre for more detailed comprehension exercises and more practice of the key phrases.

Classroom option

1 Ask students to spend a minute or two reading the questions. Play the *Talk2Me* video for students to complete the exercise. Play the video again, if necessary, before checking their answers.

2 Play the *Talk2Me* video again, so students underline the phrases in the *Phrase expert* box. Pause the video from time to time if necessary. Check answers in open class.

Talk2Me worksheet

Ask students to complete the *Talk2Me* worksheet on the Resource Centre for more detailed comprehension exercises and more practice of the key phrases.

Answers

The transcript and answer key for the *Talk2Me* video exercises and Worksheet can be found on the Teacher's Resource Centre.

Lead-in

Ask each student to write an interesting statement about him or herself, using the present perfect (and *never* if appropriate), e.g. *I've entered lots of competitions, but I've never won anything.* Have students take turns reading their statements to you. For some of the statements, give a very bored, uninspired response (*Oh. Aha.*), or keep silent with an unimpressed look (without being rude) and nominate the next student. To the other statements, sound as interested as you can. At the end, ask students if they noticed the difference in your responses. Point out how important body language is when deciding if the listener is interested or not.

3 In pairs, students ask and answer the questions. Encourage students to show that they are interested in their partner's information by responding to their comments as well as using suitable body language. Elicit answers from different students around the class and invite other students to respond appropriately.

EXAM SKILL

Describing and expressing opinions

Ask students to read the tips.

- Point out that students need to describe activities, locations, things, etc. and express their opinions about them in the speaking test.
- Explain that before giving an opinion, they can describe what they are talking about first as this helps their partner understand what they are talking about.
- Encourage students to talk about their personal preferences and to listen to what their partner has to say. They can say if they agree or disagree with their partner's opinion and this can keep the conversation flowing.

4 2.15 Tell students to listen to the audio and complete the exercise. Then check answers in open class.

Answers / Audioscript

1 bike shop / bikes **2** clothes shop / trousers **3** grocery store / tomatoes and potatoes **4** chemist / medicine **5** butcher's / sausages and other meat

5 Play the audio a second time so students can answer the questions. Then get pairs to compare their answers before going over the answers in open class.

Answers

1 Boy: likes / Girl: doesn't like **2** Girl: loves / Boy: boring **3** Boy: interesting / Girl: interesting **4** Girl: boring, doesn't like / Boy: boring, doesn't like **5** Boy: likes / Girl: hates

OPTIMISE YOUR EXAM

Discussion (pictures)

Ask students to read the tips.

- In speaking exams, examiners will be looking to see how candidates interact with each other, and speakers need to show they are interested in the speaker and the topic (even if they aren't interested).
- Point out how important it is to use appropriate phrases in discussion tasks to ask for repetition (*Sorry, I missed that.*), to ask for time to think (*Let me see, …*) and to self-correct (*No, sorry, what I mean is …*). To get the best possible marks in an exam, students also need to use phrases to show interest.
- Tell students that they will see five pictures about the same topic, and they should give their opinions about the visual prompts. If they don't know the word for an illustration, then encourage them not to avoid saying anything about that image. Emphasise that students should still talk about the image (e.g. *I'm not sure what this sport on snow is called. I think it looks dangerous.*).

Optional extension

Ask students to write down descriptions of the fashion they like the most and like the least in Exercise 6. Encourage them to use adjectives related to the different fashions and to include their opinions.

▾ Exam task

6 Assign each student a letter, A or B, and put them into A/B pairs to discuss the questions. Time them (two minutes) and give them an update, e.g. *One minute to go …* Remind students to use phrases from the *Phrase expert* box as well as phrases to show interest. Walk round, monitoring students for good use of language and errors to go over at the end of the activity.

▼ Exam task

7 In the same pairs, give students a moment to look at their questions. Time them again (two minutes) and give them an update, e.g. *One minute to go* … Walk round, monitoring students for good use of language and errors to go over at the end of the activity.

Write any errors on the board and go through them with students, eliciting corrections from them where possible. After the class feedback, students could then repeat Exercises 6 and 7 with another partner, to try to improve their performance.

THINK | **RESEARCH** | CULTURE | LEARN | ME

If you have access to the internet, students can research information in class. Alternatively, they could prepare this for homework and present their information at the start of the next lesson.

Homework

OWB

Assign students Speaking exercises 1 and 2 on page 48 of their Workbook.

LANGUAGE IN USE

3-option multiple-choice cloze

→ Student's Book, page 65 SB

Lesson aims

- Focus on identifying compound nouns and collocations
- Practise a 3-option multiple-choice cloze exam task
- Discuss different types of exhibitions

Lead-in

Write the following statements on the board:
Buying the latest fashionable clothes is a total waste of money – it's better to buy clothes in a supermarket.
Buying cheap, ugly clothes is stupid – it's better to spend more and get something fashionable.

Divide the class into two groups and allocate a statement to each group. Have a class discussion – students can only make points that reflect the statement of their group. Encourage the class to come to a consensus at the end of the discussion.

1 In pairs, students discuss and complete the exercise. Check answers in open class.

Answers

1 Do you want to go shopping tomorrow?
2 Yes, sure. Everything's on sale now, isn't it?
3 Yeah, we could really save money!
4 OK. I'll ask my mum for my pocket money!

EXAM SKILL

Identifying words that go together

Ask students to read the tips.

- Remind students that they have learnt useful collocations and compound nouns in previous units.
- Tell students that it is important to learn words as part of a whole phrase rather than just individual words.
- Point out that this part of the exam tests knowledge of vocabulary, which can include collocations, compound nouns, fixed phrases, phrasal verbs, etc. It's important that they read the words surrounding each gap to see which option fits best.

2 Tell students to complete the exercise and then check answers in open class.

Answers

save money, go shopping, pocket money, on sale

3 Ask students to complete the exercise and then compare their answers in pairs. Elicit answers from volunteers in the class.

Answers

1 d **2** f **3** b **4** c **5** a **6** e

OPTIMISE YOUR EXAM

3-option multiple-choice cloze

Ask students to read the tips.

- Encourage students to skim the text first before looking at the questions to understand the main idea of the text.
- Tell students that for each question they should try all of the options in the sentence with the missing word to see which one sounds best.
- Point out that they should pay attention to the words directly after the gap to see if the option is a collocation, fixed phrase, phrasal verb or compound noun.

▼ Exam task

4 Ask students to complete the exercise individually. Check answers as a class. Answer any doubts students may have about incorrect answers.

Answers

1 A **2** A **3** C **4** B **5** C **6** A

Fast finishers

Have students who finish quickly underline the words that helped them to choose the correct words for the gaps. As you check the answers to Exercise 4, ask individual students to explain which words or collocations helped them (e.g. question 1 is a phrasal verb so 'have on' and 'make on' don't work here: *'Many museums **put on** special exhibitions …'*)

THINK | RESEARCH | CULTURE | LEARN | ME

Put students in pairs to ask and answer the questions. Encourage them to use the collocations they identified in Exercise 2.

Homework

OWB

Assign students Language in Use exercises 1, 2 and 3 on page 49 of their Workbook.

WRITING
Guided writing (a note)

→ Student's Book, pages 66–67 SB

Lesson aims

- Focus on using a variety of tenses
- Plan and write a note

Lead-in

Divide the students into two teams. Ask teams to make a list of as many words as possible connected to clothes and personal possessions. Set a time limit and then go through students' lists as a class. Award a point for every word both teams have. Award two points for unique words. Then have teams add up their scores. The team with the most points wins.

1 After students discuss the questions in pairs or groups, have them share their ideas with the class.

EXAM SKILL

Using a variety of tenses

Ask students to read the tips.

- Remind students that the present perfect can be used to introduce experiences and the past simple can be used for giving more details.
- Tell students that they may need to use a variety of tenses in their answer. To decide which tense or tenses to use, they need to pay attention to the instructions.

2 Ask students to complete the exercise in pairs and then check answers in open class.

Answers

1 B **2** A

3 Tell students to revise both texts while they are comparing answers. Have pairs report any major disagreements they have to the class.

Answers

1 A week ago **2** bought **3** Unfortunately **4** can't **5** Do you think

OPTIMISE YOUR EXAM

Guided writing (a note)

Ask students to read the tips.

- Stress the importance of answering all parts of the question within the word limit and tell students to make sure they know exactly what information they need to give.
- Tell students to use appropriate language for specific functions the task asks for. Explain that otherwise, they are unlikely to get top marks on the exam.

Exam task

4 Ask students to complete the exercise and then compare their answers with a peer before checking answers in open class.

Answers

1 one of your grandparents **2** go shopping with you **3** what you want to buy **4** 25 or more **5** past simple, present simple, present continuous for future **6** words and phrases related to shopping

5 **Plan** Ask students to complete the table. You may want to look at the students' plans to check them and give advice and suggestions for improvement before students take the next step.

Extra support

If some students are struggling to come up with ideas, it may help to collate students' ideas on the board at the planning stage.

6 **Write** Remind students to keep all the exam tips in mind while writing. Students write their note. If there is not enough time, set this and the subsequent checklist exercise for homework.

7 **Check** Students complete the checklist before they hand in their notes.

Homework

OWB

Assign students Writing exercises 1, 2, 3 and 4 on page 50 of their Workbook and Progress check 6 on page 51.

Answers PROGRESS CHECK Units 5–6

Exercise 1
1 walked **2** Have, worked **3** bought **4** Did, wear
5 've/have lost **6** 've/have never shopped **7** haven't seen
8 didn't like

Exercise 2
1 start **2** software **3** on **4** open **5** for **6** send **7** cash **8** screen

Exercise 3
1 A **2** B **3** C **4** A **5** A **6** A **7** A **8** C

Exercise 4
1 has **2** in **3** ever **4** much **5** lots **6** than **7** biggest **8** older
9 never **10** some

Exercise 5
1 a few **2** many **3** lots **4** many **5** Some **6** little **7** much **8** any

Exercise 6
1 supermarket **2** software **3** online **4** customers **5** credit card
6 graphics **7** keyboard **8** download

7 The future of learning

UNIT AIMS

Exam preparation in Unit 7:

- multiple-choice questions
- think about the missing information in a gap fill exercise
- talk about the future
- commonly confused words
- use adjectives

TEACHER'S PRESENTATION KIT

- *Talk2Me* videos
- Speaking test videos
- Class and Workbook audio
- Workbook pages and answer key

UNIT OVERVIEW

Student's Book / Digital Student's Book SB		Workbook / Online Workbook OWB
LESSON / EXAM TASK	EXAM SKILLS / LANGUAGE FOCUS	CONSOLIDATION
Reading **3-option multiple choice (long text)**	Multiple-choice questions 3-option multiple choice (long text)	Workbook, pp 52–53, Exercises 1, 2, 3, 4 Unit 7, Reading, Exercises 1, 2, 3, 4
Grammar 1	*going to*	Workbook, p 54, Exercises 1, 2 Unit 7, Grammar 1, Exercises 1, 2
Vocabulary	Words connected with *school and studying* Words + prepositions Collocations with verbs	Workbook, pp 54–55, Exercises 1, 2, 3 Unit 7, Vocabulary, Exercises 1, 2, 3
Listening **Gap fill**	Thinking about the missing information	Workbook, p 56, Exercises 1, 2 Unit 7, Listening, Exercises 1, 2
Grammar 2	*will* and *going to*	Workbook, p 55, Exercise 1 Unit 7, Grammar 2, Exercise 1
Speaking **Questions**	Talking about the future	Workbook, p 56, Exercises 1, 2, 3 Unit 7, Speaking, Exercises 1, 2, 3
Language in Use **3-option multiple-choice cloze**	3-option multiple-choice cloze	Workbook, p 57, Exercises 1, 2, 3 Unit 7, Language in Use, Exercises 1, 2, 3
Writing **Picture story**	Using adjectives	Workbook, p 58, Exercises 1, 2, 3, 4, 5, 6 Unit 7, Writing, Exercises 1, 2, 3, 4, 5, 6
		Workbook, p 59, Progress check and Cumulative progress Progress check and Cumulative progress

Additional material

PRESENTATION KIT	TEACHER'S / STUDENT'S RESOURCE CENTRE RC	TEST GENERATOR
Talk2Me video *In one year's time …*	**Unit 7 worksheets:** *Optimise your grammar* (Standard and Higher), *Optimise your vocabulary* (Standard and Higher), *Talk2Me* video, *Say it right* **Units 7–8 worksheets:** CLIL, Culture, Everyday English (TRC only), Grammar communication (TRC only)	Unit Test 7 (Standard and Higher)

READING

3-option multiple choice (long text) | A news article

→ Student's Book, pages 70–71 SB

Lesson aims

- Focus on multiple-choice question strategies
- Practise a 3-option multiple-choice (long text) exam task
- Think about ways computers can help you learn

Lead-in

Ask students to look at the unit title ***The future of learning*** and the picture and say what they think the unit will be about (*how education may change in the future*). Ask students to talk about the possible advantages and disadvantages of learning with technology. Ask students how they have used technology for education in, or outside, school.

1 After students discuss the questions, elicit the advantages and disadvantages of having technology in the classroom. Encourage different students in the class to participate.

EXAM SKILL

Multiple-choice questions

Ask students to read the tips.

- Encourage students to skim the text to find out what the topic and general gist are.
- Tell students to read the question before reading the three options and look for this information in the text. Then when they think they have found the answer to the question, look for the option that is the closest paraphrase to the information they have found in the text.
- Point out that they should also check the other options and decide why they are wrong.

2 Ask students to complete the exercise. Get them to underline the section of the text that answers the question. Ask them to compare in pairs, but wait to check their answers in open class in Exercise 3.

3 Ask students to complete the exercise and then check answers in open class.

Answers

a, b and c are correct.

a) (*They use video chat in their homes to have their lessons and it feels like they're all in a normal classroom*)

b) (*for children in Australia who live far away from cities and towns and can't get to school*)

c) (*They use video chat / they can see each other on their screens*)

OPTIMISE YOUR EXAM

3-option multiple-choice (long text)

Ask students to read the tips.

- Tell students the order of the questions follows the order of the information in the text unless there is a global question. In some cases, the final question could test the whole idea of the text. This could be, for example, a purpose question (e.g. *Why has the writer written this article?*). The other questions (1–4) follow the sequence of the text.

▼ Exam task

4 2.16 **Note: The reading text is also available on the audio CD. You may want to have students listen and read the text after doing the exam task to check their answers.**

Tell students to read the instructions before completing the task. Check answers in open class.

Answers

1 B (*Technology is helping young people to learn about the world …*)

2 A (*… for schools in the countryside / has helped many classes … to use computers.*)

3 B (*… two mobile computer classrooms, and they travel all over the country …*)

4 C (*large battery … produces solar energy for the computers …*)

5 B (*… they are going to build computer classrooms in 55 Ugandan schools.*)

5 Ask a strong student to scan the text and find the word for the first definition. Then have students complete the exercise and compare their answers in pairs before checking in open class.

Answers

1 adults **2** battery **3** tablets **4** job **5** libraries **6** lucky **7** drivers **8** countryside

Mixed ability

Pair weak and strong students together. Have stronger students cover Exercise 5 and weaker students read each definition to their partner for him/her to guess. Then have students look for the words their partner couldn't guess together. Check answers in open class.

THINK | RESEARCH | CULTURE | LEARN | ME

After students make their lists, encourage them to share their ideas with the class, and write students' ideas on the board. Have students make a note of the ideas they didn't think of, and encourage them to make comments.

Homework

Assign students Reading exercises 1, 2, 3 and 4 on pages 52–53 of their Workbook.

OWB

GRAMMAR 1
going to

→ Student's Book, page 72 SB

Lesson aims

- Understand the correct usage of *going to*
- Practise making future plans and predictions

Lead-in

Tell the class about three things that you have arranged to do at the weekend, e.g. *At 10 o'clock on Saturday, I'm playing badminton with some friends. On Saturday evening, I'm having dinner in a new Japanese restaurant near my house. On Sunday, my cousins from Madrid are coming to visit.* Tell students to guess which two of the sentences are true and which one is false. Then ask students to write their own sentences using the present continuous to describe arrangements they have made for the weekend. Two should be true and the other should be false. In pairs, students read them to their partner who guesses which are true/false.

Grammar in context

Ask students to complete the task. Check their answers and ask students to read more about *going to* in the *Remember* box. Remind students that in Unit 2 they saw the present continuous to talk about the future; elicit that the present continuous is usually used for arrangements that we see as definite.

Remind students that they can find more information in the Grammar reference, Unit 7, page 150.

Answers

c) the future

Language note

Going to is used for the future. We use *going to* when we have made a personal plan or when we make a prediction based on evidence. Therefore, an action using *going to* is less likely to happen than an action using present continuous, which usually implies firm plans or arrangements. For example, you could say *I'm going to see a film with Sue on Friday.*, which means you want to go but haven't bought the tickets yet. Or you could say *I'm seeing a film with Sue on Friday.* In this case you have tickets.

1 Before students complete the exercise, elicit what type of text it is (*a conversation*). Have students complete it individually and then check answers by practising in groups of three. Have one group practise in front of the class.

Answers

2 's/is going to **3** are going to **4** isn't / is not going to **5** 's/is going to **6** 're/are going to **7** 's/is going to **8** Are you going to **9** 'm/am not going to **10** 's/is going to

2 Ask students to complete the exercise individually. Then ask different volunteers to read out a sentence to check answers.

Answers

1 's/is going to study **2** aren't / are not going to win **3** is, going to do **4** 'm/am not going to go **5** 's/is going to be **6** 's/is going to snow

Fast finishers

Have students rewrite the sentences using their own ideas. For example, *Guilio is going to study French in Paris.*

3 Ask students where the largest school in the world is (*India*). Then have them complete the exercise individually. Have students compare answers in pairs before checking in open class.

Answers

1 are going to be **2** aren't / are not going to use **3** 're/are going to have **4** 'm/am going to study **5** 's/is going to be **6** 'm/am not going to go **7** 're/are going to meet **8** 's/is going to be

SAY IT RIGHT

Pronunciation of *going to*

For the *Say it right* pronunciation activity and instructions, go to the Teacher's Resource Centre.

TRC

Cultural note

The City Montessori School in Lucknow, India, opened in 1959. It currently has over 50,000 students and, in 2010, broke the Guinness World Record for the largest school in the world. It uses the educational philosophy of the Italian specialist Maria Montessori who believed that great emphasis should be placed on play at school and on encouraging students' natural abilities. She opened her first school, the Casa dei Bambini, in Rome in 1907. Her ideas quickly spread to the USA and there are now Montessori schools all around the world.

Homework

Assign students Grammar 1 exercises 1 and 2 on page 54 of their Workbook.

OWB

VOCABULARY
Topic vocabulary | Word patterns | Collocations

→ Student's Book, page 73 SB

Lesson aims

Understand the correct usage of:

- words connected with school and studying
- verb + preposition word patterns
- verb + noun collocations
- Discuss school and homework

Lead-in

Tell students they are going to play a guessing game. Tell them to write down a word related to the school and two clues/descriptions of it: one that's obvious and one not so obvious. Tell students your not-so-obvious clue first: *This is a place in the school.*, and encourage the students to guess. Then say your more obvious clue: *You spend your break time there.* Have the student who guesses correctly (*playground*) continue, and keep going so that more students can participate.

Words connected with *school and studying*

1 2.17 Focus students' attention on the words in the box. Tell them to read them and check that they know the meaning of each one before completing the exercise. Then play the audio for students to listen and check their answers.

Answers/Audioscript

things in the classroom: board, bookshelf, desk, dictionary, eraser

school subjects: biology, geography, history, maths, music, physics

verbs for things people do at school: learn, practise, remember, study, teach

2 Ask students what their favourite school subjects are and why. Ask students to complete the exercise. Then have them compare their answers in pairs before you check them in open class.

Answers

1 history **2** geography **3** biology **4** maths **5** physics **6** music

Refer students to the Vocabulary reference, page 160, for more information on topic vocabulary.

Words + prepositions

3 2.18 Elicit from students what word patterns are (*two or more words that go together to form a 'chunk' of language*). As an example, ask students what word or phrase comes after *revise for* (*an exam/test*). After the exercise, play the audio for students to check their answers.

Answers/Audioscript

1 (C) You can learn a lot *from* books.
2 (A) You need to use technology when you study or are *at* work.
3 (C) Today we're going to learn *about* how the stomach works.
4 (B) Do you need any help *with* your homework?
5 (C) I usually arrive *at* school just before 9 am.
6 (A) You can borrow three books *from* the library at one time.

Refer students to the Vocabulary reference, page 160, for more information on word patterns.

Collocations with verbs

4 2.19 Go through the example as a class. Ask students to complete the exercise individually. Before you play the audio, ask students which options were difficult to match. Have them focus on those while they listen.

Answers/Audioscript

1 (d) do homework **2** (f) draw a picture **3** (a) take a course **4** (c) leave school **5** (b) go to university **6** (e) learn a foreign language

5 Ask students to complete the exercise individually. Then have them check their answers in pairs.

Answers

1 draw a picture **2** learn a foreign language **3** take a course **4** go to university **5** do homework **6** leave school

Extra support

Give stronger students one minute to memorise the collocations in Exercise 4 and then tell them to cover it and complete the sentences in Exercise 5 from memory. Give less confident students the verbs in the order they appear in Exercise 5 (*draw*, *learn*, *take*, *go*, *do*, *leave*) and tell them that they need to change the form of one of the verbs and one of the nouns. Check answers by reading each sentence up to and including the verb and then eliciting the missing noun from the class.

Refer students to the Vocabulary reference, page 160, for more information on collocations.

THINK | RESEARCH | CULTURE | LEARN | **ME**

Tell students to make a list of the things they like most about school and number them in order of preference. Then have them discuss the other questions.

Homework

OWB

Assign students Vocabulary exercises 1, 2 and 3 on pages 54–55 of their Workbook.

LISTENING
Gap fill

→ Student's Book, page 74 SB

Lesson aims

- Listen to missing information in gap-fill exam tasks
- Practise a gap-fill exam task
- Think about questions to ask someone in India

Lead-in

Ask students, *How do you communicate?* and write the words *friends*, *family* and *teachers* on the board. Encourage students to say why they use different ways of communicating with different groups and what they think the best ways of communicating are. Have them give reasons for their answers.

1 Have students discuss the questions in pairs. Then elicit some answers from different students around the class.

EXAM SKILL

Thinking about the missing information

Ask students to read the tips.

- Remind students that predicting the kind of information they are listening for – and the different formats that information could be given in – is a very important skill for listening exams.
- Tell students that they will need to find words that fit in the phrases they are given. Remind them of the work they did on the previous page with word patterns. For example, if they had to complete the phrase *learn from*, it could be completed with a thing or a person.

2 Write the word *in* on the board followed by *January, London, the morning* and have students brainstorm other words that follow *in*. After students finish the exercise, go through answers in open class.

Answers

in: March, 2018; Amsterdam, Paris; afternoon
on: Wednesday
at: 3:20, night; Halloween

3 Before students complete the exercise, tell them that in two sentences the words are not possible because they don't fit with the prepositions, and in three sentences the words are not possible because they are illogical. Check their answers and ask students to identify which is which.

Answers

1 a computer (illogical – no-one lives in a *computer*) **2** evenings (not possible after *on*) **3** London (the answer should be a time) **4** study (illogical – *study* is not a subject) **5** online (illogical – you can't take photos of *online*)

Optional extension

Ask students to add other possible words to each group, e.g. *1 a house/flat, 2 summer courses*, etc. Have them share their ideas with the rest of the class after you check the answers.

OPTIMISE YOUR EXAM

Gap fill

Ask students to read the tips.

- Remind students to use their preparation time sensibly and think about what type of information to expect for each answer. Point out that, although they did some work on this in exercises 2 and 3, the answers may not be what they saw there.
- Remind students that it is very common in listening exams for the recording to include words that sound like they could be correct answers but are not.

Exam task

4 2.20 Ask students to read the instructions and the information in the notes. Tell them to think about what sort of word will fit in each gap. Play the audio and then ask students to compare their answers in pairs. Wait until Exercise 5 to check the answers in open class.

5 2.20 Play the audio again so students can check their answers. Go over the answers in open class. Have students share their thoughts on how easy or difficult the task was.

Answers

1 children **2** SOLEVINE **3** January **4** 34 **5** history

THINK | RESEARCH | CULTURE | LEARN | ME

Before students write their questions, brainstorm different topics they could ask about. Then have students share their questions with the class and number them in order of importance.

Homework OWB

Assign students Listening exercises 1 and 2 on page 56 of their Workbook.

GRAMMAR 2
will and *going to*

→ Student's Book, page 75 SB

Lesson aims

- Understand the correct usage of *will* and *going to*
- Practise using *will* for spontaneous decisions, offers/requests and for predictions based on opinion
- Practise using *going to* for future plans and for predictions based on evidence

Lead-in

Draw a weekly planner on the board with the days of the week listed on the left and the heading *Things to do* on the right. Tell students about some of your arrangements and plans for the week, using the present continuous and *going to*. For example, *On Monday evening I'm going to relax at home with my family. On Tuesday it's my son's birthday so we're having dinner in a restaurant.*, etc. Then tell students to create their own planner in their notebooks. Give them a time limit and then have them share their lists with the class.

Grammar in context

Remind students that *I'm* is a contraction for *I am*. Elicit that *I'll* is the contraction for (*I will*). Then ask students to complete the task, and refer them to the information in the *Remember* box if they aren't sure.

Remind students that they can find more information in the Grammar reference, Unit 7, page 150.

Answers

1 b **2** d **3** c **4** e **5** a

Language note

Students have already seen how *going to* is used for personal plans and to make predictions based on evidence. Students will now see how *will* is used for spontaneous reactions, to make offers or requests and predictions based on opinions.

1 Ask students to complete the exercise individually. Then have them check their answers with a partner.

Answers

1 'm going to **2** 'll **3** Will you **4** aren't going to go **5** 'll **6** aren't going to

Mixed ability

Give weaker students the function that corresponds to each item (**1** *a plan,* **2** *an instant decision,* **3** *a request,* **4** *a plan,* **5** *an offer/instant decision,* **6** *a plan*). When stronger students have finished, ask them to make a list of the function for each item. Check the functions as you go through the answers in open class.

2 Ask students to look at the conversation and tell you what the friends are talking about (*planning an end-of-term party*). Have students complete the exercise individually. Check answers in open class and then put students into groups to practise the conversation. Walk round the class, monitoring students for pronunciation and helping them where necessary.

Answers

1 're/are going to make **2** 'm/am going to sell **3** Will, choose **4** 'll buy **5** 's/is going to prepare **6** are going to come **7** will, check **8** 's/is going to be

3 Before students complete the exercise, ask them how they get to school. Have students check in pairs before you check their answers in open class. Then have the class compare their own journey with that of the students in Atuler.

Answers

1 going **2** going **3** are **4** will **5** will **6** to **7** will **8** will

Homework

OWB

Assign students Grammar 2 exercise 1 on page 55 of their Workbook.

Assign students the Flipped classroom tasks on page 76 of their Student's Book if you'd like them to prepare for the next lesson. To complete this task, students need to watch the *Talk2Me* video which can be found on the Resource Centre.

SPEAKING
Questions

→ Student's Book, page 76 SB

Lesson aims

- Focus on talking about the future and making predictions
- Practise answering personal questions in an interview
- Research what students plan to do when they finish school

The *Talk2Me* video in this unit focuses on jobs and job interviews. The people in the video talk about getting a part-time job, preparing for a job interview and their plans for when they leave school.

Students answer some comprehension questions and then listen for key phrases in the video.

The video can be used in one of two ways:

Flipped classroom

Flipped classroom option

Using this approach, students watch the video and complete the exercises for homework. This prepares students for the speaking lesson by introducing them to the topic and the key phrases to use in the exam task. Teachers who use this method will find they have more class time to spend on activating the target language and developing fluency for the final task.

***Talk2Me* worksheet**

Ask students to also complete the *Talk2Me* worksheet on the Resource Centre for more detailed comprehension exercises and more practice of the key phrases.

Classroom option

1 Ask students to spend a minute or two reading the questions. Play the *Talk2Me* video for students to complete the exercise. Play the video again, if necessary, before checking their answers.

2 Play the *Talk2Me* video again, so students underline the phrases in the *Phrase expert* box. Pause the video from time to time if necessary. Check answers in open class.

***Talk2Me* worksheet**

Ask students to also complete the *Talk2Me* worksheet on the Resource Centre for more detailed comprehension exercises and more practice of the key phrases.

Answers

The transcript and answer key for the *Talk2Me* video exercises and Worksheet can be found on the Teacher's Resource Centre.

Lead-in

Revise some of the personal questions students have already seen on the course. Write the following groups of question prompts around the unit numbers on the board:

Unit 1 – *How much / free time / you / have / ?*

Unit 3 – *What / be / favourite type of food / ?*

Unit 5 – *What / you / do / next weekend / ?*

Have students use the prompts to ask and answer the questions in pairs. Tell them to ask other personal questions they can remember. Walk round the class, monitoring students' use of English and helping them to form questions if necessary.

Answers

Unit 1 – How much free time do you have?

Unit 3 – What's your favourite type of food?

Unit 5 – What are you doing next weekend?

3 In pairs, students ask and answer the questions. Elicit answers from different students around the class and encourage a class discussion.

EXAM SKILL

Talking about the future

Ask students to read the tips.

- Explain to students that personal questions in speaking exams are usually chosen so candidates can use a variety of different verb tenses in their answers. On this page, for example, they are given opportunities to use both *going to* and *will* to talk about the future.
- Tell students that examiners are listening for candidates' correct use of grammar, but remind them that they can increase their marks by using appropriate phrases like those in the *Phrase expert* boxes.

4 2.21 Rearrange the first question as a class and elicit tips on how to do this from the class. For example, *The question should start with 'Are'.* Have students complete the rest of the exercise. Then play the audio for students to listen and check.

Answers

1 Are you going to take exams this term? **2** Will your classmates pass the test? **3** What languages will you study next year? **4** Are you going to study in the summer holidays?

Fast finishers

Ask students to cover Exercise 5 and brainstorm possible answers to the questions in Exercise 4. After matching the questions and answers in the next exercise, they can compare their ideas with the model answers.

5 2.21 After students complete the exercise, have them practise asking and answering the questions in Exercise 4 in pairs.

Answers

1 next term **2** 're/are going to **3** perhaps **4** 'm/am going to

OPTIMISE YOUR EXAM

Questions

Ask students to read the tips.

- Stress the importance of candidates answering the question they are asked and not something completely different. Remind students that if they are unsure about the question, they should use an appropriate phrase to confirm their understanding, e.g. *Sorry, could you repeat the question, please?*
- Remind students to listen for the tense used in the questions, as this will give them an idea of what the examiner is expecting. In many cases students will need to use the same tense in their answer as the examiner used in the question.
- Remind students to give extra information in their answers. Answering with short answers, even if these are grammatically correct, will not be enough to get top marks. It is much better to expand their answer to show their knowledge of the language even if the answer they give isn't true.

Exam task

6 Remind students to use time expressions from the *Phrase expert* box in their answers and to give appropriate additional information or reasons for their answers. Walk round the class, monitoring students for good use of language, making notes of any errors you hear. Write any errors on the board and go through them with students, eliciting corrections from them. After the class feedback, students could repeat this activity with another partner, to try to improve their performance.

Suggested answers

1 My favourite subjects at school are history and geography.
2 I'm going to study economics and biology (in the future).
3 I'm going to do 7 hours of homework this week.
4 I'm going to relax and watch TV at home.
5 When I leave school, I think I'll get a job at a bank.

Optional extension

Divide the class into small groups. Have students pick three or four personal questions to ask you that they think they could be asked in the speaking exam. Allow students to take turns asking you their questions. Make sure your model answers are the type of answers that you would expect students at this level to be able to produce themselves.

THINK | **RESEARCH** | CULTURE | LEARN | ME

Ask students to interview students from a different class and present their information to the class in the next lesson.

Homework

OWB

Students use their notes from Exercise 6 to write a summary of what they found out about their partner. Remind them to be particularly careful with the use of future tenses.

Assign students Speaking exercises 1, 2 and 3 on page 56 of their Workbook.

LANGUAGE IN USE

3-option multiple-choice cloze

→ Student's Book, page 77 SB

Lesson aims

- Focus on commonly confused words
- Practise a 3-option multiple-choice cloze exam task
- Discuss ideas for playing *Classcraft*

Lead-in

Revise some of the collocations students have already seen in the course. Write the following words in random order in two circles on the board:

Circle 1 – *board, cinema, do, DVD, make, newspaper, send, start, take, TV*

Circle 2 – *a conversation, a mistake, a text message, a train, article, game, player, programme, screen, the washing-up*

Tell students to look at the words in both circles. Then read a word out from Circle 1 and elicit the word it goes with from Circle 2. Continue with more students from around the class.

Answers

verb + noun: do the washing-up, make a mistake, send a text message, start a conversation, take a train

noun + noun: board game, cinema screen, DVD player, newspaper article, TV programme

1 After students discuss the questions, have them share their ideas with the rest of the class.

EXAM SKILL

Commonly confused words

Ask students to read the tips.

- Remind students how important it is to learn language in chunks, i.e. studying groups of words that go together, rather than lists of isolated words.
- Explain that multiple-choice cloze tasks often test collocations and other word phrases, such as verb + preposition phrases. Tell students to think about the meaning of the word they need to complete the gap and its correct form.
- Remind students to include some example phrases or sentences when they record new vocabulary.

2 After students complete the exercise, make a note of any common errors to focus on straight away or at a later date.

Answers

1 did **2** have **3** learn **4** do **5** make **6** take

3 Ask students to complete the exercise. Have them compare their answers in pairs after they finish.

Answers

1 do **2** make **3** did **4** had **5** take

Optional extension

Split the class into four groups. Assign each group one of the verbs *make*, *do*, *have* and *take*. Set a strict time limit of two minutes. In their groups, students brainstorm all the collocations they can think of with the verb. Regroup students into groups of four so there is one student who has prepared each verb in each group. Students share their collocations and take notes if they wish.

4 Have students scan the text quickly and then work in pairs to answer the question.

Answer

b

OPTIMISE YOUR EXAM

3-option multiple-choice cloze

Ask students to read the tips.

- Remind students that they need to think carefully about 'chunks' of language as these are commonly tested.
- Remind students of the process they practised earlier in the course: read the text first for general understanding; complete the gaps and leave difficult options until the end; check the words before or after the gaps to confirm answers; guess the best answer for all the gaps, even the ones they are not sure of.
- Point out that as they become more familiar with the language, they will develop their intuition and will recognise whether or not their chosen option 'sounds right' / makes sense when they read through the text for the final time.

Exam task

5 Tell students to implement the tips they have learnt to complete this task type. Ask students to complete the exercise individually and then compare their answers in pairs. Check answers in open class.

Answers
1 B **2** A **3** C **4** C **5** C **6** A

Mixed ability

Tell weaker students one incorrect option for each question so that they only have two options to choose from. Have stronger students complete the task as it appears in the Student's Book.

THINK | RESEARCH | CULTURE | LEARN | ME

After groups complete the exercise, have them present their ideas to the rest of the class. Have the groups evaluate each other and then vote for the best idea.

Cultural note

Classcraft was created by Canadian physics teacher Shawn Young in 2013. He decided to harness his students' love of video games to help with classroom management. In the game, students create virtual characters who can gain experience and skills, just like the characters do in the games they play. These characters inhabit an impressive virtual world, but the key difference is that students gain points to improve their learning in the real world of the classroom. This outcome has dramatic implications on students' motivation and interaction with their classmates. The platform has more than 1 million users and it is in more than 20,000 schools in more than 75 countries around the world.

Homework

OWB

Assign students Language in Use exercises 1, 2 and 3 on page 57 of their Workbook.

WRITING
Picture story

→ Student's Book, pages 78–79 SB

Lesson aims

- Focus on using adjectives when writing a story
- Practise a picture story exam task

Lead-in

Write the words *school trip* on the board and encourage the class to brainstorm all the places they can think of. Tell them to think of places they have been with the school and places they would like the school to take them.

1 After students complete the exercise, have them share their experiences with the class.

2 Ask students to work in pairs or small groups to discuss what they think the story is about. Then invite students to share some of their ideas with the class.

Answers
Students' own answers

3 Ask students to complete the table. Monitor and offer suggestions if necessary.

Suggested answers
Picture 1
nouns: museum, teenagers, TV, radio, mobile phone, (home) phone
verbs: go to, see, visit
adjectives: happy, excited, old
Picture 2
nouns: robot, chess
verbs: watch, see, play
adjectives: amazed, amazing, awesome
Picture 3
nouns: (gift) shop, present, money, T-shirt
verbs: buy, pay
adjectives: interesting, unusual

EXAM SKILL

Using adjectives

- Tell students they can make their stories more interesting by describing the people, places and things in the images.
- Encourage students to include adjectives throughout their story and to include how the characters feel in the images.

4 Ask students to complete the exercise and then check answers in open class.

Answers
1 surprised **2** excited **3** interesting

5 Tell students to work in pairs or small groups and complete the exercise. Then check their answers.

Answers
1 afraid, bored, excited, sad, tired, worried **2** awesome, awful, fantastic, great, interesting, scary, strange, unusual

6 Ask students to complete the exercise. Then have them check their answers in pairs before going over the answers in open class.

Answers
1 happy/excited **2** awesome/fantastic/great/strange/unusual
3 fantastic/great **4** awesome/interesting

OPTIMISE YOUR **EXAM**

Picture story

Ask students to read the tips.

- Encourage students to decide when their story took place in the past and to let the reader know this in the opening sentence by using a time expression (e.g. *Late last night …*).
- Point out that students need to refer to all three pictures in their story. They shouldn't focus on the smaller details in the pictures but the main ideas, in 35 words or more.

7 Ask students to refer to the pictures in Exercise 8 and answer the question before checking the answer in open class.

Answer

b

Homework

OWB

Assign students Writing exercises 1–6 on page 58 of their Workbook and Progress check on page 59.

Exam task

8 Ask students to look at the exam task and complete the exercise. Elicit from students some of the adjectives they came up with for each of the pictures.

Suggested answers

Picture 1: happy, excited

Picture 2: awesome, fantastic

Picture 3: hungry, tired

9 Plan Students should complete the table while referring to the pictures in Exercise 8. Monitor and offer suggestions as appropriate.

10 Write Ask students to write a story in 35 words or more. Tell them to refer to their notes in Exercise 9 to help guide them.

Fast finishers

Ask students to underline the words in Alex's notes and the words in the exam texts that mean the same, e.g. *begin* = *start*, *don't take* = *leave*. Check these words while going through the answers.

11 Check Students complete the checklist before they hand in their stories.

8 It's only a game

UNIT AIMS

Exam preparation in Unit 8:

- find ideas that mean the same
- listen for important information
- give opinions
- use modal verbs
- write an email in an informal style

TEACHER'S PRESENTATION KIT

- *Talk2Me* videos
- Speaking test videos
- Class and Workbook audio
- Workbook pages and answer key

UNIT OVERVIEW

Student's Book / Digital Student's Book (SB)		Workbook / Online Workbook (OWB)
LESSON / EXAM TASK	EXAM SKILLS / LANGUAGE FOCUS	CONSOLIDATION
Reading **3-option multiple-choice (short texts)**	Finding ideas that mean the same Notices and messages	Workbook, pp 60–61, Exercises 1, 2, 3, 4, 5 Unit 8, Reading, Exercises 1, 2, 3, 4, 5
Grammar 1	Modals (1): ability, necessity, obligation, possibility	Workbook, p 62, Exercises 1, 2, 3 Unit 8, Grammar 1, Exercises 1, 2, 3
Vocabulary	Words connected with *sport* Verbs/nouns Collocations with verbs	Workbook, pp 62–63, Exercises 1, 2, 3 Unit 8, Vocabulary, Exercises 1, 2, 3
Listening **Matching**	Listening for important information	Workbook, p 64, Exercises 1, 2, 3 Unit 8, Listening, Exercises 1, 2, 3
Grammar 2	Modals (2): advice, permission, polite requests, prohibition	Workbook, p 63, Exercises 1, 2, 3 Unit 8, Grammar 2, Exercises 1, 2, 3
Speaking **Discussion (pictures)**	Giving opinions	Workbook, p 64, Exercises 1, 2, 3 Unit 8, Speaking, Exercises 1, 2, 3
Language in Use **Open cloze**	Using modal verbs	Workbook, p 65, Exercises 1, 2 Unit 8, Language in Use, Exercises 1, 2
Writing **Guided writing (an email)**	Writing in an informal style	Workbook, p 66, Exercises 1, 2, 3, 4 Unit 8, Writing, Exercises 1, 2, 3, 4
Progress check	Check language progress for Units 7 and 8	Workbook, p 67, Progress check and Cumulative progress Progress check and Cumulative progress

Additional material

PRESENTATION KIT	TEACHER'S / STUDENT'S RESOURCE CENTRE (RC)	TEST GENERATOR
Talk2Me video *Can I buy …?*	**Unit 8 worksheets:** *Optimise your grammar* (Standard and Higher), *Optimise your vocabulary* (Standard and Higher), *Talk2Me* video, *Say it right* **Units 7–8 worksheets:** CLIL, Culture, Everyday English (TRC only), Grammar communication (TRC only)	Unit Test 8 (Standard and Higher) Progress Test (Standard and Higher)

READING
3-option multiple choice (short texts) | Notices and messages

→ Student's Book, pages 80–81 SB

Lesson aims

- Focus on identifying paraphrases
- Practise a 3-option-multiple choice (short texts) exam task
- Research famous sports people

Lead-in

In pairs, ask students to look at the unit title ***It's only a game*** and brainstorm what the *it* in the question could refer to, e.g. *football, tennis, volleyball, cricket.* Explain that we sometimes say *It's only a game* when people get really excited about something, more than necessary – perhaps like the people in the photo celebrating their victory.

1 In pairs or as a group, students ask and answer the questions. Elicit answers from different students around the class and open out to a class debate about whether it's more important to enter sports competitions or to win them.

2 Ask students to think of different sports and to write them in the correct list.

Possible answers

Team sports: basketball, cricket, football, rugby, volleyball

Sports you do alone: athletics, badminton, skiing, surfing, tennis

EXAM SKILL

Finding ideas that mean the same

Ask students to read the tips.

- Tell students that they need to understand the main meaning of the text and decide which option is the closest paraphrase to the meaning of the text.
- Tell them that they should look for parts of the text that have similar ideas in an option. They shouldn't assume that if the same word or phrase appears in both the text and option, they have found the correct answer.

3 Ask students to complete the task and then check answers in open class.

Answers

a, c

4 Ask students to complete the exercise. Check answers in open class.

Answers

1 c **2** a **3** b **4** d

OPTIMISE YOUR EXAM

3-option multiple-choice (short texts)

Ask students to read the tips.

- Encourage students to read the information before and after any new words they encounter. Then they should try to figure out what the whole sentence means as this may help them to decode the meaning of the new word. They can use this strategy to keep learning new words and building their vocabulary.
- Point out that they should first decide what type of message it is (notice, text, advert, etc.) and who the message is meant for (the public, a friend, club members, etc.), then decide the main idea of the message.

▼ Exam task

5 2.22 **Note: The reading text is also available on the audio CD. You may want to have students listen and read the text before doing the exam task.**

Ask students to complete the exercise. Have students compare in pairs before you check in open class.

Answers

1 A (*I'm tired and I haven't finished my homework*)
2 B (*I'm having a party … Can you and Karen come?*)
3 A (*Are you feeling better?*) **4** C (*Thanks for the book, I love it!*) **5** C (*Must bring trainers*) **6** B (*… you must be able to swim well*)

Extra support

Ask students to underline the words or phrases in the text that helped them to arrive at the correct answer. Then get pairs to compare and discuss which paraphrases helped them to figure out the answers to Exercise 5.

6 Ask students to complete the exercise. Students compare in pairs before you check in open class.

Answers

1 won **2** rackets **3** coach **4** winners **5** tired **6** sailing

Fast finishers

Have students write an email to a friend using the vocabulary in Exercise 6.

THINK | **RESEARCH** | CULTURE | LEARN | ME

If you have access to the internet, students can research this information in class. It could be a collaborative project with students working in pairs or groups. To avoid repetition, you may prefer to brainstorm famous sports people and then assign these yourself.

Homework

OWB

Assign students Reading exercises 1, 2, 3, 4 and 5 on pages 60–61 of their Workbook.

GRAMMAR 1

Modals (1): ability, necessity, obligation, possibility

→ Student's Book, page 82 SB

Lesson aims

- Understand the correct usage of modals of ability, necessity, obligation and possibility
- Practise using modal verbs to talk about ability, necessity, obligation and possibility

Lead-in

Write these jumbled questions on the board and ask students to reorder them:

1 well / you / sports / what / do / can / ?

2 sports / what / do / at all / can't / you / ?

In pairs, students ask and answer the questions. Circle the words *can* and *can't* and elicit what kind of words they are and what they mean (*modal verbs; they are used to talk about abilities you have or don't have*).

Answers

1 What sports can you do well? **2** What sports can't you do at all?

Grammar in context

Ask students to complete the task and refer them to information in the *Remember* box if they aren't sure. Check their answers.

Remind students that they can find more information in the Grammar reference, Unit 8, page 151.

Answers

1 d, obligation **2** e, necessity **3** c, possibility **4** a, ability
5 b, obligation **6** a, ability

Language note

Modal verbs, also called modals, 'help' other verbs to express a meaning. Point out that modal verbs have no meaning by themselves.

1 Ask students to complete the exercise. Check answers in open class.

Answers

1 couldn't **2** must **3** might **4** have to **5** needn't **6** must

Extra support

Write *Present or past?* and *Ability? Possibility? Necessity? Obligation? No obligation or necessity?* on the board. Look at the sentences in Exercise 1 with the students and analyse each one, answering the questions. Check students understand the type of modal verbs: Ability: *can, could*; Possibility: *may, might, could*; Necessity: *need to*; Obligation: *must, have to*; No obligation or necessity: *not have to, needn't*

2 Ask students to complete the exercise. Students compare in pairs before you check in open class.

Answers

1 Can **2** can't **3** might **4** needn't **5** have **6** don't have

3 Ask students to look at the photo and say what sport they can see (*athletics/running*). Ask them to complete the exercise. Have students compare in pairs before you check their answers in open class.

Answers

1 couldn't **2** may/might **3** had **4** needn't/mightn't
5 have/need **6** can't **7** needn't **8** might/may

Fast finishers

Write these numbers on the board for students to find out what they refer to in the text: *15, 2nd, 1952, 5,000, 10,000, 42*

Answers

15 the age Zátopek was when the factory sports coach told him to run in a race
2nd the position he came in that first race
1952 the year he participated in the Olympic Games
5,000/10,000 the distances in metres of the races he ran and won at the Olympics
42 the length of a marathon, in kilometres

Homework

OWB

Assign students Grammar 1 exercises 1, 2 and 3 on page 62 of their Workbook.

VOCABULARY

Topic vocabulary | Word formation | Collocations

→ Student's Book, page 83 SB

Lesson aims

Understand the correct usage of:

- words connected with sport
- verbs and nouns from the same word family
- verb collocations

Lead-in

In small groups, students take turns to mime sports for the other students in their group to guess.

Words connected with *sport*

1 2.23 Ask students to complete the exercise. Play the audio for students to listen and check.

Answers/Audioscript

1 You need a small plastic ball to play this game. *table tennis*
2 You can go swimming here. *pool*
3 You can do this sport on snow in the mountains. *skiing*
4 You can watch a football game here. *stadium*
5 This is the person who is first in a competition or race. *winner*
6 You need a racket to play this game. *badminton*

2 2.24 Read the first sentence with students and establish that all three answer options refer to people. The correct answer is the one that best fits the context. Encourage students to look for clues in the rest of the sentences to help them choose the correct word.

Ask students to complete the exercise individually. Play the audio for students to listen and check their answers.

Answers/Audioscript

1 (B) The *coach* told us what exercises to do and helped us play better.
2 (C) Can you *ride* a horse?
3 (A) You need a *ticket* to go to the basketball game tonight.
4 (A) I can't go swimming because I haven't got my *swimsuit*.
5 (A) Ed was the winner of the 800-metre *race*.
6 (C) They played in a rugby *match* yesterday, and won 35-3!

Fast finishers

Ask students to explain what the incorrect alternatives mean and how they could be used, e.g. a *team* refers to a group of people who play a sport together, whereas a *member* is someone who belongs to a club or group: *Some members of the hockey team are friends of mine.*

Refer students to the Vocabulary reference, page 160, for more information on topic vocabulary.

Verbs/nouns

3 2.25 Look at the first line of the table with students as an example. Ask them to complete the exercise. Play the audio for students to listen and check their answers.

Answers/Audioscript

verb: win, **noun:** winner
verb: *surf*, **noun:** surfer
verb: swim, **noun:** *swimmer*
verb: *run*, **noun:** runner
verb: play, **noun:** *player*

4 Ask students to complete the exercise. Check students have spelt the words correctly.

Answers

1 swimmers **2** won **3** runners **4** player **5** surf

Mixed ability

Give less confident students the words in the correct form and ask them to put them into the correct sentences. Ask stronger students to complete the exercise as given and then brainstorm additional verbs/nouns for people which they already know, e.g. *act/actor, teach/teacher, write/writer.*

Refer students to the Vocabulary reference, page 160, for more information on word formation.

Collocations with verbs

5 2.26 Write *run* in the centre of the board. And ask students to tell you what might come after *run*, e.g. *a race, a marathon, 5,000 metres.* Remind students that learning combinations of words which are often used together (collocations) is a very effective way of learning vocabulary.

Ask students to complete the exercise. Play the audio for students to listen and check their answers.

Answers/Audioscript

1 Greg *threw* the ball into the road.
2 My class *goes* swimming at the city pool every Wednesday.
3 Everyone can *enter* the competition, but only one person can win.
4 In the summer, lots of people in England *play* cricket.
5 Do I need to practise a lot before I *climb* a mountain?
6 Emil Zátopek was very happy when he *won* the 5,000-metre race at the Olympic Games.

Refer students to the Vocabulary reference, page 160, for more information on collocations.

Homework

OWB

Assign students Vocabulary exercises 1, 2 and 3 on pages 62–63 of their Workbook.

LISTENING
Matching

→ Student's Book, page 84

Lesson aims

- Listen for important information
- Practise a matching exam task
- Discuss summer camps

Lead-in

Recycle the collocations from the previous lesson.

Call out a verb (*climb, enter, go, play, throw, win*) and ask students to work in pairs or small groups to think of a grammatically correct sentence using the verb and an appropriate collocation. Repeat with other verbs.

1 In pairs, students ask and answer the questions. Elicit answers from different students around the class. Ask students which verb usually collocates with each of the sports they mention.

Answers

1 table tennis, volleyball, trampolining
2 and 3 Students' own answers

EXAM SKILL

Listening for important information

Ask students to read the tips.

- Remind students that in listening exams it is not necessary to understand everything to be able to complete the task. If students prepare before listening by reading the questions carefully, they will then have an idea of what the recording is going to be about and can relax and will understand a lot more.
- In listening exams, students usually have 30 seconds before the first listening to prepare – in tasks like the one in Exercise 2, it can be useful to think of vocabulary which they expect to hear in connection with the topic, e.g. *running – athletics, a race, a stadium, winner; windsurfing – water, sea, (bad/good) weather*, etc.

2 2.27 Play the track for students to listen and complete the exercise. Elicit answers from students around the class.

Answers

1 e **2** d **3** b **4** a **5** c

3 2.27 Play the track again for students to identify the other sports the people talk about in the conversations.

Answers

1 football, rugby **2** volleyball **3** fishing **4** swimming **5** tennis

Optional extension 2.27

Write these questions on the board. Play the track again for students to answer them.

1 *What sort of sports does Dan enjoy?*
2 *Where did Lorna go cycling?*
3 *Does Chris often go windsurfing?*
4 *Why didn't Lily enjoy going running?*
5 *Was Pete good at playing badminton before?*

Answers

1 Sports where you run around. **2** in the mountains **3** No, it was his first time. **4** Because it was cold. **5** Probably not, because someone taught him how to play.

OPTIMISE YOUR EXAM

Matching

Ask students to read the tips.

- Explain that in this type of task there are often distractors, i.e. items which look like they could be correct answers but in fact are not needed. In Exercise 4, for example, there are five days of the week but there are eight sports. Some or all of the distractors may be included in the recording, so students need to remember that they might hear a word that they don't actually need to use in an answer.
- Remind students that they will usually hear the recording twice, so they shouldn't panic if they aren't sure of some of the answers after the first listening. They should check carefully in the second listening that the answer they have chosen is correct and that they haven't been tricked by a distractor.

Exam task

4 2.28 Play the audio for students to listen and complete the exercise. Ask students to compare their choices in pairs but wait until Exercise 5 to check answers in open class.

Answers

1 C **2** B **3** E **4** G **5** A

5 2.28 Play the audio again and check answers in open class.

Answers

1 C (*Then I played volleyball in the afternoon*) **2** B (*A coach taught us to play badminton in the sports centre*) **3** E (*One of the instructors took us sailing*) **4** G (*We had a cricket competition*) **5** A (*The camp leader says we can go to the pool … enjoy your swim*)

Extra support

Give students a copy of the audioscript. Play the track again and ask students to identify the distractor, e.g. *I wanted to play tennis on Tuesday, but it was raining so I couldn't.*

THINK | RESEARCH | **CULTURE** | LEARN | ME

Ask students to discuss the questions. Point out that there are no right or wrong answers. Open out to a class discussion, if there is time, and find out if any students in the class have been on a summer camp.

Homework OWB

Assign students Listening exercises 1, 2 and 3 on page 64 of their Workbook.

GRAMMAR 2

Modals (2): advice, permission, polite requests, prohibition

→ Student's Book, page 85 SB

Lesson aims

- Understand the correct usage of modals of advice, permission, polite requests and prohibition
- Practise using modal verbs to talk about advice, permission, polite requests and prohibition

Lead-in

Write these sentences on the board:
If you feel ill, you should …, If you work hard this morning, you can …, Can I go …?, In school, you mustn't …
Model a possible completion for the first sentence, e.g. *If you feel ill, you should go to see the nurse.* In pairs or small groups, students try to complete the sentences in as many different ways as possible. Elicit answers around the class.

Circle the modal verbs in the sentences and elicit the function of each (***should*** *= to give advice;* ***can*** *= to talk about permission, or to make a request;* ***mustn't*** *= to talk about prohibition*). Explain that in this lesson students will be learning about more modal verbs and their functions.

Grammar in context

Ask students to complete the task. Refer them to the information in the *Remember* box if they aren't sure. Then check their answers. Ask students to think of personalised sentences of their own, using the modals in the box. Elicit a few examples around the class.

Remind students that they can find more information in the Grammar reference, Unit 8, page 152.

Answers

1 d **2** a **3** c **4** e **5** b

Language note

Students have to be able to use a limited range of modal and semi-modal verbs for exams at this level.

On page 82 of their Student's Book, students saw how *can/can't* and *could/couldn't* are used to talk about ability. In this lesson, they will see that these same modals are also used to say that something *is/isn't* or *was/wasn't allowed*. Be prepared to give students further explanations and examples to help them distinguish *ability* (something that you are able to do because you have a natural talent, or that you have taught yourself to do) from *permission* (something that is allowed because another person or the rules say that this is acceptable).

The verb *have to*, like *need to*, is a semi-modal verb and can be problematic.

- In terms of form, negatives and questions are formed with the auxiliary verbs *do/does* or *did/didn't*, not with the addition of *n't* to the end of the verb.
- Students may mistakenly use the negative *don't have to* to talk about things that are not allowed, so you need to clarify that in these cases the opposite of *have to* is *can't* (*In football, you can't touch the ball with your hands.*)
- The negative *don't have to* is used to talk about things which it is not necessary to do, but which you can do if you choose.

1 Ask students to complete the exercise. Check in open class.

Answers

1 can **2** mustn't **3** could **4** shouldn't **5** should

Mixed ability

Tell students five things you *have to* and *don't have to* do as a teacher, e.g. *I have to correct my students' homework. I don't have to work at weekends.* Ask weaker students to work in pairs and write sentences about what they *have to* and *don't have to* do as students. Ask stronger students to work in small groups and take turns to think of a job and make five sentences about it with *have to* and *don't have to*. The other students in their group have to guess the job. In both cases, walk round monitoring students for good use of language and errors to go over at the end of the activity.

2 Ask students to complete the exercise. Have students check in pairs before you check their answers in open class.

Answers

1 a **2** c **3** c **4** a **5** b **6** b

3 Ask students to complete the exercise. Students compare in pairs before you check in open class.

Answers

1 should bring **2** can't do **3** could you bring **4** should bring **5** can use **6** shouldn't arrive **7** could you ask **8** mustn't leave

Fast finishers

Ask students to expand the first paragraph of the text in Exercise 3 with additional ideas of things they should or shouldn't take to the camp, e.g. *You can bring a mobile phone, but you should leave it in your locker during the day.*

Homework OWB

Assign students Grammar 2 exercises 1, 2 and 3 on page 63 of their Workbook.

Assign students the Flipped classroom tasks on page 86 of their Student's Book if you'd like them to prepare for the next lesson. To complete this task, students need to watch the *Talk2Me* video which can be found on the Resource Centre.

SPEAKING
Discussion (pictures)

→ Student's Book, page 86 SB

Lesson aims

- Focus on asking and answering questions to exchange information
- Practise a discussion (pictures) exam task
- Discuss learning new sports

The *Talk2Me* video in this unit focuses on mobile phones and communication problems. The people in the video ask their phones questions using the voice recognition function, but the phones misunderstand.

Students answer some comprehension questions and then listen for key phrases in the video.

The video can be used in one of two ways:

Flipped classroom

Flipped classroom option

Using this approach, students watch the video and complete the exercises for homework. This prepares students for the speaking lesson by introducing them to the topic and the key phrases to use in the exam task. Teachers who use this method will find they have more class time to spend on activating the target language and developing fluency for the final task.

***Talk2Me* worksheet**

Ask students to also complete the *Talk2Me* worksheet from the Resource Centre for more detailed comprehension exercises and more practice of the key phrases.

Classroom option

1 Ask students to spend a minute or two reading the questions. Play the *Talk2Me* video for students to complete the exercise. Play the video again, if necessary, before checking their answers.

2 Play the *Talk2Me* video again, so students underline the phrases in the *Phrase expert* box. Pause the video from time to time if necessary. Check answers in open class.

***Talk2Me* worksheet**

Ask students to also complete the *Talk2Me* worksheet on the Resource Centre for more detailed comprehension exercises and more practice of the key phrases.

Answers

The transcript and answer key for the *Talk2Me* video exercises and Worksheet can be found on the Teacher's Resource Centre.

Lead-in

Create a word web to revise and extend the unit vocabulary. Write *SPORT* in the middle. To the right, draw a circle with *VERBS* in it, and to the left draw a circle with *EQUIPMENT* in it. Invite students to come up and add words.

EXAM SKILL

Giving opinions

Ask students to read the tips.

- Tell students that in this part of test they need to keep a discussion going for up to two minutes.
- Point out that they need to give their opinions about five pictures throughout the conversation. The phrases in the *Phrase expert* box can help them to discuss and share their opinions.
- Tell students that the examiner is not assessing them on their actual opinions but the language and accuracy they use to express their ideas. In other words, they won't receive higher marks by giving an opinion that they think will please the examiner.

3 Ask students to complete the table and then compare their answers with a partner. Elicit from students some of their opinions and reasons for them in open class.

Answers

Students' own answers

Language note

All the questions students are required to formulate in Exercises 4 and 6 follow standard word order. Remind students of the standard word order pattern, QASI, by writing the following table on the board and talking them through some of the questions from the *Talk2Me* video:

Question word	Auxiliary verb	Subject	Infinitive
How often	*do*	*you*	*do* sports at school?
What sports	*would*	*you*	*like* to do at school?
–	*Do*	*you*	*like* sport?

4 Put students into pairs to complete the exercise. Monitor and take note of any pronunciation or grammatical errors. Then give class feedback after students have asked each other the questions.

SAY IT RIGHT

Intonation in questions

For the *Say it right* pronunciation activity and instructions, go to the Teacher's Resource Centre. TRC

Extra support

Tell students that they may be asked to give their opinions about any of these topics for the exam: clothes, daily life, entertainment and media, food and drink, health, medicine and exercise, hobbies and leisure, house and home, language, people, personal feelings, opinions and experiences, personal identification, places and buildings, services, shopping, social interaction, sport, the natural world, transport, travel and holidays and weather. Ask students to work in pairs to create a similar table to the one in Exercise 3 after choosing one of these topics. Then have them practise giving their opinions about their chosen topic.

OPTIMISE YOUR EXAM

Discussion (pictures)

Ask students to read the tips.

- Students should look at the five visual prompts and immediately engage in conversation with their partner, talking about their likes/dislikes in relation to the five activities, places or things.
- In this part of the exam, students should be looking at each other. Eye contact is important as it indicates that you are listening and interested in what your partner has to say. Students should avoid looking at the examiner in this part of the exam, as they should be paying attention to the visual prompts while holding a discussion.

Exam task

5 2.29 Put students in pairs to discuss the images. If you have a timer, time this task so that pairs discuss the images for two minutes. After students have finished their discussions, play the audio of two students doing the task. Ask students to note down if the speakers agree with any of their opinions.

Answers

Students' own answers

6 Assign each student a letter, A or B, and put them into A/B pairs. Give them a moment to look at their questions. Time students (two minutes) and give them an update, e.g. *One minute to go …* Remind students to use phrases from the *Phrase expert* box and to ask for any necessary clarification. Walk round, monitoring students for good use of language and errors to go over at the end of the activity.

Write any errors on the board and go through them with students, eliciting corrections from them where possible. After the class feedback, students could then repeat this activity with another partner, to try to improve their performance.

Suggested answers

Student A's questions

When are they?
Are there classes for children?
What's the price? / How much are they?
Do I need a bat?
What's the telephone number?

Student B's questions

What's its name? / What's it called?
Where is it?
Is it open on Sunday evening?
Does it sell tennis rackets?
Can I/you buy things online?

Homework

OWB

Assign students Speaking exercises 1, 2 and 3 on page 64 of their Workbook.

LANGUAGE IN USE

Open cloze

→ Student's Book, page 87 SB

Lesson aims

- Focus on modal verbs in a gap-fill exercise
- Practise an open-cloze exam task
- Research street games

Lead-in

Put students in pairs. Have them take turns to imagine they are a popular sports personality. Their partner asks them a series of questions to find out which sports personality they are. Make sure the students asking the questions use the modal verbs they have learnt so far in this unit (*can*, *could*, *need to*, *have to*, etc.).

1 In pairs or as a group, students ask and answer the questions. Elicit ideas from different students around the class.

EXAM SKILL

Using modal verbs

Ask students to read the tips.

- Stress that learning to understand and use modal verbs is important for all exam skills. They can be tested in open-cloze and multiple-choice cloze exam tasks.

2 Students complete the exercise individually. Check answers in open class.

Answers

1 shouldn't **2** can **3** may **4** must **5** Could

3 Ask students to complete the exercise. Check their answers.

Answers

1 C (*It's a way for young people to do more sport …*) **2** B (*The events are held in the streets …*)

Extra support

Ask students to read the text quickly to get the general idea of the text before completing Exercise 4. Point to the gap for question 1 and elicit from the class possible words to complete the sentence. Write all the possibilities on the board and repeat the process for all items if necessary.

OPTIMISE YOUR EXAM

Open cloze

Ask students to read the tips.

- In the exam, students should always read the text for general understanding first. They will do this in Exercise 4. Remind them that when they have finished the task, they should read the text again and make sure it makes sense with all the answers in place.
- This type of exam task is testing grammatical structures, and modal verbs and linking words can be tested. Students will need to look carefully before and after each gap to help them decide on the correct answer.
- Remind students that marks are not deducted for incorrect answers so they should not leave the answer sheet blank for any questions.

Exam task

4 Ask students to complete the exercise. Students compare in pairs before you elicit answers in open class.

Answers

1 get **2** where **3** too **4** like **5** should / must **6** have / need

THINK | **RESEARCH** | CULTURE | LEARN | ME

If you have access to the internet, students can research this information in class. Alternatively, they could prepare this for homework, asking parents, grandparents, etc. what they played when they were younger. They can then present their findings at the start of the next lesson.

Cultural note

StreetGames started life in England in 2005 when a group of workers in local community regeneration programmes decided to found a charity to encourage young people to do more sport and physical activity, particularly in disadvantaged inner city areas. In 2009, it expanded into Wales and in 2011 a new programme called *Us Girls* was added to target young women and encourage them to participate in sport.

Homework

Assign students Language in Use exercises 1 and 2 on page 65 of their Workbook. OWB

WRITING

Guided writing (an email)

→ Student's Book, pages 88–89 SB

Lesson aims

- Focus on writing in an informal style
- Plan and write an informal email

Lead-in

Play ***Hangman*** with some of the vocabulary from the unit. Suggested words: *competition, racket, badminton, winner, because, cricket, skiing, table tennis, surfer.*

1 In pairs, students ask and answer the questions. Elicit answers from different students around the class.

EXAM SKILL

Writing in an informal style

Ask students to read the tips.

- In writing exams, students need to demonstrate a basic understanding of the concept of 'register', i.e. using formal or informal language depending on what they are writing and who is to read it.
- Point out that informal style does not mean incorrect English. Although emails tend to be less formal in style than paper-based communication, students should still avoid the use of 'text-speak', e.g. acronyms such as 'LOL' or smileys.

2 Ask students to complete the exercise. Check the answers in open class and write the contractions on the board to make sure students have written them correctly.

Answers

2 Sally's **3** They'll **4** weren't **5** didn't **6** Who's **7** I'm **8** We've

Fast finishers

Ask students to think of all the other contractions they know. Students then share the additional contractions with the rest of the class when everyone has finished.

3 Ask students to complete the exercise. Have students compare in pairs before you check their answers in open class.

Answers

1 F **2** I **3** I **4** F **5** I **6** I **7** F **8** F **9** I **10** F

4 Students read the email and answer the questions. Get them to compare in pairs before checking answers in open class.

Answers

1 football, cricket, hockey, basketball, athletics **2** at least one **3** when the weather is good **4** use the gym

5 Students complete the exercise and then compare their answers in pairs. Check in open class.

Answers

1 Hi, Write soon **2** everyone's

OPTIMISE YOUR **EXAM**

Guided writing (an email)

Ask students to read the tips.

- In writing exams, students are sometimes asked to write a short email to a friend, including pieces of specific information. In Exercise 6, for example, they are required to answer three questions their friend has asked. If they only answer two, they will lose marks.
- Top marks will be given to candidates who include all the information they were asked to, and use an appropriate style. In Exercise 6, students need to make sure they use informal language, if possible including examples of contractions and phrasal verbs, and start and finish their email appropriately.

▼ Exam task

6 Ask students to complete the exercise. Check answers in open class.

Answers

1 the clothes he has **2** the person who will give you the money **3** the amount of time (they practise)

7 Plan Ask students to complete the writing plan. You may want to look at students' plans to check them and give advice and suggestions for improvement before they take the next step.

8 Write Students write their email. If there is not enough time, set this and the subsequent checklist exercise for homework.

9 Check Students complete the checklist before they hand in their email.

Optional extension

For a slightly longer writing task, refer students to the task in the Writing reference (SB page 163). It includes an annotated sample text and related writing task to challenge your students a little more.

Homework OWB

Assign students Writing exercises 1, 2, 3 and 4 on page 66 of their Workbook and Progress check 8 on page 67.

Answers PROGRESS CHECK Units 7–8

Exercise 1

1 are, going to **2** 'm/am going to **3** 'm/am going to **4** Are, going to **5** 'm/am going to **6** 'll **7** 'm/am going to **8** Will **9** 'll **10** 'm/am not going to

Exercise 2

1 B **2** A **3** B **4** C **5** A

Exercise 3

1 could **2** couldn't **3** may **4** can't **5** should **6** can **7** shouldn't **8** don't have to **9** can **10** has to **11** don't have to **12** may

Exercise 4

1 and **2** play **3** in **4** going **5** to **6** before **7** but **8** make **9** because **10** go

Exercise 5

1 do **2** take **3** climb **4** win **5** go **6** throw **7** make **8** ride

Exercise 6

1 tennis **2** cricket **3** swimming **4** volleyball **5** surfing

9 Whatever the weather

UNIT AIMS

Exam preparation in Unit 9:

- think logically
- understand the speakers' questions
- talk about a topic
- identify conditional sentences
- express preferences

TEACHER'S PRESENTATION KIT

- *Talk2Me* videos
- Speaking test videos
- Class and Workbook audio
- Workbook pages and answer key

UNIT OVERVIEW

Student's Book / Digital Student's Book SB		Workbook / Online Workbook OWB
LESSON / EXAM TASK	EXAM SKILLS / LANGUAGE FOCUS	CONSOLIDATION
Reading **3-option multiple matching**	Thinking logically Blog posts	Workbook, pp 68–69, Exercises 1, 2, 3 Unit 9, Reading, Exercises 1, 2, 3
Grammar 1	Zero conditional, first conditional	Workbook, p 70, Exercises 1, 2, 3 Unit 9, Grammar 1, Exercises 1, 2, 3
Vocabulary	Words connected with *weather and nature* Words + prepositions Nouns/adjectives	Workbook, pp 70–71, Exercises 1, 2, 3 Unit 9, Vocabulary, Exercises 1, 2, 3
Listening **3-option multiple choice (pictures)**	Understanding the speakers' questions	Workbook, p 72, Exercises 1, 2, 3 Unit 9, Listening, Exercises 1, 2, 3
Grammar 2	Second conditional	Workbook, p 71, Exercises 1, 2 Unit 9, Grammar 2, Exercises 1, 2
Speaking **Questions**	Talking about a topic	Workbook, pp 72–73, Exercises 1, 2 Unit 9, Speaking, Exercises 1, 2
Language in Use **3-option multiple-choice cloze**	Identifying conditional sentences	Workbook, p 73, Exercises 1, 2, 3 Unit 9, Language in Use, Exercises 1, 2, 3
Writing **An email**	Expressing preferences	Workbook, p 74, Exercises 1, 2, 3, 4 Unit 9, Writing, Exercises 1, 2, 3, 4
		Workbook, p 75, Progress check and Cumulative progress Progress check and Cumulative progress

Additional material

PRESENTATION KIT	TEACHER'S / STUDENT'S RESOURCE CENTRE RC	TEST GENERATOR
Talk2Me video *It's a fun place to live.*	**Unit 9 worksheets:** *Optimise your grammar* (Standard and Higher), *Optimise your vocabulary* (Standard and Higher), *Talk2Me* video, *Say it right* **Units 9–10 worksheets:** CLIL, Culture, Everyday English (TRC only), Grammar communication (TRC only)	Unit Test 9 (Standard and Higher)

READING
3-option multiple matching | Blog posts

→ Student's Book, pages 92–93 SB

Lesson aims

- Focus on thinking logically about information in texts
- Practise 3-option multiple matching exam task
- Research unusual weather

Lead-in

Ask students to look at the unit title ***Whatever the weather*** and the photo and say what they think the unit will be about (*the weather, the seasons, what people do at different times of the year*). Explain to students that *Whatever the weather* is a phrase which gives the idea that we won't let bad weather stop us from doing what we want to do. For example, if I plan to meet you on Friday, I could say something like *Don't worry. I'll be there to meet you on Friday, whatever the weather!* Encourage some discussion about what students can see in the photo.

1 Have students stand up and look out of the window or door to see what the weather is like before completing the exercise. Elicit answers from different students around the class and encourage a class debate about what the best season is and why.

EXAM SKILL

Thinking logically

Ask students to read the tips.

- Tell students that if they think logically about the information in the text, this can help them when they read parts of a text that aren't clear to them at first.
- Encourage students to think of the sequence of events in the text as this can help them as well. For example, if there were 'dark clouds', then, logically, the next thing that could happen in the text is a rain storm.

2 Set a time limit of one minute and ask students to complete the exercise. Check answers in open class.

Answers

1 b is the correct answer because it is logical to assume that if the sun is shining in the morning, it's going to be a warm day. Option a is incorrect because there is no logical connection between a sunny morning and the usual warm weather in May.

2 a is correct because it is logical that if there was ice on the ground, it would make walking difficult. Option b is incorrect because it is a statement of fact that is not connected to the main sentence.

3 a is correct because if the person was woken by the thunderstorm, it must have been a loud storm to disturb his/her sleep. Option b is incorrect because it is a statement of fact about an aspect of the storm, but it doesn't explain why it woke the person up.

3 Ask students to read the three texts quickly and to underline the parts of the text where they get their answers from. Then check answers in open class.

Answers

Students should tick:

2 (*Because of the snow, we were without electricity …*)

4 (*… very quickly, it became windy and dark as clouds covered the sky. Then the storm started.*)

5 (*… strong winds began to slowly push the ice …*)

OPTIMISE YOUR EXAM

3-option multiple matching

Ask students to read the tips.

- Encourage students to skim the text quickly to understand the general idea and topic of the three texts.
- Ask students to look at the seven questions and underline the key words in each question.
- Next, students should look for paraphrases of the words or phrases they have underlined in the questions in each of the texts. Then they should underline them in the text to help narrow down which of the three texts answers the question.

▼ Exam task

4 3.01 **Note: The reading text is also available on the audio CD. You may want to have students listen and read the text after doing the exam task to check their answers.**

Tell students to read the instruction carefully before completing the exercise. After checking students' answers, elicit which tips they used to complete the task.

Answers

1 C (*It was the strangest thing I've ever seen.*)
2 B (*… we waited in the rain until it finished.*)
3 A (*We couldn't go outside for three days.*)
4 B (*If you go sailing often, be careful!*)
5 A (*… it was dark and cold in the house.*)
6 C (*The ice went into people's houses …*)
7 B (*… stopped at a beach to have lunch.*)

Optional extension

Have students explain why the answers are correct, e.g. *Question 1 is C because the text says 'It was the strangest thing I've ever seen'.* As you check the answers to Exercise 4, ask individual students to explain the reasons behind the correct answers. Alternatively, you could have students give reasons for their answers before sharing the correct answers. (Details are given in brackets in the key.)

5 Ask students to complete the exercise. Check answers in open class.

Answers

1 c **2** e **3** b **4** d **5** h **6** f **7** a **8** g

THINK | **RESEARCH** | CULTURE | LEARN | ME

Have students work in groups to create a poster. Tell them to prepare their posters to share what they have learnt with the class in the next lesson. If you have access to the internet, have students research information in class. Alternatively, you could have students prepare this for homework.

Cultural note

The expression *raining cats and dogs* often intrigues students. No one is clear about its origin. The most common belief is that hundreds of years ago, people kept their animals outside. Often small animals would live in the thatched roofs of houses and when the rain was very heavy, they would either be washed off or jump off in order to hide from the rain. Others suggest that it may be because primitive sewage systems overflowed in heavy rain and dead animals floated out amongst other rubbish. Some believe it may be because the god Odin (responsible for storms in Norse mythology) had two pet dogs, or because witches fly with their cats on brooms.

Homework

OWB

Assign students Reading exercises 1, 2 and 3 on pages 68–69 of their Workbook.

GRAMMAR 1

Zero conditional, first conditional

→ Student's Book, page 94 SB

Lesson aims

- Understand the correct usage of zero and first conditionals
- Practise talking about things that are usually true and possible in the future
- Discuss future plans

Lead-in

Ask students to present their posters about the weather from the last lesson to the class. Encourage them to give detailed information about the poster and, if time, what parts of the creation process they found easy or difficult. Have the other groups ask questions and then have the class vote for the best poster.

Grammar in context

After students complete the task, test their understanding by asking them what we use each conditional for. Ask students to read the information in the *Remember* box to help them.

Remind students that they can find more information in the Grammar reference, Unit 9, page 152.

Answers

a 1 **b** 2

Language note

Explain that conditional sentences are divided into two clauses: a condition/cause and a result/effect. Tell students that we need both of these clauses to form conditional sentences and they can refer to different times. Point out that the clauses in both the zero and first conditional can be reversed, but that when the conditional (*if*) clause comes second, you don't use a comma, i.e. *If you heat water, it boils. Water boils if you heat it.*

1 After students complete the exercise, have them share their answers in pairs. Then check answers in open class.

Answers

1 is, changes **2** is, fall **3** feel, shines **4** don't, don't **5** Do, snows **6** have, don't

Mixed ability

Pair weaker and stronger students together and ask them to share answers. The stronger students should explain their answers using the examples on the board if necessary to reinforce which tense is used in which clause.

2 Before students complete the exercise, point out that the clauses in sentences 3, 4 and 6 are reversed. Make sure students are aware that when clauses are reversed, the grammar moves with the clauses. This is an important issue with the first conditional where the two clauses use different tenses. Highlight the fact that sentences 3, 4 and 6 do not have a comma separating the two clauses. Have students compare answers in pairs before checking in open class.

Answers

1 rains, won't **2** gets, will die **3** won't be, snows **4** Will, go **5** go, will need **6** won't, is

Optional extension

Give students a starter sentence, e.g. *If I fail my exam next week, my parents will get really angry.* Elicit a second sentence, connected to the first and starting with *If my parents get really angry, …* e.g. … *they won't give me any pocket money.* Then elicit another sentence, e.g. *If my parents don't give me any pocket money, …* When students have understood the idea, put them into pairs or small groups to see how long a 'conditional chain' they can make.

3 Ask students to complete the exercise. Have them compare in pairs before you check their answers in open class.

Answers

1 go **2** keep **3** is **4** feel **5** isn't **6** sleep **7** think **8** are **9** will grow **10** stops

Cultural note

The experiment described in the text in Exercise 3 was carried out in December 2013 by a group of 14- and 15-year-old schoolgirls from Hjallerup school in Denmark. They used 12 trays of cress plants and despite having the same conditions, the six trays near the two wi-fi routers didn't grow while those in another room did. Scientists are now looking into the potential negative effects of the radio waves in the air around us. However, it is also thought that the heat from the two routers might have killed the cress.

THINK | RESEARCH | CULTURE | LEARN | **ME**

After students discuss the questions, encourage them to report their answers to the class using full first conditional sentences in order to consolidate the structure. Give feedback on students' use of language at the end of the task if necessary.

Homework

OWB

Assign students Grammar 1 exercises 1, 2 and 3 on page 70 of their Workbook.

VOCABULARY

Topic vocabulary | Word patterns | Word formation

→ Student's Book, page 95 SB

Lesson aims

Understand the correct usage of:

- words connected with weather and nature
- word patterns with infinitives (*to*) and *-ing* form
- nouns and adjectives from the same word family

Lead-in

Draw a giant thermometer on the board and mark *0° C* at the bottom and *100° C* at the top. Write the words *boiling, cold, cool, freezing, hot, warm* under it. Have students copy the thermometer in their notebooks and, in pairs, write the words in order next to the thermometer. Check answers in open class. Use gestures to show the differences in meaning from the coldest (shivering, blowing on hands) to the hottest (fanning yourself, wiping your forehead) if necessary.

Answers

From top to bottom: boiling, hot, warm, cool, cold, freezing

Words connected with *weather and nature*

1 3.02 Focus students' attention on the illustration and elicit what the image is (*a weather map*). After students complete the exercise, play the audio for them to check their answers.

Mixed ability

Ask stronger students to cover the sentences in Exercise 1. They look at the pictures for the eight cities and write a sentence about the weather in each of them before checking their ideas against the items in Exercise 1.

Answers/Audioscript

1 It is warm and *sunny* in Madrid. **2** There is *snow* in Stockholm. **3** It is *rainy* in Dublin. **4** It is *sunny and windy* in Lisbon. **5** There is *fog* in Berlin. **6** There *are thunderstorms* in Prague. **7** It's *cloudy* in London.

2 3.03 After the exercise, ask students to write their own descriptions of the words in the box. Have volunteers share their descriptions and have the rest of the class guess the word.

Answers/Audioscript

1 A large area of trees and other plants. *forest*
2 It is very tall and sometimes there is snow on the top. *mountain*
3 It takes water from the mountains to the sea. *river*
4 It's by the sea and people go there in the summer. *beach*
5 The space above you that you see when you look up into the air. *sky*
6 It is smaller than a mountain. *hill*

Refer students to the Vocabulary reference, page 161, for more information on topic vocabulary.

Words + prepositions

3 3.04 After students complete the exercise and listen to check their answers, ask them to write new alternatives for the second parts of the sentences. Have students share what they wrote with the class.

Answers/Audioscript

1 (c) The students did experiments to see if wi-fi was dangerous.
2 (b) It is important to protect our forests and rivers.
3 (e) The students were good at thinking of new science experiments.
4 (f) Scientists want to find out why things happen.
5 (a) Summer is the best time to visit the beach, because it's sunny.
6 (d) They learnt about animals by visiting the zoo.

Refer students to the Vocabulary reference, page 161, for more information on word patterns.

Nouns/adjectives

4 3.05 Ask students to follow the example to complete the exercise. Play the audio for students to check their answers. Elicit the relevant spelling rules, i.e. *for most nouns, add -y; for nouns which end consonant + vowel + consonant, double the second consonant and add -y; for nouns which end in -e, change the -e to -y.*

Answers/Audioscript

noun: cloud, **adjective:** cloudy
noun: fog, **adjective:** *foggy*
noun: *ice*, **adjective:** icy
noun: rain, **adjective:** *rainy*
noun: *snow*, **adjective:** snowy
noun: sun, **adjective:** *sunny*

5 Remind students that one of the forms is a noun and the other is an adjective before they complete the exercise. Check answers in open class.

Answers

1 clouds **2** icy **3** sunny **4** fog **5** snow **6** rainy

Fast finishers

Ask students to write their own sentences using the nouns and adjectives in Exercise 4.

Refer students to the Vocabulary reference, page 161, for more information on word formation.

SAY IT RIGHT

/əʊ/ and /aʊ/ TRC

For the *Say it right* pronunciation activity and instructions, go to the Teacher's Resource Centre.

Homework OWB

Assign students Vocabulary exercises 1, 2 and 3 on pages 70–71 of their Workbook.

LISTENING

3-option multiple choice (pictures)

→ Student's Book, page 96 SB

Lesson aims

- Listen to understand speakers' questions
- Practise a multiple-choice (pictures) exam task
- Discuss winter free-time activities

Lead-in

Divide the board in half and write *Summer holidays* on one side and *Winter holidays* on the other side. Read out the following items and ask students to classify them into the two groups in their notebooks.

beaches blue skies grey clouds ice creams mountains rainy skiing snow sunny swimming

Check answers as a class and complete them on the board. Ask students if any of the words can be classified into both groups and elicit why (e.g. *mountains: people can go skiing on a winter holiday and camping on a summer holiday*).

Suggested answers

Summer holidays: beaches, blue skies, ice creams, mountains, sunny, swimming

Winter holidays: grey clouds, mountains, rainy, skiing, snow

1 After students discuss the questions, elicit some answers from different students around the class. Encourage students to say what they usually do and how next summer will be similar or different.

EXAM SKILL

Understanding the speakers' questions

Ask students to read the tips.

- Questions in listening exam tasks can test the candidates' ability to understand what the speaker says and how they say it. Students should listen out for the speaker's intonation and word choice for clues about the speaker's feelings.
- Speakers may avoid answering 'No' or 'I don't agree' in order to be polite, but their intonation can still make it clear what their real feelings are.

2 3.06 Before students listen, remind them to listen to the complete conversations before they choose their answer. Play the track and then check answers in open class.

Answers

1 yes **2** don't know **3** no **4** yes **5** don't know

3 After students complete the exercise, have them check their answers in pairs and then practise the conversations.

Answers

1 idea **2** sure **3** really **4** Maybe

Optional extension 3.06

Write the five expressions (*I'm not sure. Maybe. Good idea! Great. Not really.*) from Exercise 3 on the board in random order. Play the first conversation and ask students to focus on the intonation of the answer. Repeat the conversation, pausing for the class to repeat the answer with the appropriate intonation. Repeat the process with the other four conversations.

OPTIMISE YOUR EXAM

3-option multiple choice (pictures)

Ask students to read the tips.

- Remind students to use the preparation time productively. Encourage them to use this time to read the questions carefully, underline the important words and check exactly what they will listen for. Tell them to also look at the pictures carefully and try to predict what words or phrases they expect to hear about each one in the recording.
- Remind students to listen to the complete conversation before selecting an answer. Explain that speakers may say more than one possible answer, but only one will be correct. Remind students that they will have a second opportunity to listen to the recording to make sure they have chosen the right answers.

Extra support

Before students complete the exam task, give them time to make notes about the questions. Write the following set of notes on the board as an example and ask students to match them to the A/B/C options in one of the questions.

i autumn, wind/windy, trees, leaves, park

ii summer, sun/sunny, blue sky, beach, sunbathing
iii winter, snow/snowy/snowing, mountain, skiing

Split the class into four groups. Assign each group one of the remaining questions in Exercise 4, i.e. questions 1–4, and ask them to prepare a set of notes to match each picture, using the notes on the board as a model. Regroup students and have them share their notes, checking for similarities and differences. Encourage students to justify their notes with reasons.

Answers
The notes match question 5 in Exercise 4
A ii **B** iii **C** i

▼ Exam task

4 3.07 Tell students to read through each question and look at the three pictures for each one before they listen. Play the audio. Then have students compare their answers in pairs. Wait to check answers in open class in Exercise 5.

5 3.07 Play the audio again and check answers in open class.

Answers
1 B (*Then why don't we go to the lake? It's beautiful there in the sun.*) **2** C (*… it's very cloudy. It isn't sunny at all.*) **3** C (*We'd go to the beach in Spain if we had more money … we'll probably go somewhere nearer home this year.*) **4** A (*… after lunch there's going to be a big storm.*) **5** C (*Autumn is my favourite time of year.*)

THINK | RESEARCH | **CULTURE** | LEARN | ME

Give examples of popular free-time activities in different countries from around the world. Then discuss the question as a class. Write down students' ideas on the board and then come to a consensus on the most popular one.

Homework OWB
Assign students Listening exercises 1, 2 and 3 on page 72 of their Workbook.

GRAMMAR 2
Second conditional

→ Student's Book, page 97 SB

Lesson aims

- Understand the correct usage of the second conditional
- Practise talking about impossible situations in the present and hypothetical future events
- Think about living in the forest

Lead-in

On the board, draw a rough map of your students' country and the countries surrounding it. Draw weather symbols like those on Student's Book page 95 next to different countries. Have students work in pairs and practise giving a weather forecast for the area. Walk round, monitoring students for good use of weather vocabulary and helping with the names/pronunciation of country names if necessary.

Grammar in context

Ask students what they remember about the listening in the previous lesson. Then have them complete the task individually. Refer them to information in the *Remember* box if they aren't sure. Check their answers to ensure students' understanding.

Remind students that they can find more information in the Grammar reference, Unit 9, page 153.

Answers
1 a no **b** no **2 a** no **b** no **3 a** yes **b** no

Language note

Point out that the clauses in the second conditional can be reversed in the same way as in zero and first conditional sentences. Remind them that the comma disappears when the second clause is the *if* clause.

1 Go through the first sentence as a class. Then say the first clause with a different effect as a model, *If there was lots of snow outside, we would build a snowman.* Elicit other ideas from students. Have students complete the exercise and then check answers in open class.

Answers
1 was **2** wouldn't **3** didn't **4** would **5** were

2 Before students complete the exercise, explain that we can use the abbreviation *I'd* instead of *I would* and the same goes for the other pronouns: *you'd*, *we'd*, etc. Check answers in open class.

Answers
1 could, 'd/would visit **2** didn't own, wouldn't / would not cycle **3** go, lived **4** had, 'd/would buy **5** stopped, would be

Extra support

Write the second conditional structure on the board with the clauses in both positions and highlighting the use/omission of the comma:

If + past simple, *would* + infinitive

would + infinitive *if* + past simple

Before students complete Exercise 2, ask them to circle *'if'* in each sentence. Then refer them to the structures on the board while completing the exercise. With weaker classes, leave this on the board for students' reference to complete exercises 3 and 4. Before completing Exercise 3, brainstorm possible ideas/verbs for them to use to complete the sentences, e.g. *fly around the world, be very rich, have a quiet life, be a pop star, live by the sea.*

3 Encourage students to use their imagination. After they complete the exercise, have them share their ideas with the class. Ask the class to say which idea was the most original for each sentence.

4 Focus students' attention on the photos and the title and elicit what they can see (*somebody living 'with nature' in a tent in a forest, and a highland cow – a traditional breed in Scotland*). After students complete the exercise, have them compare answers in pairs before checking in open class.

Answers
1 do **2** wash **3** didn't have **4** could **5** be able to **6** would be

THINK | RESEARCH | CULTURE | LEARN | ME

Have students brainstorm some ideas before discussing the questions in pairs. Develop into a class discussion to get a general indication of students' thoughts.

Homework OWB

Assign students Grammar 2 exercises 1 and 2 on page 71 of their Workbook.

Assign students the Flipped classroom tasks on page 98 of their Student's Book if you'd like them to prepare for the next lesson. To complete this task, students need to watch the *Talk2Me* video which can be found on the Resource Centre.

SPEAKING
Questions

→ Student's Book, page 98 SB

Lesson aims

- Talk about the weather and other topics
- Practise answering personal questions in an interview
- Research the weather in different countries

The *Talk2Me* video in this unit focuses on talking to an exchange student and describing places. The people in the video talk about where they live and what they like to do there.

Students answer some comprehension questions and then listen for key phrases in the video.

The video can be used in one of two ways:

Flipped classroom

Flipped classroom option

Using this approach, students watch the video and complete the exercises for homework. This prepares students for the speaking lesson by introducing them to the topic and the key phrases to use in the exam task. Teachers who use this method will find they have more class time to spend on activating the target language and developing fluency for the final task.

Talk2Me worksheet

Ask students to also complete the *Talk2Me* worksheet on the Resource Centre for more detailed comprehension exercises and more practice of the key phrases.

Classroom option

1 Ask students to spend a minute or two reading the questions. Play the *Talk2Me* video for students to complete the exercise. Play the video again, if necessary, before checking their answers.

2 Play the *Talk2Me* video again, so students underline the phrases in the *Phrase expert* box. Pause the video from time to time if necessary. Check answers in open class.

Talk2Me worksheet

Ask students to also complete the *Talk2Me* worksheet on the Resource Centre for more detailed comprehension exercises and more practice of the key phrases.

Answers
The transcript and answer key for the *Talk2Me* video exercises and Worksheet can be found on the Teacher's Resource Centre.

Lead-in

Review some of the geographical features from the Topic vocabulary section and the use of infinitives for purpose from the Words + prepositions section on page 95. Write the following sentence starters on the board:

It was hot and there wasn't a cloud in the sky, so we went to the … to …

There was a lot of snow and the sky was blue, so we went to the … to …

We love seeing animals and being close to nature, so we went to the … to …

Have students work in pairs to complete the sentences. Elicit some answers from different students around the class.

Suggested answers
beach, go for a swim / sit in the sun / play volleyball
mountains, go skiing/snowboarding
forest, have a long walk / go camping

3 Before students complete the exercise, ask them if the weather plays a part in their plans and if so, how. After students discuss the questions, elicit their answers with reasons.

EXAM SKILL

Talking about a topic

Ask students to read the tips.

- Remind students that after answering some personal questions in the Speaking test, they will be asked to talk about a topic. These can include aspects of their daily routine, hobbies and interests, favourite places or food, their hometown or school, the weather, etc.
- Encourage them to think about common topics that might come up and to learn some useful vocabulary and expressions about each one. Point out that it is very important to learn the part of speech of a new word so that they can use it correctly in a sentence.
- Remind them that giving examples allows them to expand on their answers, demonstrate more fluency and impress the examiner with a wider range of language.

4 3.08 Have students read the topics before you play the audio. Check answers in open class.

Answers

1 places you go on holiday **2** family and friends **3** technology **4** city where you live

5 3.08 Play the track again for students to listen and write the examples. Have students compare their answers in pairs before you check them in open class.

Suggested answers

1 They sometimes visit a new city like Paris or Berlin.

2 At weekends and the school holidays, her best friend usually comes to stay.

3 Last night, everyone was in the living room, but all using different gadgets.

4 The sports centre is very big and there's a new shopping centre with restaurants, cinemas and shops.

6 3.09 Play the audio for students to listen and complete the exercise. Have them compare their answers in pairs before you check them in open class.

Suggested answers

Topic: places you go on holiday

Examples: this year he cycled for six days around the coast, and he went on a walking trip to the mountains

Correction phrase: sorry, I mean …

OPTIMISE YOUR EXAM

Questions

Ask students to read the tips.

- Tell students that at this level, examiners do not expect candidates to speak perfect English. Explain that candidates are able to correct themselves with an appropriate phrase if they make a mistake. Tell them that this can increase their mark, as it shows they feel confident and 'in control' of the situation.
- Encourage them to use phrases to correct themselves when they are speaking in class. This will help them feel more confident about using them in a Speaking test.

Exam task

7 Give students one minute to make some brief notes for their answers. Then, in pairs, students take turns to talk about the topics. Remind them to use phrases from the Phrase expert box as well as phrases for self-correction. Walk round, monitoring students for good use of language and errors to go over at the end of the activity.

Write any errors on the board and go through them with students, eliciting corrections from them where possible. After the class feedback, students could then repeat this activity with another partner, to try to improve their performance.

Fast finishers

Remind students that the questions in Speaking tests are not taken from a fixed pool, so they need to be prepared for all sorts of questions. Ask students to brainstorm as many questions about the weather as they can.

THINK | **RESEARCH** | CULTURE | LEARN | ME

Have students look up the weather for homework. To vary students' answers have each student choose two different cities from around the world to compare. Tell them they can choose one city from the book and one of their own. Tell them to write a report of their findings to present in the next class.

Homework

OWB

Assign students Speaking exercises 1 and 2 on pages 72–73 of their Workbook.

LANGUAGE IN USE

3-option multiple-choice cloze

→ Student's Book, page 99 SB

Lesson aims

- Focus on identifying conditional sentences
- Practise a 3-option multiple-choice cloze exam task
- Discuss experiencing bad weather

Lead-in

Ask students to present the information they found on the cities they investigated. Remind students to use the vocabulary they have learnt in the unit.

1 Ask students what the highest mountain in the world is (*Mount Everest*). Then elicit other mountains they know before they discuss the questions. Elicit answers from different students around the class.

EXAM SKILL

Identifying conditional sentences

Ask students to read the tips.

- Tell students that we use different conditional sentences to express different things. They have looked at zero, first and second conditionals in Unit 9. Encourage students to review these structures as they can be tested in all parts of an exam.
- Encourage students to pay attention to the tenses in both clauses to help them identify which conditional is being used and the meaning of the sentence.

2 After students complete the exercise, have them practise saying them in pairs.

Answers
1 c **2** e **3** a **4** d **5** b

3 Ask students to complete the exercise in pairs and then elicit students' reasons for their answers in open class.

Answers
1 U (past tense *lived* = less possible or impossible) **2** L (future tense *will* = will probably happen) **3** U (past tense *didn't work* = less possible or impossible) **4** F (present tense *is* = true) **5** U (past tense *would* = less possible or impossible)

4 Ask students to work in pairs to complete the exercise before checking in open class.

Answers
1 if **2** will/may/might **3** would **4** don't **5** are

OPTIMISE YOUR EXAM

3-option multiple-choice cloze

Ask students to read the tips.

- Tell students that the gap in the sentence can appear at the beginning, middle or end of a sentence.
- Point out that if a conditional sentence is being tested, students should decide if it is a zero, first or second conditional sentence so they know how likely a situation might be.

Exam task

5 After students complete the exercise, have them explain their reasons to the class.

Answers
1 C **2** A **3** B **4** B **5** A **6** C

Extra support

Put students in pairs or small groups to identify the part of speech for each of the options (1–6). After checking answers in open class, tell students that adjectives, nouns and verbs are often tested in this type of exam task.

Answers
1 adjectives **2** nouns **3** adjectives **4** nouns **5** verbs **6** verbs

THINK | RESEARCH | CULTURE | LEARN | ME

Share your worst experience with the class or invent one in order to give them a model of what to write. After the activity, encourage students to share their experiences with the class.

Homework

OWB

Assign students Language in Use exercises 1, 2 and 3 on page 73 of their Workbook.

WRITING
An email

→ Student's Book, pages 100–101 SB

Lesson aims

- Focus on expressing preferences
- Plan and write an email

Lead-in

Write *Summer camp activities* in the middle of the board and the following word skeletons around it:

c _ _ _ _ _ g
t _ _ _ e t _ _ _ _ s
v _ _ _ _ _ _ _ _ l
s _ _ _ _ _ g
b _ _ _ _ _ _ _ n
r _ _ _ _ _ g
w _ _ _ _ _ _ _ _ _ g

Put students into teams to complete the words. Award one point for each correct word. The team with the most points wins. You may wish to set a time limit to make it more exciting.

Answers
cycling/camping, table tennis, volleyball, sailing/surfing, badminton, running, windsurfing

1 In pairs or as a group, students ask and answer the questions. Elicit answers in open class.

EXAM SKILL

Expressing preferences

Ask students to read the tips.

- Tell students that when they need to express their preference, they should explain the reason for their preference. For example, *I prefer swimming at the local swimming pool because it's opposite where I live.*
- Remind students to review the phrases they have learnt to express preferences in Units 5 and 9. This will help them if they need to reply to a question about preferences in an email task.

Language note

Explain to students about the use of *were* rather than *was* in the conditional clause: *If I were you, …* Tell them that we often use *if* + *were* instead of *was* in the phrase *If I were you, …* for giving advice and making suggestions.

2 After students complete the exercise, ask them to practise asking and answering speaker A's questions in pairs. Have students swap partners a few times asking and answering the questions.

Answers

1 prefer **2** would prefer

Mixed ability

Ask confident students to share their reasons for their preferences in Exercise 2 with the class. After each student gives their reason, ask the whole class to do the following: stand up if they agree with a student's opinion, sit down and put hands on their heads if they disagree with them.

3 Have students complete the task in pairs. Then go over the answers in open class.

Suggested answers

Brilliant!: it's brilliant (great) that they're going on a trip

Explain …: explain if they prefer to go to the beach or the countryside

Suggest …: suggest a day to go on the trip

Tell Mrs Smith: tell Mrs Smith whether they think the class should have a picnic or go somewhere for lunch

4 Ask students to complete the exercise individually. Then check answers in open class.

Answers

1 is brilliant **2** going to the beach and the countryside
3 they should go **4** wants to do for lunch

5 Ask students to complete the exercise in pairs. Then check answers in open class.

Answers

Students should underline:

1 That's the best way to end the year!

2 The weather is usually very nice in June.

3 Lots of people go to the beach at the weekend, so it's always very crowded then.

4 Then everyone could bring different dishes to share.

OPTIMISE YOUR EXAM

An email

Ask students to read the tips.

- Remind students that if they are asked to write an email to a friend, examiners want to know that candidates can write in an informal style. Remind them to think about who they are writing the email to, why they are writing it and which words and phrases are the most appropriate.
- Remind students to answer the three questions in the word limit. Explain that if they write too few words, they will receive a lower grade.

Exam task

6 Tell students to read the email and the four notes and to tick the things that John asks about. Then check answers in open class.

Answers

Students should tick: the best way to get to the camp, what clothes to take, where to sleep

7 Plan After students complete their plans, check them and give suggestions for improvements before they take the next step.

8 Write Students write their email. If there is not enough time, set this and the subsequent checklist exercise for homework.

9 Check Students complete the checklist before they hand in their email.

Optional extension

For a slightly longer writing task, refer students to the task in the Writing reference (SB page 163). It includes an annotated sample text and related writing task to challenge your students a little more.

Homework

OWB

Assign students Writing exercises 1, 2, 3 and 4 on page 74 of their Workbook and Progress check 9 on page 75.

10 Looking after yourself

UNIT AIMS

Exam preparation in Unit 10:

- decide the general message
- identify incorrect answers
- give yourself time to think
- use the present perfect
- write a good ending

TEACHER'S PRESENTATION KIT

- *Talk2Me* videos
- Speaking test videos
- Class and Workbook audio
- Workbook pages and answer key

UNIT OVERVIEW

Student's Book / Digital Student's Book SB		Workbook / Online Workbook OWB
LESSON / EXAM TASK	EXAM SKILLS / LANGUAGE FOCUS	CONSOLIDATION
Reading **3-option multiple choice (short texts)**	Deciding the general message Notices and short messages	Workbook, pp 76–77, Exercises 1, 2, 3, 4 Unit 10, Reading, Exercises 1, 2, 3, 4
Grammar 1	Present perfect simple: *for, since, already, just, yet*	Workbook, p 78, Exercises 1, 2, 3 Unit 10, Grammar 1, Exercises 1, 2, 3
Vocabulary	Words connected with *health* Words + prepositions Collocations with verbs	Workbook, pp 78–79, Exercises 1, 2, 3 Unit 10, Vocabulary, Exercises 1, 2, 3
Listening **3-option multiple choice (monologues and dialogues)**	Identifying incorrect answers	Workbook, p 80, Exercises 1, 2, 3 Unit 10, Listening, Exercises 1, 2, 3
Grammar 2	Verb patterns: verb + infinitive / *-ing*	Workbook, p 79, Exercises 1, 2 Unit 10, Grammar 2, Exercises 1, 2
Speaking **Discussion**	Giving yourself time to think	Workbook, p 81, Exercises 1, 2, 3, 4 Unit 10, Speaking, Exercises 1, 2, 3, 4
Language in Use **Open cloze**	Using the present perfect	Workbook, p 81, Exercises 1, 2 Unit 10, Language in Use, Exercises 1, 2
Writing **Picture story**	Writing a good ending	Workbook, p 82, Exercises 1, 2, 3, 4, 5, 6, 7 Unit 10, Writing, Exercises 1, 2, 3, 4, 5, 6, 7
Progress check	Check language progress for Units 9 and 10	Workbook, p 83, Progress check and Cumulative progress Progress check and Cumulative progress

Additional material

PRESENTATION KIT	TEACHER'S / STUDENT'S RESOURCE CENTRE RC	TEST GENERATOR
Talk2Me video *Let me think …*	**Unit 10 worksheets:** *Optimise your grammar* (Standard and Higher), *Optimise your vocabulary* (Standard and Higher), *Talk2Me* video, *Say it right* **Units 9–10 worksheets:** CLIL, Culture, Everyday English (TRC only), Grammar communication (TRC only)	Unit Test 10 (Standard and Higher)

READING

3-option multiple choice (short texts) | Notices and short messages

→ Student's Book, pages 102–103 SB

Lesson aims

- Focus on deciding what the general message is for notices and short texts
- Practise a 3-option multiple-choice (short texts) exam task

Lead-in

Ask students to look at the unit title ***Looking after yourself*** and describe what they can see in the photos and what they think the lesson will be about (*health*). Elicit the meaning of the phrasal verb *look after* (*take care of someone, either by helping them when they are ill or by giving them things they need*). Ask students what they do to look after themselves.

1 After students answer the questions, elicit answers from different students around the class. Don't push them to discuss health and illness if they don't want to, as this might be a sensitive area for some.

EXAM SKILL

Deciding the general message

Ask students to read the tips.

- Tell students that short messages often have the function of telling or asking people to do something.
- Point out that students should decide what the general message is when reading notices and short messages. This will help them to decide which of the three options is correct.

2 3.10 **Note: The reading text is also available on the audio CD. You may want to have students listen and read the text after doing the scanning task.**

After students complete the exercise, have them compare answers in pairs before checking their answers in open class.

Answers

1 T **2** A **3** T **4** A

3 After students complete the exercise, check their answers in open class.

Suggested answers

1 a) cook something healthy **1 b)** order a pizza **2 a)** you see / have seen a nurse **2 b)** you haven't seen a nurse

OPTIMISE YOUR EXAM

3-option multiple choice (short texts)

Ask students to read the tips.

- Remind students to be careful when deciding which option is correct. Explain that incorrect options may contain words or phrases that make them look like the right answer.
- Remind students to guess any items they are not sure of.

▼ Exam task

4 3.10 **Note: The reading text is also available on the audio CD. You may want to have students listen and read the text after doing the scanning task.**

Ask students to read the short messages. Then have them scan the texts and options, underlining any key words that seem similar in meaning before deciding which option is correct. Go through the answers in open class.

Answers

1 B (*Students … have their parents contact the school.*) **2** A (*Can we go to the cinema at 8 instead of 6?*) **3** C (*Let's buy her a present. Have you got any ideas?*) **4** B (*You must be fit.*) **5** B (*I'm interested. Are you? Let me know.*) **6** A (*I'm so upset! … I can't swim this Saturday.*)

5 Have students complete the exercise and then check the answers in open class.

Answers

1 checked **2** local **3** contact **4** appointment **5** fit **6** upset

Mixed ability

Have weaker students complete the task as it appears in the Student's Book. Ask strong students to cover the definitions in Exercise 5 and write the meanings of the highlighted words in their own words.

Cultural note

The Royal Flying Doctor Service of Australia is one of the biggest organisations of its type in the world. It was started by the missionary Reverend John Flynn as a one-year experiment in 1928. Since then it has grown to become a highly valued non-profit organisation, which is largely sustained through donations. As well as GP and nursing services, it attends emergencies 24 hours a day and covers an area of around 7.3 million km^2. The RFDS flies a total of nearly 75,000 km each day allowing its doctors and nurses to see around 750 patients.

Homework

OWB

Assign students Reading exercises 1, 2, 3 and 4 on pages 76–77 of their Workbook.

GRAMMAR 1
Present perfect simple: *for, since, already, just, yet*

→ Student's Book, page 104

Lesson aims

- Understand the correct usage of the present perfect simple with *for, since, already, just, yet*
- Practise talking about events in the past that are important now and situations in the past that continue in the present
- Write about being injured and needing help

Lead-in

Test the vocabulary from Exercise 5 on page 103. Write the following sentences on the board and ask students to say which words they define.

1 You need to make an _____ before you can see a doctor.

2 If a friend cancelled plans with you at the last minute, you might feel _____.

3 A person who does regular exercise and eats a healthy diet is probably _____.

4 Places that are near your home are in your _____ area.

Answers

1 appointment **2** upset **3** fit **4** local

Grammar in context

After students complete the task, check their answers. Then read through the *Remember* box with the class.

Remind students that they can find more information in the Grammar reference, Unit 10, page 153.

Answers

a) 3 **b)** 1 **c)** 2 **d)** 5 **e)** 4

Language note

The present perfect is often the hardest tense for students to understand fully. Explain that perfect tenses can be used to link two points in time.

In the case of the present perfect, the tense links the past to the present. In this section, students see the two most common examples of this – past events with present results and situations that started in the past and continue in the present – and five of the most common words used with the present perfect: *for, since, just, already* and *yet*.

1 After students complete the exercise, ask them to work in pairs to discuss why each sentence uses the words in the box. For example, in question 1, the answer is *just* because the action happened a short time ago.

Answers

1 just **2** yet **3** since **4** already **5** for **6** yet **7** since **8** already

2 Ask students to complete the exercise individually before checking answers in open class.

Answers

1 haven't seen, yet **2** have, had, for **3** has, just, hurt **4** haven't eaten, since **5** has, already, taken

Optional extension

Students play ***Participle tennis*** in threes. Two students work together with their books closed (Students A and B) and the third (Student C) acts as judge. Student A says a verb and Student B has to say the corresponding past participle and then a new verb. Student A has to respond with the past participle and so on. Student C monitors and checks the verbs against the Irregular verbs reference on Student's Book page 167. Students must maintain a regular rhythm. If one student pauses for too long, the other student wins a point and students change roles so they all take turns as referee.

3 Ask students to complete the exercise. Have students compare in pairs before you check their answers in open class.

Answers

1 has fallen **2** have phoned **3** already **4** hasn't arrived **5** yet **6** has been **7** has changed **8** for **9** since **10** just/already

Fast finishers

Ask students to look at all the verbs in exercises 1 and 3 and check they know all forms from memory. Tell them to think about both spelling and pronunciation and to look at the Irregular verbs reference on Student's Book page 167 if they are not sure. In pairs, students could test each other: one gives the infinitive and the other has to think of the past participle.

THINK | RESEARCH | CULTURE | LEARN | **ME**

Remind students to use the language they focused on in the lesson where possible. Then have them share their stories with a partner.

Homework

Assign students Grammar 1 exercises 1, 2 and 3 on page 78 of their Workbook.

VOCABULARY
Topic vocabulary | Word patterns | Collocations

→ Student's Book, page 105

Lesson aims

Understand the correct usage of:

- words connected with health
- word patterns with prepositions
- verb + noun collocations

Lead-in

Have students choose partners to work with in pairs or groups. Ask them to interview each other to find out how healthy they are. They should ask and answer questions about their diet and exercise regime and find out how long they have had these habits. Remind students that they don't have to answer any questions that they may feel uncomfortable about and they can make up their answers.

Words connected with *health*

1 3.11 After students complete the exercise, have them check their answers in pairs. Then play the audio for students to listen and check. Play the track again to practise pronunciation.

Answers/Audioscript

1 eye **2** ear **3** nose **4** face **5** throat **6** neck **7** back **8** stomach **9** arm **10** finger **11** leg **12** hand **13** knee **14** ankle **15** foot

2 Have students complete the exercise. Then check the answers in open class by asking different students to read out a sentence.

Answers

1 stomach **2** ankle **3** foot **4** throat **5** neck **6** eyes **7** knees **8** hand

Language note

Point out the words *headache* and *toothache* in exercises 1 and 2, on page 104 and explain that *ache* is commonly used with some parts of the body to indicate pain in that area. Most of these are written as one word, e.g. *headache, toothache, earache, backache*, but some are written as two, e.g. *stomach ache*. You might want to explain that *heartache* is used to mean a great sadness rather than physical pain.

Refer students to the Vocabulary reference, page 161, for more information on topic vocabulary.

Words + prepositions

3 3.12 Before students complete the exercise, remind them to guess the answer if they don't know. Play the audio for students to check their answers.

Answers/Audioscript

1 (C) I had a bad pain *in* my foot this morning.
2 (B) Ashley has a problem *with* his stomach so he can't eat bread.
3 (B) This is a hospital *for* children and babies.
4 (A) Sitting down all day can be a danger *to* your health.
5 (B) I'd like an appointment *with* the doctor, please.
6 (C) Have you got any medicine *for* a bad cold?
7 (A) What's the matter *with* you?
8 (B) I hope to do a course *in* nursing.

Refer students to the Vocabulary reference, page 161, for more information on word patterns.

Collocations with verbs

4 3.13 After students complete the exercise, ask them questions using the collocations, e.g. *Have you ever broken your leg? How often do you brush your teeth?*

Answers/Audioscript

1 (e) take your temperature **2** (d) make an appointment
3 (a) break your leg **4** (f) brush your teeth **5** (c) catch a cold
6 (b) feel ill or feel better

5 After students complete the exercise, ask them what clues they used from the sentences as you check answers in open class (details given in brackets in key below).

Answers

1 caught a cold (*stay in bed*) **2** broke his leg (*couldn't walk*)
3 made an appointment (*see the doctor*) **4** take your temperature (*head feels warm*) **5** brush your teeth (*so they are clean*)
6 feel ill (*tell the school nurse*)

Mixed ability

Give less confident students the nouns from Exercise 4 in the order they appear in the items in Exercise 5. They then concentrate on completing the sentences with the correct verb in the correct form. Ask stronger students to cover the verbs and nouns in Exercise 4 and try to remember the verb + noun collocations and also put the verbs in the correct form.

Refer students to the Vocabulary reference, page 161, for more information on collocations.

Homework OWB

Assign students Vocabulary exercises 1, 2 and 3 on pages 78–79 of their Workbook.

LISTENING

3-option multiple choice (monologues and dialogues)

→ Student's Book, page 106 SB

Lesson aims

- Focus on identifying incorrect answers
- Practise a 3-option multiple-choice (monologues and dialogues) exam task
- Learn words to agree and show interest

Lead-in

Review vocabulary for health problems. Either a) use gestures to elicit the words or b) give each student a health problem on a slip of paper and have them walk round the class miming their health problem for their classmates to guess. If you give each student a slip of paper, have students report what they learnt about each other after the exercise.

Suggested vocabulary:
backache, broken arm, broken leg, cold, earache, stomach ache, temperature, toothache

1 After students brainstorm their ideas in pairs, have them share their ideas with the class. Don't push students to discuss health and illness if they don't want to participate, as this might be a sensitive area for some.

EXAM SKILL

Identifying incorrect answers

Ask students to read the tips.

- Encourage students to think of different paraphrases for the options that they might hear in the audio. For example, *watch football = see the football match, look after her pet = take the dog for a walk*, etc.
- Tell students that they must listen very carefully for the meaning of what is being said. They may hear the exact words that are in the incorrect options, so they need to understand how they are being used in the context of the monologue or dialogue.

2 3.14 Before students listen, tell them to read the questions. Play the audio. Then elicit answers from students around the class.

Answers

1 A **2** B **3** B **4** A

OPTIMISE YOUR EXAM

3-option multiple choice (monologues and dialogues)

Ask students to read the tips.

- Remind students to pay attention to the information given in the question. Each question includes details of context, the question and the three options. The details of context are important as they give students valuable information before they listen to the audio. It can tell them the relationship of the speakers, whether there are one or two speakers, and some situational information so they generally know what the conversation or monologue will be about.
- Point out to students that in this type of task they will usually hear distracting information or information that is tempting them to select the wrong option.
- Encourage students to pay attention both times they listen so they can check if they have chosen the correct option and confirm why the other two options are incorrect.

Exam task

3 3.15 Have students read the five questions before listening. Encourage them to underline key words and to think of possible paraphrases for the words they underline. Then play the audio and ask students to compare their answers. Ask pairs to compare answers but wait until Exercise 4 to check them in open class.

Answers

a routine event or habit (present simple): 2, 3
a time in the past (past simple): 4, 6
an unknown time in the past (present perfect): 1, 5

4 3.15 Play the audio again and then check answers in open class.

Answers

1 A (*I'd rather do something – like play tennis. … Oh, OK, let's do that.*) **2** A (*I can't do any sports for a week.*) **3** C (*… you haven't taken the dog for a walk yet, have you? … Not until you take your pet out. It needs some exercise.*) **4** B (*I offered to take him to the doctor …*) **5** B (*I'm afraid Peter was ill today. … he looked terrible and he kept coughing.*)

Optional extension 3.15

Play the audio a final time and have students write which information helped them to figure out the answers. Ask students to compare their notes in pairs before going over answers in open class.

Answers

headphones, MP3 players, tablet, app, smartphones, electronic gadgets, internet, online video games in virtual worlds, texts, DVDs, email

THINK | RESEARCH | CULTURE | **LEARN** | ME

3.15 Play the audio and then check answers in open class.

Answers

1 Good **2** Yeah **3** pity **4** dear

Homework OWB

Assign students Listening exercises 1, 2 and 3 on page 80 of their Workbook.

GRAMMAR 2

Verb patterns: verb + infinitive / *-ing*

→ Student's Book, page 107 SB

Lesson aims

- Identify verbs followed by the infinitive or *-ing* form
- Practise using verbs followed by the infinitive or *-ing* form
- Write about getting fit and being healthier

Lead-in

Give the class a spelling test. Read out ten *-ing* forms of different verbs for students to write down. Check answers with the class, asking students to spell the words out as you write them on the board.

Suggested vocabulary:

finishing, chatting, inviting, becoming, stopping, watching, travelling, brushing, practising, succeeding

Grammar in context

Knowing which verbs are followed by an infinitive and which by *-ing* is important in all parts of official exams.

Tell students to refer to the information in the *Remember* box to help them complete the task. Check their answers. Explain that some verbs are followed by an infinitive and some are followed by an *-ing* form and students have to learn which verbs go with each form.

Remind students that they can find more information in the Grammar reference, Unit 10, page 153.

Answers

a offer, decide, tell **b** hate, keep

Language note

Most verbs need to be followed by either the infinitive (e.g. *decide, hope, learn, refuse, plan, want*) or the *-ing* form (e.g. *avoid, enjoy, finish, keep, mind, stop*). However there are some verbs that can be followed by either (e.g. *like, love, start, try*). Sometimes there is little or no difference in meaning between the two, and sometimes there is quite a large difference. For example, *He tried to eat healthier food.* (= but this was very hard for him and he wasn't able to do it) is not the same as *He tried eating healthier food.* (= he experimented with this to see what effect it had).

1 Ask students to complete the exercise individually. Check answers in open class.

Answers

1 decided **2** to help **3** didn't mind **4** hoped **5** stopped **6** kept

Extra support

Point out that in Exercise 1 the verb choice usually depended on the form of the verb **after** the options in bold, e.g. *1 My dad* ***decided / enjoyed*** *to do* … Explain that in Exercise 2, the form of the verb will depend on the verbs that come **before** the gaps, e.g. *1 Leo decided* … Ask students to underline these before starting the exercise (*stopped, enjoyed, wanted, didn't mind, spent time*).

2 After students complete the exercise, have them compare answers in pairs before checking answers in open class.

Answers

1 to make **2** taking **3** hearing **4** to eat **5** taking **6** putting on

3 Focus students' attention on the picture and ask students if they like to travel by car. Encourage them to give reasons for their answers.
Then have students complete the exercise individually. Check answers in open class.

Answers

1 to visit **2** to feel **3** travelling **4** to try **5** to enjoy **6** getting / to get **7** running **8** doing

Fast finishers

Ask students to make two lists: *verbs + infinitive* and *verbs + -ing* and include all the verbs they have seen in exercises 1–3.

Answers

verbs + infinitive: agree, begin, choose, decide, help, hope, need, offer, try, want

verbs + -ing: enjoy, finish, keep, not mind, spend time, stop, try

SAY IT RIGHT

/ɪ/ and /iː/ TRC

For the *Say it right* pronunciation activity and instructions, go to the Teacher's Resource Centre.

THINK | RESEARCH | CULTURE | LEARN | **ME**

Have students make a list of their ideas individually. Then have students share their ideas with a partner.

Homework

OWB

Assign students Grammar 2 exercises 1 and 2 on page 79 of their Workbook.

Assign students the Flipped classroom tasks on page 108 of their Student's Book if you'd like them to prepare for the next lesson. To complete this task, students need to watch the *Talk2Me* video which can be found on the Resource Centre.

SPEAKING
Discussion

→ Student's Book, page 108 SB

Lesson aims

- Focus on using phrases to give yourself time to think
- Practise a discussion exam task
- Keep an English diary for a day

The *Talk2Me* video in this unit focuses on buying tickets for a concert. The people in the video talk about a concert, the price of the tickets and queueing to buy tickets over the phone.

Students answer some comprehension questions and then listen for key phrases in the video.

The video can be used in one of two ways:

Flipped classroom

Flipped classroom option

Using this approach, students watch the video and complete the exercises for homework. This prepares students for the speaking lesson by introducing them to the topic and the key phrases to use in the exam task. Teachers who use this method will find they have more class time to spend on activating the target language and developing fluency for the final task.

Talk2Me worksheet

Ask students to also complete the *Talk2Me* worksheet on the Resource Centre for more detailed comprehension exercises and more practice of the key phrases.

Classroom option

1 Ask students to spend a minute or two reading the questions. Play the *Talk2Me* video for students to complete the exercise. Play the video again, if necessary, before checking their answers.

2 Play the *Talk2Me* video again, so students underline the phrases in the *Phrase expert* box. Pause the video from time to time if necessary. Check answers in open class.

Talk2Me worksheet

Ask students to also complete the *Talk2Me* worksheet on the Resource Centre for more detailed comprehension exercises and more practice of the key phrases.

Answers

The transcript and answer key for the *Talk2Me* video exercises and Worksheet can be found on the Teacher's Resource Centre.

Lead-in

Write these jumbled words on the board and ask students to reorder the letters in them:

kareb na mar *acarehe* *chatc a locd* *geandab* *ampereretut* *nicedime*

Answers

break an arm, earache, catch a cold, bandage, temperature, medicine

3 3.16 Have students complete the exercise before checking answers in open class.

Answers

1 example **2** opinion and example **3** opinion **4** example

4 3.16 Play the audio again so students can complete the exercise. Have them compare answers before checking in open class.

Answers

1 I used to … **2** well, I think … / I only eat it when … **3** let me see / Probably … **4** … for example …

5 Put students in pairs to complete the exercise. Tell them to use the phrases in the *Phrase expert* box.

Answers

Students' own answers

EXAM SKILL

Giving yourself time to think

Ask students to read the tips.

- Point out that candidates are not usually given time to prepare what they are going to say in Speaking tests, so learning useful phrases to stall for time is essential. Using these phrases also demonstrates to the examiner that they have the confidence and ability to express what they want to say.
- Give students some useful phrases, e.g. *Let me see, Just give me a moment, Well …, That's a good question.* Try to use these phrases yourself in the classroom and encourage students to get used to using them when necessary.

6 3.16 Play the track again for students to listen and complete the exercise. Check answers in open class.

Answers

Speaker 2: Erm … well
Speaker 3: Hmm – let me see

OPTIMISE YOUR EXAM

Discussion

Ask students to read the tips.

- Explain that there is a part in many Speaking tests where students work together in a discussion without the examiner, who may even look away to discourage candidates from addressing conversation to him/her.
- It is important that the candidates develop and sustain a conversation taking turns to speak and respond to each other, showing interest and being careful not to interrupt each other.
- To avoid long silences, encourage students to ask their partner a question, e.g. *Is there anything else that you would like to know? Are you interested in …?*

▾ Exam task

7 Assign each student a letter, A or B, and put them into A/B pairs. Give them a moment to look at their questions. Time students (two minutes) and give them an update, e.g. *One minute to go …* Remind students to use phrases from the *Phrase expert* box for giving themselves time to think. Walk round, monitoring students for good use of language and errors to go over at the end of the activity.

Write any errors on the board and go through them with students, eliciting corrections from them where possible. After the class feedback, students could then repeat this activity with another partner, to try to improve their performance.

Suggested answers

Student A's questions

What's the address?
What does it sell?
Is it big or small?
Is it closed on Sundays?
What's the telephone number?

Student B's questions

What can I/you learn?
When are the classes for 14 year olds?
How much does a class cost?
What's the telephone number?
Who can I contact about the classes?

Extra support

Put students with different partners to complete Exercise 7 again. Time the students as before. Then put students in different pairings to complete the two-minute timed task one last time. Finally, elicit some students' reasons for their opinions.

THINK | RESEARCH | CULTURE | LEARN | **ME**

If appropriate, you could ask students to discuss their diary entries in pairs. Otherwise you may wish to have a class discussion on healthy food and exercise in general.

Homework OWB

Assign students Speaking exercises 1, 2, 3 and 4 on page 81 of their Workbook.

LANGUAGE IN USE

Open cloze

→ Student's Book, page 109 SB

Lesson aims

- Focus on using the present perfect
- Practise an open-cloze exam task
- Research foods that are good for your body

Lead-in

Ask students to work in pairs and role play different situations at the doctor's. One student is a doctor and the other is a patient. Have the patients describe their problems to the doctor, using *ache*, *pain*, *hurt* or *feel* and have the doctors give advice, e.g.

Doctor: *What's the problem today, Mr García?*

Patient: *My back aches doctor. It hurts a lot.*

Doctor: *Oh dear. You should lie down and rest. And don't do sports!*

Have students change roles. Walk round, monitoring students' use of the words *ache*, *pain*, *hurt* and *feel* and their suggestions. Give students feedback at the end of the exercise.

1 After students complete the exercise, have them share their ideas with the class, giving reasons and examples.

EXAM SKILL

Using the present perfect

Ask students to read the tips.

- Remind students that they have studied the present perfect in Unit 6 and in this unit. Tell them that a range of tenses, including the present perfect, can be tested in all sections of exams.
- Encourage students to refer to the Irregular verb reference on page 167. This is where they can find a list of high-frequency verbs to help them remember the past participle when using the present perfect.

2 After students complete the exercise, have them practise asking and answering the questions in pairs.

Answers

1 c **2** e **3** a **4** g **5** d **6** f

Extra support

Ask students to underline the past participles in Exercise 2.

Answers

Students should underline:

1 eaten **2** eaten **3** made **4** had **5** done, left **6** tried

3 Have students complete the exercise, and then compare answers in pairs before checking in open class.

Answers

1 already **2** for **3** Have **4** taken **5** have **6** since

Optional extension

Draw a large + on one side of the board and a large – on the other side. Ask all students to stand up. Choose a strong student and ask, *Do you like going to the dentist's?* and point to the negative sign on the board. If the student answers with the correct short answer, i.e. *No, I don't,* he or she stays standing. If the student answers incorrectly, he or she is eliminated and sits down. Repeat the process, nominating students at random. Any student who hesitates too long or makes a mistake is knocked out. Continue until only one student is left standing.

OPTIMISE YOUR EXAM

Open cloze

Ask students to read the tips.

- Remind students that they have learnt some of the time expressions that indicate when the present perfect tense is being used. Tell them to look for these clues when completing open-cloze exam tasks.
- Tell students that they only need to write one word in each gap, never two words or any contracted words (can't, isn't, haven't, etc.) as they count as two words.

Exam task

4 Before students complete the exercise, ask them to scan the text to understand the type of message (an email) and general topic (Kerry's health). Ask students to complete the exercise. Then have them compare their answers in pairs before checking them in open class.

Answers

1 had **2** for **3** since **4** of **5** to

THINK | **RESEARCH** | CULTURE | LEARN | ME

If you have access to the internet, students can research information and prepare lists in class. Alternatively, students could prepare this for homework. If you wish, divide the class into three groups and ask each group to research one area. Regroup students so there is one student who has prepared each area in each group. Then have students present their findings to each other.

Homework OWB

Assign students Language in Use exercises 1 and 2 on page 81 of their Workbook.

WRITING
Picture story

→ Student's Book, pages 110–111 SB

Lesson aims

- Focus on writing a good ending
- Plan and write a picture story exam task

Lead-in

Write the phrase *being healthy* on the board. Divide the class into pairs and ask students to think of as many different ways to be healthy as they can, e.g. *doing sport and exercise, eating fruit and vegetables, drinking water, getting enough sleep,* etc. Have students share their lists with the class to see if they have similar or different lists of ideas.

1 Have students look at the photo and elicit what they see. After students discuss the questions, elicit answers from different students around the class.

2 Ask students to complete the exercise in pairs or groups. Monitor and offer suggestions if appropriate.

Answers

Students' own answers

EXAM SKILL

Writing a good ending

Ask students to read the tips.

- Tell students that their stories should have a clear beginning, middle and end. Tell them that they will be assessed on the organisation of their ideas. Other common assessment criteria are content and language.
- When they conclude their stories, ask students to think of a sentence that says how the main character(s) felt. This can make a good ending.

Optional extension

Put students into pairs. Have them label some of the vocabulary they see in Exercise 2 in three categories: nouns, verbs, adjectives. Elicit answers from different students around the class and write them on the board under each category.

Suggested answers

Nouns: skateboards, skate park, helmets, boys, mobile/phone, nurse/doctor, hospital

Verbs: skate, fall, call, hurt, help

Adjectives: fun, excited, sore/painful, worried, nice/kind

3 Ask students to work in pairs to complete the exercise before checking answers in open class.

Answers

1 E **2** S **3** E **4** E **5** S

4 After students complete the exercise, have them correct each other's work, checking for any grammar or spelling mistakes. If you have time, ask students to read their stories to a new partner or the whole class.

Answers

Students' own answers

OPTIMISE YOUR EXAM

Picture story

Ask students to read the tips.

- Tell students that they need to refer to all three images in their story or they will receive lower marks.
- Point out that they must refer to the pictures in chronological order. For example, they need to write about the first image, then the second image and finally the third image and only in this order.

Exam task

5 Ask students to complete the exercise and then check answers in open class.

Suggested answers

Picture 1: cold, rainy, unhappy
Picture 2: sick/ill, not well/unwell, unhappy
Picture 3: sick/ill, hot/warm, happy

6 Ask students to complete the exercise and then check answers.

Answers

1 because **2** so **3** because **4** so

7 Plan Ask students to complete the writing plan. You may want to look at their plans to check them and give advice and suggestions for improvement before students take the next step.

8 Write Students write their stories. If there is not enough time, set this and the subsequent checklist exercise for homework.

9 Check Students complete the checklist before they hand in their stories.

Optional extension

For a slightly longer writing task, refer students to the task in the Writing reference (SB page 164). It includes an annotated sample text and related writing task to challenge your students a little more.

Homework

OWB

Assign students Writing exercises 1–7 on page 82 of their Workbook and Progress check 10 on page 83.

Answers PROGRESS CHECK Units 9–10

Exercise 1
1 lived **2** lie **3** gives **4** 'd/would be **5** 'll/will go **6** won **7** pass **8** 'll/will enjoy **9** 'd/would feel **10** won't need

Exercise 2
1 for **2** taking **3** with **4** feels **5** trying

Exercise 3
1 nose **2** ears **3** stomach **4** feet **5** neck **6** hand **7** legs **8** dentist **9** back **10** bandage

Exercise 4
1 for **2** to work **3** yet **4** just **5** going **6** already **7** eating **8** taking **9** since **10** learning

Exercise 5
1 G **2** F **3** D **4** E **5** A

Exercise 6
1 sunny **2** river **3** snow **4** thunderstorm **5** clouds **6** ice **7** foggy **8** hill **9** wet **10** forest

11 The world of work

UNIT AIMS

Exam preparation in Unit 11:

- identify incorrect answer options
- take notes
- talk about jobs
- use indefinite and relative pronouns
- plan an article

TEACHER'S PRESENTATION KIT

- *Talk2Me* videos
- Speaking test videos
- Class and Workbook audio
- Workbook pages and answer key

UNIT OVERVIEW

Student's Book / Digital Student's Book (SB)		Workbook / Online Workbook (OWB)
LESSON / EXAM TASK	EXAM SKILLS / LANGUAGE FOCUS	CONSOLIDATION
Reading **3-option multiple choice (long text)**	Identifying incorrect answer options A magazine article	Workbook, pp 84–85, Exercises 1, 2, 3, 4 Unit 11, Reading, Exercises 1, 2, 3, 4
Grammar 1	Indefinite pronouns	Workbook, p 86, Exercises 1, 2 Unit 11, Grammar 1, Exercises 1, 2
Vocabulary	Words connected with *work and jobs* Words with *-ian / -ress / -ist / -er / -r* Words + prepositions	Workbook, pp 86–87, Exercises 1, 2, 3 Unit 11, Vocabulary, Exercises 1, 2, 3
Listening **Gap fill**	Taking notes	Workbook, p 88, Exercises 1, 2 Unit 11, Listening, Exercises 1, 2
Grammar 2	Relative clauses: *who, which, that*	Workbook, p 87, Exercises 1, 2 Unit 11, Grammar 2, Exercises 1, 2
Speaking **Questions**	Talking about jobs	Workbook, pp 88–89, Exercises 1, 2, 3 Unit 11, Speaking, Exercises 1, 2, 3
Language in Use **Open cloze**	Using indefinite and relative pronouns	Workbook, p 89, Exercises 1, 2, 3 Unit 11, Language in Use, Exercises 1, 2, 3
Writing **An article**	Planning an article	Workbook, p 90, Exercises 1, 2, 3, 4, 5, 6 Unit 11, Writing, Exercises 1, 2, 3, 4, 5, 6
		Workbook, p 91, Progress check and Cumulative progress Progress check and Cumulative progress

Additional material

PRESENTATION KIT	TEACHER'S / STUDENT'S RESOURCE CENTRE (RC)	TEST GENERATOR
Talk2Me video *My mum is a …*	**Unit 11 worksheets:** *Optimise your grammar* (Standard and Higher), *Optimise your vocabulary* (Standard and Higher), *Talk2Me* video, *Say it right* **Units 11–12 worksheets:** CLIL, Culture, Everyday English (TRC only), Grammar communication (TRC only)	Unit Test 11 (Standard and Higher)

READING

3-option multiple choice (long text) | A magazine article

→ Student's Book, pages 114–115 SB

Lesson aims

- Focus on identifying incorrect answer options
- Practise a 3-option multiple-choice (long text) exam task
- Think about working on the Children's Railway

Lead-in

Ask students to look at the unit title ***The world of work*** and the photos, and ask them what they think the unit will be about (*different types of work and jobs*). Ask them to think of jobs that are typically 'nine to five' jobs, e.g. *secretary, accountant* and elicit why they think those jobs have specific working hours. Elicit the jobs they can see represented in the photos. (*architect/builder, businessman, chef, comedian/singer, doctor, farmer, firefighter, nurse, pilot, police officer, sailor, student*)

1 After students discuss the questions, elicit some answers from the class and try to develop a class discussion on students' future job plans.

EXAM SKILL

Identifying incorrect answer options

- Tell students the three options for each question may contain the same or similar words in the text.
- Encourage students to underline the section where they have found the answer to the question, then ask themselves which option accurately reflects the underlined section of the text.

2 Check students' answers.

Answers

A, B and C are correct.

3 After students complete the exercise, go through the reasons for their answers as you check them in open class.

Answers

1 C **2** A **3** B **4** The trains must leave and arrive on time

OPTIMISE YOUR EXAM

3-option multiple choice (long text)

Ask students to read the tips.

- Remind students that they can decide which option is correct by using a process of elimination, as they did in Exercise 3.
- Encourage students to check if the option isn't stated in the text or if it doesn't match the information in the paragraph. This process can help them to choose the correct option.

Exam task

4 3.17 **Note: The reading text is also available on the audio CD. You may want to have students listen and read the text before doing the exam task.**

Remind students that the questions come in chronological order in relation to the text. However, question 5 can be a question related to the main idea or purpose of the text. After students complete the exercise, check answers in open class and elicit the evidence.

Answers

1 B (*… nearly everyone who works there is a child.*)
2 B (*… 11 kilometres, through the hills in the west of the city.*)
3 A (*All the workers have to wear a smart uniform …*)
4 C (*Anyone who doesn't get good marks at school won't get a job.*)
5 A (*… over 300,000 customers use the railway to get to work …*)

Fast finishers

Ask students to find evidence in the text for their answers.

Cultural note

The first section of the Children's Railway in Budapest opened in 1948 and this was followed by two further sections in 1949 and 1950. The line closed briefly in the 1950s but has been operational ever since. The narrow gauge railway has eight stations and holds the Guinness World Record for the longest children's railway in the world. Workers are local schoolchildren who have achieved excellent grades and as a reward are allowed to miss school two days a month to work on the railway. All the children receive four months training before they start and are under adult supervision. The railway is a popular excursion into the Buda Hills.

5 Go through the first definition as a class and then have students find the rest of the words individually. Check answers in open class.

Answers

1 uniform **2** clean **3** transport **4** ticket **5** late **6** staff **7** timetable **8** safe

Mixed ability

Pair less confident and stronger students together. Stronger students cover Exercise 5 and less confident students read each definition to their partner. Students agree to each answer together before continuing.

Homework

OWB

Assign students Reading exercises 1, 2, 3 and 4 on pages 84–85 of their Workbook.

GRAMMAR 1
Indefinite pronouns

→ Student's Book, page 116 SB

Lesson aims

- Understand the correct usage of indefinite pronouns
- Practise using indefinite pronouns to talk about people, places, things and actions without saying who or what they are
- Discuss how young people prepare for the world of work

Lead-in

Write *On the railway* on the board and the following word skeletons around it:

_ng_n_ _r
p_ss_n g_r
tr_ _n dr_v_r
t_ck_t s_ll_r
st_t_ _n m_n_g_r

Put students into pairs to complete the words. Check their answers in open class. Then ask students what they remember about the article they read in the previous lesson.

Answers
engineer, passenger, train driver, ticket seller, station manager

Grammar in context

While students are completing the exercise, focus their attention on the indefinite pronouns in items 1–5. Check their answers and ask students to read the information in the *Remember* box. Ask students questions to check their understanding, e.g. *What do engineers have to check?* (*Everything.*) *Did you bring everything you need to school today?*

Remind students that they can find more information in the Grammar reference, Unit 11, page 154.

Answers
a -thing **b** -one **c** -where

Language note

Tell students that we use indefinite pronouns to replace nouns without specifying which noun they replace. Explain that they are made up of two parts: The first part, *every-*, *some-* and *any-*, indicates the number of things/places/people we are referring to, and the second part, *-thing*, *-one* and *-where*, indicates what we are talking about.

1 If necessary, encourage students to refer back to the Grammar in context box to help them complete the exercise. Check answers in open class.

Answers
1 everywhere **2** anything **3** everything **4** someone **5** somewhere **6** something

2 After students complete the exercise, have them check their answers in pairs before checking in open class.

Answers
1 Everyone **2** anything **3** everywhere **4** Someone **5** anywhere **6** something

Mixed ability

Ask all students to cover the box in Exercise 2. Have stronger students complete the exercise with appropriate words without looking at the options in the box. Give weaker students the first part of the word for items 1, 3 and 5 (*1 Every-*, *3 every-*, *5 any-*) and the second part of the word for items 2, 4 and 6 (*2 -thing*, *4 -one*, *6 -thing*).

3 Tell students to look at the words before and after the gaps to help them complete the exercise. Have different students read out the text to check answers in open class.

Answers
1 B **2** A **3** B **4** B **5** B **6** B **7** C **8** A

SAY IT RIGHT

/θ/ TRC

For the *Say it right* pronunciation activity and instructions, go to the Teacher's Resource Centre.

THINK | RESEARCH | **CULTURE** | LEARN | ME

Have students work in pairs to brainstorm ideas. Then have them share their ideas with the class and encourage a class discussion if there is time.

Homework OWB
Assign students Grammar 1 exercises 1 and 2 on page 86 of their Workbook.

VOCABULARY
Topic vocabulary | Word formation | Word patterns

→ Student's Book, page 117 SB

Lesson aims

Understand the correct usage of:

- words connected with work and jobs
- suffixes used to form jobs
- word patterns with prepositions

Lead-in

Write the following sentences on the board:

1 My mum _____ in an office – she's a lawyer.

2 My dad doesn't really like his _____. He says it's boring.

3 My sister is a sales assistant. She has a lot of _____ at the weekend.

Have students discuss which word they think completes each sentence. Check their answers and make sure students understand that *work* can be a verb, as in the first sentence, or an uncountable noun, as in the last sentence. Point out that *job* is always a noun and can be singular, as in the second sentence, or plural (*My sister has two jobs – in the mornings she works at the swimming pool and in the afternoons in a local café.*).

Answers

1 works **2** job **3** work

Words connected with *work and jobs*

1 3.18 After students complete the exercise, play the audio for them to listen and check their answers. Then ask them to write a description of another job. Have them share their descriptions with the class and encourage students to guess.

Answers/Audioscript

1 someone who writes articles for a newspaper: *journalist*
2 someone who flies planes: *pilot*
3 someone who cleans an office or a home: *cleaner*
4 someone who is a member of the police: *police officer*
5 someone who works in a theatre or in films: *actor*
6 someone who helps you in a shop: *shop assistant*
7 someone who stops fires: *firefighter*
8 someone who designs or builds things such as roads, bridges or machines: *engineer*

2 3.19 Have students complete the exercise individually. Then ask them to compare answers in pairs before playing the audio for them to check.

Answers/Audioscript

Thousands of us love using social networking. But have you ever thought of it as a *career*? There are jobs for young people in most of the big social media *companies*. As a new *worker*, you might be a *social media officer*, for example – working with some of the social media *managers*, working on the website and going to *meetings*. And if you're good at what you do, you'll get the chance to do different jobs and *earn* more money. So instead of being a social media *customer*, why not think about becoming a member of *staff*?

Refer students to the Vocabulary reference, page 162, for more information on topic vocabulary.

Words with *-ian / -ress / -ist / -er / -r*

3 3.20 After students complete the exercise and check their answers, elicit what each profession does, e.g. *A musician plays an instrument.*

Answers/Audioscript

-ian: musician
-ress: waitress
-ist: artist, chemist, dentist, journalist, receptionist
-er: cleaner, engineer, farmer, footballer, photographer, waiter
-r: driver, explorer, manager, writer

4 After students complete the exercise, ask them to write a similar sentence about a member of their family.

Answers

1 farmer **2** musician **3** receptionist **4** waiter/waitress **5** dentist **6** manager

Refer students to the Vocabulary reference, page 162, for more information on word formation.

Words + prepositions

5 3.21 Ask students to complete the exercise individually. Then play the audio for them to check their answers.

Answers/Audioscript

1 (A) Alex is the manager *of* a clothes shop in the city centre.

2 (B) Charlie hopes to get a diploma *in* music from a college in London.

3 (B) Steph is a receptionist and she works *for* a company that makes computers.

4 (C) Judy is the singer *in* a local rock band.

5 (C) Michael is a writer *of* children's books.

6 (B) We have an important meeting today *with* the manager.

Extra support

Write and explain the following items on the board as a reference for students to complete Exercise 5:

i be the [secretary] for a company that [makes sweets]

ii be the [writer] of [popular novels]

iii be the [lawyer] of [his sister's company]

iv have an [interview] with [the accountant]

v have a [degree] in [physics]

vi be the [drummer] in [a famous group]

Point out that the sections in brackets can be changed for other similar words or phrases. Elicit some examples as you check the answers.

Refer students to the Vocabulary reference, page 162, for more information on word patterns.

Homework OWB

Assign students Vocabulary exercises 1, 2 and 3 on pages 86–87 of their Workbook.

LISTENING
Gap fill

→ Student's Book, page 118

Lesson aims

- Listen and take notes of specific information
- Practise a gap-fill exam task
- Research young business people

Lead-in

Play the game ***The Alphabet Race***. Divide the class into teams to make a list of a job for every letter of the alphabet. Give students a three-minute time limit and encourage them to use their imagination. Point out that some letters of the alphabet are very difficult or impossible, so students shouldn't spend too long on any one letter. Go through students' answers, giving two points for unique words and one point for words shared by two or more teams. The team with the most points wins.

Possible answers

High-level items in brackets

actor, **b**uilder, **c**leaner, **d**entist, **e**lectrician, **f**irefighter, (**g**eologist), **h**airdresser, (**i**nterpreter), **j**ournalist, (**k**indergarten teacher), **l**awyer, **m**anager, **n**urse, (**o**ptician), **p**olice officer, **q**ueen, **r**eceptionist, **s**cientist, **t**eacher, (**u**mpire), **v**et, **w**aitress, (**x**-ray technician), (**y**ard manager), (**z**oo keeper)

1 Ask students to look at the photo and describe what is happening (*A young woman has made some doughnuts and she is …*). Then have students discuss the questions. Elicit some answers from different students around the class and come to a consensus on the best business idea.

EXAM SKILL

Taking notes

Ask students to read the tips.

- Tell students that learning how to take useful notes is an important technique both for English exam tasks and for their everyday lives.
- Tell students it is impossible to write down everything they hear and is unproductive if they try. Remind them to write just the important words and phrases and encourage them to focus on these when listening.
- Remind students that bullet points, arrows, etc. can also be as useful as words to help show how things connect to each other and to give structure to their notes.

2 3.22 Before playing the audio, tell students that they need to listen very carefully and write the words that are spelled out. Elicit answers from students from around the class.

Answers

1 Armitage **2** Bicester **3** Vaughan **4** Chloe **5** Edinburgh

3 3.23 Tell students that they are going to hear Ed giving information about something he organised. Play the audio for students to listen and correct the information in the notes. Have them compare answers in pairs before you check them in open class.

Answers

1 July **2** garden **3** 80 people **4** Jayveeland **5** £200

Extra support

Give students a pool of information on the board containing the five answers to Exercise 3 and two incorrect answers/ distractors for each item:

June garden Jaybeeland 280 £220 18 town July £2200 £200 80 house Jayveeland Jay Jay Land April

Tell students to refer to the information on the board while they complete the task in Exercise 3. Remind them that some of the items are distractors.

OPTIMISE YOUR EXAM

Gap fill

Ask students to read the tips.

- Stress that in this type of exam task, students are expected to write only one word, a number, a date or a time in the gaps.
- Remind students that in this type of task, they should check that the answer they have written is correct during the second listening.

Exam task

4 3.24 Ask students to read the notes before they start. Remind them that they should write only one word, a number, a date or a time for each answer. Play the audio for students to complete the exercise. Ask them to compare answers in pairs, but don't check answers in open class until Exercise 5.

5 3.24 Play the audio again and then check answers in open class.

Answers

1 Guangzhou **2** fruit **3** Saturday(s) **4** 5/five **5** 52

THINK | **RESEARCH** | CULTURE | LEARN | ME

If you have access to the internet, students can research information in class. Alternatively, they could prepare this for homework and present their information at the start of the next lesson.

Homework

OWB

Assign students Listening exercises 1 and 2 on page 88 of their Workbook.

GRAMMAR 2
Relative clauses: *who, which, that*

→ Student's Book, page 119 SB

Lesson aims

- Focus on relative clauses with *who, which* and *that*
- Practise giving more information about a person or a thing

Lead-in

Ask students what they remember about the listening they heard in the previous lesson. Write what they say on the board, making notes of the most important points. Then reflect on what they learnt about note-taking by having them look at the notes you took.

Grammar in context

While students are completing the task, encourage them to refer to the information in the *Remember* box if they aren't sure. Check answers in open class.

Remind students that they can find more information in the Grammar reference, Unit 11, page 154.

Answers

a) buying **b)** the factory **c)** a business

Language note

Explain that relative pronouns refer to the people or thing(s) we are describing. Tell students that the information we add after a relative pronoun must be about the same people or thing(s) we are talking about.

1 While students are completing the exercise, remind them to identify what the relative pronouns are describing. Ask students to compare their answers with a partner before checking in open class.

Answers

1 which **2** who **3** that **4** which **5** which **6** who **7** who **8** who

2 Go through the example as a class. Tell students that in some cases there is more than one possible way to combine sentences. Explain that in this case, *Alex, who works in his dad's office, is a manager.*, is also a possibility. Ask students to compare their answers in pairs before checking answers in open class.

Answers

2 There is a factory near here which/that makes cars. / There is a factory which/that makes cars near here.
3 Fred is the waiter who/that took our order.
4 I would like a desk which/that is near the window.
5 They had a meeting which/that was with the new manager.

Mixed ability

Give less confident students the first two words and the last two words of each sentence and the relative pronoun(s) they should use in each case, e.g. *1 Alex is … dad's office. (who/that) 2 There is … near here. (which/that).* Students who finish early can look back at the sentences in Exercise 1 and see how they could separate them into two sentences, e.g. *1 It's a question. No-one has the answer to it. 2 The secretary works in our office. He is away today.*

3 Focus students' attention on the article and have them complete the exercise individually. Check answers in open class.

Answers

1 who/that **2** which/that **3** who/that **4** that/which **5** that/which **6** who/that **7** that/which **8** who/that

Fast finishers

Write these definitions on the board and ask students to find the words in the text in Exercise 3.

1 This is a group of firefighters who work together.
2 This is the building that firefighters work in.
3 These are the people who are staying in a hotel.

Answers

1 watch **2** fire station **3** guests

Homework OWB

Assign students Grammar 2 exercises 1 and 2 on page 87 of their Workbook.

Assign students the Flipped classroom tasks on page 120 of their Student's Book if you'd like them to prepare for the next lesson. To complete this task, students need to watch the *Talk2Me* video which can be found on the Resource Centre.

SPEAKING
Questions

→ Student's Book, page 120 SB

Lesson aims

- Focus on talking about jobs and work
- Practise answering personal questions

The *Talk2Me* video in this unit focuses on arranging a guest list for a birthday party at a restaurant. The people in the video talk about who they would like to invite to the party and the number of people who can attend.

Students answer some comprehension questions and then listen for key phrases in the video.

The video can be used in one of two ways:

Flipped classroom

Flipped classroom option

Using this approach, students watch the video and complete the exercises for homework. This prepares students for the speaking lesson by introducing them to the topic and the key phrases to use in the exam task. Teachers who use this method will find they have more class time to spend on activating the target language and developing fluency for the final task.

Talk2Me worksheet

Ask students to also complete the *Talk2Me* worksheet on the Resource Centre for more detailed comprehension exercises and more practice of the key phrases.

Classroom option

1 Ask students to spend a minute or two reading the questions. Play the *Talk2Me* video for students to complete the exercise. Play the video again, if necessary, before checking their answers.

2 Play the *Talk2Me* video again, so students underline the phrases in the *Phrase expert* box. Pause the video from time to time if necessary. Check answers in open class.

Talk2Me worksheet

Ask students to also complete the *Talk2Me* worksheet on the Resource Centre for more detailed comprehension exercises and more practice of the key phrases.

Answers

The transcript and answer key for the *Talk2Me* video exercises and Worksheet can be found on the Teacher's Resource Centre.

Lead-in

Stand with your back to the board. Ask for a volunteer to come to the front and write a job on the board for the rest of the class to see. You mustn't look at what's on the board. Nominate a student and ask him or her a closed, *yes/no* question to try to find out 'your' job, e.g. *José, do I work in an office?* Elicit a complete short answer, e.g. *No, you don't.* Tell students you have a maximum of ten questions to guess what your job is and nominate a different student to answer each question. When you have guessed correctly, repeat that activity with a volunteer and continue with more students.

3 Ask students to complete the exercise in pairs. Set a strict time limit of one minute each for questions 1 and 2. Then, after each question, elicit answers from students around the class. The pair with the most correct answers wins. Then give students time to tell each other what their family members do.

4 3.25 Have students read the sentences before you play the audio. Check answers in open class and elicit the correct information.

Answers

1 F (She's got two brothers and two sisters.) **2** F (He's a photographer.) **3** F (He doesn't work in an office.) **4** T **5** F (Her mum is a journalist. Her dad is a lawyer.)

EXAM SKILL

Talking about jobs

Ask students to read the tips.

- Encourage students to learn language in chunks, e.g. phrases or collocations including the word *work.* (This is the type of language that is often tested in Language in Use exam tasks.)
- Remind students the present simple is often used with the adverbs of frequency *never, sometimes, often, usually* and *always* to talk about jobs and routines.
- Also remind them that the present continuous is used with expressions like *at the moment* and *right now* to talk about what someone is doing now.
- Explain that the present continuous can also be used to talk about something that is temporary. Point out that sentences can combine the present simple (to talk about the normal situation) with the present continuous (to talk about a different situation that is just happening for a short time), e.g. *We usually have basketball practice on Wednesdays, but this month we're meeting on Thursdays.*

5 3.25 Ask students to complete the exercise. Then play the audio for students to listen and check their answers.

Answers

1 works **2** meets **3** is cooking **4** 's visiting

Optional extension

Have students work in pairs and choose a job from the list they made in Exercise 3. Tell them to write a short text about the job using language from the *Exam skills* box, imagining they had that job. For example, *I work as a shop assistant. I usually work in the shopping centre in the city centre, but at the moment, I'm working in a shop at the railway station because …* Walk round, monitoring students' use of the language.

OPTIMISE YOUR EXAM

Questions

Ask students to read the tips.

- Remind students that it is important that they practise talking about topics that they may be asked about in a Speaking test. These include general information about their family members and their jobs.
- Remind them that in a Speaking test they need to show the examiner how much English they know. This is more important than struggling to explain a complicated job, so it is fine for them to change some details to make a job easier for them to talk about.
- Remind students that while they can make a good impression by using grammatically correct short answers, they should always add more information to their answers when possible.

▾ Exam task

6 In pairs, students complete the exercise. Remind students to use phrases from the *Phrase expert* box and to use the present simple and present continuous correctly. Walk round, monitoring students for good use of language and errors to go over at the end of the activity.

Write any errors on the board and go through them with students, eliciting corrections from them where possible. After the class feedback, students could then repeat this activity with another partner, to try to improve their performance.

Fast finishers

Regroup students into new pairs. Have students use their notes to tell each other what they found out about their partner. For example, *Jennifer's brother works in a museum.*

Homework

OWB

Assign students Speaking exercises 1, 2 and 3 on pages 88–89 of their Workbook.

LANGUAGE IN USE
Open cloze

→ Student's Book, page 121 SB

Lesson aims

- Focus on using indefinite and relative pronouns
- Practise an open-cloze exam task
- Discuss which country you would most like to work in

Lead-in

Imagine you do a specific job (e.g. firefighter, train driver), talk to the class about what you do. Include answers to some of the questions from Exercise 6 on Student's Book page 120, and aim to include examples of *work with/for/in/as* and the present simple and present continuous. Ask students to listen to you and identify which of the questions you answer.

1 Focus students' attention on the photo. Then have students discuss the questions in pairs. Elicit answers from different students around the class.

Suggested answers

1 She is counting birds / looking at wildlife. She might be an explorer.
2 Students' own answers

EXAM SKILL

Using indefinite and relative pronouns

Ask students to read the tips.

- Tell students that both indefinite and relative pronouns can be tested in the open-cloze exam task, so they need to know the function of pronouns and rules related to them (e.g. relative pronouns go after a noun, *that* and *which* are used to talk about places and things, etc.).
- Remind students that they have completed exercises related to indefinite pronouns in this unit in the Grammar section on page 116 and relative pronouns on page 119.

2 Ask students to complete the exercise and then check answers in open class.

Answers

1 a **2** b **3** b **4** a **5** b

3 Ask students to complete the exercise individually and check their answers in pairs.

Answers

1 who / that **2** somewhere **3** which / that **4** no-one /nobody **5** everywhere

OPTIMISE YOUR EXAM

Open cloze

Ask students to read the tips.

- Remind students that open-cloze exam tasks focus mostly on grammar, so answers will almost always focus on function words, e.g. auxiliary verbs, adjectives, adverbs, pronouns, conjunctions, prepositions and articles.
- Remind students of the process they practised earlier in the course: read the text first for general understanding; think about what type of word is missing in each gap; try to complete the gaps and leave any difficult ones until the end; go back and check the words before and/or after the gaps in order to confirm the answers; make a guess about any gaps that cannot be deduced.
- Remind students to reread their answers to check they have the correct answers and that they are spelled correctly.

▾ Exam task

4 Tell students to complete the exercise taking all the exam tips into consideration. Ask students to compare in pairs before you elicit answers in open class.

Answers

1 everywhere **2** someone **3** while **4** meeting **5** who / that **6** but

Extra support

Give students the six possible words they need to complete the gaps in a jumbled order along with two distractors (*so, everyone*). Tell them that one question has two possible answers. Ask them to choose words from the pool to complete the text. Write these words in jumbled order: *everywhere, someone, meeting, while, who/that, but, so, everyone.*

Fast finishers

Ask students to think of the good things and the bad things about Sara's job as an explorer for a travel magazine, e.g. *good – see lots of places in the world, they pay you to travel; bad – away from your family and friends, some places can be dangerous*, etc.

THINK | RESEARCH | CULTURE | LEARN | **ME**

Have students discuss the question in pairs. Then open the discussion to a class debate if there's time. Have students do more research on the country and job they discussed for homework.

Homework

OWB

Assign students Language in Use exercises 1, 2 and 3 on page 89 of their Workbook.

WRITING
An article

→ Student's Book, pages 122–123 SB

Lesson aims

- Focus on organising information into paragraphs
- Plan and write an article

Lead-in

Have a class discussion about jobs. Find out the following information from students: What jobs are they interested in doing after school? What would they need to study to get a job in that area? Do they need to get some specific experience while they are still at school to do that job? Where can they get information to help them decide what jobs they might enjoy? etc.

1 Ask students to complete the exercise. Then check answers in open class.

Answers

1 Advert

1 walk/look after dogs Advert **2** be a waiter/serve food (in a restaurant)/work Friday and Saturday from 5–8 pm

2 Students' own answers

2 Put students in small groups to discuss the statements. Encourage students to give reasons for their opinions. Monitor and note any pronunciation or grammatical errors and give feedback after they complete the discussion.

Answers

Students' own answers

EXAM SKILL

Planning an article

Ask students to read the tips.

- Tell students that when writing an article, they should first look at the advert asking for articles carefully to identify what they should write about.
- Encourage students to plan a rough draft so they make sure they are covering all the points for the article and organise each main point into a separate paragraph.

3 Ask students to complete the exercise individually. Have them check their answers in pairs before checking in open class.

Answers

1 four **2** Students should underline: if students should work / What jobs are best for teenagers? / good for students to work? / Why / Why not? **3** two **4** The first two points (if students should work and what jobs are best for teenagers) can go in the first paragraph and the last two points can go in the second paragraph (good for students to work and why or why not).

Optional extension

Put students into teams. Have each team write a list of ten jobs that they think would be suitable for teenagers. Then have teams rank their list of jobs with 1 being the best job to 10 being the worst job. Finally, have teams compare their lists and rankings with each other.

4 Tell students to read the whole text before completing the task. Then have students check their answers with a partner.

Answers

1 however **2** prefer **3** In **4** Also

5 Ask students to read the article again and decide if the statements are true or false.

Answers

1 T **2** T **3** T

OPTIMISE YOUR EXAM

An article

Ask students to read the tips.

- Tell students that giving their article an interesting introductory sentence will make the reader want to continue reading.
- Encourage students to ensure that the main points are each in a separate paragraph and they include a concluding sentence to round off their article.

Exam task

6 Ask students to complete the task and then check answers in open class.

Answers

which job you'd like to do / why you think it's a good job / a job that pays well or one that you enjoy / why

7 **Plan** Ask students to complete the table and go round giving any necessary advice or suggestions.

8 **Write** Students write their article. If there is not enough time, set the article writing task and the subsequent checklist exercise for homework.

9 Ask students to use the Checklist before they hand in their articles.

Optional extension

For a slightly longer writing task, refer students to the task in the Writing reference (SB page 166). It includes an annotated sample text and related writing task to challenge your students a little more.

Homework

OWB

Assign students Writing exercises 1–6 on page 90 of their Workbook and Progress check 11 on page 91.

12 Home time

UNIT AIMS

Exam preparation in Unit 12:

- understand words with opposite meanings
- check your answers
- agree and disagree
- identify words that show the order of events
- write a story

TEACHER'S PRESENTATION KIT

- *Talk2Me* videos
- Speaking test videos
- Class and Workbook audio
- Workbook pages and answer key

UNIT OVERVIEW

Student's Book / Digital Student's Book SB		Workbook / Online Workbook OWB
LESSON / EXAM TASK	EXAM SKILLS / LANGUAGE FOCUS	CONSOLIDATION
Reading **3-option multiple matching**	Understanding words with opposite meanings Blog posts	Workbook, pp 92–93, Exercises 1, 2, 3, 4 Unit 12, Reading, Exercises 1, 2, 3, 4
Grammar 1	Present simple passive	Workbook, p 94, Exercises 1, 2 Unit 12, Grammar 1, Exercises 1, 2
Vocabulary	Words connected with *houses and homes* Phrasal verbs Collocations with verbs	Workbook, pp 94–95, Exercises 1, 2, 3 Unit 12, Vocabulary, Exercises 1, 2, 3
Listening **3-option multiple choice (dialogue)**	Checking your answers	Workbook, p 96, Exercises 1, 2, 3 Unit 12, Listening, Exercises 1, 2, 3
Grammar 2	Past simple passive and *by*	Workbook, p 95, Exercises 1, 2, 3 Unit 12, Grammar 2, Exercises 1, 2, 3
Speaking **Discussion (pictures)**	Agreeing and disagreeing	Workbook, pp 96–97, Exercises 1, 2, 3, 4 Unit 12, Speaking, Exercises 1, 2, 3, 4
Language in Use **3-option multiple-choice cloze**	Identifying words that show the order of events	Workbook, p 97, Exercises 1, 2, 3 Unit 12, Language in Use, Exercises 1, 2, 3
Writing **A story**	Writing a story	Workbook, p 98, Exercises 1, 2, 3, 4, 5, 6 Unit 12, Writing, Exercises 1, 2, 3, 4, 5, 6
Progress check	Check language progress for Units 11 and 12	Workbook, p 99, Progress check and Cumulative progress Progress check and Cumulative progress

Additional material

PRESENTATION KIT	TEACHER'S / STUDENT'S RESOURCE CENTRE RC	TEST GENERATOR
Talk2Me video *How much is …?*	**Unit 12 worksheets:** *Optimise your grammar* (Standard and Higher), *Optimise your vocabulary* (Standard and Higher), *Talk2Me* video, *Say it right* **Units 11–12 worksheets:** CLIL, Culture, Everyday English (TRC only), Grammar communication (TRC only)	Unit Test 12 (Standard and Higher) End-of-year Test (Standard and Higher)

READING
3-option multiple matching | Blog posts

→ Student's Book, pages 124–125 SB

Lesson aims

- Focus on understanding words with opposite meanings
- Practise a 3-option multiple matching exam task
- Research people who live somewhere different

Lead-in

Ask students to look at the photo and elicit the meaning of the unit title ***Home time*** (this is the typical way to refer to the end of the school day when it is time to go home). Ask students what they think the unit will be about (*different types of homes and what we have in them*).

1 Encourage students to be honest and give reasons for their answers. Elicit answers from different students around the class and open out to a class debate.

2 Ask students to complete the exercise and then check answers in open class.

Answer

1 V **2** C **3** V **4** V **5** C **6** C **7** V **8** C

3 Tell students to complete the exercise individually and then put students into groups to discuss their reasons.

Answers

Students' own answers

Optional extension

Divide students into two or more groups: those who prefer living in a city and those who prefer a village. Have students write down all the reasons for their preferences on a mind map. Then get a spokesperson from each group to present their mind maps to the opposing groups.

EXAM SKILL

Understanding words with opposite meanings

Ask students to read the tips.

- Tell students that they need to notice when an answer is expressed as an opposite word or phrase in the text. This requires them to process the information more carefully. For example, *The show wasn't boring …* is the same as *It was interesting*.
- Encourage students to think about antonyms with adjectives (*good/bad, expensive/cheap*, etc.) as this can help them with reading exam tasks.

4 Tell students to use the text to help them complete the exercise. Have students share their answers with a partner before checking answers in open class.

Answers

1 clean **2** tiny **3** bored **4** beautiful **5** modern **6** warm

OPTIMISE YOUR EXAM

3-option multiple matching

Ask students to read the tips.

- Remind students not to simply match key words that they see in the questions with the text. They need to understand the meaning of the text rather than scan for the same word.
- Point out that they should underline where they locate the answer in a text and then check the other two texts to see if they still think the answer is correct.

▼ Exam task

5 3.26 **Note: The reading text is also available on the audio CD. You may want to have students listen and read the text after doing the exam task to check their answers.**

Tell students to complete the task as they read through it. Check answers in open class.

Answers

1 C (*if you … don't need to … use a laptop every time you're bored*)

2 A (*the house is heated by a fire …*)

3 B (*cinemas and cafés … a big festival*)

4 C (*Life on a farm isn't for everyone.*)

5 A (*… I share with my sister*)

6 C (*… grow lots of fruit and vegetables … they're sold in the local market*)

7 B (*… with fantastic new houses and some older ones too that aren't as nice.*)

6 Ask students to complete the exercise. Check their answers in open class.

Answers

1 middle **2** land **3** wood **4** heated **5** blankets **6** breathe **7** shelves **8** share

THINK | RESEARCH | CULTURE | LEARN | ME

If you have access to the internet, students can research information in class. Alternatively, students could prepare this for homework and present their information at the start of the next lesson.

Homework

OWB

Assign students Reading exercises 1, 2, 3 and 4 on pages 92–93 of their Workbook.

GRAMMAR 1
Present simple passive

→ Student's Book, page 126 SB

Lesson aims

- Understand the correct usage of the present simple passive
- Practise talking about actions that are more important than the person who does them
- Discuss moving house

Lead-in

Write down the headings for each blog post from Exercise 5 on the board: *1 Gala, Russia 2 Luiza, Brazil 3 Lara, UK*. Then put students in pairs or small groups to brainstorm what they remember from the three blog posts on page 125. Invite pairs/groups to summarise what they can remember from the blog posts.

Grammar in context

Start by looking at the three sentences and eliciting how the passive is formed, i.e. verb *to be* in the correct form + past participle. Then ask students to complete the task. Check their answers and read through the *Remember* box together.

Remind students that they can find more information in the Grammar reference, Unit 12, page 155.

Answers

a) W **b)** R **c)** R

1 Tell students that active actions are the things we usually do and passive actions are the things that happen to us. Then have them complete the exercise before checking answers in open class.

Answers

1 grow **2** are made **3** are cleaned **4** stay

2 After students complete the exercise, elicit how often some household jobs are done in their house.

Answers

1 The grass is cut every month.

2 The houses are made from wood.

3 This kitchen is cleaned every week.

3 Ask students to complete the exercise individually. Have them compare answers in pairs before you check in open class.

Answers

1 are cooked **2** 's/is kept **3** 's/is opened **4** isn't / is not used
5 are made **6** isn't / is not turned on

4 Ask students to skim the text quickly and find out why the house moves described are unusual (*Because 'moving house' usually means you take your things and go to live in a different house. In these cases people actually move their houses from one place to another.*). Have students complete the exercise. Check their answers and ask students if there are any groups of people in their country that 'move houses' in this way.

Answers

1 are packed **2** 's/is carried **3** is moved **4** are made
5 are picked up **6** are taken **7** isn't / is not done

Optional extension

Explain that the present simple passive is often used to describe a process, like moving house, and allows us to focus the description on the process rather than on the people who do it. Have students work in pairs or small groups and think of a simple process, e.g. *How to make a cup of tea*, and write sentences using the present simple passive to explain how to do it. Walk round, helping students and monitoring them for the correct use of the passive. When students have finished, have them read their sentences to the class.

THINK | RESEARCH | **CULTURE** | LEARN | ME

Put students into groups to discuss the questions. Have them report back what they found out to the class.

Homework OWB

Assign students Grammar 1 exercises 1 and 2 on page 94 of their Workbook.

VOCABULARY
Topic vocabulary | Phrasal verbs | Collocations

→ Student's Book, page 127 SB

Lesson aims

Understand the correct usage of:

- words connected with houses and homes
- phrasal verbs
- verb + noun collocations

Lead-in

Divide the class into five groups and allocate a room in the house to each group: *kitchen, living room, dining room, bedroom, bathroom*. Set a strict time limit of one minute for students to brainstorm the things you usually find in their room. Regroup students so there is one student from each room in each group. Then have students share the vocabulary they thought of.

Words connected with *houses and homes*

1 3.27 After students complete the exercise, play the audio for them to listen and check. Then have them add other items to the lists. Draw students' attention to the picture and elicit what they can see (all items except *armchair, bath, fridge, toilet* and *towel*).

Answers/Audioscript

kitchen: chair, cooker, fridge, sink, table
living room: armchair, bookcase, chair, lamp, sofa, table
bathroom: bath, shower, sink, toilet, towel
bedroom: bed, blanket, bookcase, chair, lamp, pillow

2 Ask students to work in pairs to discuss and decide which item is the odd one out in each group. Check the answers in open class and elicit the reasons. Accept any answers that are properly justified by students.

Suggested answers

1 sofa (all the others are found in a bathroom)
2 fridge (all the others are found in a bedroom)
3 cooker (all the others are found in a living room)
4 bed (all the others are found in a kitchen)
5 blanket (all the others are found in a kitchen)

Refer students to the Vocabulary reference, page 168, for more information on topic vocabulary.

Phrasal verbs

3 3.28 Ask students to complete the exercise. Play the audio for students to listen and check their answers.

Answers/Audioscript

1 (A) My dad grew *up* in a small wooden house in a village.
2 (B) In the evenings, I often lie *down* on my bed and read a book.
3 (B) If you go *out* tonight, take a front door key.
4 (B) My bed is really comfortable so I find it very difficult to get *up* in the morning.
5 (C) Please tidy the dining room and wash *up* your things in the sink before you leave.
6 (C) Can you find *out* how much those new flats cost?

Mixed ability

Give less confident students a paraphrase of the meaning for each of the phrasal verbs in the exercise to help them choose the correct answer (**1** *become an adult,* **2** *get yourself into a horizontal position,* **3** *leave the house to do something nice,* **4** *leave your bed,* **5** *clean objects from the kitchen using water and soap,* **6** *get information about*).

Ask stronger students to cover Exercise 3 and work through each item as follows: They look at sentence 1, but keep the A–C options covered. They decide what they think the meaning of the phrasal verb is and what they think the missing word could be, then compare their ideas with the A–C options and choose the correct answer. They repeat with items 2–6.

Language note

These phrasal verbs belong to three different categories.

Grow up, lie down, go out and *get up* are intransitive phrasal verbs (with no object). *Find out (information)* is a non-separable phrasal verb, and the object, whether it is a noun or pronoun, will always come after the particle.

Wash up could be problematic as the object can go between the verb and the particle (*wash your things up*) or after the particle (*wash up your things*) when it is a noun, but has to go between the verb and the particle when it is a pronoun (*wash them up*).

4 Ask students to complete the exercise. Have students compare their answers in pairs and then check them in open class.

Answers

1 grew up **2** wash up **3** got up **4** lie down **5** went out

Refer students to the Vocabulary reference, page 162, for more information on phrasal verbs.

Collocations with verbs

5 3.29 Remind students that verb + noun collocations are very common in English and that they have seen sets of these in Units 3, 5, 7 and 10. Ask students to complete the exercise, and play the audio for them to check their answers.

Answers/Audioscript

1 (e) wash the floor **2** (d) tidy your room **3** (b) make my bed
4 (c) do the washing-up **5** (f) have a shower **6** (a) move house

6 Give students one minute to try to memorise the collocations in Exercise 5. Then ask them to cover them and try to complete the exercise. Students can look back and check their answers at the end. Check answers in open class.

Answers

1 do the washing-up **2** has a shower **3** tidy your room
4 wash the floor **5** move house **6** makes my bed

Refer students to the Vocabulary reference, page 162, for more information on collocations.

Homework OWB

Assign students Vocabulary exercises 1, 2 and 3 on pages 94–95 of their Workbook.

LISTENING
3-option multiple choice (dialogue)

→ Student's Book, page 128 SB

Lesson aims

- Listen to check that your answers are correct
- Practise a 3-option multiple-choice (dialogue) exam task

Lead-in

Divide the students into two teams. Call out letters randomly. Ask teams to think of a word they've learnt on the course, which begins with that letter (don't use the letters *I*, *Q*, *X*, *Y* or *Z* as students haven't seen any words beginning with these as part of the active vocabulary on the course). Have students put up their hand when they can think of a word. Choose the first student who puts their hand up and ask him or her to say the word out loud. If it is correct, their team gets a point. Play for a set time. At the end, the team with the most points wins.

1 Ask students to look at the photo and say which country they think the boat is in (*the UK/ England*). Have students work in pairs to discuss the questions. Then elicit some answers from different students around the class.

EXAM SKILL

Checking your answers

Ask students to read the tips.

- Remind students they usually hear recordings twice in listening exams, and that they should use both listenings productively. On the first listening, they should only mark answers if they are completely sure. Tell them that if they think they are sure, they should still use the second listening to double-check that they haven't been distracted by words from incorrect options.

2 3.30 Give students enough time to read the instructions, question and possible answers. Play the track twice. Remind students to check their answer, and then check in open class.

Answers

b) in an apartment

3 3.30 Ask students which of the incorrect options they also heard mentioned (*both of them*) before playing the track again. Check answers by asking the opinion of different students.

Answers

a) … *I love watching the boats* …

c) *When I was younger, I lived in a house in the countryside* …

4 After students complete the exercise, have them check their answers in pairs.

Answers

a 2 **b** 4 **c** 5 **d** 3 **e** 1

OPTIMISE YOUR EXAM

3-option multiple choice (dialogue)

Ask students to read the tips.

- Remind students that before they hear the recording, they will be given time to read through the questions and the possible answers. Tell them to think of other words that have the same meaning if they have time.
- Explain that a good technique to help them choose the right answers is to listen the first time for **all** the words that are in the options. Tell them to tick or cross out the words to indicate if the information helps ✓ or distracts ✗ them.

Exam task

5 3.31 Tell students they will hear Heidi speaking to her friend. Elicit what they will talk about (*living on a boat*). Play the track. Ask students to compare answers in pairs and wait until Exercise 6 to check answers in open class.

Answers

1 A **2** C **3** C **4** B **5** A

Optional extension 3.31

Write these true/false sentences on the board to check students' comprehension. Play the track again and then check students' answers.

1 Heidi is thirteen years old.

2 There aren't many differences between living on a boat and living in a house.

3 Things on the river change a lot.

4 It is always very cold on the boat in the winter.

Answers

1 F (She says *four years ago, when I was ten* so she must be 14.)

2 F (*It's very different from living in a house.*)

3 T (*Every day, you see something different on the river.*)

4 F (She says *in the winter we have a fire in the living room* and that *with the heating, it's nice and warm inside in the winter.*)

6 3.31 Play the audio again and then check answers in open class.

Answers

1 B (… *four years ago* …)

2 C (… *We haven't got a dining room on the boat* …)

3 C (… *my favourite thing is what you can see out of the windows* …)

4 B (… *the worst thing is that we don't have a washing machine.*)

5 A (… *the river is very beautiful and quiet.*)

SAY IT RIGHT

/b/ and /v/

TRC

For the *Say it right* pronunciation activity and instructions, go to the Teacher's Resource Centre.

Homework

OWB

Assign students Listening exercises 1, 2 and 3 on page 96 of their Workbook.

GRAMMAR 2

Past simple passive and *by*

→ Student's Book, page 129

SB

Lesson aims

- Understand the correct usage of the past simple passive with *by*
- Practise talking about past actions where the action is more important than the person who did it
- Design a small home on wheels

Lead-in

Write these jumbled questions on the board and ask students to reorder them:

a / like / What's / living / on / boat / it / ?

boat / a / What / do / most / you / about / living / on / like / ?

Tell students that the questions are from the interview with Heidi on the listening page. Ask them if they can remember how she answered.

Answers

What's it like living on a boat? (it's very different from living in a house) What do you like most about living on a boat? (you see something different every day)

Grammar in context

Ask students to read the extract from the audio and look at the sentences below it. Check their answers and read through the sentence in the *Remember* box together. Answer any questions students have about the grammar point.

Remind students that they can find more information in the Grammar reference, Unit 12, page 155.

Answers

a) No, they didn't. **b)** Yes, we do. **c)** No, we don't.

1 After students complete the exercise, check answers in open class. Then explain that in each case, the passive is used because we are more interested in the first part of the sentence than the person mentioned.

Answers

1 my grandmother **2** the manager **3** the pupils in Year 8 **4** my mother **5** a man from Scotland **6** a team of 30 men

Extra support

Write these sentences halves on the board for students to match:

1 Romeo and Juliet was written

2 The Mona Lisa was painted

3 The Taj Mahal was built

4 The Pompidou centre in Paris was designed

5 The opera Tosca was composed

a) by Shah Jahan.

b) by Leonardo Da Vinci.

c) by Giacomo Puccini.

d) by William Shakespeare.

e) by Richard Rogers.

Check answers in open class. Explain to students that if they look up information about, for example, *Romeo and Juliet*, they might find a sentence like this one. However, if they look up 'William Shakespeare', they will probably find sentences like *William Shakespeare wrote many famous plays, including* Romeo and Juliet …. Point out that the passive is often used to help us put the thing we are most interested in at **the start** of the sentence.

Answers

1 d **2** b **3** a **4** e **5** c

2 Ask students to complete the exercise. Have them compare their answers in pairs before checking them in open class.

Answers

1 were given **2** was interviewed **3** were written **4** were taught **5** was made **6** was moved

3 Have students complete the exercise individually. Then check answers in open class.

Answers

1 The fruit trees were bought by my father.
2 My parents were driven home by a taxi driver.
3 The beds were made every morning by the hotel staff.
4 Our new house was designed by a man called Jasper.
5 The English tests weren't marked by our teacher.

4 Before students start reading, elicit the meaning of the word *trailer* by asking them to scan the article very quickly to find the definition (*a metal floor on wheels*). Then have students complete the exercise in pairs before you check their answers in open class.

Answers

1 wasn't given **2** was told **3** was helped **4** were given **5** were used **6** was spent **7** was finished **8** was made **9** is asked **10** is known

Fast finishers

Ask students to write definitions for the words *chance* (*opportunity*), *tree house* (*a house for children built in a tree*) and *documentary* (*film about real events or people*). As you check the answers to Exercise 4, encourage students to explain the meaning of these words if other students are unsure of them.

5 After students complete the exercise, have them work in pairs to practise asking and answering the questions.

Answers

1 his dad and his friends **2** friends and family **3** a journalist, Kirsten Dirksen **4** local schools

THINK | RESEARCH | CULTURE | LEARN | **ME**

Have students design their home and label their plans individually. Divide the class into pairs or small groups to show each other their homes and explain the features they have chosen. Display homes around the classroom and have students vote for the one they like best.

Homework

OWB

Assign students Grammar 2 exercises 1, 2 and 3 on page 95 of their Workbook.

Assign students the Flipped classroom tasks on page 130 of their Student's Book if you'd like them to prepare for the next lesson. To complete this task, students need to watch the *Talk2Me* video which can be found on the Resource Centre.

SPEAKING
Discussion (pictures)

→ Student's Book, page 130 SB

Lesson aims

- Focus on agreeing and disagreeing
- Practise a discussion (pictures) exam task

The *Talk2Me* video in this unit focuses on a visit from a relative. The people in the video talk about their favourite school subject, art, and a visit from a relative.

Students answer some comprehension questions and then listen for key phrases in the video.

The video can be used in one of two ways:

Flipped classroom

Flipped classroom option

Using this approach, students watch the video and complete the exercises for homework. This prepares students for the speaking lesson by introducing them to the topic and the key phrases to use in the exam task. Teachers who use this method will find they have more class time to spend on activating the target language and developing fluency for the final task.

***Talk2Me* worksheet**

Ask students to also complete the *Talk2Me* worksheet on the Resource Centre for more detailed comprehension exercises and more practice of the key phrases.

Classroom option

1 Ask students to spend a minute or two reading the questions. Play the *Talk2Me* video for students to complete the exercise. Play the video again, if necessary, before checking their answers.

2 Play the *Talk2Me* video again, so students underline the phrases in the *Phrase expert* box. Pause the video from time to time if necessary. Check answers in open class.

***Talk2Me* worksheet**

Ask students to also complete the *Talk2Me* worksheet on the Resource Centre for more detailed comprehension exercises and more practice of the key phrases.

Answers

The transcript and answer key for the *Talk2Me* video exercises and Worksheet can be found on the Teacher's Resource Centre.

Lead-in

Write *agreeing* and *disagreeing* on the board and elicit their meaning in open class. Then elicit and write some phrases to express how to agree or disagree with someone. Write the sentence *I love spending time in the countryside.* Then ask pairs or small groups to discuss whether they agree or disagree with this statement using the phrases on the board and to give reasons for their opinions.

3 Put students in pairs to complete the task and then check answers in open class.

Answers

1 Just a minute, please. **2** But can I just say **3** I remember you

EXAM SKILL

Agreeing and disagreeing

Ask students to read the tips.

- Remind students to use the phrases in the *Phrase expert* box. In this part of the exam, students must talk about their likes and dislikes. They should say if they agree or disagree with their partner's opinions to show they are listening to what their partner says.
- Explain that students must be able to deal with situations in exams where they don't understand everything. Point out that using appropriate phrases to check understanding or asking their partner to repeat something can improve their mark, as it shows they can manage a conversation.

4 3.32 Have students complete the task and then check answers in open class.

Answers

1 A **2** D **3** D **4** A **5** A

OPTIMISE YOUR **EXAM**

Discussion (pictures)

Ask students to read the tips.

- Tell students to look at the five images and to focus on having a conversation about their likes/dislikes and their reasons for these preferences as well as agreeing/disagreeing with each other.
- Point out that in an actual exam, the images will only be in black and white so they wouldn't be expected to talk about colours of the objects.

Exam task

5 Assign each student a letter, A or B, and put them into A/B pairs. Give them a moment to look at the pictures. Time students (two minutes) and give them an update, e.g. *One minute to go* … Remind students to use phrases from the *Phrase expert* box for giving themselves time to think. Walk round, monitoring students for good use of language and errors to go over at the end of the activity. Write any errors on the board and go through them with students, eliciting corrections from them where possible. After class feedback, students could then repeat this activity with another partner, to try to improve their performance.

Answers
Students' own answers

6 Assign a different pairing of students with a letter, A or B, and put them into A/B pairs. Give them a moment to look at the questions. Time students (two minutes) and monitor. Then have pairs swap roles, A/B is now B/A. Time the two-minute task and monitor.

Optional extension

Put students in teams and give them one minute to write down as many phrases as possible to agree and disagree with someone.

Homework

OWB

Assign students Speaking exercises 1, 2, 3 and 4 on pages 96–97 of their Workbook.

LANGUAGE IN USE

3-option multiple-choice cloze

→ Student's Book, page 131 SB

Lesson aims

- Focus on words that show the order of events
- Practise a 3-option multiple-choice cloze exam task
- Learn new vocabulary by writing sentences

Lead-in

Write the words *first, then, after that, finally, while* and *during* on the board. Have students work in pairs and tell each other the order of things they did yesterday morning. Give them an example about yourself, e.g. *First I got out of bed, then I had a shower and after that I got dressed. The phone rang while I was having breakfast.*

1 After students complete the exercise, have them report any similarities or differences to the class.

EXAM SKILL

Identifying words that show the order of events

Ask students to read the tips.

- Explain to students that they should pay attention to words that show the order of events, such as *first, then, finally*, etc. Linking words help them to follow the sequence of events in a story.
- Remind students that they have seen a lot of different types of collocations and phrases in this course, and that it is important to learn them as 'chunks of language'. These are commonly tested in exams, particularly in multiple-choice cloze and open-cloze exam tasks.

2 Ask students to complete the exercise. Check their answers.

Answers
1 b **2** d **3** e **4** a **5** c

3 Ask students to complete the exercise. Then have them compare their answers in pairs before you check them in open class.

Answers
1 first **2** then **3** While **4** Finally **5** by

Optional extension

Ask students to write about something they did yesterday using the words from the box in Exercise 3. Then have students swap their sentences with a partner. Encourage students to underline any spelling or grammar errors they see in their partner's writing before returning it to be corrected.

OPTIMISE YOUR EXAM

3-option multiple-choice cloze

Ask students to read the tips.

- Remind students that common collocations and fixed phrases are often tested in this part of the exam so they need to pay attention to the words surrounding the gaps.
- Tell students to use their instinct when choosing options they don't know the answers to. Remind them that it is always best to justify an answer, but if this is not possible, guess.

Exam task

4 Have students complete the exercise. Check answers in open class.

Answers

1 C **2** A **3** A **4** B **5** C **6** B

THINK | RESEARCH | CULTURE | **LEARN** | ME

Before students write their sentences, remind them that it is always a good idea to write an example sentence when they record new vocabulary. Using the language in context helps them to remember it better. When they have finished, have them share their sentences in pairs.

Homework

OWB

Assign students Language in Use exercises 1, 2 and 3 on page 97 of their Workbook.

WRITING
A story

→ Student's Book, pages 132–133 SB

Lesson aims

- Focus on ways to structure a story
- Plan and write a story

Lead-in

Draw the following table on the board:

	city	*village*
good		
bad		

Elicit a few examples to show students how to complete the table, e.g. *good–city: lots of places to go out, public transport; good–village: very quiet, clean air.*

Have students work in pairs to complete the table with good and bad aspects of city and village life. Have them share their answers with the class, and then collate their ideas on the board.

1 Tell students to answer the questions, giving reasons for their answers. Elicit answers from different students around the class.

EXAM SKILL

Writing a story

Ask students to read the tips.

- Tell students they should always make a plan before writing their stories. First, they should decide who is in the story as well as when and where the story takes place.
- Point out that they should use time expressions and linking words and phrases to tell their story, so the story is cohesive and well organised.

2 Ask students to complete the exercise and then check answers in open class.

Answers

1 c **2** b **3** a

3 Have students work in pairs or small groups to complete the exercise before checking answers.

Answers

1 Students should underline:

Beginning: Nick got out of his parents' car and looked at the house.

Middle: It all started a month ago when his parents won the house in a competition.

End: Then they went inside and explored the house.

2 because (reason), so (result)

3 Students should circle:

Paragraph 1: amazing, huge, beautiful

Paragraph 2: surprised

Paragraph 3: excited, happy

4 Then

OPTIMISE YOUR EXAM

A story

Ask students to read the tips.

- Remind students that they are assessed in three key areas to get the best possible mark. They are content, language and organisation.
- Students should demonstrate a basic understanding of how to write a story that has a clear beginning, middle and end. Emphasise that the first line of the story must be the line they are given, word for word.
- Finally, tell students that they need to include as much variety in their description as possible by using adjectives.

4 Ask students to complete the exercise. Monitor and offer suggestions and feedback when necessary.

Answers

Students' own answers

5 Plan Ask students to complete the writing plan. You may want to look at students' plans to check them and give advice and suggestions for improvement before they take the next step.

Extra support

Look at the plan with students. Put students into pairs or small groups to brainstorm ideas to add further details to their tables. Encourage them to share their ideas with the class and collate them on the board, so all students have plenty to choose from before they start writing.

6 Write Students write their story. If there is not enough time, set this and the subsequent checklist exercise for homework.

7 Check Students complete the checklist before they hand in their story.

Optional extension

For a slightly longer writing task, refer students to the task in the Writing reference (SB page 164). It includes an annotated sample text and related writing task to challenge your students a little more.

Homework

OWB

Assign students Writing exercises 1–6 on page 98 of their Workbook and Progress check 12 on page 99.

Answers PROGRESS CHECK Units 11–12

Exercise 1
1 pilot **2** journalist **3** farmer **4** shop assistant **5** engineer **6** dentist **7** firefighter **8** waiter/waitress **9** cleaner **10** receptionist

Exercise 2
1 cooker **2** fridge **3** sink **4** lamp **5** pillow **6** table **7** armchair **8** bath **9** cupboard **10** blanket

Exercise 3
1 A **2** C **3** C **4** B **5** A **6** B **7** A **8** C

Exercise 4
1 was closed **2** was given **3** bought **4** aren't taught **5** didn't repair **6** was taken **7** weren't told **8** moved **9** are worn **10** was paid **11** wrote **12** are made

Exercise 5
1 that/which **2** that/which **3** who **4** of **5** for **6** to **7** up **8** in **9** with **10** is

OPTIMISE YOUR EXAMS

The ***Optimise your exams*** pages are designed to give your students extra training in exam tasks. Each task includes OPTIMISE boxes, which contain tips for students. Remind students to read these boxes before they start each of the exam tasks.

Students can work on the tasks in class or for homework, and the tasks can be done at whatever stage you feel is most appropriate for your class.

Your students should complete these pages before they move on to the Practice test in the Workbook.

READING AND WRITING SB pages 136–139

1

1 B **2** C **3** A **4** A **5** B **6** A

2

1 B **2** A **3** C **4** B **5** C **6** A **7** C

3

Sample answer

It's about an 18-year-old American snowboarder called Chloe Kim. She has won lots of medals.

4

1 C **2** B **3** C **4** A **5** B

5

1 A **2** B **3** A **4** C **5** A **6** C

6

1 for
2 there
3 were
4 to
5 part
6 not

7

Students' own answers

8

Students' own answers

LISTENING SB pages 140–141

1

1 B **2** B **3** B **4** A **5** C

2

1 Thursday
2 7:30
3 War horse
4 Troubadour
5 15

3

1 A **2** C **3** B **4** C **5** A

4

1 B **2** B **3** A **4** C **5** A

5

1 D **2** F **3** H **4** B **5** E

SPEAKING SB pages 142–143

1

✓ What's your name?
✓ Where do you live?
✓ Where do you go at the weekend?
✓ What time do you get up on a Sunday morning?
✓ Who do you spend time with at the weekend?
✓ What do you do on Saturday evening?
✓ Tell me something about what you did last weekend.
✓ What's your favourite type of food?
✓ Do you like pizza?
✓ What did you have for breakfast this morning?
✓ What do you usually eat for dinner?
✓ When do you go out to eat in restaurants?
✓ Tell me something about what you like to eat at the weekend.
✓ Do you like to eat in restaurants?

2

Students' own answers

3

Students' own answers

4

Suggested answers

	Marie	Eva
cinema	Funny – likes watching comedy	Interesting – like watching films with family and friends
park	Likes going with friends, family, dog. Likes doing sport there.	Very cool – likes walking with family friends and dog.
museum	Agrees with Eva. Likes fashion museum.	Likes some but not all. Some are boring
library	Boring – you can't speak and have to work	Russian libraries are different – you don't work in them
mountains	Amazing sport but very difficult.	View is cool and beautiful. Difficult to go up.

5

1 because
2 me too
3 think
4 but
5 agree with

6

1 R **2** A **3** O **4** C **5** A

7

Students' own answers

8

1 cinema, expensive
2 mountains, exciting
3 museum, interesting
4 park, fun

9

Students' own answers

10

1 to
2 going, to, playing
3 the

11

1 interesting
2 city, countryside
3 fun
4 prefers

12

Students' own answers

Workbook Answer Key

UNIT 1

Pages 4–5

Reading

Exercise 1
1 F **2** T **3** F

Exercise 2
1 painting **2** sport/skiing **3** photography **4** baking/cooking **5** collecting **6** travelling

Exercise 3
Sam – playing tennis, going to the cinema, watching football

Exercise 4
1 C **2** B **3** C **4** B **5** A **6** C **7** A

Exercise 5
1 planning **2** foreign **3** often **4** join **5** online **6** favourite **7** member **8** video games

Page 6

Grammar 1

Exercise 1
1 f **2** d **3** a **4** e **5** b **6** c

Exercise 2
1 Joanna never goes to bed after 10pm.
2 You don't play computer games every day.
3 My parents often go shopping on Saturday.
4 Mike usually goes cycling three times a week.
5 We always take photos on holiday.
6 I sometimes visit the museum at the weekend.

Exercise 3
1 D **2** F **3** A **4** B **5** E **6** C

Page 7

Vocabulary

Exercise 1
1 collect **2** photograph **3** tent **4** magazines **5** swimming **6** rock climbing

Exercise 2
1 painter **2** music **3** photograph **4** guitar **5** games **6** musicians

Exercise 3
1 a **2** b **3** c **4** c **5** c **6** b

Page 7

Grammar 2

Exercise 1
1 My mother's favourite hobby is painting.
2 Please look after Anna's camera. It is new.
3 Do you know Mike's brother and sister?
4 Greg's daughter is only three years old.
5 Would you like to see my sister's holiday photos?
6 This is Jim's book. He needs it for his homework.

Exercise 2
1 B **2** C **3** B **4** A **5** A **6** C **7** C **8** B **9** A **10** C

Page 8

Listening

Exercise 1
1 C **2** B **3** A

Exercise 2
1 A **2** B **3** B **4** B **5** C

Page 8

Speaking

Exercise 1
1 f **2** d **3** b **4** a **5** e **6** c

Exercise 2
1 What's/is your name? **2** Where do you live? **3** What are your hobbies? **4** What's/is your favourite sport? **5** What do you usually do in the summer holiday? **6** How often do you play video games?

Exercise 3
Students' own answers

Page 9

Language in Use

Exercise 1
1 f **2** c **3** a/g **4** h **5** d **6** g **7** b **8** e

Exercise 2
1 with **2** There **3** in **4** a **5** front **6** it

Page 10

Writing

Exercise 1
Students should tick:
c, e, f

Exercise 2
1 A **2** B **3** B **4** A

Exercise 3
where, meet; what time, meet; which film

Exercise 4
Students' own answers

Page 11

Progress check

Exercise 1
1 magazines **2** guitarist **3** turn off **4** join **5** look after **6** painting **7** get off **8** member

Exercise 2
1 b **2** b **3** a **4** b **5** c **6** c **7** b **8** a

Cumulative progress

Exercise 3
1 C **2** A **3** B **4** A **5** B

UNIT 2

Pages 12–13

Reading

Exercise 1
an arts festival for young people all around the world

Exercise 2
1 happens, summer
2 different country, every year
3 All singers, dancers, from Britain

Exercise 3
happens, festival; C

Exercise 4
1 A **2** A **3** B **4** A **5** B

Exercise 5
1 festival **2** shows **3** musicians **4** instrument **5** plays **6** concerts

Page 14

Grammar 1

Exercise 1
1 are you doing **2** 'm watching **3** love **4** think **5** prefer **6** are **7** are showing **8** Do you want

Exercise 2
1 goes **2** 's/is making **3** are having **4** wants **5** plays **6** isn't / is not raining **7** comes, lives **8** acts, 's/is acting

Page 14

Vocabulary

Exercise 1
1 art gallery **2** concert hall **3** gaming café **4** opera house **5** theatre **6** museum

Exercise 2
1 in **2** in **3** at **4** out **5** with **6** to

Exercise 3
1 a **2** c **3** a **4** c **5** b

Page 15

Grammar 2

Exercise 1
1 's/is moving **2** 's/is meeting **3** are selling **4** starts **5** are playing **6** 's/is singing

Exercise 2
1 'm/am meeting **2** are, doing **3** 's/is happening **4** want **5** are playing **6** are, playing **7** do, want **8** don't think **9** are visiting **10** 're/are going

Page 16

Listening

Exercise 1
1 f **2** e **3** a **4** b **5** d **6** c

Exercise 2
C The Carltons are an excellent band.
Exercise 3
1 C **2** F **3** A **4** H **5** E

Page 16
Speaking
Exercise 1
1 Do you have **2** are you doing **3** do you spend **4** Are you going **5** do you see **6** do you do **7** do you prefer **8** do you enjoy
Exercise 2
a 5 **b** 1 **c** 7 **d** 8 **e** 6 **f** 2

Page 17
Language in Use
Exercise 1
Students' own answers
Exercise 2
1 watching, cinema **2** library, borrow **3** eating, restaurant **4** plays, café **5** singing, concert **6** buy, gallery **7** museum, learn **8** see, theatre
Exercise 3
1 B **2** A **3** C **4** C **5** B **6** A

Page 18
Writing
Exercise 1
Students should tick: 2, 3, 5
Exercise 2
B
Exercise 3
1 What are you doing on Sunday afternoon? **2** Do you know where that is? **3** Would you like to come with us?
Exercise 4
Students' own answers

Page 19
Progress check
Exercise 1
1 gallery **2** act **3** article **4** concert **5** looking **6** player **7** hip hop **8** programme
Exercise 2
1 live **2** opens **3** are getting **4** Are you playing **5** are waiting **6** think **7** are you listening **8** practises
Cumulative progress
Exercise 3
1 A **2** B **3** A **4** C **5** B **6** C **7** B **8** C

UNIT 3

Pages 20–21
Reading
Exercise 1
1 present **2** past **3** past **4** present **5** past
Exercise 2
1 e **2** d **3** a **4** b **5** c
Exercise 3
1 E **2** H **3** D **4** B **5** F
Exercise 4
1 business **2** healthy **3** salad **4** cooks **5** customers

Page 22
Grammar 1
Exercise 1
1 worked **2** started **3** baked **4** cooked **5** cleaned **6** walked **7** needed **8** invited **9** liked **10** learnt
Exercise 2
1 Who did you invite for dinner tonight? **2** Where did you buy those cakes? **3** What did you order for dessert? **4** When did the restaurant open? **5** Which cupcakes did you buy? **6** What can we cook on the barbecue?
Exercise 3
1 Who **2** Where **3** What **4** When **5** Why **6** What

Page 22
Vocabulary
Exercise 1
1 honey **2** cereal **3** Strawberries **4** salt **5** oil **6** steak **7** tomatoes **8** onion
Exercise 2
1 fry **2** boil **3** bake **4** grilled **5** baked
Exercise 3
1 a **2** b **3** a **4** c **5** b **6** c

Page 23
Grammar 2
Exercise 1
1 went **2** bought **3** ate **4** drank **5** did **6** came **7** met **8** got up **9** took **10** made
Exercise 2
1 bought **2** didn't / did not get up **3** didn't / did not eat **4** did, go **5** met **6** drank **7** made **8** didn't / did not do
Exercise 3
Students' own answers

Page 24
Listening
Exercise 1
1 spent a week, Lyon, village, school
2 teacher, course, women, father, daughter, Daniel
Exercise 2
1 Abi, where **2** Teacher, who
Exercise 3
Suggested key words:
3 weren't, lessons, biscuits, bread, cakes and students' own answers
4 Ingmar, cooking holiday, easy, funny, difficult, started, finished and students' own answers **5** Ingmar, favourite, friends, learning, eating and students' own answers
Exercise 4
1 A **2** B **3** A **4** C **5** C

Page 24
Speaking
Exercise 1
1 What's/is your favourite food? **2** What do you like for breakfast? **3** What did you have for dinner last night? **4** How often do you eat fast food? **5** Which do you prefer, pizza or burgers?
Exercise 2
Students' own answers
Exercise 3
Students' own answers

Page 25
Language in Use
Exercise 1
2 and **3** because **4** and **5** so **6** but
Exercise 2
1 and **2** it **3** but **4** of **5** the **6** or

Page 26
Writing
Exercise 1
B
Exercise 2
1 make/prepare **2** prefer **3** ask/invite
Exercise 3
2 like / prefer **3** like to eat? **4** Students' own answers **5** favourite **6** Students' own answers **7** about **8** Would
Exercise 4
Students' own answers

Page 27
Progress check
Exercise 1
1 cereal **2** bakes **3** boiled **4** tomato **5** fried **6** boil **7** yoghurt **8** roast **9** oil **10** grilled
Exercise 2
1 baked **2** decided **3** did, buy **4** looked **5** did, meet **6** didn't / did not go **7** didn't / did not eat **8** took **9** did, think **10** invited
Cumulative progress
Exercise 3
1 In **2** was **3** to **4** son **5** do **6** made/prepared **7** Then **8** his **9** out **10** after

UNIT 4

Pages 28–29
Reading
Exercise 1
1 b **2** a **3** b **4** a **5** a **6** a
Exercise 2
1 Jake **2** Kyle **3** Peter

Exercise 3
1 B **2** C **3** A **4** C **5** A **6** B **7** A
Exercise 4
1 journey **2** paths **3** guide **4** countryside **5** airport **6** tourists

Page 30
Grammar 1
Exercise 1
1 were sitting **2** was selling **3** were, doing **4** was raining
5 were, walking **6** weren't / were not talking **7** were getting
8 Were, making
Exercise 2
1 when **2** but **3** and **4** because **5** When **6** because

Page 30
Vocabulary
Exercise 1
DOWN
1 traffic **3** bridge
ACROSS
2 roundabout **4** miss **5** railway **6** delay
Exercise 2
1 licence **2** news **3** station **4** guide **5** ride **6** machine **7** park **8** boat
Exercise 3
1 b **2** c **3** c **4** b **5** c **6** a

Page 31
Grammar 2
Exercise 1
1 happened **2** were staying **3** was buying **4** asked **5** told
6 was leaving **7** found **8** were walking **9** got **10** found

Page 32
Listening
Exercise 1
1 Present **2** Karol **3** 524
Exercise 2
1 4 hours 15 minutes **2** 1787 **3** 1822 **4** 162
Exercise 3
2 Gary **3** 1822 **4** 524 **5** lunch/going to a restaurant

Page 32
Speaking
Exercise 1
1 I'm sorry, I don't understand **2** Could you explain, please? / Could you please explain? **3** What do you mean? **4** Please could you say that again?
Exercise 2
Students' own answers
Exercise 3
Students' own answers

Page 33
Language in Use
Exercise 1
1 b **2** c **3** a **4** a **5** b **6** c
Exercise 2
1 C **2** A **3** B **4** C **5** A **6** A

Page 34
Writing
1

	A	B
All the questions are answered clearly.	✓	✗ Carla didn't answer the question: 'How long did it take?'
It's easy to understand what the writer means.	✗	✓
There are no spelling mistakes.	✗ aeroplanes	✓
A word needs a capital letter because it is a name.	✗ Madrid	✓
There is an apostrophe missing from a contraction.	✗ wasn't	✓
There is a mistake with a preposition.	✗ with plane ⟶ by plane	✓

Exercise 2
Mistakes are: went in ⟶ went to; mexico ⟶ Mexico; fly ⟶ flight; next the ⟶ next to the; didnt ⟶ didn't
Exercise 3
Students' own answers
Exercise 4
Students' own answers

Page 35
Progress check
Exercise 1
1 b **2** d **3** f **4** c **5** h **6** e **7** a **8** g
Exercise 2
1 a **2** c **3** a **4** b **5** c **6** b **7** c **8** a
Cumulative progress
Exercise 3
1 on **2** were **3** went **4** was **5** at **6** near **7** there **8** in/inside **9** at **10** who

UNIT 5

Pages 36–37
Reading
Exercise 1
1 text message **2** email **3** notice
Exercise 2
1 a **2** c **3** b
Exercise 3
1 Max **2** Anna **3** Ben **4** Mr Jones **5** Students **6** parents
Exercise 4
1 B **2** A **3** B **4** C **5** C **6** A
Exercise 5
1 video **2** laptops **3** website **4** uploaded **5** shared **6** chat

Page 38
Grammar 1
Exercise 1
1 some **2** A few **3** much **4** A lot of **5** many **6** many **7** a few **8** any
Exercise 2
1 c **2** b **3** b **4** a **5** b **6** a **7** c **8** a

Page 38
Vocabulary
Exercise 1
1 keyboard **2** printer **3** laptop **4** mouse **5** screen
6 download, stream **7** software **8** graphics
Exercise 2
1 mobile **2** file **3** DVD **4** site
Exercise 3
1 a **2** c **3** b **4** c **5** a **6** a

Page 39
Grammar 2
Exercise 1
1 faster **2** the best **3** longer **4** more attractive **5** the easiest
6 more interesting **7** the most expensive **8** more popular
Exercise 2
1 The Wave 4.1 is the cheapest.
2 The Kiwi 7 is more popular than the Saphora X2.
3 The Saphora X2 is heavier than the Wave 4.1.
4 The Wave 4.1 is the most popular.
5 The Saphora X2 is lighter than the Kiwi 7.
6 The Kiwi 7 is the most expensive.
7 The Wave 4.1 is bigger than the Saphora X2.

Page 40
Listening
Exercise 1
1 Do you prefer **2** the best **3** talking **4** to watch **5** to **6** That's why
Exercise 2
1 A **2** B **3** C **4** C **5** B

Page 40
Speaking
Exercise 1
1 better **2** faster, lighter **3** interesting **4** cheapest
5 worse **6** most boring
Exercise 2
1 Do you prefer tablets to PCs? / Do you prefer PCs to tablets?
2 Do you like to chat / chatting online? **3** Do you prefer to go out or to stay at home / going out to staying at home / going out or staying at home?

Exercise 3
Students' own answers

Page 41
Language in Use
Exercise 1
1 this **2** theirs **3** them **4** Those **5** a **6** many **7** That **8** few **9** the **10** these
Exercise 2
1 mine **2** it **3** her **4** them **5** The **6** much
Exercise 3
1 your/the **2** a **3** Would **4** me **5** something **6** This/Here

Page 42
Writing
Exercise 1
1 a **2** b **3** c **4** b **5** a
Exercise 2
1 C **2** D **3** A **4** B
Sentence C
Exercise 3
Sample answer
It was a cold and rainy Saturday. Max and Cathy were at home and they couldn't go out. That's why they decided to watch videos. They went online and then they found some really funny ones on YouTube.
Exercise 4
Students' own answers
Exercise 5
Students' own answers
Exercise 6
Students' own answers
Exercise 7
Students' own answers

Page 43
Progress check
Exercise 1
1 a **2** c **3** c **4** a **5** b **6** c **7** b **8** c **9** a **10** c
Exercise 2
1 many **2** any **3** the biggest **4** faster **5** much **6** cheaper **7** the most **8** many
Cumulative progress
Exercise 3
1 B **2** C **3** B **4** A **5** C **6** B **7** A **8** C

UNIT 6

Pages 44–45
Reading
Exercise 1
1 but **2** finally **3** also **4** so **5** for example **6** then **7** because
Exercise 2
1 F **2** A **3** E **4** C **5** G
Exercise 3
1 suit **2** tie **3** necklace **4** jumper **5** scarf **6** earrings

Page 46
Grammar 1
Exercise 1
1 's/has lost **2** 's/has tried on **3** hasn't / has not brought, 's/has left **4** Have, worn, haven't / have not
Exercise 2
1 've/have gone/been **2** 've/have bought **3** 've/have visited **4** 've/have, seen **5** haven't / have not gone/been **6** 's/has rained **7** Have, watched **8** 's/has given **9** haven't / have not forgotten **10** 've/have found
Exercise 3
1 ever, never **2** ever **3** never **4** ever **5** ever, never **6** ever

Page 47
Vocabulary
Exercise 1
1 credit card **2** receipt **3** department store **4** customer **5** cash **6** shopping centre **7** change **8** supermarket **9** market **10** shopper
Exercise 2
1 down **2** on **3** back **4** for **5** off **6** in
Exercise 3
1 catch **2** keep **3** saving **4** going **5** do **6** for **7** caught **8** been

Page 47
Grammar 2
Exercise 1
1 's/has been, bought **2** got, hasn't / has not worn **3** Did, go, haven't / have not heard **4** opened, 've/have sold **5** 've/have seen, got
Exercise 2
1 did, get **2** bought **3** haven't / have not been **4** opened **5** Have, bought **6** 've/have been **7** haven't / have not had

Page 48
Listening
Exercise 1
A
Exercise 2
driver found it, glad you found it
Exercise 3
1 C **2** B **3** C **4** A **5** B

Page 48
Speaking
Exercise 1
1 In **2** ever **3** to design **4** always
Exercise 2
Students' own answers
Exercise 3
Students' own answers

Page 49
Language in Use
Exercise 1
1 d **2** h **3** f **4** b **5** j **6** a **7** i **8** g **9** e **10** c
Exercise 2
1 credit card **2** shopping centre **3** Shop assistants **4** department store **5** online shopping **6** pocket money
Exercise 3
1 B **2** A **3** C **4** B **5** C **6** A

Page 50
Writing
Exercise 1

	A	B
What you bought		✓
Why you bought it	✓	
Why you were surprised	✓	✓

Exercise 2
1 because **2** unfortunately **3** really **4** back
Exercise 3
Students' own answers
Exercise 4
Students' own answers

Page 51
Progress check
Exercise 1
1 store **2** centre **3** assistant **4** customers **5** shopping **6** try **7** costs **8** for **9** credit **10** receipt
Exercise 2
1 b **2** a **3** a **4** a **5** c **6** c **7** b **8** c
Cumulative progress
Exercise 3
1 B **2** B **3** A **4** B **5** C

UNIT 7

Pages 52–53
Reading
Exercise 1
Sample answer
It is believed that students don't learn well if they are stressed so they should spend more time doing their own activities at home.
Exercise 2
A
Exercise 3
1 C **2** B **3** C **4** A

Exercise 4
1 secondary schools **2** pupils **3** scientists **4** break **5** lessons **6** homework

Page 54
Grammar 1
Exercise 1
1 Are, going to **2** isn't / is not going to **3** am, going to **4** aren't / are not going to **5** 'm/am going to **6** 's/is going to **7** Are, going to **8** isn't / is not going to **9** aren't / are not going to **10** 's/is going to
Exercise 2
1 Brad's/is going to visit relatives.
2 Mo's/is going to study for the exams.
3 Katie's/is going to work in a shop.
4 Brad and Mo are going to go to summer camp.
5 Katie isn't / is not going to go to summer camp.
6 Brad and Katie are going to go to the beach.
7 Mo and Brad aren't / are not going to work in a shop.
8 Mo isn't / is not going to visit relatives.

Page 54
Vocabulary
Exercise 1
1 desk **2** bookshelf **3** maths **4** dictionary **5** geography **6** history **7** board **8** biology
Exercise 2
1 from **2** at **3** with **4** from **5** about **6** at
Exercise 3
1 f **2** d **3** e **4** a **5** c **6** b

Page 55
Grammar 2
Exercise 1
1 's/is going to leave
2 'll/will show
3 's/is going to rain
4 won't / will not break
5 aren't / are not going to win
6 are, going to do

Page 56
Listening
Exercise 1
1 a name **2** a year **3** a price **4** a thing **5** a thing
Exercise 2
1 Attic **2** September **3** 5,000 **4** computers **5** TV

Page 56
Speaking
Exercise 1
1 When **2** Tomorrow **3** future **4** plan **5** years' time **6** Next
Exercise 2
1 future plans **2** future plans **3** predictions **4** future plans **5** predictions **6** future plans
Exercise 3
Students' own answers

Page 57
Language in Use
Exercise 1
1 b **2** a **3** c **4** b **5** a **6** b
Exercise 2
1 have **2** make **3** learn **4** on **5** study **6** take **7** opens **8** studies
Exercise 3
1 A **2** C **3** B **4** C **5** B **6** A

Page 58
Writing
Exercise 1
1 interested **2** surprising **3** excited **4** surprised **5** interesting **6** exciting
Exercise 2
1 C **2** B **3** A
Exercise 3
Suggested answers
1 tired, sleepy **2** worried, afraid **3** pleased, surprised

Page 59
Progress check
Exercise 1
ACROSS
3 board **5** remember **8** library **9** help
DOWN
1 dictionary **2** course **4** geography **6** biology **7** taught
Exercise 2
1 a **2** c **3** a **4** b **5** c **6** c **7** b **8** a
Cumulative progress
Exercise 3
1 take/do **2** about **3** on **4** many/any **5** at **6** not **7** started **8** from **9** lot **10** will

UNIT 8

Pages 60–61
Reading
Exercise 1
1 usually **2** tells **3** don't usually **4** doesn't know **5** some information
Exercise 2
1 can't **2** giving Jack **3** opens after the last lessons **4** would like to go on Friday **5** write back to Becky
Exercise 3
1 a **2** b **3** a **4** b
Exercise 4
1 C **2** B **3** A **4** B **5** C **6** A
Exercise 5
1 look after **2** coach **3** beginners **4** meeting **5** competition **6** wet

Page 62
Grammar 1
Exercise 1
1 can **2** couldn't **3** Could **4** could **5** can't **6** couldn't **7** can't **8** Can
Exercise 2
1 have to **2** don't have to **3** have to **4** has to **5** don't have to **6** have to
Exercise 3
1 may stay **2** needn't / don't need to drive **3** mustn't / must not run **4** must stay **5** Do, need to bring **6** may win

Page 62
Vocabulary
Exercise 1
1 racket **2** swimsuit **3** ticket **4** ride **5** coach **6** kit
Exercise 2
1 swims **2** won **3** runner **4** player **5** surf
Exercise 3
1 e **2** f **3** d **4** a **5** c **6** b

Page 63
Grammar 2
Exercise 1
1 Could/Can **2** can **3** can't **4** could **5** Can **6** could
Exercise 2
1 shouldn't eat **2** should wear **3** should get **4** shouldn't talk **5** shouldn't worry **6** should play
Exercise 3
1 couldn't / could not go **2** Could/Can, open **3** should buy **4** mustn't / must not use

Page 64
Listening
Exercise 1
1 d **2** e **3** a **4** b **5** c
Exercise 2
1 a **2** b **3** b **4** b **5** a
Exercise 3
1 F **2** D **3** E **4** G **5** C

Page 64
Speaking
Exercise 1
1 think **2** boring **3** you **4** agree **5** really **6** about **7** do **8** prefer
Exercise 2
Students' own answers
Exercise 3
Students' own answers

Page 65
Language in Use
Exercise 1
1 must **2** Can **3** couldn't / could not **4** shouldn't / should not **5** may
Exercise 2
1 should/must **2** own **3** start **4** could/did **5** may/might **6** read

Page 66

Writing

Exercise 1

Students should tick: 1, 3, 4

Exercise 2

	A	B	C
1	✗	✓	✓
2	✗	✗	✓
3	✗	✓	✓
4	✗	✗	✓
5	✗	✗	✗

The best email is C.

Exercise 3

1 I'm / I am **2** teacher's / teacher is **3** a **4** is **5** have to wear

Exercise 4

Student's own answers

Page 67

Progress check

Exercise 1

1 play **2** teams **3** winner **4** throw **5** kit **6** club **7** coach **8** ticket

Exercise 2

1 can't **2** should **3** could **4** shouldn't **5** Can **6** should **7** Can I **8** don't have to

Cumulative progress

Exercise 3

1 B **2** B **3** A **4** A **5** C

UNIT 9

Pages 68–69

Reading

Exercise 1

1 B **2** C **3** B **4** A **5** C

Exercise 2

1 C **2** A **3** A **4** A **5** B **6** C **7** B

Exercise 3

1 moon **2** grass **3** countryside **4** sky **5** mountains **6** clouds **7** storm **8** lie down

Page 70

Grammar 1

Exercise 1

1 is, runs **2** are, grow **3** is, go **4** swim, is **5** becomes, gets **6** snows, close

Exercise 2

1 feel, 'll/will go **2** Will, play, snows **3** are, 'll/will drive **4** 'll/will get, don't / do not take **5** Will, wait, 'm/am **6** will happen, rains

Exercise 3

1 Rain changes into snow when it's/is very cold.
2 She'll/will take a taxi if it rains.
3 If we get lost, we'll/will phone our parents.
4 When it's/is sunny, I always wear a hat.
5 If the weather gets better, we'll/will have a picnic.
6 Everyone will be happy if it's/is sunny tomorrow.

Page 70

Vocabulary

Exercise 1

1 sky **2** sun **3** river **4** beach **5** clouds **6** rain **7** snow **8** mountain **9** hill **10** forest

Exercise 2

1 We learnt about bears by visiting the forest.
2 Miranda did an experiment to find out about clouds.
3 Scientists are good at finding answers to problems.
4 It's really important to protect nature.
5 The best time to eat this fruit is in September.
6 Martin wants to go to South Africa in the spring.

Exercise 3

1 rainy **2** sun **3** snow **4** foggy **5** ice **6** cloudy

Page 71

Grammar 2

Exercise 1

1 b **2** c **3** a **4** b **5** c **6** c

Exercise 2

2 If there were/was snow on the mountains, I'd/would go skiing.
3 If there were any sheep on the hill, we'd/would see one/them/some.
4 If our teacher liked the sun, we'd/would have lessons outside.
5 If it were/was (very) windy today, we'd/would go sailing.
6 If it weren't / were not / wasn't / was not going to rain, I wouldn't / would not have this umbrella.

Page 72

Listening

Exercise 1

1 T **2** T **3** F

Exercise 2

Mark: Zoe and I <u>got so wet when we went camping</u> last week.
Jen: Did you get caught in that big storm?
Mark: <u>Of course!</u> We were <u>walking to the café</u> for dinner and had to wait under some trees.
Jen: Well, <u>next time, I hope you'll take an umbrella</u> with you!

Exercise 3

1 C **2** B **3** B **4** C **5** A

Page 72

Speaking

Exercise 1

1 your family **2** the places you go on holiday **3** the place where you live **4** your friends
Expressions used to introduce examples: One example is; For example; Let me give you an example

Exercise 2

Students' own answers

Page 73

Language in Use

Exercise 1

1 will **2** feel **3** gets **4** are **5** Does **6** won't be **7** lived **8** move

Exercise 2

1 were **2** if/when **3** goes/sits/stays **4** would **5** could/would **6** rains **7** would **8** will

Exercise 3

1 C **2** A **3** C **4** B **5** B **6** A

Page 74

Writing

Exercise 1

1 Don't forget to take your boots. **2** If I were you, I'd arrive early. **3** Don't walk in the mountains by yourself. **4** It would be better if you didn't drive. **5** Be careful, the roads are icy. **6** I'd read the instructions before you start.

Exercise 2

Have you tried your new bike yet? Where did you get your jacket from? When should we leave on Sunday? What food are you bringing with you?

Exercise 3

1 Hi/Hello **2** this morning / yesterday **3** great / very comfortable **4** pleased/happy **5** bought/got **6** department store / shop **7** morning/park **8** sandwiches **9** fruit/snacks **10** next week / soon

Exercise 4

Students' own answers

Page 75

Progress check

Exercise 1

1 sky **2** foggy **3** forest **4** snow **5** river **6** sun **7** rainy/rains **8** thunderstorm **9** windy **10** beach

Exercise 2

1 a **2** b **3** b **4** a **5** c **6** a **7** b **8** a

Cumulative progress

Exercise 3

1 A **2** B **3** B **4** C **5** A **6** B **7** C **8** A

UNIT 10

Pages 76–77

Reading

Exercise 1

1 let Mum know about the appointment **2** meet him at the dentist's at 4 o'clock **3** she shouldn't be late **4** bring his kit to practice **5** look in his room for the kit **6** look in the car for the kit

Exercise 2
1 A 2 C 3 B
Exercise 3
1 C 2 D 3 B 4 F 5 G
Exercise 4
1 footwear 2 expensive 3 closes 4 outdoor wear 5 for hire

Page 78
Grammar 1
Exercise 1
1 We've already done our English homework and now we're doing maths.
2 Carrie isn't feeling well, but she hasn't been to the doctor yet.
3 Nick's had a terrible headache since this morning.
4 Pete isn't ill. I've just seen him playing football in the park!
5 My grandad has had this problem for many years.
Exercise 2
1 I can't write because I've/have just hurt my hand.
2 I haven't / have not eaten since breakfast because I have a stomach ache.
3 Josh's/has had a cold for three days so he isn't coming to school.
4 Have you brushed your teeth yet?
5 Nermine's/has just hit her head and now she has a headache.
6 Mike's/has already watched six films today and now his eyes hurt.
Exercise 3
1 for 2 since 3 already 4 just 5 yet

Page 78
Vocabulary
Exercise 1
ACROSS
2 hand 3 nose 6 hospital 7 neck 9 eyes
DOWN
1 throat 4 stomach 5 finger 8 knee
Exercise 2
1 in 2 for 3 to 4 with 5 with 6 for
Exercise 3
1 e 2 b 3 a 4 f 5 d 6 c

Page 79
Grammar 2
Exercise 1
Verbs + infinitive: choose, hope, need, offer, stop, try
Verbs + *-ing*: don't mind, finish, keep, spend time, stop, try
Exercise 2
1 taking 2 to find 3 to brush 4 to eat 5 waiting 6 eating 7 to pay 8 to use

Page 80
Listening
Exercise 1
1 telling 2 giving 3 opinion 4 asking 5 offering 6 explaining
Exercise 2
1 a 2 b 3 b 4 b 5 a
Exercise 3
1 B 2 C 3 A 4 B 5 C

Page 81
Speaking
Exercise 1
1 Just a minute, please. 2 Let's have a look at the advert.
3 Looking at the information, it says … 4 Let me think …
Exercise 2
Sample answers
1 Is it open on Mondays? 2 Are there tennis courts? 3 What's the address? 4 What's the telephone number? 5 What's the cost?
Exercise 3
a) 5 **b)** 4 **c)** 2 **d)** 3 **e)** 1
Exercise 4
Students' own answers

Page 81
Language in Use
Exercise 1
1 Have, ago 2 for, am 3 Have, never 4 did, yet, will 5 yet, going 6 did, since
Exercise 2
1 when/if 2 much 3 been 4 but 5 going

Page 82
Writing
Exercise 1
1 because 2 so 3 so 4 Because 5 Because 6 so
Exercise 2
1 so 2 because 3 C
Exercise 3
Sample answers
1 she felt bad 2 her mum called the doctor 3 After she took the medicine, she felt much better!
Exercise 4
1 Hi 2 normal 3 sure 4 think 5 some fruit / breakfast / vegetables / a salad 6 some fruit / vegetables / a salad 7 about 8 some fruit / vegetables / a salad 9 fast food / fried food 10 luck
Exercise 5
Students' own answers
Exercise 6
Students' own answers
Exercise 7
Students' own answers

Page 83
Progress check
Exercise 1
1 c 2 a 3 a 4 b 5 b 6 a 7 c 8 a 9 c 10 b
Exercise 2
1 Darren offered to take me to hospital yesterday when I felt ill.
2 Has Carla seen the doctor yet?
3 I usually don't mind helping my grandparents.
4 Lily's/has had the pain for 10 days.
5 Reuben hopes to be a doctor in 10 years' time.
6 When I was in hospital last year, I didn't enjoy eating the food.
7 Zara hasn't had a stomach ache since Monday.
8 Everyone tried to help me when I fell off my bike last night.
9 Pedro has already brushed his teeth and (he's/he) is now in bed.
10 The doctor's/has just arrived.
Cumulative progress
Exercise 3
1 A 2 C 3 B 4 A 5 B

UNIT 11

Pages 84–85
Reading
Exercise 1
1 e 2 a 3 c 4 d 5 f 6 b
Exercise 2
B
Exercise 3
1 B 2 C 3 A 4 C 5 B
Exercise 4
1 business 2 customers 3 shampoos 4 poor 5 article 6 earn

Page 86
Grammar 1
Exercise 1
1 c 2 c 3 a 4 b 5 c 6 a
Exercise 2
1 anywhere 2 everything 3 something 4 everyone 5 someone 6 anything

Page 86
Vocabulary
Exercise 1
1 receptionist 2 musician 3 police officer 4 pilot 5 dentist 6 firefighter
Exercise 2
1 actor 2 engineer 3 waiter 4 journalist 5 manager 6 cleaner
Exercise 3
1 in 2 for 3 of 4 with 5 of 6 at

Page 87
Grammar 2
Exercise 1
1 who 2 which 3 which 4 who 5 which 6 which
Exercise 2
1 that 2 who 3 that 4 that 5 that 6 who

Page 88
Listening
Exercise 1
1 d **2** a **3** e **4** c **5** b
Exercise 2
1 Rightstar **2** Madrid **3** three/3 **4** games **5** 2,000
Page 88
Speaking
Exercise 1
1 I have **2** only **3** there are **4** for **5** in **6** as
Exercise 2
1 get ready **2** work **3** am usually **4** am learning **5** enjoy **6** work **7** usually start **8** bring **9** love **10** am saving
Exercise 3
Students' own answers.
Page 89
Language in Use
Exercise 1
1 indefinite pronoun **2** relative pronoun **3** article **4** preposition **5** verb
Exercise 2
1 something **2** who/that **3** the **4** up **5** work
Exercise 3
1 for **2** who **3** everyone **4** are **5** the
Page 90
Writing
Exercise 1
Students' own answers
Exercise 2
what kind of job would you like to do for a summer job; is it good for teens to work during their holidays; more important to work or to relax in the summer?; Why?
Exercise 3
Students' own answers
Exercise 4
Students' own answers
Exercise 5
Students' own answers
Exercise 6
Students' own answers
Page 91
Progress check
Exercise 1
1 meeting **2** boss **3** uniform **4** factory **5** journalist **6** customers **7** receptionist **8** staff **9** dentist **10** farmer
Exercise 2
1 who **2** which **3** anyone **4** someone **5** which **6** Everywhere **7** something **8** who **9** everything **10** anywhere
Cumulative progress
Exercise 3
1 C **2** A **3** B **4** C **5** A **6** C **7** C **8** B

UNIT 12

Pages 92–93
Reading
Exercise 1
1 have my own **2** isn't cheap **3** isn't quiet **4** hasn't found **5** isn't messy **6** bought
Exercise 2
1 F **2** T **3** T **4** F **5** F **6** T
Exercise 3
1 C **2** A **3** B **4** A **5** C **6** A **7** B
Exercise 4
1 pillows **2** carpet **3** blanket **4** mirror **5** screen **6** lamp
Page 94
Grammar 1
Exercise 1
1 is usually made before breakfast **2** flats aren't built **3** is opened with a key **4** are washed every week **5** are watered **6** is made in that factory
Exercise 2
1 is owned **2** is often heard **3** is looked after **4** are turned on **5** are shown **6** aren't eaten **7** are eaten **8** is cleaned

Page 94
Vocabulary
Exercise 1
1 bed **2** pillows **3** lamp **4** blanket **5** bath **6** armchair **7** sofa **8** shower **9** towel **10** toilet **11** bookcase **12** cupboard **13** table **14** fridge **15** sink **16** cooker
Exercise 2
1 out **2** up **3** up **4** out **5** down **6** up
Exercise 3
1 do **2** tidied **3** move **4** makes **5** has **6** washes
Page 95
Grammar 2
Exercise 1
1 was asked to tidy my room by my parents **2** were taken by my sister **3** was built by **4** were given that plant by our neighbour **5** were given some money to buy their house by my parents **6** were broken by some children
Exercise 2
1 was stolen **2** was found **3** were sold **4** stopped **5** drove **6** was repaired **7** was returned **8** sold
Exercise 3
1 a man **2** the police **3** a man who lives near us **4** a mechanic **5** the police **6** my dad
Page 96
Listening
Exercise 1
B
Exercise 2
Instead, we visited the post office; and also Hotel 71
Exercise 3
1 C **2** B **3** A **4** C **5** A
Page 96
Speaking
Exercise 1
1 a minute, please **2** right **3** what you mean **4** good point **5** I don't agree **6** sure about that **7** I agree **8** add something
Exercise 2
1, 4
Exercise 3
Students' own answers
Exercise 4
Students' own answers
Page 97
Language in Use
Exercise 1
1 while **2** first **3** finally **4** During **5** next **6** By
Exercise 2
1 make **2** up **3** for **4** move **5** with **6** First
Exercise 3
1 C **2** B **3** A **4** B **5** A **6** C
Page 98
Writing
Exercise 1
1 b **2** c **3** a
Exercise 2
1 excited **2** fantastic, best, gold, awesome
Exercise 3
Students' own answers
Exercise 4
Students' own answers
Exercise 5
Students' own answers
Exercise 6
Students' own answers
Page 99
Progress check
Exercise 1
1 a **2** a **3** b **4** c **5** c **6** c **7** a **8** a **9** b **10** a
Exercise 2
1 was built **2** moved **3** was repaired **4** isn't / is not used **5** grow **6** are often given **7** are kept **8** leaves
Cumulative progress
Exercise 3
1 said **2** by **3** look **4** which/that **5** lot **6** were **7** had **8** about **9** for **10** who

OPTIMISE PRACTICE TEST

Page 100

Reading and Writing

Part 1
1 A **2** C **3** A **4** A **5** B **6** B
Part 2
7 C **8** B **9** A **10** B **11** A **12** C **13** A
Part 3
14 B **15** A **16** C **17** B **18** A
Part 4
19 B **20** C **21** A **22** C **23** B **24** A
Part 5
25 about **26** to **27** a **28** my **29** they **30** them
Part 6
Sample answer
Hi, Taylor
Do you want to play badminton at the sports centre on Sunday? I have piano lessons in the morning, but we could meet after 12pm. We can go to the café in town afterwards.
Tom
Part 7
Sample answer
Yesterday, a girl saw a notice about a lost cat. Then she saw the cat in a tree. It looked scared. The girl called the number on the notice. The man who lost his pet cat came to the park. The man was happy to see his cat.

Page 111

Listening

Part 1
1 C **2** C **3** B **4** C **5** B
Part 2
6 Bellentyne **7** 11th July **8** swimming **9** 16/sixteen **10** bus
Part 3
11 B **12** C **13** C **14** B **15** C
Part 4
16 A **17** B **18** A **19** C **20** B
Part 5
21 A **22** C **23** F **24** B **25** D

Page 116

Speaking

Part 1
Phase 1
My name is Leo.
Phase 2
A: I like to play football and video games with my friends.
I see my friends every weekend and sometimes during the week.
B: My friends and I go to cafés, parties, the cinema and the stadium.
Most of my friends live in my neighbourhood.
Extended response A
My best friend is Marie. I've known her for seven years. She's 12 years old. She lives in my street and we are in the same class at school. Marie is tall and thin. She's got two brothers. She's a very kind person and she's good at sport.
B: My favourite subject at school is maths.
I usually walk to school. It's near my house.
A: I go to the cafeteria with my friend and have something to eat. Sometimes I'll have time to do some homework then too. I start school at 9am.
Extended response B
My classroom is on the first floor of the school building. There are twenty desks for the students and a bigger one for the teacher. There are two large windows and we have a view of the playground. There are lots of posters on the walls.

Part 2
Phase 1
Sample answers
A: I don't cook because I don't really like it. I don't read magazines very much because I read a lot online, but I read books in my bedroom and I enjoy it. Chess is fun – my grandfather taught me to play it when I was ten. I love running in the park with my friends because we always have a good time, and it's healthy. My parents think I'm too young to go to concerts, but when I'm older I'd really like to go because I love music.
B: I don't think cooking is easy. I think it's difficult to cook a really good meal.
Well, some magazines are boring, but when I read an interesting magazine, I really enjoy it.
Yes, chess is difficult to play and you need to practise a lot to be good at it.
Yes, running in the park is great fun especially if you go with your friends.
Of course I enjoy listening to music and watching the musicians play their instruments. It makes me really happy.

Phase 2
Sample answers
B: Well, I prefer indoor activities in the winter – like playing basketball at a gym or playing video games at home. But in the summer, I enjoy outdoor activities more, like running, swimming or cycling.
A: I'm very sporty so I prefer outdoor activities in winter too. I like to go skiing and snowboarding. In the summer, I swim and play outdoor sports like tennis.
A: I'm very sporty, but I prefer going to a concert to running in the park. You can sing and dance at a concert and have more fun.
B: I agree that concerts are more fun than going to the cinema. I think it's really exciting to watch a band performing on a stage, especially if it's one of your favourite bands. You can see your heroes live on the stage!

Audioscripts

UNIT 1 | STUDENT'S BOOK

1.01 | Reading, page 4

The right hobby for you

Kareem

I often play video games, but I don't spend all my free time playing online. I also write a blog about new video games every month. I enjoy blogging because I love writing and the blog gives me the chance to share what I write. It's also great to read the comments that people leave on my blog. They say they are better players after they read it. It's nice to know that they're learning something from my hobby.

Jake

I like adventure and I love trying new activities. It's a good idea to look at websites for ideas about different clubs and activities in your area. People don't usually find the perfect hobby immediately, but it's fun trying out new things. My favourite hobby is skateboarding. I found out a lot about it on the internet after watching a TV show. My friends and I always go skateboarding in the park after school even when it rains. It's really exciting!

Amaya

Hobbies help you to make friends. Just think about what you usually like doing. Do you prefer big or small groups? Outdoor or indoor activities? I like being outdoors with other people and I enjoy taking photos inside interesting buildings or outdoors of nature. This year, I wanted to meet new people, so when I got a new camera, I became a member of a photography club. We meet every Thursday evening to discuss new ideas and post our photos online. It's simple to choose the right hobby.

1.07 | Listening, page 8, Exercises 4 and 5

1

What game do they play?

Girl: Let's play a video game – but not that football game we played last time.

Boy: Good idea! My brother's new video game is good. Or I've got a great new adventure game. You choose.

Girl: The adventure game, please.

Boy: OK, we can play the racing game next time.

2

What does Helen like to read?

Boy: Do you often read magazines, Helen?

Helen: No, I don't really like them. I sometimes look at my sister's pop magazine. But … I think it's boring.

Boy: I agree! So did you bring anything to read on holiday?

Helen: Yes, my book. It's great!

3

What time does football practice usually start?

Girl: When does football practice usually start? Is it 9:15?

Boy: No, it's not. It always begins at 9:30.

Girl: So what time do you get home after practice, then?

Boy: Ryan's dad brings us home in the car. I'm usually home by 11 o'clock.

4

What do they have for dinner?

Man: What do you want for dinner this evening? We could have burgers … or pizza? It's your sister's favourite.

Girl: What about fish and chips? That's Mum's favourite. We had pizza on Monday.

Man: OK. We can go to that place next to the hotel. They do good fish.

Girl: Great. Yes, their food is very good.

5

When does the girl have art lessons?

Boy: Do you have art and English on Wednesday afternoons?

Girl: I have art on Wednesday, yes. But English is always on Thursday afternoons and Friday mornings.

Boy: I have English lessons on Thursdays and Fridays too, but I have art on Monday mornings.

Girl: That's a nice way to start the week!

1.09 | Unit 1, Speaking, page 10, Exercises 4 and 5

Examiner: Good morning. What's your name?

Student A: My name is Victor.

Examiner: How old are you?

Student A: I'm 12.

Examiner: Thanks. And what's your name?

Student B: My name's Eleanor.

Examiner: And how old are you?

Student B: I'm 13 years old.

Examiner: Now, let's talk about free time. Victor, do you have any hobbies?

Student A: Sorry, can you say that again, please?

Examiner: Sure. Do you have any hobbies?

Student A: Yes, I really like swimming and I'm in the school swimming team. And I also love skateboarding. I go skateboarding every day.

Examiner: And, what do you usually do in the evenings?

Student A: I usually get home from school at around 6pm. Then I do my homework and have a meal with my family. I usually go to bed at 9pm.

Examiner: Eleanor, what do you like doing at the weekend?

Student B: I often go to the beach. I swim in the sea or play volleyball at the beach.

Examiner: And, who do you usually spend time with at weekends?

Student B: I usually spend time with my brothers and my friends. They like going to the beach too so we all go together.

Examiner: Now Victor, tell me about what you did last weekend.

Student A: I went to visit my grandparents in the countryside with my family. It was really good fun. We saw a lot of animals and I helped my grandad in the garden.

UNIT 2 | STUDENT'S BOOK

1.14 | Unit 2, Listening, page 18, Exercises 6 and 7

Kacey: Hi Paul. I'm doing a school project on entertainment. Can I ask you some questions?

Paul: Sure. No problem.

Kacey: OK, thanks. So – do you watch much TV?

Paul: I always watch the sports channel on TV. I find it really interesting to watch people doing different sports. But I also go online to watch things, too.

Kacey: Do you watch cartoons on TV?

Paul: Well, I sometimes watch anime, with my friend, Jack. He likes them a lot. They're cartoons from Japan. I think they are beautiful to look at, but a bit boring after a while. We're watching a new one tonight. I hope it won't be boring! I prefer watching funny cartoons that make me laugh. I watch a lot of those on TV!

Kacey: Right! What about films?

Paul: Sometime I watch films online, but I mostly watch them on TV. I like anything really. I enjoy funny films, but action films are my favourite. I like them because they're exciting.

Kacey: How about the news? Do you watch that on TV, or online?

Paul: I watch the news online. Some people think it's boring, but I think it's important to know what's happening. I often don't feel happy when I watch some news stories, though. They make me feel sad.

Kacey: Do you watch anything else online? I sometimes watch vloggers on YouTube.

Paul: Yes, my brother and I are watching a good video gaming channel at the moment. The guy on it is very loud, but some of the things he shows you are really excellent.

Kacey: And what about music videos?

Paul: Oh, no. They're terrible. Pop stars think they're so important. I don't like watching them at all – I think they're really bad.

Kacey: What about other entertainment online?

Paul: I take lots of photos and post them for my friends. That's a lot of fun. What are you doing later? I can show you some.

Kacey: Sorry, I'm working on my project this afternoon.

UNIT 3 | STUDENT'S BOOK

1.16 | Unit 3, Reading, page 27, Exercise 7

KIDS IN THE KITCHEN

In the UK, 60% of 18-year-olds can't cook five easy meals. There are, however, many different ways young people can learn to cook. Some people learn by watching TV cooking competitions like *Junior MasterChef*. The programme started in the UK 20 years ago. The idea for it was simple – to help people think about the food they eat. In the show, young people prepare different delicious dishes every week. The one who cooks the best food is the winner. And some of the food is amazing. Everyone remembers the famous alligator chilli one junior chef made!

Junior MasterChef winners can help people learn to cook by sharing their recipes online. One winner said she actually learnt to cook by watching YouTube videos. However, many winners learnt to cook when they helped their parents at home.

There are also cooking courses and schools for teenagers in the UK. At one school, the teacher, Ben Coyle-Larner, isn't a chef. He's a successful rapper called Loyle Carner. Thanks to his music he is now teaching kids to cook. When Ben was a teenager, he found it difficult to study. Ben says, 'My brain is always busy, but with cooking there is no time to think about other things.' In 2016, Ben opened his cooking school to help teenagers like him.

So, next time you're online, why not look up the recipe of your favourite dish or watch a video about how to cook it? Or watch the latest cookery to get some great ideas.

Then start cooking!

1.21 | Unit 3, Listening, page 30, Exercise 4

Kay: Hi Matt. Are you free to come for coffee with Liz and me on Saturday morning?

Matt: Hello Kay! That sounds like a nice idea. Where are you thinking of going?

Kay: There's a really good cafe on Lion Street and they play great music, too.

Matt: Sounds good. Is it quite cheap?

Kay: It's not that cheap, but the coffee is really good – and you get a free cake! The staff there are helpful, too.

1.22 | Unit 3, Listening, page 30, Exercises 6 and 7

Simon: Hi Clare, I'm just phoning to say happy birthday.

Clare: Oh, thanks Simon. That's really nice of you.

Simon: So did you go to the new music café with Kristy on Friday evening?

Clare: Well, we planned to go then, but in the end we went on Saturday afternoon.

Simon: I went last week and really liked it. What did you think of it?

Clare: It was good, but it was a bit small.

Simon: I know, there are only five tables and when I went there were people at four of them.

Clare: We were lucky it wasn't too busy and there were only two of us.

Simon: Was the music good?

Clare: Yes, it was, but the food wasn't great.

Simon: Really, I'm surprised. I just had an omelette as a snack and it was good! What did you have?

Clare: Well, I had the grilled fish as a main and Kristy had the vegetable curry. The drinks were fantastic, though.

Simon: What did you have to drink?

Clare: I was thirsty so I ordered a glass of lemonade. It was sweet and had lots of fruit in it. It was almost a dessert!

1.23 | Unit 3, Speaking, page 32, Exercises 4 and 5

Examiner: What's your favourite type of food?

Student: Definitely pasta – I love pasta! All sorts of pasta, with any type of sauce. It's my favourite meal because it's tasty and easy to make.

Examiner: And what type of food don't you like?

Student: Mmm … there aren't many things that I dislike, but I really hate pears. We have a pear tree in the garden and so Mum makes us eat them in the autumn. We have pear juice, pear in salads, pear for dessert, pear for breakfast … so I really don't like pears because I have to eat so many of them!

Examiner: Tell me about the food you eat at festivals and parties.

Student: Well we have a festival in winter and it's very cold and dark so we make hot things like special hot bread. And also we have some meat that my mum cooks for three days – it's delicious. The meat is very expensive so that's why we only have it once a year.

UNIT 4 | STUDENT'S BOOK

1.24 | Unit 4, Reading, page 36, Exercise 2

Useful travel tips

Readers share their experiences

A

I hate long journeys. Last winter I went to Mexico City with my family. When we arrived at the airport in London, our flight was delayed because there was a terrible storm. Luckily, I had my tablet with me, so I downloaded an eBook. We were waiting there for five hours, but I was reading an exciting story, so the time went quickly.

Kat

B

Last July, I went to a language school in the UK. I made some new friends and when I wasn't studying, we spent time together. One weekend we went to a music festival for teenagers. It was raining all day, but we had a lot of fun. Most people were wearing boots, but I didn't pack any, so my new sandals got really wet and muddy. The music was brilliant, and I kept my dirty sandals as a souvenir!

Jess

C

Last summer I went on a school trip to Edinburgh. On the first day we went sightseeing – my favourite place was Edinburgh Castle, but it was really busy because it's so popular. However, I was walking all day in uncomfortable shoes, so by late afternoon my feet were hurting. That evening I decided to stay in the hotel to rest. What were my friends doing while I was in the hotel? A tour guide took them on an exciting night tour of the city – by bus!

1.28 | Unit 4, Listening, page 40, Exercises 2 and 3

1

Boy: Which house do you live at?

Girl: I don't live in a house. I live in a flat – 32a.

2

Boy: Maria, I thought there were some biscuits left.

Maria: Well, there were four, but I ate three … and Jo ate one as well.

3

Girl: Hello, is that Jon?

Martin: No, this is Martin Williams, sorry – I think you called the wrong number. This is 786 954.

Girl: Oh, sorry. I wanted 786 934.

4

Girl: So, is Paul having a party?

Boy: Yes he is – it's his 16th birthday on Saturday.

5

Boy: So, when does your train get in?

Girl: It gets in at 12:14.

Boy: 12:40. OK – see you then.

Girl: No, 12:14. And remember, it's platform two.

1.29 | Unit 4, Listening, page 40, Exercise 4

1

A: My name's Jeremiah Gayle, that's J-E-R-E-M-I-A-H, then G-A-Y-L-E.

B: Did you say G-A-L-E?

A: No, G-A-Y-L-E.

2

A: My address is 5 Solomon Street, that's S-O-L-O-M-O-N Street.

B: S-O-L-M-O-N?

A: No, there are three 'O's – it's S-O-L-O-M-O-N.

3

A: I'm calling from Cambourne School.

B: Can you spell that, please?

A: Of course. It's C-A-M-B-O-U-R-N-E.

4

A: It's Alisha Pieters, that's A-L-I-S-H-A, then P-I-E-T-E-R-S.

B: OK – A-L-I-S-H-A … P-E-T-E-R-S.

A: No, my last name is spelt P-I-E-T-E-R-S.

5

A: I'm from Leicester.

B: Is that L-E-S-T-E-R?

A: No, it's L-E-I-C-E-S-T-E-R.

6

A: So you get off the train at Clapham Junction, that's C-L-A-P-H-A-M then J-U-N-C-T-I-O-N.

B: OK, I'll write that down … C-L-A-P-A-M … J-U-N-C-T-I-O-N. Right?

A: No, you missed out an H. It's C-L-A-P-H-A-M, then J-U-N-C-T-I-O-N.

7

A: I live in Borough Road.

B: Is that B-U-R-R-O-W?

A: No, it's B-O-R-O-U-G-H.

8

A: It's Tom Maltravers. M-A-L-T-R-A-V-E-R-S.

b: OK, so T-O-M … M-A-T-L-A-V-E-R-S.

a: No, Maltravers is M-A-L-T-R-A-V-E-R-S.

1.30 | Unit 4, Listening, page 40, Exercises 5 and 6

Hello everyone. I'm going to give you some information about the sailing trip on Monday. The bus leaves at eight thirty in the morning. We are going to meet in front of the Nunthorpe building – that's N-U-N-T-H-O-R-P-E in the centre. We won't wait if you are late, so please be there early! It's a day trip and we are away for about seven hours and only get back late afternoon. We will be on the boat from eleven am until three p m. You can buy snacks from different shops before you get on the boat, but we're eating lunch together at the activity centre on the island. Remember while we are on the boat, we are at sea so it can be dangerous. Last year while we were sailing, someone fell into the water. You must go to the toilet in pairs. Also, it's going to be quite sunny, so make sure you wear a cap and don't forget to bring some water with you. OK, any questions?

1.31 | Unit 4, Speaking, page 42, Exercise 4

Examiner: Here are some pictures that show different types of holidays. Do you like these different types of holidays? Say why or why not. All right? Now, talk together.

Student A: OK, so let's start with cycling holidays. They're great because you get a lot of exercise and I love being outside.

Student B: Me too, a cycling holiday sounds fun. What about going on a cruise? You know, travelling on a ship to different places? What do you think about doing that?

Student A: Hmmm. Well you often get to see lots of cities or countries, but I think it might get a bit boring when you're on the ship for days.

Student B: Sorry, did you say it was boring?

Student A: Yes, I don't think it's that much fun.

Student B: Oh, I don't agree with you. There's always lots to do. Sometimes these big ships have restaurants and swimming pools.

Student A: Well, what about a coach trip?

Student B: Well I think that way of travelling is a bit slow if there's lots of traffic. Also, you can't walk around much while you're travelling on a coach or a bus.

Student A: Yes. I agree. I also like the idea of a walking holiday. It's always good to go around cities on foot or to walk around the countryside because you get to see more.

Student B: I did that last year with my family. It's quite a nice way to explore new places, but you can't really go to lots of different areas without using a car or bus, so I wouldn't go again. This picture is of a horse-riding holiday. I'm not sure about that because I can't ride. I think it would be too scary for me to do that.

Student A: Yes, me too. I don't know how to ride a horse.

UNIT 5 | STUDENT'S BOOK

2.01 | Unit 5, Reading, page 49, Exercise 5

1

From: Liam
To: Jenny
Call me tonight after seven about football practice. Don't call my mobile – it's broken. My home number is 96507699.

2

Kids' Store:
New video games
Lots of books for kids
Half-price computers for school

3

Hi Carly
The new football stadium is open! Let's go and watch the match this Sunday. Let me know before Friday.
Alan

4

From: Sofia
To: Luke
Hi from Spain! I'm spending every day at the beach. Here are a few photos I took.
See you next week!

5

Customers can now buy tickets online but must collect them at the cinema
www.Prices-Cinema.com

6

Hi Tony
I've got some ideas for our history project. Let's discuss them tonight. Do you have any free time for a video chat?
Bella

2.06 | Unit 5, Listening, page 52, Exercises 4 and 5

1

Boy: Do you write letters to your pen friends in other countries, Sarah?

Sarah: No! I never write letters anymore.

Boy: So, how do you contact them, then? Do you send them emails?

Sarah: Yes, I do, I've always got lots of things I want to tell them about, so texts are no good.

2

Kirsty: Are we going to listen to music later?

Boy: Let's do something different. How about playing this game online? I was talking to Dan yesterday and he said it's great!

Kirsty: Yes, OK, then. But I hope it's better than the football game we played last week! Dan told me that was a good game, but it wasn't.

Boy: Oh, I'm sure this one's better!

3

Dad: There are some good laptops here, but they're expensive. I prefer to get your brother a new camera.

Girl: But Dad, look at this smartphone. It's amazing … and it's got a camera.

Dad: Your brother's got a good phone already. I think this camera will take better photos. I'm going to get him this.

Girl: Well, OK. But I think the phone's nicer than the camera.

4

Boy: Sorry I wasn't free this afternoon. Was the chat room really busy?

Girl: There were about 13 people in it.

Boy: That's not too bad. Sometimes there are thirty people chatting at the same time.

Girl: I think that's too many. It's better when there aren't so many people.

5

Mum: Can you help me, please? I want to download a new app.

Girl: Yes, of course, Mum. Is it that new music app I told you about?

Mum: No, it's an exercise app. I can use it when I go running.

Girl: Oh, right. My friend's got an app like that. Hers takes photos too.

2.07 | Unit 5, Speaking, page 54, Exercises 4 and 5

1

Examiner: Do you prefer to be with your friends or to chat with them online?

Student A: Well I don't have a lot of free time. Chatting online is great as I can talk to friends anywhere and at any time of day, but I think I still prefer to spend time with my friends so we can go to different places together. So I like being with my friends the best.

2

Examiner: Do you prefer to watch a film or to go on your computer?

Student B: Uhm, well … I think I prefer watching films to going on my computer. It's my favourite way to relax.

3

Examiner: Do you prefer shopping with friends or shopping online?

Student C: Online shopping is OK and I think it's quicker, but I prefer going shopping with friends. You can ask them for their opinion and it's more fun to be with other people.

4

Examiner: Do you prefer blogging or playing games online?

Student D: Well, I use my laptop most days for lots of different things. However, I like playing games online more than anything else. I think it's a bit more interesting than blogging and since I play games a lot, I've become quite good at it.

2.08 | Unit 5, Language in Use, page 55, Exercise 1

1

Peter: I spend a lot of time using social networking sites. I chat to lots of different people. A few months ago I started taking pictures and making short videos to share with my friends. You don't need a special camera or anything. You just use your phone to make the video then upload it. I think it's the best way to show people my new skateboarding moves!

2

Chloe: I like to contact my friends and tell them what I'm doing, without spending lots of money. All of us have mobile phones so this is how we keep in touch. Sometimes we have a group chat, so the same message goes to lots of different people. It's really good. I think it's the fastest way to share information and a great way to stay in touch with friends.

3

Sam: A lot of people in my family live in foreign countries. I don't see them very often. But when I use this app on my laptop, I can talk to my cousins and see them, too. Sometimes the sound is slow, so it can be difficult to understand what someone is saying. But most of the time it's the easiest way to speak to my family.

UNIT 6 | STUDENT'S BOOK

2.09 | Unit 6, Reading, page 59, Exercise 6

Fashion changes

Online shopping has changed the world of fashion. We can buy clothes from all over the world, compare prices and find the best places to shop. What other things have changed the fashion world?

There are a lot of new people starting new trends, especially teenagers. Some of them are famous, like Romeo Beckham, but many are normal teenagers who use social media to show people how to dress well. A lot of people follow them on social media. So clothing companies now look at their ideas. These teens don't just follow fashion, they make it. To them, it doesn't matter if something is old or new. The most important thing is that it looks good.

Have you ever worn a T-shirt made from old plastic bottles? Clothes are often made from different things these days. This is because many people are interested in looking after the world, and some customers think carefully about this when buying fashion. They choose clothes made of different plants, like bamboo, coconut and banana, or from recycled materials like bottles, tyres and coffee. And now you can even buy shoes that make electricity when you walk. They're amazing!

Many people buy their clothes online, but shopping centres are still very busy. There are lots of clothes shops to choose from. Some shops use unusual ideas to try and get more customers. For example, Johnny Cupcakes is a clothes shop that smells of cakes! And it's an experience they won't forget. The shop assistant puts your clothes in special boxes. I've never visited the store, but it must make you hungry!

2.13 | Unit 6, Listening, page 62, Exercise 2

Speaker 1

I know you're probably busy, but I'd really like you to help me with the shopping this afternoon. I hope that's OK.

Speaker 2

Mike has just broken his computer so he's gone to the shop. I'm not sure how long he'll be.

Speaker 3

I don't know what to do. I bought this dress and it's too big for me, but I haven't got time to find something else for the party.

Speaker 4

I'm going to work at home all day tomorrow, but you can call me if you need me.

2.14 | Unit 6, Listening, page 62, Exercises 3 and 4

1 **You will hear a customer talking to a shop assistant. What's the problem with the trousers?**

Customer: I'd like to return these boy's trousers please.

Shop Assistant: OK, can you tell me why? Are they too small?

Customer: I'm afraid my son needs blue ones. I didn't realise until I got back home and my son told me.

Shop Assistant 1: OK.

2 **You will hear a girl, Maisie, talking to her father. What does Maisie want to do later?**

Dad: Maisie, can you come and help me with the cooking?

Maisie: I can't. I've got to finish my homework.

Dad: You can do that later while Mum and I are out.

Maisie: But I've saved that time for practising the piano. It's important!

Dad: Oh, I see. OK.

3 **You will hear a mother talking to her son about their holiday. What does she want her son to do?**

Mother: Oh goodness, come on. Why aren't you ready?

Boy: I am. I've just given the cat some food and finished packing.

Mother: Well, your sister put her clothes in her suitcase last night! I need you to put the luggage in the car!

Boy: OK, OK! Give me five minutes and then I'll help you.

4 **You will hear two friends talking about their weekend plans. Why is the boy happy?**

Girl: Let's go camping by the lake this weekend.

Boy: Yes, sure. As long as I don't have to light the fire or put up the tent!

Girl: I'll do that. And we can go swimming in the lake.

Boy: OK. I'm really pleased that I can bring my dog – I miss him when he can't come with me.

5 **You will hear a boy talking to his friend. What does the boy need to buy?**

Boy: I can't wait to start playing badminton. I wasn't sure what racket to get, so I asked the coach and he said he would lend me one to try before I spend any money. I have already got some good trainers, so all I need now is the team's shirt and then I'll have all the kit.

2.15 | Unit 6, Speaking, page 64, Exercise 4

Boy: OK so for homework, we've got to decide if we like these shops. Let's look at this one first. It's a bicycle shop because you can see bikes outside it. I like bike shops actually.

Girl: Hmm, I'm not sure I do – I only go when my bike is broken so I don't really like them. This next one is a clothes shop. Look you can see some trousers in the window. I love clothes shopping. I go every week with my mum.

Boy: I think clothes shopping is boring. Then there's a grocery store here. I can see tomatoes and potatoes in the front of the window. Well, that's quite nice because it's always interesting to buy food.

Girl: Yes, I agree. I think this one is a chemist because I can see some medicine. I only go there to buy boring things so I can't say I like it!

Boy: Yes, that's true! And this final one is a butcher's because, look, there are some sausages and other meat in the window. I quite like going there to help choose what we have for dinner.

Girl: Do you? I don't eat meat so I hate going in there!

UNIT 7 | STUDENT'S BOOK

2.16 | Unit 7, Reading, page 71, Exercise 4

Technology for all

In classrooms around the world, many students now have computers or tablets on their desks instead of books. Technology is helping young people to learn about the world, and preparing them for work. But in poorer countries, there aren't any computers available for students.

That was a problem for schools in the countryside in Uganda, in East Africa. But since 2007, the Mobile Solar Computer Classroom has helped many classes of children and adults at schools and libraries to use computers. There are two mobile computer classrooms, and they travel all over the country in two large cars, going to schools to give computer lessons. Later today, one of them is going to visit a village in the west of the country. It's a long way down a difficult road, but the drivers are lucky because it isn't going to rain, and that helps. In the car, there are 15 laptop computers, desks and chairs, two ICT teachers and a large battery. This produces solar energy for the computers, because many of the villages don't have electricity.

More than 200 people a day can have computer lessons from the two mobile classrooms. This means over 5,000 people have these lessons each year! What are they going to do next? Well, over the next few years, they are going to build computer classrooms in 55 Ugandan schools. Teachers and students know how important computers will be in the future and these classrooms will really help students prepare for a job in tomorrow's world.

2.20 | Unit 7, Listening, page 74, Exercises 4 and 5

You will hear a woman talking about how she helps children in Argentina.

My name's Alice, I'm 69 and I'd like to tell you how I help children in Argentina from my home in England.

I have an unusual job because I work as a 'cloud granny'. I do this for a company called SOLEVINE– that's S-O-L-E-V-I-N-E.

I talk online to schoolchildren for an hour on Mondays and Wednesdays. I help them with their schoolwork, and they ask me about life and they talk about their lives too.

I saw an advert for cloud grannys in December, and I thought this job sounded interesting! By January, I was teaching children who live on the other side of the world!

I usually teach small groups of two or three children, but I also have classes of 34 children!

So, what am I going to teach them today? Well, I'll start the lesson by discussing their homework, before I give them English and history lessons. Sometimes, I show them photos of the trees and plants in my garden which they always enjoy.

2.21 | Unit 7, Speaking, page 76, Exercises 4 and 5

1

A: Are you going to take exams this term?

B: No, we're not going to take any exams until next term.

2

A: Will your classmates pass the test?

B: Yes, they are studying really hard, so I think they're going to pass.

3

A: What languages will you study next year?

B: I think I'll study French and English perhaps.

4

A: Are you going to study in the summer holidays?

B: No, when school finishes for the holidays, I'm going to work at a summer camp.

UNIT 8 | STUDENT'S BOOK

2.22 | Unit 8, Reading, page 81, Exercise 5

1

Hi Tim
Sorry, but I can't practise for the match today. I'm tired and I haven't finished my homework. Can we go tomorrow?
Adele

2

From: Alex
To: Sue
We are the winners!
My team won the competition, so I'm having a party on Saturday. Can you and Karen come?

3

Hi Rob
Are you feeling better? Do you want me to visit you? I can show you what we did in art class today.
Helena

4

From: Alice
To: Marc
Thanks for the book, I love it! As you know, I'm Usain Bolt's biggest fan. The photos are amazing!

5

Tennis coach
Beginners: £10 a lesson
Can lend rackets to students
Must bring trainers

6

Sailing trip
To go on the trip, you must be able to swim well.

2.27 | Unit 8, Listening, page 84, Exercises 2 and 3

1

Mum: What did you do yesterday when it rained?

Dan: We couldn't go outside, so we played table tennis. It wasn't very good. I prefer sports where you run around, like football or rugby.

2

Dad: What happened on Sunday, Lorna?

Lorna: Well some of the girls played volleyball, but I went cycling in the mountains. I didn't get tired and I had a great time.

3

Mum: Did you go fishing this morning, Chris?

Chris: No, we went windsurfing this morning. It was my first time, but I loved it.

4

Dad: Did you have a good time yesterday, Lily?

Lily: Not really. I wanted to go swimming, but we had to go running outside. It was very cold and no-one wanted to do it.

5

Friend: Did they teach you how to play tennis at the club yesterday?

Pete: No, they taught us how to play badminton. It was really good fun ... and I was quite good!

2.28 | Unit 8, Listening, page 84, Exercises 4 and 5

Bea: Hi Dad.

Dad: Hi Bea. How's summer camp?

Bea: It's great! I'm doing lots of different sports. So, on Monday, we went for a long run in the morning. I don't like running, but it was OK because we were all together. Then I played volleyball in the afternoon.

Dad: That sounds great!

Bea: I wanted to play tennis on Tuesday, but it was raining so I couldn't. So, instead of tennis, a coach taught us to play badminton in the sports centre.

Dad: Did you enjoy it? I played badminton years ago and I liked it a lot.

Bea: Yes, I loved it! You should start playing again, Dad – it's good exercise and we could play together.

Dad: *[laughs]* Good idea. I might do that. Anyway, what did you do on Wednesday?

Bea: On Wednesday we went to the sea. It's a long walk to the beach, so we have to get up really early when we go there ... and you know how much I like getting up early!

Dad: Haha – it's not something you enjoy, I know that! So, did you go swimming?

Bea: No. I wanted to, but it was too windy. Camp rules say we mustn't swim if there is a strong wind – it's not safe.

Dad: So, what did you do?

Bea: One of the instructors took us sailing. It was amazing.

Dad: Your mum loves sailing, too. Umm ... Bea – could you take some photos of the boats, please? I'm sure Mum would really like to see them.

Bea: Yes, no problem.

Dad: Thanks. And, what happened yesterday?

Bea: Yesterday ... that was Thursday. Oh, yes ... we had a cricket competition. That was fun. Today the plan was for us to play football, but it's really hot here.

Dad: Well, you shouldn't be out in the sun all day if it's very hot.

Bea: I know. The camp leader says we can go to the pool today instead.

Dad: OK, enjoy your swim, Bea! See you on Sunday.

Bea: Bye Dad!

2.29 | Unit 8, Speaking, page 86, Exercise 5

Narrator: Here are some pictures that show different sports. Do you like these sports? Say why or why not.

Boy: So, let's discuss these sports. What do you think about basketball?

Girl: Hmm, well I like watching it, but I've never played it. I think you need to be tall so it would probably be difficult for me.

Boy: I've played it a few times and I really enjoyed it. It's a very fast game so you need to be very fit.

Girl: What about football?

Boy: I quite like it, but it's not my favourite sport. What about you?

Girl: I agree. I don't really like team sports. I think activities like swimming are more relaxing.

Boy: Yes. I like swimming but only in the summer. What about playing tennis?

Girl: I think tennis is fun and it's probably very good for you as you need to run around a lot.

Boy: I like playing it with my family actually. My brother is a really good player.

Girl: What about climbing?

Boy: Well I'm afraid of high places so I don't think climbing is for me. Do you like it?

Girl: I've never gone climbing before, but I think I'd like it because you can do it on your own or with friends. I'm sure it feels really good when you reach the top of the climbing wall or the mountain.

UNIT 9 | STUDENT'S BOOK

3.01 | Unit 9, Reading, page 93, Exercise 4

Crazy weather!

Max

Do you like snow? I do, but sometimes it can cause problems! One morning when I woke up, there was snow. It covered our car and the garden. Because of the snow, we were without electricity, and it was dark and cold in the house. For me, it was an adventure, but my parents were very worried. We couldn't go outside for three days. Now that I'm older, I think I would be scared if it happened again.

Ian

If you go sailing often, be careful! One Saturday, it was warm and sunny, so my family decided to go out in our boat. We spent the morning sailing. Then we stopped at a beach to have lunch. But very quickly, it became windy and dark as clouds covered the sky. Then the storm started. It wasn't safe to sail, so we waited in the rain until it finished. We were lucky that we weren't at sea when it happened!

Joe

My village is near a lake and, a few winters ago, something very dangerous happened: strong winds began to slowly push the ice on the lake towards the village! Nothing could stop it. The ice went into people's houses, covered the roads and moved their cars. People were afraid, but luckily nobody was hurt. It was the strangest thing I've ever seen. If it happens again, I'll film it and put it on YouTube!

3.06 | Unit 9, Listening, page 96, Exercise 2

1

Man: Would you like to go for a walk in the forest today?

Woman: Good idea!

2

Girl: It's a lovely sunny day. Do you want to go swimming?

Boy: I'm not sure. I'll think about it.

3

Boy: Do you want to play tennis?

Boy: Not really. I'm tired.

4

Dad: Why don't we go to the beach?

Girl: Great. I'll get my swimsuit.

5

Girl: Do you want to go for a bike ride?

Girl: Maybe.

3.07 | Unit 9, Listening, page 96, Exercises 4 and 5

1

Mum: Would you like to go to the mountains this weekend, Sophie?

Sophie: Not really. If it's raining, can we go to the cinema?

Mum: Maybe. But I think it's going to be sunny.

Sophie: Great. Then why don't we go to the lake? It's beautiful there in the sun.

2

Jack: Is it raining again?

Anna: No, but it's very cloudy. It isn't sunny at all.

Jack: If it was sunny, I would go to the beach today.

Anna: Me too, but not when the weather is like this. Do you want to watch a film instead?

3

Granddad: Are you and your parents going on holiday this summer?

Arthur: I think so. We'd go to the beach in Spain if we had more money. We loved it there last year. But we'll probably go somewhere nearer home this year.

Granddad: Well you could all go camping in the countryside. It's not expensive.

Arthur: Great idea! And after that, maybe we'll go to the mountains.

4

Man: It looks like it's going to be warm and sunny in the north tomorrow.

Woman: Yes, but we aren't in the north! What's it going to be like here?

Man: It's going to be cloudy in the morning. But after lunch there's going to be a big storm.

Woman: Oh, dear. I don't think I'll go out then.

5

Boy: I can't wait till summer. I love the hot weather. What about you?

Girl: I don't really like the hot weather.

Boy: Do you prefer winter, then? Or autumn?

Girl: Autumn is my favourite time of year. It's beautiful. I don't like snow, so I don't like winter very much at all.

3.08 | Unit 9, Speaking, page 98, Exercises 4 and 5

1

Well we usually go to the same place every summer because we go to visit my grandparents who live by the sea. Then in the winter, we usually have a short break for two or three days. We go to different places. For example, we sometimes visit a new city like Paris or Berlin.

2

I'm an only child, and I don't have any cousins, so I spend more time with my friends. One example is at weekends and the school holidays my best friend usually comes to stay. It's almost like having a sister.

3

We have lots of gadgets in our house as my parents, my brother and sister and I all love tablets, phones and computer games. Let me give an example – last night when I got home, everyone was in the living room, but all using different gadgets.

4

It's a big place with lots of things to do. For example, the sports centre is very big and there's a new shopping centre with restaurants, cinemas and of course, shops.

3.09 | Unit 9, Speaking, page 98, Exercise 6

I love where I live, but I love visiting other places even more. Every year I try to visit new places, for example this year I cycled for six days around the coast with the cycle club. We saw lots of beautiful scenery. I also went on a walking trip to the beach, sorry I mean to the mountains. It was amazing.

UNIT 10 | STUDENT'S BOOK

3.10 | Unit 10, Reading, page 103, Exercise 4

1

Students who are ill should stay home and have their parents contact the school.

2

From: Anna
To: Julie
I've just remembered I have an appointment today. Can we go to the cinema at 8 instead of 6?

3

Ben
Tina has been in hospital since Saturday. Let's visit her and buy her a present. Have you got any ideas?
Rob

4

42km Running Competition
Have you entered the race yet? You must be fit.

5

Hi Joe
Did you know the local hospital has had first-aid courses for six months? I'm interested. Are you? Let me know.
Cathy

6

From: Meg
To: Lorna
I'm so upset! The doctor's checked my eyes and I can't swim this Saturday. I've already missed so many races this year!
Meg

3.14 | Unit 10, Listening, page 106, Exercise 2

1

Hi, I'm sorry to come back to see you, Doctor, but I've had a really bad headache. The tablets you gave me for the earache were good though so that's better now.

2

I'm fed up with my broken arm. It was so stupid. I left my school bag at home, then because I was late, I was running and tripped on the steps that lead to the main entrance.

3

I can't play football this week because I've hurt my ankle. It happened yesterday while I was at tennis practice. It's so sore I can't run!

4

At the end of the day I've always got a headache. I can't see the board properly because my eyes hurt. I try to listen really carefully to the teacher so I can understand what to do. I must have a check-up.

3.15 | Unit 10, Listening, page 106, Exercises 3 and 4

1 **You will hear two friends talking about their plans. What do they decide to do at the weekend?**

Boy: Do you want to go to see the football match this weekend?

Girl: Who's playing?

Boy: The city team. It's going to be good.

Girl: Actually, I'd rather do something – like play tennis.

Boy: Oh OK, let's do that. We could go swimming afterwards?

Girl: Mmm we don't have lots of time. Let's just do one thing.

Boy: OK.

2 **You will hear a boy, Sam, talking to his football coach. Why is Sam feeling unhappy?**

Sam: I went to see the doctor yesterday because I've had a bad stomach ache for a week. The doctor gave me some medicine. I feel a lot better today, but I can't eat anything sweet or spicy. He also said I can't do any sports for a week so I won't be able to play football on Saturday.

3 **You will hear a father talking to his daughter, Sarah. What is Sarah's dad asking her to do?**

Dad: Sarah, have you tidied your room yet?

Sarah: Yes, I have, Dad. I did it a while ago.

Dad: Good, but you haven't taken the dog for a walk yet, have you?

Sarah: But Mum's going to show me how to fix my flat tyre in a minute.

Dad: Not until you take your pet out. It needs some exercise.

Sarah: Yeah, OK.

4 **You will hear two friends talking about their friend David. How did Anna try to help her friend?**

Boy: I heard David was ill and didn't play at the concert. Is he OK?

Anna: Yes, he caught a cold and has a cough.

Boy: Oh, what a pity!

Anna: Yes I offered to take him to the doctor, but he didn't want to go because he hates taking medicine.

Boy: That's why he keeps getting ill.

5 **You will hear a teacher talking to Peter's mother. Why's the teacher talking to his mum?**

Mrs Brown: Sorry I'm late.

Teacher: Oh Mrs Brown. I'm afraid Peter was ill today.

Mrs Brown: Oh dear! What was wrong?

Teacher: I'm not sure, but he looked terrible and he kept coughing. I told him to drink lots of water and not do his homework.

Mrs Brown: OK, thanks. I'll take his temperature when I get home and see how he's doing.

3.16 | Unit 10, Speaking, page 108, Exercises 3, 4 and 6

1

Examiner: What do you think of running?

Student A: Oh I really love it. I used to get headaches all the time and then I started running three times a week. Now I feel much better.

2

Examiner: What kind of healthy food do you like?

Student B: Erm … well, I don't eat much healthy food. I think most of it tastes horrible. I only eat it when my mum makes me eat salad at the weekend.

3

Examiner: Do you prefer doing exercise alone or with other people?

Student C: Hm – let me see. Probably with other people because in my view it makes you try much harder – and it's more enjoyable.

4

Examiner: Which do you like better – shopping or cooking?

Student D: Oh definitely cooking! I'm quite good because my mother taught me how to make some good dishes so now, for example, I cook for the family quite often.

UNIT 11 | STUDENT'S BOOK

3.17 | Unit 11, Reading, page 115, Exercise 4

All aboard the children's railway

Are you interested in trains? Have you ever thought about all the jobs people do on a railway? It isn't easy. All the trains have to be clean, the engineers need to check everything is working, someone needs to sell the tickets and take the money, and the trains mustn't be late. The trains must leave and arrive on time and this must match the timetable. And, very importantly – the trains must be safe. Almost everywhere in the world, railway staff are adults. But in Budapest, there is a special railway and nearly everyone who works there is a child.

The Gyermekvasút, or Children's Railway, in Hungary, first opened to customers in 1948. And it is still taking passengers on journeys from a few hundred metres to 11 kilometres, through the hills in the west of the city. The train drivers and engineers are adults, but all the other staff, from the ticket sellers to the station managers, are between 10 and 14 years old. All the workers have to wear a smart uniform, and they are all volunteers, which means they don't get paid. Every year, lots of children want to work on the railway, but they don't give jobs to everyone. Anyone who doesn't get good marks at school won't get a job. The children who get jobs have two days off school every month to work on the railway.

The Children's Railway isn't a toy or a model railway. It is part of the national railway system of Hungary and an important part of Budapest's transport system. Each year over 300,000 customers use the Railway to get to work, visit friends or just to see how well the children do their jobs!

3.22 | Unit 11, Listening, page 118, Exercise 2

1 My name is Tom Armitage – that's A-R-M-I-T-A-G-E.

2 I live with my family in a place called Bicester – you spell that B-I-C-E-S-T-E-R.

3 We live in Vaughan Way – Vaughan is spelt V-A-U-G-H-A-N.

4 My best friend is Chloe Green. Can you spell Chloe? It's C-H-L-O-E.

5 Next summer, Leo and I are going to visit Edinburgh in Scotland – that's E-D-I-N-B-U-R-G-H.

3.23 | Unit 11, Listening, page 118, Exercise 3

I really like going to concerts, but I live in a small town and there aren't many places where musicians can play. So, in July last year, I decided to plan a concert myself. My friend Dan said I could have it in his large garden. I put a message on Facebook and asked lots of musicians to come and play. About 80 people came and six bands played. The best band was Jayveeland – that's J-A-Y-V-E-E-L-A-N-D. We sold food and drink and we earned about £200. It was great. We're going to do it again this year as well.

3.24 | Unit 11, Listening, page 118, Exercises 4 and 5

Hi my name's Zi Yang Chen and I want to tell you about a business that I started a year ago. People are surprised I have my own business because I'm only 15. I got the idea because my dad works in a big factory which is near Guangzhou, that's G-U-A-N-G-Z-H-O-U. There aren't any supermarkets near the factory and my dad told me that he couldn't buy any healthy snacks, so I decided to start a fruit business. Every morning except Saturdays, people can visit our website before 5pm and choose what they would like for the next day. We buy all the fruit and then my mum takes them to the people the next morning. We take food to three factories and six offices at the moment. Altogether there are 52 people who buy from us every week. Next year, we hope to have four or five people working for the business, and a lot more customers.

3.25 | Unit 11, Speaking, page 120, Exercises 4 and 5

Well, I come from a large family with five children. I have an older brother and sister and a younger brother and sister. My older brother, Matthew, is a photographer for a magazine and my sister, Marta works in a theatre. She's worked there for ten years. Matthew can work very long hours, but unlike my mum and dad he doesn't work in an office. Matthew often meets his manager in the morning in a coffee bar or on location. My dad is a lawyer in Manchester. My mum is a journalist, but it's the school holidays, so she isn't working this week. We're at home. My sister, Anna is cooking lunch at the moment and my younger brother, Jake is playing computer games. I'm talking to Marta's friend on the phone. Jane usually works in an office, but this month she's visiting customers. She's going to come and visit us while she's in the area.

UNIT 12 | STUDENT'S BOOK

3.26 | Unit 12, Reading, page 125, Exercise 5

This is where I live

Gala, Russia

My village is in a beautiful forest. I love it because I wake up to the sounds of birds and the wind in the trees. Our house isn't modern, but it has everything we need. There's one big room with the kitchen and living area, a bathroom and two bedrooms – one for my parents and another that I share with my sister. In my bedroom there are shelves for books and our beds have lots of blankets. In winter, the house is heated by a fire and it stays nice and warm.

Luiza, Brazil

There are many towns in Brazil. Mine is near the Amazon river. It's a big town with fantastic new houses and some older ones too that aren't as nice. The older houses are made from wood and they're tiny. My house is new and it's very comfortable. I live here with my parents and my two brothers. My best friend lives next door. It's great here. There's a nice square in the middle of the town with cinemas and cafes. We also have a big festival every year. I don't want to live anywhere else!

Lara, UK

I live on a farm, far away from a town or city. My parents are farmers and they grow lots of fruit and vegetables on the land and sell them in the local market. We also have some sheep and cows – they're my pets! Everything we eat is healthy and the air we breathe is fresh and clean. Life on a farm isn't for everyone. But if you want to live close to nature and don't need to turn on the TV or use a laptop every time you're bored, life on a farm is great!

3.30 | Unit 12, Listening, page 128, Exercises 2 and 3

When I was younger, I lived in a house in the countryside with my parents and brother. Two years ago, we moved to a large apartment by the sea. It's smaller than our old house, but I love watching the boats on the water every day.

3.31 | Unit 12, Listening, page 128, Exercises 5 and 6

Jed: So, when did your family first live on the water Heidi?

Heidi: Well, I grew up in a house by the river so I've always lived near water. But four years ago, when I was ten, my parents were given a boat by their cousins and we went to live on it.

Jed: What it's like living on a boat?

Heidi: It's very different from living in a house. The kitchen is much smaller and there isn't a bath in the bathroom. But I don't mind. We haven't got a dining room on the boat, but that's OK because we usually eat outside in the summer.

Jed: What do you like most about it?

Heidi: Well, in the winter we have a fire in the living room. I love it. And my bedroom is really cool. But my favourite thing is what you can see out the windows. Every day, you see something different on the river.

Jed: That must be amazing.

Heidi: Yes, it is. But there are some problems. For example, it's nice and warm inside in the winter, but in the mornings before we light the fire, it's very cold. But the worst thing is that we don't have a washing machine.

Jed: Hmm ... I don't think I'd like to live on a boat. Maybe it's OK for some people, but there isn't much space, although the river is very beautiful and quiet.

3.32 | Unit 12, Speaking, page 130, Exercise 4

Woman: Are you moving?

Man: Yes we're going to live in the countryside. I don't want to leave the city though, it's such fun here.

Woman: Wow! I agree. I would hate to move. But you can have a good time in the countryside too in the summer.

Man: I'm not so sure. There's not much to do. I *really really* liked living right in the centre of the city. It's the best place.

Woman: Hm. I'm not sure about that. It's very noisy and expensive. But at least the transport is good and fast.

Man: That's true. It'll be terrible in the countryside! I won't be able to go anywhere!

Woman: Never mind. You can come back and stay with my family sometimes. We aren't going to move away!

Man: Ah thanks! I'll miss you and living in the city so much. The countryside just won't be the same especially as you won't be there!

OPTIMISE YOUR EXAMS STUDENT'S BOOK

3.33 | Optimise your exams, Listening, page 140, Exercise 1

1

Girl: Have you seen my bag, Jim?

Jim: Is it under your desk? I think I saw it there in our maths lesson.

Girl: No, it was there, but after the lesson I left it by the door.

Jim: Look – there it is. It's by the window.

2

Boy: What time does the film start? Is it eight fifteen?

Girl: No, it's not. It begins at quarter to eight.

Boy: Are you sure? If you're right, we should leave here at seven fifteen so we get there on time.

Girl: Yes, it's definitely at seven forty-five. I checked on the internet. So, we need to go soon.

3

Kevin: Are we going to the shopping centre again on Saturday, Sal?

Sal: Let's do something different, Kevin. How about going to the skate park?

Kevin: Yes, OK then. Anything's better than shopping.

Sal: *[laughs]* Really? How about studying in the library all day – is that better than shopping? *[laughs]*

4

Dad: There are some nice watches here, but they're expensive. I think Mum might prefer some new jewellery.

Girl: Dad, look at this tablet. It looks fantastic. Mum could read her books on it.

Dad: No, I'm not buying Mum a tablet for her birthday. How about this necklace? It's not too expensive.

Girl: Yes, it's pretty. I think she'll like that.

5

Woman: It looks like it's going to be cold and snowy in some places tomorrow.

Man: Really? Is it going to snow here?

Woman: No, the weather forecast says it will be cold and icy here, but not snowy.

Man: Well ... I don't like cold weather. I think I'll be staying in the house tomorrow!

3.34 | Optimise your exams, Listening, page 140, Exercise 2

Teacher: Next week Thursday we're going on a school trip to the theatre in London. I know we usually have football practice on Tuesdays and Thursdays, but Mr Jones has agreed to change it to Monday and Wednesday this week. This will allow the boys on the football team to go on the trip too. Everyone has to be at school at six fifteen because the bus leaves at six thirty and we don't want to be late. The play starts at 7:30. We're going to see War Horse at the Troubadour Theatre. That's T-r-o-u-b-a-d-o-u-r. It's a famous play with the same story as the book by Michael Morpurgo. The play is about two hours forty minutes long with a 20 minute break. You can look online to read more about the play. The tickets are not too expensive as we have a special price for students of 15 pounds. Tickets are usually cost a lot more and the cheapest tickets are usually 19 pounds, but those seats are not very good.

3.35 | Optimise your exams, Listening, page 141, Exercise 3

Matt: Hi Joanna, are you free on Friday? Tim and I are going to *The Birds* concert, would you like to come? I asked Peter and Jill, but they're both busy.

Joanna: I'd love to come, but I don't really know much about *The Birds*. What kind of music do they play? Is it dance or rock with classical guitars?

Matt: It's rock music, but they use violins too.

Joanna: It sounds really interesting. It's not the kind of music I usually listen to, but I think I will enjoy it.

Joanna: Shall we meet at the concert hall? I'll get the train there or I can get the bus.

Matt: No, don't do that. My dad's going to drive me, so you can come with us.

Joanna: OK, thanks.

Matt: Do you remember the last concert we went to? It was terrible.

Joanna: Oh yes. I remember.

Matt: *The Birds* should be much better, they are always thinking of new ways to play music. Peter has been before and says they're amazing.

3.36 | Optimise your exams, Listening, page 141, Exercise 4

Dialogue 1:

You will hear two friends talking about their day. What did they do first?

Girl 1: Ah, what a busy day! That was so much fun and it's nice to end the day at the shopping centre.

Girl 2: Yes, I enjoyed it, too. The tennis was great.

Girl 1: Yes, it was. It was a good idea to do that before going shopping. It was too hot for tennis this afternoon.

Girl 2: I know. I'm looking forward to dinner now. I'm so hungry!

Dialogue 2:

You will hear a teacher talking to a student. What does she want him to do?

Teacher: Oh Craig, you have answered the wrong question for your homework.

Craig: Oh no, do I need to do it again?

Teacher: I don't think there's time now. You need to stop talking to your friends in class while I am telling you what to do for homework.

Craig: OK, I'm sorry.

Teacher: You will do much better if you listen more!

Dialogue 3:

You will hear a man talking about feeling ill. What should he do?

Man: I haven't felt very well this week. I have a cough so I went to the doctor this morning. She said I didn't need any medicine just some rest. She said it was important not to stay in bed all day though and the best thing I can do to get better is to drink a lot more water. I had wanted her to give me some medicine but she didn't.

Dialogue 4:

You will hear a boy talking to his friend about shopping. Why did he buy the T-shirt?

Girl: Hey James. Have you been shopping today?

James: Yeah I bought a T-shirt.

Girl: Can I see it? Oh, Matt's got one just like that!

James: I know, he got his for his birthday.

Girl: Why did you buy the same one?

James: Oh, because I have to wear it for the next game I'm playing in. We all have to have a blue T-shirt.

Dialogue 5:

You will hear a father talking to his daughter. Why is he unhappy?

Dad: Where have you been, Livi?

Livi: I just went to the shop to get some milk because mum asked me to buy some this morning.

Dad: OK, thanks, but I wish you would take your boots off when you come in. Look at the carpet, I'll need to clean it now! And that's not how I like spending my time.

Livi: Oh, sorry, Dad!

UNIT 1 | WORKBOOK

01 | Listening, page 8, Exercise 2

1

Carl: Where are Zach and Emma?

Laura: They're at a picnic in the park with some friends from school.

Carl: Remember, we all have a barbecue this evening.

Laura: It's OK, the picnic finishes before five. They can cycle back.

2

Paul: What do you do in your free time, Linda?

Linda: I watch movies and listen to music. My brother plays guitar and sometimes I sing with him.

Paul: Do you like reading?

Linda: I read a lot of books, but I never read magazines.

3

Andy: Is there a club meeting tonight?

Mina: Yes, there is, but it isn't in the school. It's closed.

Andy: Oh, OK. Is it at Matt's house again?

Mina: No, it's at Gina's. She lives opposite the new café on George Street.

4

Jo: Who do you go camping with?

Angus: It's usually just my parents and my brother and me.

Jo: And your cousins?

Angus: No, they never come. They don't like camping.

5

Emma: I want to go to your party tonight, but I have an art class.

Jeff: What time is it?

Emma: It starts at 7. It's for an hour and a half.

Jeff: Well, the party starts at half past seven. But it's OK, you can come later.

UNIT 2 | WORKBOOK

02 | Listening, page 16, Exercise 2

Katie: It's the best festival of the year. And so many great bands are playing this year.

James: Who do you want to see?

Katie: Well, The Carltons are my favourite. They play here every year. They're amazing. They've got so many great songs. The guitarist is also in The Plastic Cups.

03 | Listening, page 16, Exercise 3

Katie: It's the best festival of the year. And so many great bands are playing this year.

James: Who do you want to see?

Katie: Well, The Carltons are my favourite. They play here every year. They're amazing. They've got so many great songs. The guitarist is also in The Plastic Cups.

James: I don't know them.

Katie: They're very different to The Carltons. Their music is really quick and the songs are very loud.

James: I really like Lonely Phones. They're playing tomorrow, I think.

Katie: Yes, they're cool. And really good-looking too!

James: What about The Tea Lions?

Katie: Don't go and see them! They play really slow and sad music.

James: Sounds boring. I prefer something that's happy.

Katie: Mexico Sun are never boring. Their music is really exciting. They're playing on Sunday afternoon.

James: Great. Let's go and see them together then.

UNIT 3 | WORKBOOK

04 | Listening, page 24, Exercise 4

Ingmar: Where did you go on your cooking holiday?

Abi: I flew to Lyon and met the group there. We then travelled by coach to the small village of Chassagny, where we stayed for a week in an old house. The house was lovely and we had the cooking lessons in the kitchen.

Ingmar: Who was the teacher?

Abi: There was a young woman called Margot. She was really friendly. She taught most of the lessons. And also her father, Daniel. He was a chef, and he also helped with the teaching.

Ingmar: It sounds great. I also went on a cooking holiday last year to Italy.

Abi: Really? What did you learn?

Ingmar: We learnt about baking bread and making cakes and there were two lessons on other desserts. I wanted to learn how to make biscuits, but there wasn't enough time.

Abi: Was it difficult?

Ingmar: At first it was. But I loved meeting everyone, talking about food, learning and cooking. And of course, we could eat everything we made. That was the best thing.

UNIT 4 | WORKBOOK

05 | Listening, page 32, Exercises 1, 2 and 3

Hiya. Welcome to today's Brighton Past and Present Tour. My name's Gary (that's G-A-R-Y) and I'm your guide for today, and this is Karol, that's with a K and not a C, K-A-R-O-L, and he's your driver. Before we leave, I just want to give you all some information. Is everyone listening? OK, great. So, the tour starts in a few minutes, and finishes in four hours and 15 minutes. So, we finish at about 3:45 this afternoon. OK? Lovely.

This morning we're visiting the Royal Pavilion, Brighton's most famous building. They started building it in 1787 and it was finished in 1822. It was once the summer house of the Prince Regent (R-E-G-E-N-T – just like the famous street and park in London). He was the son of King George III. After that, we're going to see the new i360 tower, which is 162 metres high, and then we're going to Brighton Pier. It's 524 metres long and it has some amazing views from the end. There's also a famous fish and chip restaurant there, and yes, we're having lunch there. That'll be at about 1:30.

After lunch, we walk through the Lanes (L-I-N, sorry I mean L-A-N-E-S), Brighton's oldest and most beautiful shopping area, so there will be plenty of time for shopping. Any questions?

UNIT 5 | WORKBOOK

06 | Listening, page 40, Exercise 2

1

Kate: I'm so sorry we are late. I know the party started at 7.

Mike: What happened?

Kate: Our train was at 6 o'clock, but it was an hour late.

Mike: I see. Well, come in. We sang *Happy Birthday* and gave Sally the cake, but the party isn't finishing until 9pm.

2

Laura: This is terrible. I should be at your house in Bristol now. I used the map on my phone for directions. I typed in the first part of the address, 26 Crescent Road, but I don't think I checked the name of the city.

Paul: But you know the way to Bristol from Swindon, don't you?

Laura: Well, no. I just followed the directions on my phone. It took me about an hour and a half to get to Crescent Road, but I'm not in Bristol. I'm in Oxford.

Paul: That's the opposite way!

3

Jon: I was really worried. I had it at the market. Then when I got on the bus it wasn't there.

Lucy: So, what did you do?

Jon: I spoke to a police officer about it. She told me to call the phone company. Then my mum got a phone call. It was an old lady. She said her granddaughter found the phone at the bus stop.

Lucy: You were really lucky.

4

Alex: Where is it? I need to use it tonight. I remember I checked my emails when we were in the café.

Glenda: Did you have it at school? Perhaps it's still in the classroom.

Alex: Yes, I know I had it at school. But I didn't take it out of my bag in the classroom. What about the library?

Glenda: Yes, I remember. You went there after the lesson to do your homework.

5

Gabby: I took it the first time I used the camera. I was walking in the countryside taking photos. Then I turned round and saw this snake eating a bird's egg. I stopped and took a photo.

Ian: It's an amazing photo, did it win the competition?

Gabby: No. But later on that day I took a photo of a bird giving some food to its baby, and this one of a wild cat sleeping in a tree which came first!

Ian: Wow, well done!

UNIT 6 | WORKBOOK

07 | Listening, page 48, Exercise 1

Kim: Have you found your wallet, Aaron?

Aaron: Yes, I have. It was on the bus. The bus driver found it under a seat. I'm really lucky. My grandad gave me that wallet, so it's really important to me.

Kim: I'm really glad you found it.

08 | Listening, page 48, Exercise 3

1 You will hear a boy, Ben, talking to his mother. What does she want Ben to do?

Mum: Ben, are those the boots you got when we went shopping last month?

Ben: Yes, Mum. Er, they're a bit dirty now. I wore them to play football in the park yesterday … But they're really comfortable.

Mum: They're covered in mud! You should look after them, Ben. They were expensive!

Ben: I know.

2 **You will hear a shop assistant talking to a customer. What is the customer not allowed to do?**

Shop assistant: The changing rooms are over there on the right. You can only take five items in with you. If you give me the red T-shirt, I can keep it for you. Try the blue one on first and if it fits then you can choose the colour you like best.

3 **You will hear two friends talking about a shirt. What does the girl tell the boy to do with the shirt?**

Boy: I'm taking this shirt back to the shop.

Girl: Why? It fits well and it looks great. And red really suits you. You should keep it.

Boy: But there's a hole here in the sleeve.

Girl: Oh! Well, don't ask for your money back. Get the same shirt if they still have it in your size.

4 **You will hear a customer in a shoe shop. What is the problem with the shoes?**

Customer: I like these shoes very much. They're a pretty style. I'm usually a size 37, but these hurt my feet. I think I need to try on a 38? I'm sure they'll fit perfectly. Oh, and can I try them on in black too? These brown ones are nice, but maybe black would be better.

5 **You will hear two friends talking about a jacket. Why is the boy wearing the jacket?**

Kim: Is that a new jacket you're wearing?

Aaron: Well, not really. It isn't mine. I found it in my brother's room.

Kim: You 'found' it? Don't you mean you took it?

Aaron: Well, he said it was OK. He doesn't wear it much.

Kim: That's nice of him. It goes well with your scarf.

UNIT 7 | WORKBOOK

09 | Listening, page 56, Exercise 2

Now class, today I'm going to tell you about an unusual school in London. You'll need to take some notes so you can look at the website later. The Attic School – that's Attic, A-double T-I-C – is in a beautiful park in the city. The school is in an old building that was built in 1880. It opened in September 2008 and it's a private school for children from three to 14 years old. Parents pay around £5,000 a year to send their children there. So what's unusual about this school? There aren't any computers in the classroom and no-one can use a mobile at school, not even the teachers. The school thinks that young people learn better when they are talking, listening and working together. Also, students can't watch any TV at home and their parents have to agree to this. The teaching and the students are excellent. So perhaps the future of learning isn't only in technology.

UNIT 8 | WORKBOOK

10 | Listening, page 64, Exercise 2

1

Boy: No, we couldn't go out on the lake yesterday in the boat because there wasn't enough wind. So we went swimming instead. I prefer sailing though – that's my favourite.

2

Girl: I love table tennis. Most of my friends prefer racket sports like tennis and they think they're more fun, but I don't agree with them.

3

Boy: Can I go cycling with you after school, please? My friends are going running, but I like riding my bike. I don't like running.

4

Dad: I played football when I was a boy, you know. All my friends did too … but I've always enjoyed rugby much more that football.

5

Girl: I walked to the top of a mountain last weekend. Climbing's OK, but I prefer more exciting sports like skiing.

11 | Listening, page 64, Exercise 3

Karen: Are you doing anything after school today?

Mark: I'm going sailing with Ben.

Karen: With Ben? But I thought he hated water sports.

Mark: Well, he doesn't like swimming very much, but he loves going out in his dad's boat. It's Harry who hates sailing. It makes him sick.

Karen: What's his favourite sport then?

Mark: Harry loved basketball when he was younger, but he prefers rugby now. I can't understand why, though.

Karen: I can't understand either. It's quite a dangerous game! What about Paula? Does she still go skiing with her family?

Mark: Yes, that's right. They go most weekends, but last year she tried surfing and she says she likes that more than skiing, now.

Karen: Really? I might try it one day. Have you seen Lisa this week?

Mark: No, she's busy practising for a table tennis competition.

Karen: Table tennis? I thought Lisa was on the school basketball team.

Mark: You're right, she is. She does both sports, but she enjoys basketball more than table tennis. She isn't sure about table tennis. The coach says she should play for a bit longer to find out if she likes it, but I know she prefers team sports.

Karen: Doesn't Steve play basketball on your team?

Mark: No, not now. Steve had to choose between basketball and cricket. He could play both sports well, but he chose cricket. Now it's his favourite sport.

Karen: Interesting! Well, enjoy your afternoon and see you tomorrow!

UNIT 9 | WORKBOOK

12 | Listening, page 72, Exercise 1

Mark: Zoe and I got so wet when we went camping last week.

Jen: Did you get caught in that big storm?

Mark: Of course! We were walking to the café for dinner and had to wait under some trees.

Jen: Well, next time, I hope you'll take an umbrella with you!

13 | Listening, page 72, Exercise 3

1

Mark: Zoe and I got so wet when we went camping last week.

Jen: Did you get caught in that big storm?

Mark: Of course! We were walking to the café for dinner and had to wait under some trees.

Jen: Well, next time, I hope you'll take an umbrella with you!

2

Carl: It sounds terrible. Were you in the mountains?

Abby: We left the mountains in the morning and drove back.

Carl: So, you were at home?

Abby: No. We were still driving when it got windy. We had to stop on the road side.

3

Ines: Why aren't you at the party tonight?

Javier: I'm sorry. It's too dangerous to drive.

Ines: Is it snowing there? It's only raining here. Is that why you're at home?

Javier: If it was just raining, I would come. But it's really foggy here. I can't see a thing.

4

Andy: Be careful. It's going to snow tomorrow.

Zach: Do you know when? If I finish work early, I'll drive down before lunch.

Andy: It won't start until the evening.

Zach: OK. It'll probably take me three hours to get there.

5

Julia: I'm just happy I'm not in the park.

Ash: Me too. So, where are you?

Julia: I was shopping when it started, but I just took a taxi home.

Ash: OK, great. I'm going to stay at work until it stops.

UNIT 10 | WORKBOOK

14 | Listening, page 80, Exercise 3

1 **You will hear two friends talking about their friend, Amber. What happened to their friend?**

Girl: Where are you going?

Boy: To see Amber. She fell and badly hurt her arm on Thursday.

Girl: Oh, no! Is it broken?

Boy: Luckily, that didn't happen.

Girl: Was she at school at the time?

Boy: No, she was in the park. For some reason, she decided to climb a tree, but that's when she fell down and hurt her arm.

2 **You will hear two friends talking about a health problem. What did the boy do to improve his backache?**

Girl: Is your backache any better, Andy?

Andy: Yes, it is. I haven't had any pain this week.

Girl: That's good. Are you doing special exercises?

Andy: I decided not to because I prefer to swim. I think that's made a difference more than anything else. Oh, and I'm getting a new chair for my desk, so that will help for sure.

3 **You will hear a mother talking to her son, John. What is John worried about?**

Mum: You've still got a temperature. I am not sending you to school today. I think another day in bed is what you need. I know you have maths test which you have studied hard for, but I have emailed Mr Jenkins and he will give you another test on Friday. Oh, and of course no football practice either!

4 **You will hear two friends talking about an eye test. Why is Jess happy?**

Boy: Did the doctor check your eyes, Jess?

Jess: Yes, she did. I had an appointment last week.

Boy: And do you have to wear glasses?

Jess: Not all the time, luckily only when I study.

Boy: Well, I suppose that's good news, isn't it?

Jess: Yes, I'm really pleased about what the doctor said because the headaches were bad.

5 **You will hear a father talking to his daughter, Helen. What was Helen going to do?**

Helen: Bye, dad. I'm going to the gym with Jamie.

Dad: Helen, have you forgotten we're meeting your grandparents and going out to a restaurant for your mum's birthday later?

Helen: Oh! That's tonight? Sorry! My exercise class finishes at 6:30.

Dad: Well, dinner is at 7. Maybe you should change your plans.

Helen: You're right, Dad. I'll let Jamie know.

UNIT 11 | WORKBOOK

15 | Listening, page 88, Exercise 2

Hello. My name's Maria Bradley and I started a new job on Monday. I'm very excited about this and want to tell you about it.

The name of the company is Rightstar. That's one word R-I-G-H-T-S-T-A-R. Because the people we are looking for are stars!

I work in the main office, which is in Madrid, but we also have offices in Berlin and London.

So what exactly do we do? We help companies find the best people for some very special jobs. Let me tell you about one of them. At the moment, we're looking for a person to video games. There are many new games that need testers. So far, over 2,000 people have applied for the job. It's a fun job, and soon, someone is going to be very happy indeed!

UNIT 12 | WORKBOOK

16 | Listening, page 96, Exercises 1 and 2

Andrea: How was your trip to Chicago?

Marco: It was great. We went on one of those tours that show you the buildings where famous movies are filmed.

Andrea: Oh, yes, I've been on one of those too. What did you see?

Marco: We visited some places where they filmed the *Batman* films. There's the famous Berghoff Restaurant, of course, but we didn't go there. Instead, we visited the post office, which was the Gotham Bank in the movies, and also Hotel 71, which most *Batman* fans will know. This is where Bruce Wayne's apartment was.

17 | Listening, page 96, Exercise 3

Andrea: How about you? Did you go anywhere during the holidays besides Bath?

Marco: Yes, I did. My family and I went to Blenheim Palace for the day. It's an old house in the countryside near Oxford. It is hard to believe that you are in England, because it feels like you are in a castle in Germany.

Andrea: Why did you go there?

Marco: Well, my dad really likes history and it is important because the famous British leader, Winston Churchill, was born there.

Andrea: That sounds interesting.

Marco: The house is fantastic. There are lots of big rooms with beautiful old tables with lamps on them. And there are bookcases with very old books in them and on the wall there's a big clock.

Andrea: It sounds amazing. How old is the building? Let me look online. Hmm, they started building in 1705 and finished in 1722, which means it's nearly 300 years old. I see it has also been in some famous films.

Marco: Yes it has been in *The Transformers* movie, *The Last Knight* and the James Bond film *Spectre*.

Andrea: Wow, I want to go too!

OPTIMISE PRACTICE TEST WORKBOOK

18 | Optimise Practice test, Listening, Part 1

1

Woman: I've never met your sister. Does she look like you?

Man: Not really. She had dark hair like mine, but she changed the colour. She's blonde now.

Woman: Oh, and is she tall, like you?

Man: No, she's not. But she wants to be! That's why she always wears very high shoes!

2

Boy: How are your exams going, Sarah?

Sarah: Hmm, I'm not sure. The last one was geography and it was quite hard. That was on Wednesday and I've got physics next Monday.

Boy: Oh, geography is my worst subject!

Sarah: Really? I think physics is the most difficult subject.

Boy: I can help you on Saturday if you want.

Sarah: Oh, that sounds great. Thanks!

3

Girl: Let's get something to eat. There's a café over there.

Boy: OK, I hope they have chips. That's what I usually eat.

Girl: You eat a lot of fried food, Alex. Why don't you get a sandwich? Or, even better, a salad? That's what I'm having.

Boy: That's boring! But you're right. Maybe I'll have a sandwich.

4

Holly: Mum, can you pick me up after school at half past three and take me to my swimming lesson?

Mum: Well, Holly, I've got a doctor's appointment at quarter past three. Can you take the bus?

Holly: I suppose so, but I don't want to be late. The coach gets upset if we aren't there at 4.

Mum: OK. Don't worry, I'll change my appointment.

5

Man 1: Wow! That's amazing! How did they build it?

Man 2: They used the most modern technology, of course.

Man 1: It's so big! How long did it take to build?

Man 2: Only a year, I think. Come on. Let's go inside. The match starts in 20 minutes.

19 | Optimise Practice test, Listening, Part 2

It's summer time here in New York and the question is what are you going to do? Are you going to stay at home and watch TV all day? Of course not! You're going to come to the best camp in the city – Camp Bellentyne. That's B-E-double L-E-N-T-Y-N-E, Bellentyne! It's open from the 11th of July to the 30th August.

At the camp you can have tennis lessons with coach Cam on Mondays and Wednesdays. You can go swimming every morning. And if you like playing football there's a weekly match that's a lot of fun.

Hundreds of teenagers have had a great time at the camp. If you're between 12 and 16, you can join in the fun and it's easy to get to there, too. There is a special bus from the city centre every day that also stops at the train station. So, don't have a boring summer! Have an exciting time at our amazing camp!

20 | Optimise Practice test, Listening, Part 3

Tom: Hi, Jane. I haven't seen you at club recently.

Jane: Hi, Tom. Oh, that's because I was in London at the weekend with my sister. We went to visit my grandparents. My brother was going to come with us, but in the end he couldn't.

Tom: Was it fun?

Jane: Oh, yes! I went to the theatre. Bradley Moore was in the play.

Tom: Bradley Moore! I've seen all his films.

Jane: Me too. He was excellent in the play, but I do like him best in his comedies.

Tom: What else did you do?

Jane: I ate a lot! I also went to a Mexican restaurant. Did you know that chicken with chocolate is a popular dish in Mexico?

Tom: That's unusual! Did you try it?

Jane: Oh, I thought it was too strange! But my sister had it with beans. I just had red rice.

Tom: And did you go to any famous places?

Jane: Yes, Big Ben and Tower Bridge. But the British Museum wasn't open when we got there.

Tom: And how was the weather?

Jane: I took an umbrella and a raincoat because I know it usually rains a lot, but it was sunny most days. I was lucky that I took my sunglasses. I didn't wear any of the jumpers I took.

21 | Optimise Practice test, Listening, Part 4

16

Vicky: Hi, Ben. It's Vicky. I'm phoning to ask about the café where you work. I've heard they're looking for a student to work at the weekends. Is that right? I'd like to get a job for the summer, so if you know anything about it, can you call me? I'll be home after seven tonight. Thanks. Bye!

17

Man: Have we got everything for your birthday party?

Girl: Let me check … orange juice, soft drinks, snacks, cups, plates … oh, we forgot the plates. Can you go back and get them? Here's some money.

Man: OK! What about candles for the cake?

Girl: There are some in the cupboard by your room. But please hurry. Everyone will be arriving soon.

18

Teacher: I have your essays here, and I must say, I'm disappointed. Please make sure your work is clear. If your writing is difficult to read, I can't mark it. And if it happens again, I'll ask you to rewrite it. In class, after school! So please, be more careful when you write.

19

Dad: You've been studying all day, Lucy. Aren't you tired? Maybe you should take a break now. How about a snack?

Lucy: I'm fine, Dad, really. Don't worry. And I had a sandwich earlier.

Dad: Well, OK, if you're sure there's nothing you want …

Lucy: Actually, a cup of tea would be great, just to keep me warm. It's freezing up here!

20

Boy: Mum, have you seen my football scarf? The match I'm going to see starts soon and I can't find it.

Mum: Isn't it with your football shirts?

Boy: No, I've looked there. I hope I haven't lost it. It's my lucky scarf. We always win when I wear it!

Mum: Look! It's on the sofa. Do you wear it when you watch TV?

22 | Optimise Practice test, Listening, Part 5

Max: Hi, Katy. You look busy! Are you ready for your barbecue tomorrow?

Katy: Nearly, Max. There's still a lot to do! I'm lucky that my family are helping me. So far I've got the chicken and the burgers.

Max: Is there anything I can do? What about drinks?

Katy: Thanks, but my brother Fred is getting lemonade, cola and juice from the supermarket.

Max: OK. What about music?

Katy: Well, my cousins Helen & Jess are bringing their guitars so we can sing some songs.

Max: What is your mum going to make?

Katy: A chocolate cake. And she's bought lots of ice cream too!

Max: Wow! I can't wait! So who's coming?

Katy: I invited everyone in our class. I hope I've got enough chairs – my dad's brought some more from my grandma's house. She's bringing some nice snacks too.

Max: You haven't forgotten anything. Well done!

Katy: Actually, someone will need to take photos of the day.

Max: Let me do that for you.

Katy: Really? Thanks, Max!

Max: No problem. I'll see you tomorrow.

Macmillan Education
4 Crinan Street
London N1 9XW
A division of Springer Nature Limited

Companies and representatives throughout the world

Optimise A2 Teacher's Book ISBN 978-1-380-03191-4
Optimise A2 Teacher's Book Premium Pack ISBN 978-1-380-03371-0

Written by Timothy Foster
Additional material by Judy Alden

This edition published 2019
First edition entitled "Optimise A2 Teacher's Book" published 2017 by Springer Nature Limited.

Concept and text design by Designers Collective
Typeset by J & D Glover Ltd and SPi Technologies Inc.
Cover design by Designers Collective
Picture research by Emily Taylor

The author and publishers would like to thank the following for permission to reproduce their photographs:
Getty Images Getty Images/Blend Images p27; **Daniel** Grill p26; **MTJ Media** pp8, 16; **Thinkstock Images** p24

Commissioned photographs by **Creative Listening** p16(tr); **MTJ Media** pp8(tl, tr), 16(l, bl).

Full acknowledgements for photographs and illustrations in the facsimile pages can be found in the Student's Book ISBN 978-1-380-03189-1, the Workbook ISBN 978-1-380-03372-7 and the Workbook with Answer Key ISBN 978-1-380-03190-7.

Printed and bound in Argentina

2022
1 2